# HEAT AND SACRIFICE IN THE VEDAS

# HEAT AND SACRIFICE IN THE VEDAS

UMA MARINA VESCI

*Under the auspices of the*
*Istituto per il Medio ed Estremo Oriente* (*Roma*)
*and the*
*Italian Embassy Cultural Centre* (*New Delhi*)

MOTILAL BANARSIDASS PUBLISHERS
PRIVATE LIMITED . DELHI

*First Edition: Delhi, 1985*
*Second Revised Edition: Delhi, 1992*



ISBN : 81-208-0841-x

Also available at:
MOTILAL BANARSIDASS
41 U.A., Bungalow Road, Jawahar Nagar, Delhi 110 007
120 Royapettah High Road, Mylapore, Madras 600 004
16 St. Mark's Road, Bangalore 560 001
Ashok Rajpath, Patna 800 004
Chowk, Varanasi 221 001



PRINTED IN INDIA
BY JAINENDRA PRAKASH JAIN AT SHRI JAINENDRA PRESS, A-45 NARAINA INDUSTRIAL AREA, PHASE I, NEW DELHI 110 028 AND PUBLISHED BY NARENDRA PRAKASH JAIN FOR MOTILAL BANARSIDASS PUBLISHERS PVT. LTD., BUNGALOW ROAD, JAWAHAR NAGAR, DELHI 110 007

ALLA MIMMI
queste pentole, tolte dal Fusco
troppo tardi per lei

# CONTENTS

# FOREWORD

Writing a foreword to an author's first book is, like the writing of the book itself, a kind of ritual. And this is all the more so if the work is the summing up of twenty years of study, and the one who introduces it has himself been deeply involved in the process. It forms part of the author's rite of passage into the realm of what the western medievals called by the solemn word 'auctores', because from then on they had 'auctoritas' i.e. the capacity to foster the intellectual and spiritual growth of the people. They were no longer interpreters of the past but shapers of the present and creators of the future. I gladly perform this ritual of presenting both the author and her work. And in fact, introductions are generally supposed to furnish that biographical background which is all too often as crucial to the deeper understanding of a book as is the immediate context furnished by the writer. So, I propose to say, first, a few words about the author and, second, something about the work.

In 1963, shortly after completing her studies at the University of Rome, Dr. Vesci left for India to begin a life that few scholars have the courage to undertake : to get lost in the new culture, to incarnate oneself in the other tradition, to live and share the destiny of the newly made friends, and to do this having cut the bridges of return. In a competitive society, even if it goes by the name of academia, an absence of decades will severely jeopardize any opportunity of being accepted back and integrated into 'business as usual'. In a modern, job-oriented civilization, *negotium* is the only thing that counts.

In India, Marina Vesci enjoyed the creative *otium* which permitted her to practice the most natural and perfect way of 'knowing' another culture : to learn as the children of any culture do, to sit at the feet of the masters, to assimilate as we do a healthy food without concerning oneself over producing immediate results and writing informative papers with hastily collected data; in a word, to incarnate oneself in the other culture. Everything she has published so far has been truly assimilated and is as much a part of her praxis as her 'theoria'. I know of her early sketches describing her first encounters with India and once even recommended that she not keep them to herself, but she considered these materials—and rightly so—as the soil out of which less anecdotal and more substantial studies would grow, as they have in course of time.

Umā, as she later became known, began to delve deeply into the culture of the South, Bengal and the North : three different worlds. She soon discovered the underlying fabric of the entire Indian tradition : Vedic culture. To be sure, it is not the only element that makes up the warp and woof of what we call the culture of the Indian subcontinent (we must also integrate the strands of pre-Aryan culture, the tribals, the later reforms and also the graftings, such as Islamic and Christian cultures and the secular world-view). But there is no doubt that the lion's share is had by that extraordinary vision which crystallizes in the Vedic culture.

It is well known that western indology and also, by repercussion Indian scholarship, was, until very recently, mainly interested in the speculative aspects of that culture. The rest was considered 'primitive', if not outright superstition. Western scholars were by and large not interested in, and Indian paṇḍits were almost ashamed of, the ritualistic literature. The Saṃhitās of the Vedas and especially the disquisitions of the Upaniṣads, so the discourse would go, are refined productions of the human mind, but most of the Brāhmaṇas, and especially the rituals, were considered 'galamatias' to say the least, when not just decadent casuistry and priestcraft. The Purāṇas, or ancient legends, have been over the last few years more and more investigated, but it is only very recently that students are beginning to take the rituals seriously.

When Marina Vesci first started for India I recommended to her the topic of *tapas* (ardor, and thus heat, zeal, concentration, spiritual power), that extraordinary symbol which cuts across the ages and schools of India. It has an existential as well as a doctrinal character, a cosmic as well as an anthropological meaning, and is certainly a divine category. Umā has been studying and practicing *tapas* since then. Most of her published articles refer directly or indirectly to this topic, and this book, as well as a forthcoming one, started, as it were, by dealing with the problem of *tapas* even if the nature itself of *tapas* compelled her to shift her main subject toward the effects of heat in sacrifice as such. Actually *tapas* has, or better *is*, a ritual element, being intimately linked with Agni and thus with the sacrifice which constitutes the core of Vedic culture. For this reason she preferred to turn her attention to the subject of rituals, and precisely to those rituals connected with cooking and heating.

This has prompted the author, and this is one of the merits of this book, to unearth an entire world that only now is beginning to be rediscovered and appreciated by scholars in India and abroad. When she first began to express interest in the topic, she was often either misunderstood or discreetly advised to choose another subject of study. Moderns tend to forget that to 'study' (*studium*) means to turn one's whole being toward an aspect of reality, having sensed the urge to integrate it into our lives. Study, in this sense, is a passionate, all-consuming activity not only of the mind, but also of the heart. It has an irreducible existential dimension.

And so I have already begun to present the book to the reader. But before doing so directly, I wish to voice a certain concern, one that will be especially understandable to the reader who happens to live in modern India, or is aware of the present situation. Such reservations or misgivings may be expressed somewhat like this.

India is a land of immense problems. More than half of its people are below the poverty line. Cultural and human deterioration is often visible. Westernization is mainly seen as harmful, yet inevitable. Should intensive work on some very specific ritual be the urgent concern of a spiritually sensitive intellectual coming to India? Can one justify having spent so many years on such a preoccupation ? There is no doubt as to the level of scholarship of the author. However the question is whether our time is better spent than in unearthing some apparently strange irrelevant subtleties of pure casuistry. We could put it in a more general way: Is indology purely asocial archaeological research? Furthermore, the problem is not with India alone. It is the question of what a truly intellectual vocation means in our times.

It is certainly true that the world is on the brink of disaster. We run the risk of nuclear holocaust. And this is qualitatively different from the danger of the extinction of a particular people or even a whole civilization. Moreover, all this is a man-made thread of catastrophe, so that appeasing the Gods is out of the question. They are certainly not responsible for the present day predicament. Given this current situation, what is the place and justification for a highly specialized book on Vedic sacrifice ?

Far be it from me to think that everything has to be justified by its utility value. The old Chinese wisdom will tell us of the highest value of uselessness. But the importance of this study is that it cuts across these pragmatic considerations, for it tells us, or rather, it invites us, to reflect upon one of the most central problems of our time: namely, the loss of ritual awareness. Perhaps, and here we are already at the centre of Dr. Vesci's study, those powers that so threaten the fate of the earth have lost the ritual vision of life and have abandoned the myth that makes us understand that only within a ritual context can any human act have its full meaning.

Traditional Man, in fact, has nearly always constructed the world he lived in by means of rituals. To do this, obviously, he needs the Gods as well as the cosmic elements and the human being. There is no ritual without a cosmotheandric cooperation. A rite, moreover, indicates a sense in life, the sense in which our lives proceed. A ritual speaks to our imagination and not just to our fantasy, let alone exclusively to our reason. Fantasy is private, a product of our individualism. The imagination is public, it reveals the unconscious, the archetypes, the contours and the movement of the intelligible contents of the mind.

On this note, then, I would like now to link these general considerations with the scholarly work of Umā Marina Vesci. Her book does not spin grand theories, but quietly, through her analysis of texts, and contexts, furnishes us with ample evidence to the fact that we need to recover a more holistic view of reality. Strictly speaking, the word 'recovery' is not accurate enough. Certainly we must first recover a more complete picture of ourselves and of the world, but after that follows the task of *recreating*, as is were, a new vision of the universe. And indeed this book not only deciphers for us the inner meaning of the Vedic world, but also hints as to its sense for our contemporary situation. This sense, only timidly insinuated by Umā Marina Vesci, speaks of the necessity of the ritual as a fundamental factor for the construction of a world in which the human being can live in peace and fulfill his destiny. She does not say it in so many words, but her insights tally with what I have been saying elsewhere: in spite of the fact that much water has run down the Ganges since Vedic times and that many tributaries have contributed to our current situation, the predominant template for our modern civilization, even in its form of *techniculture* (which is no longer agriculture), is still the ancient Indo-European culture. And precisely the ritual described by the author gives us an introduction into that Vedic world; i.e. it reveals to us the structure of reality as it was experienced by the ancestors of that Indo-European culture and by other traditional religions as well.

Furthermore, Umā Marina Vesci will explain that her reading of such a cult is based upon an insight into the primordial nature of the sacrifice as the original force of reality in the sharing of which both Gods and Men commune. And in doing this the author tells us about the true understanding of ritual when she rescues even an apparently meaningless piece of trivia from being interpreted as a mere whim of priestcraft and of power-obsessed elites who make things difficult and expensive for the mass of believers. But her book does something more. It tries to place itself before that momentous event when sacrifice has exploded into that crucial bifurcation which itself has helped to bring forth: namely, the birth of intellectual reflection, a reflection which, by giving absolute preeminence to the spirit, is imposing a different, spiritual "worldview" compared to that born, centered and maintained in and through sacrifice. And since perhaps we are still heirs of that not yet healed dichotomy, defended at that time by the *karmakāṇḍins* on one side and by the *jñānamārgins* on the other, we still do not appreciate much a discussion on rituals which gives too much value to the action, to the body of sacrifice as such. The *karmakāṇḍins*, in fact, stood for the irreducibility of the praxis to theory, but the others, who got perhaps the upper hand, wanted to co-opt the ritual in the purely intellectual 'performance' of it. From that moment onward we are witnesses to the perennial tension between action and contemplation, having assisted to the very birth of the independence of the intellect from the moorings of matter, with all it entails of space, time and the body. And yet, by placing itself before that dichotomy took place, and actually pointing out at the very moment in which such dichotomy appeared, the book reminds us that a rite has body and soul, and needs both. For Umā Marina Vesci the body of ritual is more important, if not more primordial, than the soul of doctrine. And in fact before the dichotomy alluded to before, body and soul, doctrine and practice, belong together in a real 'advaitic', non-dualistic, harmony.

The ritual is not only to be heard or spoken out, it must be performed. It belongs to the domain of gesture, song, recitation, movement, action; and like any action, it has many meanings, or rather a number of meanings may be extracted from it. Moreover, ritual in itself is also a kind of language. In this sense, language is a symbol and symbols belong to the field of ritual; it is in fact in ritual that we catch the power of the symbol. As an offshoot of this book, Dr Vesci wrote an article entitled "Qualis cultus, talis Deus", in which she showed the primacy or at least the equality of cult over, or beside, theological discourse. Cult, she observed, is at least as determining a factor in the degree of reality, and plays as central a role in the representation of the Divine, as any purely speculative theology and philosophy can do. As language does, so also rituals disclose a feature of the reality they refer to. And like any language, ritual also has its own grammar and its syntactic rules. The book describes part of the syntax of this language and goes on to show us how to begin to 'read' it.

In order to 'read' better this inner meaning of sacrifice, we are reminded that in ritual action everything matters; each smallest detail contributes to and stands in living relationship to the whole. For this reason, this study takes as the subject of its research an apparently insignificant question: the fact that fire, or heat, is used in very many sacrifices performed in the world religions—a fact that only recently has aroused the interest of some western scholars. Even more specifically the book deals with a seemingly unimportant detail that only now begins to attract some attention: namely that in Brāhmaṇism we find the sacrificial victim cooked with special care, and this cooking is not just for the sake of the priests or for those who are going to partake in the sacrifice with the Gods, but for the Gods themselves. The act of cooking even transforms the sacrificial offering into its divine status. In other words, it is an intrinsic requirement flowing from the conception of the sacrifice itself. This has borne significant consequences both for the idea of the Divine and for that of the nature of the human being. Thus, in the process of the research this seemingly small detail has revealed itself to be at the very core of Vedic culture and mainly responsible for many subsequent changes and developments in Brāhmaṇic and Upaniṣadic thinkings. But I will not anticipate here those ideas which are clearly summed up in the first and last chapters of the book. I leave it to the reader to taste firsthand the intricacies and peculiar *rasa* of the text itself.

R. PANIKKAR

# INTRODUCTION

## 1. *The Choice of Topic :*

In many religions where sacrifice is offered, the cooking of victims in huge cauldrons is one of the most important and compelling features of the ritual. But, as one would expect, it is the sacrificial portion allotted to man which is cooked as his share in the meal with the Deity. The portion allotted to the God is put on the altar fire when still raw. In India, however, ritual cooking is especially reserved for the portion due to the God which is destined to be burnt entirely on another sacred fire. This strange fact, hardly understandable at first sight, is what forms the topic of the present study. However, our aim is not to stop short at a mere description. Our research into the cooking of offerings is developed bearing in mind certain philosophical, historical and hermeneutic problems whose answers go beyond the mere exposition of rites. This study attempts to discover the philosophical and theologico-cosmological message which lies hidden in the necessary cooking of the victim as the most important part of the preliminaries of any sacrifice in the Vedic tradition.[1]

1. Cf. a preliminary bibliography about Vedic sacrifice in two main monographs, especially based on Vedic and Brāhmaṇic texts : K. P. POTDAR, *Sacrifice in the Rigveda (its nature, influence, origin and growth)*, Bombay (Bharatiya Vidya Bhavan), 1953 (Bharatiya Vidya Series Vol. 16) (out of print) ; G. U. THITE. *Sacrifice in the Brāhmaṇa-texts*, Poona (Poona University Press), 1975. Cf. also, for the various rites here taken into consideration, the related monographs: W. CALAND & V. HENRY, *L' Agniṣṭoma*, 2 vols. (Paris, 1906-7) ; P. E. DUMONT, *L'Aśvamedha* (Paris, Louvain, 1927) ; id. *L'Agnihotra*; J.A.B. van BUITENEN, *Pravargya* (Poona

Research of this sort can only be done if one supposes that the rite, and especially sacrifice, is not merely the 'practical aspect', considered as complementary but subordinate to the 'more important' religious aspect of a tradition, namely the doctrinal, theological and speculative. Nor that it is merely a *means* in the service of the Divinity, which serves, more than anything else, to characterize the Divinity by revealing its tastes and its field of action and therefore its specific physiognomy.[2] The basis of this study is the assumption that the rite is really and truly a 'language' with its own internal message, on the same level as that of any other form of spoken expression, a message which sometimes is seen to be even independent of the doctrine which should have supported it.[3] Seen in this perspective, an analysis of the effects of heat, and above all of ritual cooking in the rite which extends its import from Brāhmaṇic religion to its philosophy, is but one possible example among many which show how sacrifice, in its very liturgy, rules and position it occupies in the bosom of its own tradition, can have, and does have, an active role to play also in the theoretical field, and has a 'word' to say in the formation of the cosmological and theological vision of its culture.

This understanding of the rite as 'language' allows us to approach sacrifice as having a 'structure' which is common to

1968); and also some of the classical general works on Vedism as P. V. KANE, *History of Dharmaśāstra*, 5 vols. Poona (B.O.R.I.), 1941-1962; A. B. KEITH, *Religion and Philosophy of the Veda and Upanishads* (H.O.S. 1925, reprinted by Motilal Banarsidass, Delhi 1976); and last but not least, the general works on Vedic sacrifice as H. AGUILAR, *The Vedic Sacrifice*, Delhi (Bharatiya Vidya Prakashan), 1976; R. PANIKKAR, *Le Mystere du cult dans l'Hindouism et le Christianisme*, Paris (ed. du Cerf), 1970; id. *The Vedic Experience, Mantramañjarī*, London (Longman, Darton and Todd), 1977, where there is a selection of Vedic texts, some of which are connected with sacrifice.

2. This is the thesis of a historicist school of History and Phenomenology of Religions: cf. e.g. A. BRELICH, *Dispense sul Politeismo*, Rome, (Ed. Ateneo) 1958, pp. 132 ff. and also his contribution to the XII International Conference of I.A.H.R., Stockholm, August 1970, "Comme se forme un Dieu," in *Proceedings of the XII International Congress of International Association for the History of Religions*, edited by C. J. BLEEKER, G. WIDENGREN, E. J. SHARP, Leiden (Brill) 1975, pp. 136 ff. (Suppl. to NUMEN, n. 31).

3. B. N. Saraswati, *Ritual Language, a Transanthropological Perspective*, Varanasi (N. K. Bose Memorial Foundation), 1982.

all the various religions of the world[4]—without, however, having for that reason to postulate the certainly inadmissible existence of one basic Sacrifice of which all other concrete sacrifices are but surface phenomena. From this 'structure' certain 'syntactic' rules can be drawn which are sufficiently well defined, valid in themselves and obedient to certain laws which cannot be transgressed and which the various religious traditions have always to bear in mind in their particular practices[5]. The same could be said, for example, of music where rules of harmony and melody which govern the relations between notes, their intervals, their assonances and dissonances, while being of the greatest variety, are fixed and valid for every kind of melody, rhythm and sonorous composition on any musical system whatsoever.[6] This of course does not mean that these rules cannot, on occasion, be broken; still such transgression has to be internally motivated and justified, otherwise the result would be merely meaningless dissonances. It is precisely the same with the governing religious phenomena, particularly those concerning sacrifice. The various religions of the world employ in a manner most appropriate within the frame-work of their respective culture, certain structural rules inherent in the rite whose universality became evident only recently through scholarly compartive studies. All the religions of the world have found themselves obliged to offer an internal solution, in as satisfactory a way as possible, whenever the particular 'scheme'

4. This essay tries to apply to the rite the same process, which modern structuralist critics apply to myths looking for a possible interpretative 'grammar' of the latter. Cf. Cl. LEVI STRAUSS, e.g. *Le cru et le cuit*, Paris (Plon), 1964, and his structuralist school. Cf. also C. KERENY, *la mitologia dei greci. I racconti sugli Dei e sull'umanità*, edited by A. BRELICH, Roma (Astrolabio), 1952, pp. 9ff.

5. On the idea of a possible "syntax of sacrifice", cf. my communication at the XIII International Congress for the History of Religions : "Sacrifice seen as an ambivalent action" in *History of Religions, Proceedings of the XIII Congress of the International Association for the History of Religions, (IAHR) Lancaster* 1975, edited by M. PYE & P. McKENZIE, Series Leichester Studies and Religions 2, Leichester (Dpt. of Relig., Univ. of Leichester) 1980, pp. 115 ff. Cf. also the following note and note 24 of Ch. **VII, p. 176; and Ch. V, p. 110 f.**

6. Cf. the same parallel made for Mythology in C. KERENYI, op. cit., p. 10 ". . .Those images are the material of mythology as sounds are the material of music."

of their respective sacrifice was at variance with the general rules. If necessity at times demanded that it was the general rules which had to be broken, this had to be done in a careful way, as is the case with certain dissonances required by some musical contexts.[7]

With the intention, therefore, of bringing out these 'general' rules in full relief and at the same time of showing their adaptation to the 'particular' exigencies of a given religious context, we have chosen to concentrate our attention on the rite mentioned above and to study it in its scriptural framework provided by the Vedas, first of all trying to discover it in the collection of the Hymns, the Saṃhitās, and then proceeding to the Brāhmaṇas and the Sūtras. This aspect of the Vedic rite seemed to us, in fact, to be a determining factor in representing, and in its turn, in shaping, a characteristic of the religion under discussion.

It has been noticed, in fact, how in the sacrificial liturgy of various religions there is often an action, generally to do with the offering, which seems to keep recurring and to point in which direction the importance of the offering itself lies. Moreover, in such action there seems to reside the 'message' which the cult of a given religion wants to transmit, in such a way that if, on the one hand, such an action determines the sacrifice in question, on the other hand, it reflects the entire religious mentality in which sacrifice is inserted. This liturgical action varies from one religious tradition to another. In the Vedic religious tradition the determining and revealing action seems to consist in the cooking of offerings and, in general, in the heating of sacrificial implements, while elsewhere, for example in the semitic religious tradition, it seems to consist more in the gathering of the blood or in the way the victim has to be consumed during the ritual banquet.

In fact, the action to which we are referring can also be defined as the 'means' by which a people chooses to carry its offerings to their destination, and an examination of the various potencies of such a 'means of delivery' in its application in a

7. Examples of such adaptations of the "peculiar" to the "general" and vice versa will be given in the course of the book and especially in Chapters V and VII

concrete context could throw a lot of light on those factors which led to different formulations of religious, doctrinal and even philosophical thought in different cultures.

Moreover, our research on the cooking of offering as the 'means' of the Vedic people to carry their sacrificial action from this world to the divine world, has led us to enter into the philosophical and 'meta-physical' problem which runs down in a continuous line from the first Vedas to their Brāhmaṇas and finally to the Upaniṣads.

Seen from **this** perspective of the ritual, more than one philosophical difficulty or obscure textual passage can find, if not a solution, at least a meaning which is more coherent.[8] We therefore hope that our study inspire similar studies on liturgical 'means' chosen by other religions. We cannot exclude the possibility that such studies pursued on a large scale could show that many apparently contradictory and incompatible doctrines and theories regarding various religious phenomena are only the inevitable developments resulting from one's choice of such a ritual 'means'.

## 2. *Layout of our Study* :

This study has already been sketched out in an article.[9] In that article we proposed to examine the symbolic effects of heat in sacrifice under the following headings: I. heat as such; II. its lack; III. its excess. For various reasons, the second and third part have not been included in this volume. In the Vedic sacrifice, the importance of heat as a source of physical, spiritual and psychic energy becomes apparent when an imbalance in the ritual is supposed to occur whenever heat fails to attain its required intensity, whereas the difficulties which arise whenever heat is excessive become immediately evident to the *ṛṣis* and to the

8. As, for example, a passage of Pañcaviṃśa-Brāhmaṇa, unintelligible to W. CALAND who has translated it (cf. below note 21 of ch. II), or the fate of ritual blood not properly explained by A.B. KEITH (cf. Ch. V, par. 3) or the very evolution of Brāhmaṇic sacrifice too often explained away as 'magic' by the Indologists of the last century (cf. below Ch. IV, note 1), etc.

9. Cf. U.M. VESCI, "The Role of Heat in Vedic Sacrifice. The Place of Pain in the Act of Creation," in BIJDRAGEN, 39 (1978), Amsterdam, pp. 399-423.

priests at the very moment when they are about to produce it. This is an indication that to the brāhmaṇic consciousness and attention, the necessity of ritual heat appears at the same moment when one tries to avoid its lack or to stem its effects when its quantity becomes excessive. Still, these two other aspects of the problem will have to be omitted not to overburden the present analysis and perhaps be treated in an independent volume. But we shall not fail to give an occasional explanation in the notes wherever the problem cannot be ignored.

And now a word on the chapters of this volume.

The first chapter contains an introduction to the problem, taking its point of departure from the position Agni occupies in the Vedic Pantheon and from the special relation it has to sacrifice. The second and third chapters deal with our topic on the basis of texts from the Ṛgveda and the Atharvaveda respectively, while the fourth chapter introduces the problem as seen in the Brāhmaṇas, especially those of the Yajurveda as interpreted in its two major recensions, namely the *śukla* or *white* (which we follow in the Mādhyandina version) and the *kṛṣṇa* or *black* (which we follow in the Taittirīya version). The rest of the chapters, from the fifth to the eighth, which form the second part of the volume, are each dedicated to a particular rite in which heat plays a pre-eminent part, namely, animal sacrifice (*paśuyajña*), the kindling of the first sacrificial fire by a young head of a family (*agnyādhāna* or *agnyādheya*), the erection of a special firealtar for the Soma-pressing rite (*agnicayana* or *agniciti*), and *pravargya* rite which consists in the oblation of hot milk, also connected with the preliminaries of the Soma-pressing sacrifice The last chapter recapitulates by way of conclusion the change in status the divine and human underwent through the development of sacrifice during the Brāhmaṇic period.

The basic texts for these last chapters are taken from the Yajurveda with its exegetical and ritual commentaries, that is to say with its Brāhmaṇas and its Sūtras. Pride of place is given, in our study, to the Śatapatha Brāhmaṇa which of all the other Brāhmaṇas is the most meticulous in its treatment of ritual problems, followed by the Taittirīya version of the *kṛṣṇa* recension. At times, however, this is compared with the Ṛgvedic Brāhmaṇas (the *Aitareya* and the *Kauṣītaki*) for their different understanding of the same ritual details. Of the Vedas, the *Sāma* has not been taken into consideration; for it adds nothing new to what had already been said in the Ṛk, being mostly a rearrangement of the same *mantras* adapted for chant and hence very important from a liturgical point of view but less so from a historical one.[10] Its Brāhmaṇas also appear rarely in our study except the *Pañcaviṃśa*. As for the Sūtras, we have only taken account of the Śrautas, and from among these especially those of the *Yajurveda* in its two main divisions, the *śukla* and the *kṛṣṇa* These treatises, in fact, are those which have the closest relation to the rites we will study and provide us with the best and most detailed rites commented upon and explained by the Brāhmaṇas. For the most part we have set aside the Śrauta Sūtras belonging to the Ṛgveda and *Atharvaveda* because we wanted to cull from the more ancient Saṃhitās those direct allusions to the rites, permitting us to come as close as possible to their most ancient form.

Before we bring our introduction to a close, a word of warning would not be out of place. As our research focuses on a given point, it is logical that all our attention be concentrated on it, thus giving it a preponderant importance to the extent that it might sometimes seem to be the only thing that matters in the sacrificial economy. Hence, it would be well to remember that this biased impression is due to the limitation inherent in this kind of research. That other factors, and not only heat, have contributed to the speculative development of the sacrifice in the Brāhmaṇas is certainly not denied. Still these other factors do not concern us and hence we pass over them in silence. There can be no doubt that an enquiry into the symbolic value of heat in the sacrifice reveals the fact that the function of sacred heat is much greater than it has so far been thought to be; but it is equally true that its influence is not so exclusive as our study might lead one to believe.

10/ I may also add here a 'liturgical' peculiarity which, although it obviously was not decisive in the selection of these texts, has found nevertheless way to impose itself by other means: the recition of the sacred texts of the Sāma is normally not meant for feminine ears (and to this grammatical gender belongs the present writer).

3. *Thanksgiving* :

Warm thanks are due to my family for having to bear my absence during the most excruciating times of our life. To my guru, who was responsible for the first choice of the topic, and to late Professor V.S. Agrawala and Professor S. Bhattacharya for having enlarged my perspective of the topic itself. To Professor Salvino Azzopardi and Doctor Marc Dyczkowski for their English rendering; to Doctor H. Ranade and Professor A.N. Pandeya, for their careful reading from a liturgical and philosophical point of view respectively and their valuable suggestions; and also to Mr. K. N. Gupta a typist who has performed the miracle of typing an impossible manuscript in a record time; and to Dr. G. P. Bhatt, for having painstakingly edited it and for having prepared the Indexes.

# PART I

# THE CREATIVITY OF RITUAL HEAT IN THE VEDIC SACRIFICE (ŚRAUTA YAJÑA) ACCORDING TO THE HYMNS (MANTRAS)

# CHAPTER ONE

# PRELIMINARY PERSPECTIVES ON THE PROBLEM

## 1. *The Importance of the Sacrificial 'Means' and the Role of Fire with respect to the Divine in the Mediterranean Religions and in India* :

In almost all the religions of the world, for a sacrifice to be valid and efficacious and capable of realizing the union between the two opposite poles, the Divine and the Human, Heaven and Earth, the Infinite and the Finite, it is not enough that it be simply offered by man. For such a union of the two levels of the religious cosmos to be realized, it is necessary that the sacred action performed on earth reach the 'heavenly' destination to which it is directed and that it be there accepted.

Every religion has devised a liturgical 'means' with this end in view which, in accordance with the needs of its culture, is capable of partaking of both the spheres of the global Reality which sacrifice is intended to connect. Each one of these religions has shown great inventiveness in this respect by its choice, from among its own mythic, ritual and doctrinal motifs present within the limits of its culture, of a particular liturgical item as the specific element in the transition and transformation of the offerings made to bridge the otherwise unbridgeable abyss between the divine world and the human. The choice of the means of union is indeed very important in the religion and culture of a group of people and it is one of those determining factors with which a religious tradition gives the 'syntactic' elements of the sacred its own characteristic and personal stamp.

If fact, the means chosen by any liturgy to attain this end, that is, to establish, in accordance with the needs of the believer, a concrete contact with the Divine, is indicative of the type of religiosity of a given people and has vast repercussions, also theological ones, within each religion.

Thus, for example, in the religious visions of many peoples, water assumes a specific character with regard to man's relation to the Divine. Thus, water flows, descends from heaven, reaches unfathomable depths : it engulfs whatever is entrusted to it, concealing it in its deep bosom or dragging it away towards distant lands. Many peoples, such as the ancient Germans, entrust to it their offerings. But in northern Europe and in northern Asia, tree, pole and ladder also assume a special importance in the link between Heaven and Earth[1]. Tree is also chosen as a connecting link by the ancient Germans who entrust it with their most important sacrificial victims, namely human beings which they hang on trees[2]. Tree, however, and ladder, though they have their religious significance in the semitic world[3], are not there employed for this purpose. For the Israelite people, as also for other semitic peoples and in general for peoples of the Mediterranean lands, the principal element used for the delivery of offerings to the Divinity is rather fire—fire which necessarily occupies an important place in the mythologies of man since it is the only one of the basic elements of the mythic cosmos which is not overtly found in nature. All the others, like earth, water and air, are spontaneously *given* to man for his consumption, whereas fire has first to be found and then maintained. Because of this peculiarity, it is hardly ever considered to be man's normal heritage, but belongs to the Divine in a special way. Besides, it has a destructive power and can make disappear in a short time anything combustible which is given to it. This disappearance

1. Cf. M. ELIADE, *Patterns of Comparative Raligions*, London (Kegan Paul) 1958, Chs. V & VIII.

2. Cf. e.g. E. O. G. TURVILLE-PETRE, *Myth and Religion of the North*, London 1964.

3. Cf. Gen. ii.16ff and Gen. xxviii. 2ff.

can also be interpreted as a sign of a transference from this world to another more subtile one, namely the Divine[4]. It is logical, then, that the task of the intermediary between the human world and the supranatural one be assigned to it more than to any other element and that the offerings be delivered to it that they may thus reach their destination. Fire, generally speaking, receives the sacrificial portion which is destined for the Divinity. It destroys it and eliminates it from the human world, while, on the other hand, it cooks that other portion which is left for man as partaker of the great banquet where the victim is eaten, in equal measure, by both man and God.[5]

We have spoken of fire, but what we have said does not apply to all kinds of fire, but only to the *consecrated* fire. Unlike the profane fire, in fact, the sacred fire can, to the mind of the believer, have effects which transcend the 'natural world' since it derives its power not from its mere physical heat but from the fact that it forms part of a whole ritual complex, performed in special situations and in a place especially consecrated for the purpose, namely the altar, at a prescribed time. Moreover, such rites are performed by persons who have a special mandate to do so and who are protected by a special consecration to withstand its power, namely, the priests. In other words, if, in a certain sense, it is the physical property of a given element which is responsible for its being chosen as a 'means' to fill the abyss between Heaven and Earth, it is only by its insertion in a sacred context that this 'means' becomes efficacious in a field which is otherwise beyond its physical reach. Tree, water, fire, etc. do not possess sacral value in themselves but only in a particular action which renders them sacred. One has to bear in mind that we are here speaking of a subject which supposes the dominance of religious faith, and that the field of action of this faith is

4. Cf. the meaning of ashes in W. O'FLAHERTY, *Asceticism and Eroticism in the Mythology of Śiva*, Delhi (Oxford University Press), 1973, pp. 245-47.

5. Cf. e.g. G. van der LEEUW, *Phenomenologie der Religionen*, Tübingen (J. C. B. Mohr Paul Siebeck), 2nd ed. 1956, par. 50; A. BRELICH, *Introduzione alla Storia delle Religioni*, Roma (ed. Ateneo), 1966, pp. 43 ff.; W. BURKERT, *Homo Necans: Interpretationen altgriechischer Opferriten und Mythen*, Berlin-New York (Walter de Gruyter), 1972, Ch. II, n. 29.

governed by laws which exceed those which govern the profane, social or historical field.

Now, as for many other peoples, for the Vedic people too the 'means' through which sacrifice must pass to be brought to its fulfilment is fire. But the practical function which is here attributed to it is somehow different from that demanded from it by other religions.[6] This is already hinted at by the different position which Fire assumes as a divine element in the various Pantheons. Sometimes, it is an 'epiphany', a manifestation of the Power or the presence of God, as was the case when Yahweh called Moses or when he went before the Hebrews guiding them at night through the desert.[7] Or it is simply an element which belongs exclusively to the Divinity and which can only descend to the world of men either by being stolen or by a special divine concession, as is indicated by the Greek myth of Prometheus[8]. Among men, in any case, it is kept in the hearth, under the surveillance or protection of a particular Divinity like Hestia/Vesta of the ancient Greek-Roman world.

In any case, in many mythologies, the God of Fire, who is not identified with the element but is only related to it, is only partly connected with sacrifice and, at most, is connected with hearth or with certain arts or trades, as was the already mentioned Hestia/Vesta or Ephaistos/Vulcan. Still, its sacrificial importance is not as cultically determinant as it is in India.

The role which fire assumes in Vedic India is different both as an element in the liturgy and in its relation to the Divine. In fact, the God Agni, besides bearing a name which clearly puts him in direct relationship with the element of fire in itself without, however, being exhausted in it, contrary to what some naturalistic interpretations still maintain[9]—is directly connected with the sacred action par excellence, namely, sacrifice, and

6. A hint to this can be found in JaimBr III, 168 ff. where two Asuras are said to be able to "cook over non-fire" (*pacato'nagnau*), possibly because the only fire they could have was not a sacrificial fire. The text will be discussed at length in a subsequent study.

7. Cf. Ex. III. 1 ff. & XIII. 21 ff. and also Deut. IV. 24: Ps. L. 3 and Hebr. XII . 29; etc.

8. Cf. HESIOD, *Theog*. 535 ff; 562; ESCHYLOS, *Prometheus Bound.*

9. Cf. in this respect the closely knit and exhaustive criticism of this naturistic interpretation, in H. AGUILAR, *op cit.*, pp. 112 ff.

its place on earth is more the altar than the home (or the hearth) for domestic use. As God, the chief characteristic and principal task of Agni is that of being Mediator between Heaven and Earth, between men and gods—and this not so much because he is the 'medium' between men (amongst whom he visibly dwells in the flame) and Gods (to whom he belongs by nature) but because he is also the 'medium' or instrument by which sacrifice is accomplished[10]. His sacrificial function is precisely that of carrying the human offering to the divine world and to see that it is there accepted. Inversely, he is also the vehicle by means of which Gods themselves descend among men to enjoy the same offering.[11] However, in the course of the theological development of sacrifice, Agni becomes the Mediator between the human and the Divine in a still more profound sense, namely the means, or the instrument, by which is realized the passage from the human to the Divine and vice versa, a passage which will be, and aims to be, a slow but constant divinization of the whole universe by means of sacrifice itself.[12]

Agni, therefore, is not merely the divine element sent to consume, in the name of the Gods the sacrificial portion of the offering destined to them, or the natural element to which men commit their offering which has thus to be taken away from the human world. He is a God, a God directly connected with sacrifice and who finds in sacrifice his main *raison d'être*[13]. Why has Agni assumed this status ?

This leads us to ask what could have been that peculiar factor intrinsic to the Vedic cult which resulted in the attributing of such pre-eminence to Fire whose function in sacrifice seems to go much beyond the normal one of consuming the offering or of carrying it to its destination. This is the question we shall discuss in the following paragraph.

10. Cf. e.g., RV I. 1.1 ff; I. 145. 3; VI. 9. 2; etc.

11. Cf. e.g., RV I. 1. 2 ff; I. 189. 1 ff; etc.

12. Cf. e.g., RV VI. 9. 7; etc. Cf. also an interpretation on the same line as mine in R. PANIKKAR, *Le Mystere du cult,* op. cit.; id. *The Vedic Experience,* op. cit.

13. Cf. R. PANIKKAR, *The Vedic Experience,* op. cit.

2. *The Role of Ritual Cooking in the Vedic Sacrifice* :

In order to realize the peculiar nature of Agni, it is important to examine the location itself which Agni has on the sacrificial altar[14]. The altar on which a victim is normally offered is naturally the place proper to Agni, thus acquiring, in its turn, an importance so central, in Vedic religiosity, that it even replaces the temple found in other religions. Unlike other religions where altar is located outside temple, though in relation to, and in front of it, n the Vedic tradition the sacrificial place acquires an importance in itself and can be erected anywhere since it is related to no kind of cultic building. It is even provisional since it is erected from time to time, as the need arises, and destroyed as soon as a sacrifice is terminated.

It is not our task to consider here the complex and interesting structure of the Vedic altar, or its complicated symbolism which extends to include the whole universe—to which we shall return later[15]. It is enough to underline here the location of Fire which is generally divided into two or three different hearths (as, in fact, the kingdoms to which Agni belongs are three : the superior, the intermediate and the inferior)[16], in positions which correspond to the cardinal points. Of these fires, the one to the east, in the form of a square, the *Āhavanīya*, receives the holocaust, while the one to the west, in the form of a circle, the *Gārhapatya* is reserved for the equally important function of the ritual cooking of the offerings. Occasionally a third fire is added for the cooking which is called *Anvāhārya-pacana*. Since it is placed to the South (*dakṣiṇa*) of the *Gārha-patya* it is also called *Dakṣiṇāgni*.

The fact that there is a separate sacred fire reserved for the cooking of offerings which will be later burnt in another fire, is certainly surprising. One cannot so easily understand how food which is meant to be burnt almost in its entirety, needs

14. Cf. a small but numerous literature for the liturgy of building altars and fire-altars near temples in India, collected in Pt. Veni Ram SHARMA GAUDA, *Yajña Mīmāṃsā*, Varanasi, 1970 (3rd ed.). See also Ch. VI below.

15. Cf. Ch. VI below.

16. For an exposition of the symbolism of the fires in Vedic altars, cf. D. K. KNIPE, *In the Image of Fire*, Delhi etc. (Motilal Banarsidass) 1975, Ch. I.

to be previously submitted to a whole process which could seem at first sight to be useless. When it is committed to fire to be transferred to the divine world or, in any case, to be taken away from the human world, the offering could just as well be still raw.

This is precisely what happens in the majority of sacrifices of the religions of the world. To limit ourselves to examples taken from two among the best known and most important religions of the Mediterranean world, those of the ancient Greeks and the Israelites, we see that in both religions, the sacrificial victim, especially in its classical bloody form, is meant to be eaten in a common meal by both God and men. Of these, the portion destined to the Divinity is offered on fire while it is obviously still raw and only that portion destined to be sacrificially consumed by man is cooked.[17] Moreover, the liturgical texts, generally speaking, do not insist too much on that cooking and certainly not to the extent that it be cooked on a sacred fire especially reserved for such a purpose. In Vedic India, however, where the consumption of the offerings on the part of man is spoken of only secondarily, the cooking of the offering seems to have been so important as to demand a separate fire. Besides the importance given to the cooking of the offerings in the Vedic sacrifice would seem even more strange if we consider the fact that in ancient India the consumption of the sacrificial victim never enjoyed, it seems, pre-eminent importance in the whole sacrificial complex. The act which matters above all is *havana*, the pouring of offering into fire with extended hand, *palm upwards* and fingers pointed downwards. If, then, the priest and the sacrificer (the *ṛtvij* and the *yajamāna*, respectively) consume a part of the offering, this act of theirs remains marginal with respect to the very essence of sacrifice, which precisely consists in the offering of the victim in almost its entirety. The part which is destined to them, in any case, is the 'remnant' (*ucchiṣṭa*) and not a 'portion' in the same sense as that destined to the Divinity.

That it is the total offering and not the consumption of the victim which must be considered to be the principal and more

17. Cf. W. BURKERT, op. cit., ch. II, note 29.

common form of the whole Vedic sacrificial complex (even though the 'remnant' occasionally may be greater than the offering) is further proved, or at least indicated, by the fact that in its ritual development and in the social behaviour which resulted from it and which is still today the basis of Indian social mores, the meal in common does not form part of the orthodox Indian tradition. Whereas in the Mediterranean world, for example, where sacrifice generally took the form of a sacred banquet, there survived the custom of the convivial meal to cement unions and alliances, in India this custom is conspicuously absent. In India a meal is seen above all as an alm or as an act of hospitality. The head of the family (there is always a host who takes the initiative) offers the customary meal to his guests, whether these be a family group with whom he enters into a relationship through the marriage of a daughter, or Brāhmaṇas, or strangers to be venerated as Gods, or poor people to feed as an act of charity, he regards his act as a form of *service*. He hastens to serve them, but he certainly does not care to strengthen any further this alliance with them by joining himself to them as a fellow table-companion.

The consumption of the sacrificial portion destined to the sacrificer seems to be of this kind. The sacrificer does not eat together with his God, but, like a good Amphitrius, waits till his guest is first served to his heart's content before he eats what remains. His portion is a 'left-over' (*ucchiṣṭa*), what 'remains' after the Gods have been satisfied. From this is derived on one hand the use of *prasāda* in the modern cult where the devotee gets back a part of his offering as 'gift', as a 'left-over', imbued with the grace of the gratified God (or *guru* or *mahātmā*), and on the other hand the practice of hospitality as an act of service whereby the guest is first served properly and only afterwards can the host's family finish what eventually remains of the food.

Even so, in spite of the ritual absence of the institutionalized meal over the offerings, these are cooked on a separte fire to make sure that their specific effect is not lost. This concern, which does not seem to be felt in those religions where the offering is cooked for human consumption during the sacrificial meal, is strangely enough rather strong where such meal is not important. And cooking is so significant that what is not cooked cannot even be considered either as a proper offering to the Gods or a suitable portion for a meal, to such an extent that to eat raw food is a way of eating without breaking ritual fast (as it appears from a ritualistic advice given by Yājñavalkya).[18] Moreover, this usage of cooking the sacrificial offerings for Gods cannot be linked, in India, with the human custom of eating cooked food, because in India often human conduct is rather seen as diametrically opposed to divine conduct.[19] It would have been more logical, in fact, from the Indian point of view that the contrary should be the case: the offering destined to Gods is in no way to be cooked precisely because man cooks his food before he eats it. Since it is not so, it is clear that the Vedic people meant to convey a 'message' through their cooking of the offerings, a message that we shall try to discover now from a direct study of the texts. We shall try to find out if there is a special characteristic in the cooking which accounts for their great importance in ritual, and, if this is the case, what this characteristic is.

### 3. *Etymology and Semantics af the words denoting Heat in the Vedas :*

It is necessary to say a word about the etymology and semantics of the Sanskrit terms which recur most often in our study and which are, as it were, its pivot and indeed its very structure. These words all denote Heat in some sense. They are : *gharma* from the root *ghṛ*; *tapas* from the root *tap*; *śocis* from the root *śuc*; the conjugational forms from the root *dah*; *śṛta* from the root *śrā;* and *pakti* from the root *pac*.

*Gharma*, from the verbal root *ghṛ*[20] and the substantival

18. Cf. SatBr I. 1. 1. 9.

19. For example, the Brāhmaṇa wears the sacred thread on the left shoulder because the Devas wear it on the right; one cuts first the nails of the left hand just because the Devas start with those of their right (SatBr III. 1,2.4) and similar other details.

20. *ghṛ*, from which is also derived "*ghṛta*" (the clarified butter of the offerings), comes from the Indoeuropean root **guher* (from which are derived the adjective **guhermo*, the name **guheros* and **guhormos* in the neutral case). From this root stem the Gothic "*varmya*", the Germanic "*warm*", the Greek "*thermos*", the Latin "*formus*" and "*fornus*", the Avestic "*garama*", etc. Cf. J. POKORNY, *Indogermanisches Etymologisches Worterbuch*, Bern (Francke), 1959, pp. 493 ff.

suffix *ma*, meaning to 'shine, to 'warm', indicates the heat of the sun and that of fire and is used in connection with the physical action of the former and of the ritual activities of the latter. Since the sun is the source of heat (*gharma*) par excellence, the term is also applied to the ritual container which represents the sun as such in the cultic action with which man controls its rise and protects it from the cold and the humidity of the rainy season. At other times, *gharma* indicates the boiling liquid, generally milk, used as offering.

Modern Indian languages which are derived from Sanskrit still employ the term (written *garmī*) to signify 'heat'.

*Śocis* is derived from the verbal root *śuc*[21], meaning 'to be aflame', to 'glow' and also to 'suffer'. It is an attribute of Agni and an important means of expressing the activity of the God. It leaves visible traces of its contact. It is found in many sacrificial contexts and its association with the rite is perhaps decisive in the semantic change which the term has undergone. The heat, which the blazing flame communicates to whatever comes in contact with it, led to the meaning of 'pain' prevailing over the other meanings of the term, in such a way that from the later Brāhmaṇic and Upaniṣadic times, *śocis* is used almost exclusively to mean 'pain', 'affliction', 'suffering'.

*Śṛta* is derived from the root *Śrā*[22], meaning to 'cook', to 'boil', to make 'ripe', to 'roast'. This is the past participle. Together with *śratā*, it is one of the most often recurring terms used to indicate transformation by cooking.

*Pakti* is derived from the root *pac*[23], meaning also to 'cook', to 'boil', to make 'ripe'. It is more often found in the exegetical texts and tends to take the place of the previous term. Its meaning can be extended so as to signify anything cooked.

21. Cf. J. POKORNY, *op. cit.*, p. 597 suggesting a derivation from the Indoeuropean root **keuk*. It has correspondents in the Avestic "*saocint*" "*saocaveiti*", in the Greek "*kuknos*", etc., and properly means "to illuminate", "to inflame"; sometimes it is connected with the whiteness of a glow.

22. Cf J. POKORNY, *op. cit.*; 582. It comes from the Indoeuropean root **kera*, **kra*, meaning "to cook". Cf. the Greek *kratus* (in *demokratos*); its similarity with the Greek *kirnemi*, meaning "to mix", has been suggested.

23. From the Indoeuropean root **peku* (cf J. POKORNY, *op. cit.*, p. 798) meaning "to cook", cognate to the Greek "*pesso*" (derived from *pek-joo*), "*pelsispepto*", also to the Latin "*coquo*", Breton "*pober*", Slavic "*peka*", etc.

*Tapas* is drived from the root *tap*[24] meaning to 'irradiate heat', to 'heat', to 'shine', to 'warm', to 'consume by heat', to 'suffer'. Although it is a word of Indo-European origin, as the previous ones, it has developed in a somewhat particular manner which does not correspond to that of any other linguistic term related to it. It indicates a type of heat entailing the idea of a minimal luminosity but also the idea of a charge of energy which approaches that of the sun (with which the term is more closely linked). The sun often appears as the subject of the verb *tapati*[25] and as such it does not require a direct object on which to exert its energy. An object is required, however, when the subject is fire or any other source of heat which necessarily must have an object on which to discharge its energy[26].

As heat of the sun or of fire, *tapas* penetrates, without leaving any immediately visible traces, into the depth of those things on which it alights and transforms them from within. As a verb, or as verbal participle *tap* is directly, or more often indirectly, linked with *śṛta*. Its effects are psychologically felt by the person who experiences it and who exerts it on any given object, as, for example, the ritual implements to which the priest transmits energy, not only through the direct action of fire but also through his internal ascetic power.

*Tapas*, is as elusive as the thermic energy of which it bears the name and it can be said to have no tangible consistency or definite concreteness in itself: it reveals itself in movement, in the transmission of energy, and is experienced in an action as a result of some effort. Since the result of the acquired energy through determinate means is difficult to grasp or analyze, *tapas* is also identified with the means with which it is

24. Cf. J. POKORNY, *op. cit.*, pp. 1069 ff. who refers to the other cognate of the Celtic group: Irish "*te*"; Gaelic "*twim*"; old Corn. "*toim*" (**tepesmo*), modern Breton "*tom*"; and of the Slavic group: the Russian "*tieply*", Polish "*cieply*", Serbian-Croatian"*topao*"; etc. Cf. also the Latin "*tepesco*".

25. Cf. e.g., RV X.60.11: *nyak tapati sūryaḥ* ("the sun warms downwards") etc.; AV XIX. 53. 6: *kāle tapati sūryaḥ* ("the sun shines in time") etc. Cf. also AitBr IV. 25 etc.; KausBr XXV. 3, etc.; PancBr XII. 10. 6, etc.; SatBr II. 2.4.6, etc.; and for the character of *tapas* and *tap* Ch. BLAIR, *Heat in Rig Veda and Atharwa Veda*, New Haven, Coun. (AOS), 1961, p. 98.

26. Cf. Ch. BLAIR, *op. cit.*, p. 98 and *passim*.

produced or the action which produces it. This bi-polarity of the term, which includes both the end to be achieved and the means to achieve or produce it, remains one of its constant characteristics throughout all the develoment of its millenary history.

Besides *tapas*, the oldest derivative of the verbal root *tap*, found almost exclusively in the ancient Ṛg Veda to gradually disappear from the more recent sacred texts, is the adjective *tapus*.

*Tapus* is found in the Ṛg Veda, especially in its oldest books, sixteen times while already in the Atharva Veda proper it is found only twice.[27] In the Aitareya Brāhmaṇa, it also appears twice, whereas in the Upaniṣads it disappears altogether. It means 'intensely hot', and is often used to qualify the weapon which strikes both enemies and demons who attempt to thwart the success of sacrifice.

*Tapuṣi*, 'scorching', is fire, and also the heat of anger and of violent emotions.

*Tāpa*, 'heat', 'splendour', 'suffering', is intense heat. In modern Indian languages it has also retained the meaning of heat especially in connection with water or fever.

*Tapana*, 'burning', 'effulgent', 'causing suffering', is applied to the sultriness of the sun and also of the hot season. The term, with the passage of time, began to be used with the meaning especially of 'affliction', 'anxiety', 'pain' and even to indicate certain mental disturbances.

*Tapasyā*, 'produced by heat' is directly connected with the last meaning of *tapas*, namely 'austerity' and retains even in modern languages the meaning of 'performing harsh and severe ascetic exercises', 'abstinence' 'austerities'.

*Tapasvin*, 'he who possesses *tapas*', is one who is poor, afflicted, suffering because of privations endured for the sake of austerity, but also one who is powerful, who, by his ritual act and self-inflicted hardships, has acquired the power of *tapas*.

Finally, *tapas* and *tapasyā* are the two last months of the year, occurring between winter and spring.[28] As such they are also

27. Cf. Ch. BLAIR, *op. cit.*, Ch. II.
28. Cf. VajSam XV. 57 and SatBr VIII, 7. 1. 5.

said to be the feet of the year who is Prajāpati[29] and therfore his support. Thus they are the supporters of the whole Reality. But if the feet are the supports of the body, they are too its most humble members. So, when the caste system was fixed and codified as a specific form of the brāhmaṇic society and needed a theological justification, the *śūdras*, those belonging to the working class, were said precisely to come from the *feet of the Year*, that is from *tapas* and *tapasyā*, and then also from the personified *tapas*[30].

29. Cf. AitBr VII.7.2; KausBr VI. 15; SatBr I.2.5.13; XI.1.6.13; etc.Cf. S. LEVI, *La doctrine du sacrifice dans les Brāhmaṇas*, Paris (PUF), 1966, p. 16.

30. Cf. RV. X.90.12.

CHAPTER TWO

# RITUAL HEAT AS A SOURCE OF ENERGY IN THE ṚGVEDA

In order to try to go as far back as possible to the time when there first appeared in India the idea that cooking had a specific ritual significance, we shall examine here the Ṛgvedic hymns directly leaving aside for the present their Brāhmaṇic and ritual commentaries which are unanimously considered to be of more recent origin[1]. The hymns seem to refer to a more ancient time than that of the explanatory ritual literature, and hence, even if the Śrauta Sūtras most probably contain rules which perhaps have remained unchanged from the time of the first Vedic hymns, we have preferred to take into consideration only those hints which can be gathered from the hymns themselves to remain as far as possible closer to the more ancient times. To fall back on these hymns alone, as our first material, does not mean however that we shall have to look on them as specialized treatises capable of furnishing us with all the necessary informations about the rites with that clarity and descriptive meticulosity of the Brāhmaṇas and of the Sūtras. We must never forget that the Saṃhitās are a collection of prayers, hymns and invocations and as such they can provide us with no more than

1. The Ṛgvedic hymns, in fact, are almost unanimously considered to be much older than their brāhmaṇical and ritualistic commentaries. By 'ritualistic commentaries' we mean the Śrauta Sūtras, which, although they are later than the hymns, perhaps contain references to ritual rules which were not much changed during the course of the centuries.

hints of the rite, with which they were eventually linked, in passages which seem to refer to ritual. Supposing, then, that some of them are really *mantras* meant to accompany the offering of the sacrifice, we can be guided by their verses to discover what the corresponding cultic action could have been.

1. *The Texts* :

In the ancient ritual hymns, many offerings are repeatedly said to have been cooked (*pakta* or *śṛta*): cereal cakes, roasted corn, flesh of victims offered in honour of Indra, etc.[2] One of the most frequent offerings to Indra is the mash of cooked rice, a victual whose very name, *pakti*, testifies to the importance of its having to be cooked.[3] For Indra *pakti* is cooked and Soma pressed and thus the God blesses the one who offers them to him.[4] Three hundred buffaloes are consigned to Agni during a ceremony and he prepares them[5] so that when they are well cooked Indra can, by their means and by Soma which he drinks, acquire enough power to perform his cosmic functions. Agni cooks a hundred buffaloes for Indra while the other Gods offer Soma in libation[6] so that Indra gains strength and is thus enabled to sustain and defend the world. Besides the ceremony of Soma, but still forming part of it, there are other offerings, whether of vegetables or of animals, which have to be cooked so that the act of offering be valid and pleasing to the Divinity. Indeed the act of cooking is so closely linked to the idea of sacrifice that the Vedic poet can testify that "Indra compensates in equal measure him who presses (Soma) and him who cooks (*pakti*)"[7], thus using these two concrete terms as synony-

2. Cf. e.g., RV III.52.1 *indra prātarjuṣasva naḥ puroḷāśaṃ pacatyaṃ juṣavendrā gurasaa ca* ... ; RV V. 73.8 ... *vat samudrāti parṣathaḥ pakvāḥ pṛkṣo bharanta vām* ... etc.

3. Cf. RV V. 29.11 *ā tvam ṛjiśvā sakhyāya cakre pacan paktīr apibaḥ somam asya*... Cf. also ch. I note 23.

4. Cf. RV VII. 32. 8 . . .*sunotā somapāvne somam indrāya vajriṇe/pacatā paktīr avase kṛṇadhvamit pṛṇannit pṛṇate mayaḥ.*

5. Cf. RV V. 29.7 . . . *sakhā sakhya apacat tūyam agnirasya kratvā mahiṣā crī śatāni*. . .

6. Cf. RV VI.17.11 . . . *vardhān yaṃ viśve marutaḥ sajoṣāḥ pacac chataṃ mahiṣām indra rubhyām* . . .

7. RY IV. 24.7 *ya indrāya sunavat somam adya pacāt paktīr uta bhṛjjāti*

mous to symbolize the whole act of the offering—which is an indication that the two ritual acts are so intimately linked to their respective sacrifices that, in each case, the ritual act can be understood to represent the sacrifice itself. It is well known, in fact, that the Vedic tradition often employs the term 'pressing, (*sutyā*) to refer to the whole ceremony of Soma, and that it calls, in the technical language of the ritual, him who takes on himself the offering of Soma, as the one 'who presses'. From this it follows that the analogous use of the technical term 'to cook' to refer to the sacrifice places the act of cooking at the heart of the sacrifice itself of which it became the synonym.

Moreover, this act of cooking does not merely signify or represent a superficial warming of an offering which has in any case to be later poured into the fire; one has to make quite sure that it is really cooked before it can be offered in sacrifice lest one incurs the risk of bringing on oneself the wrath of the God or risks to have the act becoming counter-productive. It would then be better to wait[8] and pronounce the invocation only when it is entirely cooked.[9] The same thing can be said of the morning offering of hot milk to the Aśvins in *agnihotra* or in that other rite mentioned in the Saṃhitā, which later came to be known by the name '*Pravargya*'. In these rites, the Aśvins are invoked by a formula which informs them that: "the cauldron has been heated (*atāpi gharmaḥ*) in the house of man".[10] The explicit mention of this detail leads us to think that it is precisely because it is heated (*tapta*) that the offering is ready for the heralds of the dawning Sun. The fact that the milk, on this occasion as on many others,[11] has to be heated is underlined in various ways not the least of which is by the name itself both of the offering and of its container, a name which means just 'heat' (*gharma*). The *tapta gharma* (heated cauldron) is mentioned at the end of a hymn (which perhaps refers to rite) as the worthy remuneration of the officiating priest who thus

*dhānāḥ* ...; Cf. also RV II. 12. 14 sq . . . *yaḥ sunvantamavati vaḥ pacantam. sa janāsa indraḥ| yaḥ sunvate pacate dudhra ā cid* . . .

8. Cf. RV X.179.1 *yadi śrāto juhotana yadi aśrāto mamattana* . . .
9. Cf. RV X.179.2 *śrātaṃ haviro ṣvindra pra yāhi* . . .
10. RV VII.70.2 *atāpi gharmo manuṣo duroṇe.*
11. As for instance in *agnihotra.*

prides himself of it: "and we these who officiate, have received the cauldron made of metal, heated for the *pravṛje*."[12] *Pravṛje* is probably the ancient form of Pravargya or perhaps an independent rite, similar to Agnihotra, which later was incorporated as Pravargya into the preliminary ceremonies preceding the grand Soma sacrifice, as we shall see later on.[13] This vessel seems to have been exalted with almost greater pride than the other valuable gifts which the priests received from their generous sacrificers (*yajamāna*).[14] But, even if the metal (*ayas*) expressly named as the material of the container had been of solid gold as Sāyaṇa says[15], this would not explain how it would have compared with or even been held in greater esteem than the four thousand heads of cattle mentioned in the same verse.[16] Besides the symbolic value which an object can assume by representing sacrifice itself, this value is conferred on it, as we can deduce from the successive Brāhmaṇas, from the heat which it incorporated into itself during the rite which, for that matter, is stressed by the qualification *tapta* given to the *gharma*. Later, in fact, when the ritual of Pravargya will be more defined in its particulars, the function of heat during the course of the ceremony will acquire such an importance as to determine the success or failure of the sacrifice as directly depending on the quantity of heat acquired by the cauldron.[17] In any case, this sensitivity to the symbolic value of heat, which developed throughout the centuries and especially in the period following

12. RV V.30. 15 : '*gharmaś cit taptaḥ pravṛje ya āsīd ayasmayas taṃ vādāma viprāḥ*'. See also Sāyaṇa's comment *in hoc loco*, considering, as we shall see later, the cauldron as being made of gold.

13. See below Ch. VIII.

14. Cf. RV V. 30.12-15 where there is mention of four thousand cattle, of wealth and ornaments.

15. Cf. SĀYAṆA, Comm. RV V. 30. 15. It is to be noted that in this hymn, the cauldron is expressly mentioned as 'metallic' (*ayas*), although we cannot be too sure which type of metal is intended here. Later on, however, in Pravargya which is spoken of in the Brāhmaṇas, this cauldron is made of clay, and this usage has to be religiously justified and mythologically motivated. Cf. e.g. SatBr XIV. 2.2.53 ff discussed in Ch. VIII.

16. Cf. RV V. 30. 15 a: *catuḥ sahasraṃ gavyasya paśvaḥ* . . .

17. Cf. text discussed below in Ch. VIII, note 179, and qouted in Ch. IV, note 26.

the Vedic hymns, seems to have already had its seeds in the rituals of the Ṛks.

From what we have said so far, one can legitimately affirm that the cooking of the offering formed an integral part of the preliminary rites of the Vedic sacrifice from the time when the hymns were composed. From these general references, however, one cannot affirm too categorically that cooking had any specific character to distinguish it from that found in other sacrifices with a different pattern—except for the fact that here it is specifically indicated as being important for the God who receives the offering rather than for the devout person who consumes it. The buffaloes are cooked *for* Indra so that he can consume them and draw benefit therefrom; the Aśvins can come because the cauldron is hot, etc.[18]

Still, that this cooking has a function which is independent of the fact of whether or not the offering is consumed by the Divinity itself can be further deduced from those hymns which clearly indicate the bad effects which would eventually accrue if this cooking, or better, if a certain quantity of heat which is outwardly produced in the cooking, were to be lacking. This lack creates bad effects which are so serious, not only because of divine displeasure with a badly prepared meal, but also because the ritual act itself seems to be affected to the point of becoming sterile. This is a sign that the cooking does not serve merely to render the offerings edible but to impress on them, by means of the heat, a 'stamp' without which the sacrifice itself could turn out to be a failure.

### (a) *The Soma Sacrifice* (*somayajña*):

In the preparation of Soma, it is not immediately evident that the extraction of the inebriating part of it should require cooking. Indeed, it is probably not a condition for its consumption as is the cooking of the milk, the meat or the rice. The liquid can perhaps also be extracted from the raw root. And yet even here a certain amount of heat cannot be absent. Precisely because heat is probably not required in the process of preparing the liquid as a drink and yet is still considered to be so

18. Cf. notes 5, 9 etc. of this chapter.

important that it cannot be done away with, it demands an explanation as to why it is so necessary—an explanation which will be taken up and strengthened by exegetico-philosophical suggestions found in the Brāhmaṇas themselves. When, in fact, the plant in order to have its juice extracted, must pass, together with its solid mass, through a filter, this filter, in order to make the ceremony efficacious, must be intensely hot as is explicitly indicated by the adjective *tapus* qualifying it[19]. No doubt both the filter and the heat serve to purify the drink, but it is undoubtedly true also that the Vedic priest expected that something more happen to the liquid than a mere rise in temperature. After having declared that the filter **is stretched** out (*pavitraṃ te vitatam*) and that the Lord (Soma) with all his limbs passes through all its parts, the priest continues in his recital of the hymn which accompanies the ritual and says, as if to justify an action which could perhaps have seemed superfluous, "that which is cold (*āmaḥ*), whose mass has not been heated (*atapta tanūr*), does not reach it (*na...aśnute*) ; but that which is cooked (ready, *śṛtāsa*) together with those who carry it, has reached it".[20] This text has been taken up *verbatim* by the Pañcaviṃśa Brāhmaṇa which according to Caland's translation reads as follows: "the strainer, O Brahmaṇaspati, is stretched out; surpassing its members thou goest around it on all sides. No creature whose body has not been heated and who is raw, reaches it, but the cooked ones, who draw, have reached it".[21] Now, though a literal translation may seem incomprehensible, the idea becomes sufficiently clear if we consider the properties of heat as the Vedic priest most likely understood them to be. The passage through the filter, which in the succeeding verse of the Ṛgveda is called *tapus*,[22] does not only give the Soma the possiblity of being purified, as every passage through an ordinary filter does, but it also equips

19. Cf. RV IX. 83.2.

20. RV IX. 83.1: *pavitraṃ te vitatam ... ātapta tanūr na tad āmo aśnute śṛtāsa id vahantas tat samāśatā.*

21. PancBr I.2.8. W.CALAND confesses that he does not understand the meaning of what he translates: "the meaning of the verse... is not entirely clear" (Note *in hoc loco*).

22. Cf. RV IX.83.2 where *tapus* qualifies *pavitram* of the verse 1 (quoted above in note 20).

it with an energy so that it may have the power to "arrive', to *reach* its destination, therefore to *move*. Since heat is a giver of energy, the poet declares that that which remains cold (*āmaḥ*), that is, whose body has not had the benefit of having received heat, remains inert. Moreover, according to the Pañcaviṃśa Brāhmaṇa, this energy thus acquired by the offering overflows on to its carrier (the offerer ?) also, in such a way that he too may have the possibility of reaching the goal for which the sacrifice had been performed. The Pañcaviṃśa then continues to incorporate two other Ṛgvedic verses (this time from Maṇḍala VII)[23] as if to make clearer the end to be attained by the passage of the Soma through the incandescent filter. These Ṛgvedic verses, it is true, do not by themselves show any direct link with the corresponding ritual action. The Brāhmaṇic sensibility, however, still in close contact with the theology which developed concerning the effects of heat in the rite, makes this direct link clearly evident. Explaining these verses, the exegete comments : "Let the clear Goddess Prayer go forward from us as a chariot well carpentered and swift; for my long life become thou strained, for my glory become thou strained. Of Earth and Sky the origin they know, let hear the waters that flow down. Sing thou, O Soma, here as Chanter, for my long life, for my spiritual lustre, for the weal of the sacrificer, for the reign of so and so".[24] The Sūtras explain, in their turn, that these verses are recited while the Soma is being filtered[25].

Now, if the 'raw' or the 'cold' do not have in themselves the energy to move something which only the 'cooked' have— this means that it is only at the time when the Soma passes through the incandescent filter that offering and offerer find their strength and that the divine and

23. The verses are the first two of the RV VIII. 34.1-2: *pra-śukraitu devī manīṣā/asmat sutaṣṭo ratho da vājī// viduh pṛthivyā divo janitram/ sṛṇvanty āpo adha kṣarantīḥ/*.

24 PancBr 1. 2.9 (Caland's translation). We have quoted here a text belonging to the commentaries, because, although generally we prefer to avoid this type of quotations for this part of our study, sometimes, as in the present ease, the help of the tradition in explaining difficult passages may be useful.

25. Cf. LatySS I.10.21. Also W. CALAND and V. HENRY, *L'Agniṣṭoma op. cit.*, par. 131.

brilliant (*śukra*) prayer acquires the power to move, to go forward and therefore to precede the sacrificer. In fact, the Brāhmaṇa adds, in a verse of its own, that the liquid is purified and therefore strengthened, by which it means to say that in that way the liquid acquires that energy which is necessary to prolong the life of the sacrificer and to augment his glory. The song thus receives strength from the ritual and at the same time, being itself a way of infusing energy by means of the word[26], adds energy to the inebriating liquid which is being purified and heated.

But even to remain within the very ambit of the hymns as far as the transforming power of heat on the liquid is concerned, the liquid's passage through the slits (*aṇva*) of the incandescent filter makes every single drop resemble the rising sun (*sūraḥ*),[27] each acquiring the glory of the Divinity, the mythical Dawn. Moreover, the advantages obtained by those who offer it (and consume what is left over) are significantly described in terms which evoke light. The priest who communicates with the Divine by means of the drink (which is identified with the Moon) prepared in this way invokes in his chant the light, that light (*jyotis*) which belongs by right to the Divinity, and asks that he become brilliant as the fire of the sacrifice (literally: "which is produced by friction", *mathita*).[28]. The Soma, bringing us light, can make us perfect[29], give us splendour and riches,[30] heroism and treasures of all kinds[31] and also remove from us all evil together with false friends[32]. In that light, the sacrificer reaches also the supreme good of immortality, the good par excellence which is the gift of Soma[33].

26. Cf. e.g., RV VIII. 78 (89). 7, where Maruts, "energise" (*tapatā*) a *sāman* for Indra.

27. Cf. RV IX.10.5: *āpānāso vivasvato jananta uṣaso bhagam/sūrā aṇvaṃ vi tanvate.*

28. Cf. RV VIII. 48.6.

29. Cf. e.g., RV IX.4.1 ff.

30. Cf. e.g., RV IX. 31.I ff.

31. Cf. e.g., RV IX. 59.1 and 5.

32. Cf. e.g., RV IX. 104.6.

33. Cf. e.g., RV VIII.48.3 *apāma soman amṛtā abhūmāgan ma jyotir avidāma devān* . . . ("We have drunk Soma and become immortal; we have attained the light, the Gods discovered") (tr. GRIFFITH); and also RV IX. 113.8 etc.

All this gives credence to our supposition that the Vedic priest, when he entrusts his offering to Agni to 'prepare' or 'cook' it, does not mean mere cooking but rather he intends to give his offering the heat which signifies Divine energy. Such energy is indeed so essential to the sacrifice that its lack appears to him to be evidently deleterious. In fact, without this energy the sacrificed cannot reach its destination. A cold object, *āmaḥ*, has no power to move. Since the filter has already in itself a purifying function, the passage of the Soma through the heat of the filter acts on the material of the offering in three ways : it *purifies* it, it *transforms* it and it endows it with a *power to rise*. Soma, thus, rises up to the gods, only when transformed, purified and fully endowed with energy.

(b) *The Horse Sacrifice* (*aśvamedha*):

The place where these three motifs concerning the effects of heat on the offering stand out with greater evidence is in the Ṛgvedic hymn which accompanies one of the greatest sacrifices, namely the *aśvamedha* or the Horse Sacrifice.

Here cooking seems to be, after the immolation of the victim, one of the most important rites judging by the number of times it is mentioned in the first of the two hymns dedicated to it[34]. After tracing the various particulars of the rite of presentation, immolation and cutting of the victim, the hymn proceeds to emphasize in almost every verse the culminating moment of the preparation and cooking of the various parts of the horse[35]. The immolators must cook the victim (*medhaṃ śṛtapākam*) in such a way that the impure parts are purified and the foul smell of the flesh is changed into sweet perfume[36]. Indeed, it is this change of smell which signals to the sacrificer, to his priests and perhaps even to the Divinity that the preparation of the victim is finished and that the cooking has been done

34. Cf. RV I.162 and 163.
35. Cf. e.g. RV I. 62.6 and 10ff.
36. Cf. RV I. 162.10 *yad ūvadhyam udarasyāpavāti ya āmasva kraviṣo gandha asti| sukṛtā tac chamitāraḥ kṛṇvantūta medhaṃ śṛtapākaṃ pacantu ||* ("food undigested steaming from his belly, and any odour of raw flesh remaining, this let the immolators set in order and dress the sacrifice with perfect cooking"). (tr. Griffith)

well.[37] The flesh of the great principal victim, the courser, immolated in the name of the Vedic Divinities, must pass through a transformation effected by the cooking to be able to become a worthy offering to the 'sacred' world. Without this transformation, effected by the cooking, the flesh would remain impure, still inserted in the so-called 'profane' world, and so 'inert'—to use the same expression used in connection with the Soma which was said to remain 'inert', devoid of the power to move, if it were not to pass through the heat of the filter[38].

The hymn recalls at a certain stage all the equipment of the horse, especially those things which 'have served it' (*pari bhūṣantyaśvam*) for its preparation. Among these are particularly prominent the utensils used for cooking, whether by way of boiling or by way of roasting. In fact the verse specifically mentions among the things which 'serve the horse': the large fork, the container for the meat, the cauldron (*ukhā*), the soup bowls, the smoking lids, the rice-pudding (*caruṇā*) (which is the cereal offering which usually accompanies bloody offerings), the hollow skewers[39]. The fact that these are honoured by a special mention in the hymn is indicative of the great importance of their function in the economy of sacrifice and of the importance, from a liturgical point of view, of their service to the horse.

From the mention of the containers, we can also deduce that the flesh of the victim had to be boiled since many kinds of pots and bowls to drink the soup or juice are spoken of, while the presence of the skewers indicates that at least part of the

37. Cf. RV I. 162. 12: *ye vājinaṃ paripaśyanti pakvaṃ ya īmāhuḥ surabhir nirhareti||* ("They who observing that the Horse is ready call out and say the smell is good, remove it.") (tr. Griffith). H.H. Wilson (*in hoc loco*, p. 262) explains the verse as follows: "it is fragrant, therefore, give us some; or it may mean, give it to the gods; *nirhara*, take off, or give, having no government". The change of smell which is here hinted at, is an essential means to understand if the meat is cooked, because at that time as it is still nowadays, it was formally forbidden to taste the food which is being cooked. Cf. later on in Ch. V.

38. Cf. above pp. 29-30.

39. RV I.162.13: *yan nīkṣaṇaṃ māṃs pacanyā ukhāyā yā pātrāṇi yūṣṇa āsecanāni ūṣmaṇyāpidhānā carūṇām aṅkāḥ sūnāḥ pari bhūṣanty aśvam* |

offering was roasted. A glance at the *Sūtra*, which provides us with the ritual at least as it developed later, confirms the fact that the greater part of the flesh of the victim is in fact boiled in one container, and that the skewers are used especially for the heating and then the cooking of the *omentum* (*vapā*), the membrane covering the intestines, which is universally considered to be the portion of the victim specifically reserved for the Divinity[40]. Thus we can infer that the principal victim of the *aśvamedha* was cooked at the time when the hymn in question was composed[41]. This is confirmed by the poet who exalts the various containers which have been used for the purpose.

After the victim has been cooked and the smell of the raw flesh has turned to that of cooked meat, it is placed on consecrated grass[42] and the offering volted into round balls (*Piṇḍa*)[43] just as is the custom even to this day with all kinds of offerings. The victim in this form is then solicitously handed over to the fire a second time.

Without entering here into the minute details of the *aśvamedha* ceremony as elaborated successively by the Yajurveda and by its Śrauta Sūtra and which, in time, will be developed in still greater detail[44], we can already see from the formulas which are recited during the course of each of the phases of the rite, a process emerging in which cooking seems to have a determining function in such a way that the three properties of fire mentioned at the end of the previous section are brought out more forcibly than in the rite of the pressing of

40. Cf. later on pp. 117 ff. in Ch. V.

41. Namely RV I.162. Not always, in fact, can we be sure that ritual changes have not crept in the period between the composition of the hymns and the systematization of the ritual rules. The changes registered in the methods of immolation (cf. later in note 51 of this chapter) may be an example of these occurrences.

42. Cf. RV I.162.11: *mā tad bhūmyāmā śriṣan mā tṛṇeṣu devebhyas tad uśadbhyo rātam astu|*

43. Cf RV I.162.19: *tātā piṇḍānāṃ pra juhomyagnau* . . . ("this in the form of 'round balls' I offer in the fire").

44. VajSam XXII-XXV & TaittSam V.2.11 ff. with SatBr XIII. See the collection of the *śrautic* texts referring to this important sacrifice in R.N. DANDEKAR, *Śrautakośa*, Poona (Vaidika Samsodhana Mandala), 1958 ff. in various volumes which are not yet all published. Cf. also Ch. V below.

Soma. In fact, *purification* is obvious in the recovery and valorization of the less attractive parts of the animal flesh; *transformation* is especially indicated in the change of smell of the flesh when, after it was raw, it is now cooked—a change which is emphasized in the verses which are recited while the action is being performed; as for *power to rise*, which we have postulated as the more plausible reason for the specific characteristic of the Vedic rite, it appears here too in a negative way. The fact possibly seemed so obvious that there was no need to mention it. Only its lack seems to attract the attention of the priest. As is the case of the passage of Soma through the filter, so here too it seems that the normal means, to impart power to the victim to 'move' is given by fire which transforms it from raw into cooked[45]. What leads us to think on these lines is the problem which faces the *ṛṣis* regarding those parts of the horse which, either by their very nature or because of causes independent of the will of the sacrificer, cannot benefit from the cooking as a means of propulsion.

These parts are of two kinds : the first kind are the accessories of the trappings which came into contact with the victim before its immolation: the mantle, the spurs, the rope which tied its legs (perhaps at the very moment of the immolation)[46], while the second kind are those small particles of flesh which "the flies have eaten, those which remain sticking to the sacrificial post and to the hatchet, and those which remain adhering to the hands and finger-nails of the immolator"[47].

At first sight, it may seem somewhat strange to find these relatively small parts mentioned in the hymn with the injunction that these too join the rest of sacrificial victim which has already ascended to the Gods. The Vedic *mantra* which names one after another the various parts which are refractory to transformation or lost because of accidental causes, continues with the invocation: *may also these be with you* (*horse*) *with the*

45. Cf. what has been said above in notes 20 and 22.

46. Cf. RV I.162.16: *yad aśvāya vāsa upastṛṇantyadhīvāsaṃ yā hiraṇyān yasmai/ sandānamarvantaṃ paḍbīśam priyā deveṣvā yāmayanti//*

47. RVI .162.9: *yad aśvasya kraviṣo makṣikāśa yad vā svarau svadhitau riptam asti/ yaddhastayoḥ śamitur yan nakheṣu sarvā tā te api deveṣvastu//*

*Gods*."[48] It seems therefore that these parts which were not subjected to the transforming action of cooking, were considered lost in the act of offering, and hence even though the above-mentioned *mantra* strictly speaking does not mention heat, has the function of taking its place as a propelling force.

One could also suppose that these verses could not have been intended to substitute an eventual 'missing cooking'. After all, the formula "may also these be with you (horse) with the Gods" could have been pronounced when these parts were committed to the fire during the final oblation. That the verses which explicitly mention those parts of the victim which could not benefit from the action of the cooking, have this function in this important liturgical act is confirmed however by the ritual rules of the Sūtras and the Brāhmaṇas. Even if we would not want to consider these rules as already valid in all their completeness and subtlety during the more ancient period as mirrored in the Ṛgvedic hymn, it still remains a significant fact that tradition interpreted these *mantras* in this very way by applying them to the cereal cake (*paśupuroḍāśa*) which is called the "completion of the sacrifice". According to the Aitareya Brāhmaṇa, in it are gathered symbolically these lost parts to allow them also to benefit from the transforming action of heat[49]. Still, even if this rite was not yet present in the earliest times—and this is not even certain—the very fact that the religious sensibility of the following generations felt the need to provide a concrete item, which could be actually cooked, confirms us in the view that the *mantra* pronounced on the 'lost parts' had the ritual function to supply that energy which only the heat of the sacred fire could bestow.

Moreover, this insistence that the priest recovers even those smallest parts of the victim shows that no part, not even the smallest, should be missing for the sacrifice to be complete. This paved the way for another of those Vedic intuitions which, in the course of time, made clearly apparent the difference between the Brāhmaṇic cult and that of other religious cultures. The fact that the horse must go to the world of Gods whole and entire, including its equipment, makes one think

48. *Sarvā tā te api deveṣvastu*: which is the ending of both verse 9 and 16.
49. Cf. AitBr VII.1 (I.2.11) quoted below in Ch. V, note 135. The problem of the *paśupuroḍāśa* will be discussed in Ch. V, pp. 135 ff.

that it does not 'die' after the fashion of the victims offered in sacrifice in other religions. If, in fact, the victim were destined simply to disappear and to be consumed in the divine banquet, there would be no need to equip it with everything that had served it in life by way of trappings, nor would the lack of any of its parts, even of those small particles of flesh eaten by flies or those that remained stuck to the finger nails of the immolator, disturb in any way its consumption on the part of the Divinity.

The requirement that the animal be whole and entire in the divine world seems to point to a future life which awaits the immolated animal once it reaches its destination. Its death is simply a passage, a painful but necessary path towards an eternal future of glory. Beyond its slaughter, it is life which presents itself to the horse, a life in a new sphere with a different reality belonging to the stable and joyful world of the Divine. And it is in fact precisely this assurance which is given to the equine representative at the moment of its difficult crossing over through the immolation : he will not die, but he will go directly to the world of Gods to enjoy a new life.[50] His is indeed the shortest and most direct way to attain this goal, a goal coveted by all creation. He is moreover assured that he will not suffer, and lest his soul burns of fear, one prays that the hatchet be skilfully handled by the immolator so that it should not remain in contact with the body more than the few necessary seconds, while the immolator is exhorted not to be in too great a hurry so that he will be able to hit in the right place and not damage the limbs[51]. The victim is in fact subjected to a process

50. Cf. RV I.162.21: *na vā u etan mriyase na riṣyasi devāṃ ideṣi pathibhiḥ sugebhiḥ* ... ("No, here thou diest not, thou art not injured: by easy paths unto the Gods thou goest ...") (tr. Griffith).

51. Cf. RV I.162.20: *mā tvā tapat priya ātmāpiyantaṃ mā svadhitis tanva'ā tiṣṭhipat te| mā te gṛdhnuraviśasiātihāya chidrā gātrāṇyasinā mithū kaḥ||* ("Let not thy dear soul burn thee as thou comest, let not the hatchet linger in thy body. Let not a greedy clumsy immolator, missing the joints, mangle thy limbs unduly".) (tr. Griffith). We note that here one speaks of 'hatchet', *svadhiti* (f.). The term is peculiarly a Vedic one, and only rarely is it found in the Purāṇas. This leads us to think that in Vedic times (at least at the earliest period) the immolation was not performed, as in classical times beginning from the Brāhmaṇas and the Sūtras onwards, only by suffocation.

of dismemberment followed by the reunion of the parts of its body in the world of Gods. The means for this reunification, transformation and revivification is precisely the heat which changes it from raw to cooked.

The destiny which awaits the victim after its immolation and cooking is made clear by the very adjectives which qualify it : the victim is called 'the wealth of Gods' (*devānāṃ puṣṭe*) and their 'good friend' (*subandhum*)[52]. The divine world then, seems to receive power from the offering, not so much in the form of nourishment (as common elsewhere) but by welcoming in their midst a 'friend' who gives them power by his very presence full of energy[53]. If the victim were merely destined to be consumed by Gods, as is often the case in other religions, for example, in the Mediterranean ones, it would not be assured of future life. The consumed animal, in these other religions, generally speaking, does not remain alive (except in those cases where the Divinity is identified with the victim—something which is not the case in this type of sacrifice) and the eaten parts, including those eaten by the Deities, are usually destroyed. The Greek myth of Pelops illustrates our point. In the banquet of Tantalus, the resurrection of his son Pelops, who was offered as food to Gods, was possible only because the Gods themselves got to know of it in time and did not consume him. Only Demeter failed to notice it and ate her part, the shoulder, with the result that it could not be re-integrated into the whole body[54]. The Vedic horse, on the contrary, has a different destiny, and in its transformation by fire, he himself obtains the

In fact, only if the animal had to face the hatchet while still alive, would it have made sense to comfort him and to ask him not to be afraid to approach the knife. This need of exhortation and comfort would have been out of place if the hatchet had been used for the post-mortem dissection. This procedure of killing with a knife is, however, in contrast with the methods of immolation prevalent in the Brāhmaṇic period. Even a *paṇḍita* to whom I showed the passage remained uncertain about its meaning.

52. Cf. RV I.162.7 : *devānāṃ pvṣṭe cakṛmā subandhum. Puṣṭi* "riches" is a Vedic term only.

53. This does not mean, however, that because of usual expressions both in the texts and in the present study, we cannot continue to talk of the victim as "nourishment of the Gods".

54. Cf. e.g. APOLLOD MYTHOGR., *Epitome* I.10; also PLUT., *Theseus* 221; etc. For a general survey of the myth, see K. KERENYI, *Gli Dei*

immortality to which those who offer him aspire, and which he then extends both to the Gods waiting for him[55] and to the sacrificer and his family offering him.[56]

Moreover, lest the horse experiences the anxiety of death, which, no matter how beautifully represented, has always a terrific aspect, a secondary victim, a billy-goat, is placed at his side as his companion to help him crossing to the other shore. This billy-goat, of black colour, is led in procession to the place of immolation, already bleating, and placed in front of the horse[57]. It is said to be the part destined to Pūṣan, the Sun in its meridian splendour, but here probably identified with the Agni of the Sacrifice[58]. The function of this billy-goat is two-fold : on the one hand, according to its 'official' function described by the hymn itself, it is to precede the principal victim to announce its arrival to the Gods who await it[59] and

*e qli Eroi della Grecia*, vols. 2, Zurich, 1958, Ch. V; R. GRAVES, *The Greek Myths*, vols 2, Penguin Books, 1957 (Rep).

55. Cf. RV I.162.11 quoted in note 42 of this chapter.

56. Cf. RV I.162.22: *sugavyaṃ no vājī svaśvyaṃ puṃsaḥ putrāṃ uta viśvā-puṣaṃ rayim / anāgās tvaṃ no aditiḥ kṛṇotu kṣatraṃ no aśvo vanatāṃ haviṣmān//* ("may this Steed bring us all-sustaining riches, wealth in good kine, good horses, manly offspring. Freedom from sin may Aditi vouchsafe us: the Steed with our oblations gain us lordship.") (tr. Griffith). Here, as very often is the case, the desire of immortality is expressed in terms of riches, sons and cattle.

57. Cf. RV I.162.2-3: *yan nirṇijā reknasā prāvṛtasya rātim gṛbhītāṃ mukhato nayanti/ suprāñajo memyad viśvarūpa indrāpūṣṇoḥ priyam apyeti pāthaḥ // 2 // eṣa cchāgaḥ puro aśvena vājinā pūṣṇo bhāgo nīyate viśvadevyaḥ/ abhipriyaṃ yat puroḷāśam arvatā tvaṣṭedenaṃ sauśravasāya jinvati // 3 //* ("what time they bear before the Courser, covered with trappings and with wealth, the grasped oblation, the dappled goat goeth straightforward, bleating, to the place dear to Indra and to Pūṣan. 2. Dear to all Gods, this goat, the share of Pūṣan, is first led forward with the vigorous Courser, while Tvaṣṭṛ sends him forward with the Charger, acceptable for sacrifice, to glory."3) (tr. Griffith). See also RV I.163.12: *ajaḥ puro nīyate nābhir asyānu paścāt*—("... the goat who is his kin is led before him ...") (tr. Griffith).

58. Cf. RV I.162.3: *pūṣṇo bhāgaḥ*—The identification of Pūṣṇa with Agni has been suggested because of a parallel with another Ṛgvedic hymn: X. 16.4, where the he-goat is the secondary victim and is said to be "Agni's portion." See below, note 67. See furthermore H. H. WILSON, *Ṛg-Veda*, vol. II, p. 259, who makes the same identification but by another means.

59. Cf. RV I.162.4: *atrā pūṣṇaḥ prathamo bhāga eti yajñaṃ devebhyaḥ prati-*

on the other hand, (if we can take this suggestion from another hymn[60]), it is to protect the principal victim from the first destructive impact of the fire so that it should not be injured and can retain its full vitality.

(c) *The Funeral Rite* :

Now, if this process of attaining to immortality instead of death is valid for the steed of *aśvamedha* and, by extension, for the principal victim of any type of sacrifice (the secondary victim disappears as the consumed 'portion of Agni', as we have seen and shall see again), it is no wonder that the *ṛṣis* 'saw' (to use Vedic terminology)[61] the possibility of applying the underlying principle to the 'ultimate' victim of the sacrificer's ultimate grand sacrifice, namely that of the *yajamāna's* own body on the funeral pyre[62]. Here the function of fire does not seem to be what it later came to be under the influence of Upaniṣadic philosphy, namely, to eliminate the obstacle of the physical body by helping its decomposition and the dissolution of its various elements into the great elements of the universe. The Vedic hymns lay emphasis more on the revivification of the body through its sacrificial transformation than on anything else. Far from tending towards the elimination of the body, the whole process in fact aims at its reconstruction. This is clear from the very opening of the hymn, probably sung at the kindling of the fire or at the beginning of cremation, by an invocation to Agni to be gentle and "not burn nor consume the body, and not break its skin".[63] In the course of the hymn

*vedayannajaḥ* ("the goat precedes him, the share of Pūṣan, and to the Gods the sacrifice announceth".) (tr. Griffith).

60. Cf. RV X.16.4, discussed later on p. 42, and quoted in note 67.

61. The 'technical' term, in fact, used by the priests to refer to the introduction of innovations in the rites is "to see" (*paś-*); see e.g. RV VIII. 59.6 (Vālakhilya 11): *yajñaṃ tanvānās tapasābhyapaśyam* (".. weaving sacrifice, through *tapas* I saw ...").

62. We are talking here about the cremation of a sacrificer, a man who has his own fire (called *āhitāgni*). There are many funeral rites in ancient India, according to the caste and ritual situation of the deceased. Cf. P. V. KANE, *History of Dharmaśāstra*, op. cit., vol. IV, p. 190 and also ff. for the full description of the funeral rites.

63. RV X. 16.1 : *mainam agne vi daho mābhi śoco māsya tvacaṃ cikṣipo mā śarīram.*

(and therefore of the funeral ceremony) the priest continues to beg the Fire for clemency *not to destroy* what he has been entrusted with[64]. Similarly in other funeral hymns of the Atharva Veda the fire of pyre is supplicated not to destroy the corpse, but to burn it gently (evenly) (*śaṃ*) on all sides[65].

If this is the case, that is, if the ancient Vedic people desired, as it seems they did, that the body of the dead man be maintained and preserved intact, it seems strange that they should have recourse to cremation. Cremation, being a means more of destruction than of conservation, is, in fact, more consonant with the Upaniṣadic vision according to which the destruction of matter is required for the liberation of spirit. Fire, after all, is used especially to destroy not to preserve. It displays itself above all in violence and is not easily placated if its ferocious voracity is not satisfied. It seems strange, therefore, that the people who aspire to a kind of corporeal life even beyond the grave should consign their terrestrial body to the flames to maintain it. The most plausible explanation for this behaviour, which is both ritual and cultural at the same time, of these people so dependent on sacrifice in all its religious meanings, is to be found in the resemblance of the funeral rite to sacrifice itself. Throughout all his life as sacrificer, the *yajamāna* had sung, and made the priests to sing, the immortal destiny awaiting the victim offered on the sacrificial fire. Agni, he has always believed, does not destroy the victim, but prepares it and leads it to its destination. He can, therefore, believe that the same thing could be applied to his own body in its last earthly act when it passes through the same sacrificial fire on which he has offered, during his earthly life, innumerable oblations[66].

64. Cf. RV X.16.7 : *agner varma pari gobhir vyayasva saṃ prorṇuṣva pīvasā medasā ca net tvā dhṛṣṇur harasā jarhṛṣāṇo dadhṛgvidhakṣyan paryaṅkhayāte* ("shield thee with flesh against the flames of A., encompass thee about with fat and marrow, so will be the bold one, eager to attack thee with fierce glow fail to girdle and consume thee".) (tr. Griffith).

65. Cf. AV XVIII. 2.36 : *śaṃ tapa māti tapo agne mā tanvaṃ tapaḥ* . . . and also AV XVIII. 4.11 *śam agne paścāt tapa śaṃ purastāccham uttarācchamadharāt tapainam* ... "do not burn the body, burn gently Agni, your heat ..."; "gently look Agni, gently burn from rear, above, before and under ...".

66. In ancient times the fire for the funeral pyre was taken from the sacrificer's own sacred fires. Cf. P. V. KANE. op. cit., p. 210.

Since the fury of Agni launches itself with force on whatever is committed to it, the fear which fire inspires is exercised by a rite also taken from the same sacrificial tradition. The rite consists in the device of adding a secondary victim, a billy-goat, whose limbs are tied, one by one, to the corresponding members of the corpse, with the omentum on the face. This corresponds to the billy-goat similarly tied to the body of the horse in the *aśvamedha*. There, however, its function is explained, less dramatically, as that of a herald announcing the majestic arrival of the victim into the world of Gods. Here, on the contrary, the necessity of having a billy-goat appears with a task which is more subtle and at the same time more terrifying. The billy-goat is consciously offered as an authentic 'victim' (in the general meaning of the term, and not in its ritual meaning) to the fury of the first fire so that Agni launches himself on to it with all his first wrath and devours it in his flames, with his incandescent heat (the *śocis*, *arcis* and *tapas* of the Sanskrit terminology)[67].

The Vedic priest is here perhaps more aware, than he was at the *aśvamedha*, of the initial destructive power of Agni; and to make sure that Fire does not cause irremediable harm to the corpse, that is to the victim whose immortal destiny he has most at heart, he seeks to remedy the situation by giving a different interpretation to the secondary victim which, as we have already seen, is explicitly said to be the 'portion of Agni'. The fate of this billy-goat, is here, therefore, different from that of the one which, in the *aśvamedha*, is tied to the limbs of the horse; here it is to receive the first violent fury of the devouring fire. This fire, in its destructive form as 'eater of corpses' (*kravyād*), is then removed by means of a *mantra* to give place to a benevolent fire whose task is to energize and

67. Cf. RV X.16.4 : *ajo bhāgas tapasā taṃ te śocis tapatu taṃ te arciḥ* (already mentioned in note 58). The function of the he-goat was partly discussed in the context of *aśvamedha*; therefore, it need not be discussed in the present context where there are no special differences to be noted. Other functions, however, performed by the secondary victim (or victims) will become clearer—also to the priests themselves—at the time of the Brāhmaṇas. We shall discuss them in Ch. V.

transform the corpse[68]. The initial fire which sets the pyre ablaze is, in fact, at the beginning 'impure' since it comes in direct contact with a matter, the corpse, which is not yet 'prepared' and is a prey to the coldness of death and hence impure. This Agni, 'eater of corpses', has its sacrificial counterpart—as we shall see later[69]—in the fire of the immolator which is used to give a first heating to the *omentum* and to the other parts of the sacrificial offering. In this preliminary heating, the 'raw' and 'profane' element of the victim begins to be transformed into being 'sacred' in such a way that when it is brought to the fire of the altar, it will already have left behind, at least in part, its earthly nature and thus will be able to come in contact with the consecrated Agni who is ready to bestow on it its final transformation and thus to make it worthy to become an 'offering' in all respects.

The fire of the pyre, however, cannot be materially kindled twice, nor can the corpse be reasonably displaced from one fire to another as is done with the *omentum* and the other parts of a normal sacrificial victim. So it is ritually divided into two, of which the first, after having burnt the offering which is meant to placate it in its initial force, enters in contact with the members, still profane, of the deceased *yajamāna*, to be later ritually removed by means of the appropriate *mantra* with the impurities which it has absorbed[70]; while the second, which assumes the benevolent title of *jātaveda*, 'Knower of what is born' is called upon to perform the more important task of energizing the victim, in this case the body of the *yajamāna* himself, in order to revive it in the ritual transformation. The second fire thus renders the corpse 'ready' (and here too the

68. Cf. RV X.16.9 ab : *kravyādam agniṃ pra hiṇomi dūraṃ yamarājño gacchatu ripravāhaḥ* ("I send afar flesh-eating Agni, bearing off stains may he depart to Yama's subjects".) (tr. Griffith).

69. Cf. later on in Ch. V, p. 124. Not to overburden the present study, and lose sight of our main trend of thought regarding the positive agreeable use of hot energy in Vedic sacrifice, we leave it for another occasion to study the effects produced by a possible lack of the right degree of the required sacred heat, including the problems arising from profane material when it is still 'raw'.

70. The *mantra* used is the one quoted above in note 68.

Sanskrit term used is *śṛta*, cooked)[71] to be taken to its new dwelling-place in the world of the blessed[72].

From this it follows that just as Agni performs his task as the 'carrier of the offerings' from one level of Reality to another as Mediator par excellence between the human and the divine spheres, so too, by extension he includes in his task also that of being an 'escort of souls' (or of 'persons' in their integrity). But how different is this function of his from that, for example, of a Hermes *psychopompos*! Whereas Hermes is an 'escort of souls' in the sense that he guides to the divine world those who are entrusted to him, Agni absolves his task in the same way as in sacrifice, that is to say, by means of a transformation which he effects on the corpse, imparting to it the power to *ascend* to where its destiny calls it[73]. Even as *psychopompos*, Agni is always and principally a sacrificial Power who acts by means of the energizing and transforming force of his *tapas*, of his heat. In fact, as the Vedic priest had profoundly intuited during the performance of his sacrifices, the sacrificial fire is not simply destructive, but contains in itself the power of transforming and revivifying what is entrusted to it. Hence, in spite of the fact that the fire of pyre clearly burns the corpse and destroys it, it can also be seen as a valid means of revivification, if understood in the light of the analogy with sacrifice. And this interpretation is also confirmed by the use of the word *śṛta* which designates the positive action of the *jātaveda* fire on the corpse.

In fact, the use of the word *śṛta* in connection with corpse, which is surely not meant to mean 'cooked' in the usual sense

71. "O Jātavedas, when you have 'cooked' (*śṛta*) it, then you send it on the way of the fathers; when you have 'prepared' (*śṛta*) it, O Jātaveda, then you give it to the fathers" ("*yadā śṛtaṃ kṛṇavo jātavedo 'themenaṃ pra hiṇutāt pitṛbhyaḥ || 1 || śṛtaṃ yadā karasi jātavedo 'themenaṃ pari dattāt pitṛbhyaḥ . . .*") (RV X. 16.1 and 2).

72. Cf. RV X.16.9 cd : *ihaivāyamitaro jātavedā devebhyo havyaṃ vahatu prajānan* ("But let this other Jātavedas carry oblation to the Gods for he is skilful") (tr. Griffith).

73. Cf. RV X.16.3 : *sūryaṃ cakṣur gacchatu vātam ātmā dyāṃ ca gaccha pṛthivīṃ ca dharmaṇā / apo vā gaccha yadi tatra te hitamoṣadhīṣu prati tiṣṭhā śarīraiḥ* // ("The Sun receive thine eye, the wind thy spirit; go, as thy merit is, to earth or heaven; go, if it be thy lot, unto the water; go make thine home in plants with all thy members".) (tr. Griffith).

of the word, rather signifies what is required from fire by the Vedic priest whether in this particular case or in that of any other kind of sacrifice : *transformation.* 'Cooking' transforms what is cooked into a new life as a prelude to the divinization to which it aspires. This function of fire, therefore, justifies cremation even where there is the will to live and even a wish for bodily immortality[74].

And it is therefore here where a ritual language with a message of its own begins to come to light. Analyzing the probable reasons which must have led the liturgist to cremate the deceased even though he had in mind the latter's survival after death, including that of his body, one could perhaps arrive at a better knowledge of the Vedic conception, for us still dim, of what lies beyond the tomb[75]. It is not the task of this study to delay on such a problem. It is enough to indicate here how many suggestions worth considering from a theological and philosophical point of view, can be found in a study of the cult.

2. *Some Historico-religious Parallels* :

At this point it is interesting to attempt to draw a parallel with other religions and ask ourselves what specific characteristic distinguishes Vedic sacrifice from that, for example, of the Greek or Judaic sacrifice—the two more significant points of reference in the Western culture, a culture which generally speaking is unanimously considered to be a paradigm in such and other matters.

74. Archaeologists begin to be more and more certain that the first Indo-Europeans used to bury their dead. In such case the change to cremation appearing in Vedic usage confirms the hypothesis of a sacrificial influence leading one to see in the pyre's fire not a means of destroying the corpse, but of preserving through revivification. Only later on, will the evident destructive force of fire be adapted to the change in the philosophical attitude, which occurred at the time of Upaniṣads, towards death and cremation. Anyway, even nowadays cremation is not meant for all the Hindus, but is reserved, theoretically, to those entitled to have a sacrificial fire.

75. It is somewhat significant that an American scholar, having finished a thesis on *tapas,* found it meaningful to choose as theme for his next study *śrāddha,* namely the ceremony for the dead.

In both of these religions, fire plays a vital part in the preparation and consumption of the sacrificial offering. In Judaic ritual, fire is an indispensable element, but among the many ritual regulations which Yahweh himself dictates for his cult, there is no special emphasis as to how to kindle it. Indeed, in one limit-situation it is not even lit by human hand but comes down directly from Heaven as a sign of God's acceptance of the sacrificial gift[76]. Ritually it does not seem to have the same importance as that given to other liturgical particulars which are essential in the Judaic religious tradition. Here the emphasis is laid on the manner in which the sacrificial offering is to be consumed; or in the allocation of the victim's blood which is to be sprinkled on fixed places of the altar; etc.[77] Sometimes specific ways of cooking the victim are given, as for example in the Paschal commemoration, but here too the emphasis is laid not on the properties of the fire but rather on its consumption by the faithful[78]. It is in the *act of consuming* the Paschal lamb that the message expressed by the sacrifice is conveyed; it is this same act which gives spiritual and historical meaning to the rite[79].

Moreover, God seals in the sacrifice every pact which he makes with his people, so that it is in the common partaking of the offering that the covenant is cemented. As the victim is to be eaten, logically it must be cooked. However, the portion destined for Yahweh is not cooked, but having been well prepared, is put to burn in the fire while still obviously raw. When Elijah challenges the prophets of Baal, in a divine contest, the decisive factor is precisely the appearance of the fire. This fire however has nothing to do with the preparation of the victim but with its consumption. The bull is cut in pieces and laid, still raw, on the wood of the altar; it is abundantly drenched in water so that the absorbing and destructive violence of the divine fire is manifested[80].

76. Cf. below note 80.
77. Cf. e.g. *Mishna* I. 1.
78. Cf. e.g, Ex. XII. 1 ff. espec. vv. 9 and 11.
79. Cf. Deut. XVI. 2 ff.
80. Cf. I kings XVIII. 20-38 esp. from v. 33 onwards.

Similarly, in Greece fire is also the means by which the victim is offered to the Divinity[81]. Cooking has an important part to play[82]. As in Israel, it seems to be connected with the consumption of the victim by man rather than with the manner of producing an effect on the victim or on the Divinity which is to receive it. The myth of Prometheus illustrates this fact well : When Zeus discovers the trick played on him by the Titan over his own portion of the offering, he reacts by taking fire away from men so that they will have no means of consuming their part of the immolated animal[83]. Without fire it is not possible to consume the offering, so Prometheus remedies the situation by stealing again the fire from Zeus and returning it to mankind. Although this act earns him the well known punishment, he has completed his civilizing work for mankind[84]. This means that, in order to put a remedy to the effects of Zeus'

81. Cf. e.g. pertinent text in W. BURKERT, *op. cit.*, pp. 80 ff. We do not have much information about Greek sacrifices, but surely fire was very important, so much so that the altar of Zeus in Olympia was built of ashes.

82. The tripodes were very important items in sacrifices and there the flesh of the victims was boiled. Cf. W. BURKERT, *op. cit.*, note 29 of Ch. II, and p. 83 (of the It. Ed.)

83. One could recall here the well-known myth of Prometheus in HESIOD, *Theog.* vv 532 ff. The myth narrates how the Titan contrived to get for man the better portion of the victim offered in sacrifice, tricking Zeus to choose for himself the 'classical' portion, that is the long bones covered with fat. Disappointed, Zeus took fire away from men so that they be unable to consume their better portion. But Prometheus stole the fire again from the Gods, thus allowing sacrifices and civilization to proceed on their course. The myth seems to account for the 'strange' division of the portions between Gods and men. In a civilization where all the 'best' things have to be given to the Divine it is nonsensical to give to Gods the less comestible portion. This usage actually was handed down to the 'civilized' world from the prehistoric hunting period, where the vivification of the killed game was due **from the reposition of the long bones** covered with fat. But what at that time had a meaning, came to represent a 'mischievous' device in a different cultural situation. Hence the myth explaining this so-called 'cheating'. For an interpretation of this myth, see D. SABBATUCCI, *Saggi sul misticismo greco*, Roma (Ed Ateneo), 1955, pp. 77 ff.

84. The punishment of Prometheus consisted in his being bound to the Rocks of Caucasus, with an eagle daily devouring his always growing liver (Cf. ESCHYLUS, *Prometheus Bound*). The punishment of men consisted in the creation of Pandora and her subsequently being sent to the world with her famous vase full of evils including Hope. (Cf. HESIOD. *Theog.* vv 567 ff.)

anger, Prometheus although himself an inventor, could not find any other means but fire to prepare the sacrificial victim for consumption; although this cooking was not necessarily extended to the share of Gods.

The difference between this and what we have tried to bring out in our exposition of the Vedic sacrifice is clear enough. It would become clearer still if we were to consider the eventual results stemming from lack of fire and absence of cooking in both Greek and Vedic sacrifices. When Zeus took the fire away from man, perhaps he meant to deprive him of the means to participate in a sacrifice where the eating of raw meat could be simply unthinkable. Yet, in the history of the Greek religion we know of a sacrifice which dispenses with fire and with the 'civilizing' properties of cooking. This is the Orphic sacrifice in which the faithful—generally women—consume the victim raw as soon as it is killed. By means of the direct and immediate consumption of the victim when still pulsating with life, the faithful aim at entering into an immediate 'mystical' relation with the Divinity identified with the kid-victim without the mediation of fire. All the orgiastic rites of the Orphic-Dionysian mystery religion seem, in fact, to want to break out of the confines of social norms : the kid which is sacrificed is considered wild (whereas one of the actually universal conditions of the sacrifice demands that the victim be domesticated). It is chased *extra muros* (outside the limits set by society), and torn to pieces on the spot without preparation. This emphasizes the direct sacramental communion of the faithful with the Divine in a mystical thrust which projects them beyond the conventions of society. In other words, the Orphic faithful who consume the sacrificial victim without it passing through the mediating and civilizing power of fire, perform an act which, though generally disapproved by conventional society, is religiously legitimized in Greece and assumes, in contrast to the normal sacrifice, certain special characteristics which may be called 'mystical'[85].

85. We recall that the word "mystic" is originally derived from the Greek word "mysticos" connected with all that regards the Mysteries, especially the Eleusinian, but also the Orphic, Dionysian etc.

The situation is completely different in the Vedic 'sacrifice'. In the Veda, where the lack of heat and of cooking is explicitly mentioned, it always has a negative character, even for the Divinity. It is the *atapta tanūr* which lacks the power to arrive at its completion; it is that portion of the horse lost to cooking which has to be symbolically transferred on 'something' which could be subjected to cooking in order to make the sacrifice complete. Indra can be invited to receive the offering only when the priest is quite sure that it is sufficiently cooked or heated as we have seen. Besides, lack of heat is considered to be the mark of foreign peoples[86], and it is precisely because these foreigners do not boil the milk (when the animals are not milked according to the rules) that their sacrifice is considered useless for the Divine[87]. As a result the herds of cattle of alien peoples are useless and sterile from a religious, and therefore also a social, point of view, and their plunder by the Vedic peoples is seen to be more than legitimate[88]. The unheated container is characteristically that used by foreigners (*itarajanā*) and the poets of the Atharvaveda who perhaps have greater experience with 'cold' rites than their colleagues of the Ṛks, perceive the danger which lies in this lack of ritual heat and warn against its effects which they attribute to sorcery[89]. Far from seeing it as a 'mystical' expression, the Vedic people consider lack of heat as belonging to what is generally known as sorcery.

But, even without search for those rites in which lack of heat is deliberately sought with a precise aim, such as in the rites of black magic, it is enough to see the negative effect which the failure of heat to reach a required degree has on the Vedic rite itself. We have already considered some key examples which have served us to establish the specific properties of heat in the

86. Cf. e.g. AV VIII. 10.28.

87. Cf. RV III.53.14: . . . *nāśiraṃ duhre na tapanti gharmam* ("They pour no milky draught, they heat no cauldron") (tr. Griffith).

88. *Ibid.* For a comment on this and similar texts see my "Ritual as Mirror Reflecting Ṛgvedic Life" in *Bharati*, Bulletin of the Dept. of Ancient Indian History, Culture and Archaeology, vols. 12-14 (1968-71) dedicated to V.S. Agrawala, Benares (B.H.U.) 1971, pp. 281 ff.

89. Cf. AV VI.17.4; V.31.1: *yāṃ te cakrur āme pātre* . . ("That (spell) put in the raw vessel...").

Vedic sacrifice : the pressing of Soma whose plant has to receive the right quantity of heat in order to attain the *tad*, i. e. the goal to which it is directed. It is precisely here that the essential difference lies between the use of fire in the Mediterranean religions and in the Vedic. In Greece, cooking is merely indicative of being a civilizing device and therefore can be occasionally dispensed with. In India, cooking is the principal agent which provides the victim with the energy to transform itself and to ascend to its proper destination, and so is indispensable. In India, its absence does not express a mystical attitude; it renders all the rites inefficacious or even counterproductive. Its presence gives the measure of the actualizing power attributed to cooking, a power which can determine the success or failure of any sacrificial activity.

In other words : in Greece, an offering which is consumed raw has its *raisond'être* although remaining at the periphery of the official religion. It only alters one's relationship to the Divinity, but does not abolish it; on the contrary, it strengthens it. In India when a more intimate and more immediate 'mystical' relationship with the Divine is sought it is rather the celebration of the rite which is dropped altogether, but, significantly not the energy produced by it. This energy, as we are going to see, is interiorized through ascetic discipline as *tapas*.

### 3. *First Consequences of Ritual Cooking as an Agent of Transformation* :

The Vedic priest was not fully aware in the beginning of the possible liturgical and philosophical implications which his manner of handling the offering entailed. He probably only knew that the rites he performs distinguish him from the priests of the surrounding peoples who "do not heat the cauldron"[90]. But as yet no precise references—but only hints—are given to explain the effects caused by ritual heat. Still, the idea that the heat of the sacrificial fire has an 'energetic' meaning is already latent in several passages of the Ṛgvedic hymns.

90. Cf. RV III.53.14 quoted above in note 87.

The start of this Vedic interpretation of heat as an energizing element in sacrifice may have been the observation of the transforming powers of fire and its heat which are able to radically change the properties of offering, modifying it from the raw to the cooked state and transforming its unpleasant smell into sweet fragrance. The attentive priests and poets must have then extended this process from the physical realm to the realm which is more properly religious. After all, this step could not have been too difficult for the Vedic man, who is attentive to every detail and is in search of a unifying principle between the transient world, from where sacrifice departs, and the eternal, divine, world where sacrifice arrives. The energy of heat, which has the power to transform a physical object in such a way that it can become virtually unrecognizable from its previous condition, must also possess the power to effect another much more important transformation on the victim, a transformation which renders it presentable to Gods and acceptable for them as part of themselves. It is this energy which gives fire the power to bring about not only the preliminary purification of the offering but also the total transformation which is necessary for the interaction between the two realms or spheres of the global Reality : the terrestrial and the divine. These two realms are felt to be not only separate from each other but also intrinsically different, though complementary to each other. In order to come into contact, therefore, the two natures must fuse into each other, and this cannot happen except through the transformation of the imperfect part into the perfect. The Divine, in fact, cannot, by definition, 'absorb' what is extraneous to it, namely what is non-divine. Thus in order that interaction should be effected, the terrestrial sphere needs to adapt itself to the divine and to be transformed into it. Only then by the sacral transformation of its offerings which are called upon to pass over from one plane to another can human nature bridge the abyss which separates it and its presents from the divine. The discovery of the sacred properties of heat, exhibited in the sacred fire enable the Vedic priest to make use of this energy to surmount through using the transformation of the victim the distance between Heaven and Earth and to overcome the difference between Divinity and Humanity (together with all that pertains to it). It is the sacrificial fire, with its heat, which transforms, prepares, 'cooks' the offerings, consecrating them into the very 'substance' of the Sacred.

This observation, which at first sight may seem insignificant, will reveal itself, in the long run, to be full of consequences not only in determining ritual practice but also in all the subsequent Brāhmaṇic religious and cosmological speculations.

We have seen that in the Mediterranean world fire is used as the principal means to transfer, consume and eliminate the victim from the human world in order to bring it into contact with the celestial world receiving it. Theoretical speculation on the effects of sacrifice and hence too the liturgical insistence on the ritual particulars which are judged more important for cultic purposes, concentrate on the blood of the victim—which, as life element, is in direct relationship with the Divine to which it belongs by right. As for the rest, the true and great protagonists of the whole sacrificial complex are primarily the Divinity who receives the offering and by it is placated or pleased, and secondarily man who deprives himself of a part of himself to give it to the Divinity either in homage, or in expiation, or in the hope of receiving an adequate recompense. In any case, the fire and the victim are just two elements of the whole sacrificial complex and are definitely subordinate to the dominant divine Reality, so much so that for the majority of the followers of the various theistic religions of the world the offering of a sacrifice implies *ipso facto* a belief in a Divinity who receives it and who is naturally far superior to the rite which is dedicated to it. To portray graphically this conception of sacrifice in its entirety, we could represent it by the following diagram :

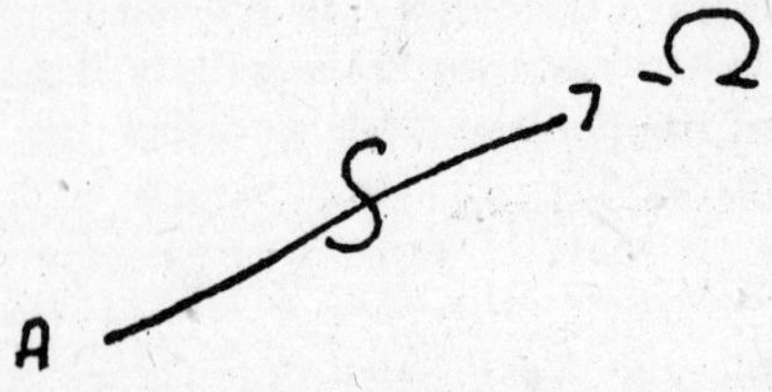


in which Alpha is man the sacrificer, Omega the Divinity who receives the offering and 'S' is the liturgical action by means of which the offering ascends, transforming itself to 'sweet fragrance' and spiritual food. The Divinity profits from this liturgical action and along the same sacrificial line sends its grace in the form of various benefits.

No doubt, the first Vedic sacrifice, in the oldest hymns of the RV, conforms more or less to the idea represented in the diagram. There we come across ṛṣis who, to obtain favours for their kings and patrons[91], offer sacrifice to Divinities who dominate the world scene and are free to listen or not to the prayers of those who offer the sacrifice according as they have been well propitiated or not[92]. The Vedic hymns are full of invocations for help addressed to the principal Divinities, which is a sign that they are considered to be powerful in themselves and clearly superior to the offering which they are implored to accept[93].

Still the methods of cooking, liturgically imposed for the preparation of the victim after its immolation, put the victim in a position which begins to distinguish it, as far as its own destiny is concerned, from other sacrificial victims in most religions of the world. In the Vedas, the victim is energized and is transferred alive to the divine world. It seems that Gods do not consume it but welcome it to their company as a friend, gaining power from the energy of the new life which is added to theirs and to their world, without having to eat it, although *yajña* is sometimes also considered to be a meal for them. In the final destiny of the immolated offering is contained the seed of the new Vedic interpretation of sacrifice, a seed which did not remain unnoticed. When the ṛṣis became aware of the transformation wrought by fire on the victim or on the ingredients of the offering an imperceptible change of accent occurred in the whole Vedic sacrificial complex which was enough to give a new direction to their entire sacred act.

Once the necessity of thermic energy in sacrifice, or better in its preparation, became clear to the ṛṣis, all the theory and

91. Cf. e.g. RV III.33; IV.30; VI.18; VII.33; VII.82; X.49; etc.

92. Cf.e.g. RV I.10 to Indra; RV III.28 to Agni; RV V . 54 to the Maruts; RV VIII.26 to the Aśvins; RV IX. 66 to Soma; etc.

93. Cf.e.g. RV III. 36 and 37 where Indra is invoked for the help he gives in battles; RV IV. 13 and 14 where the sun rises due to Varuṇa, Mitra and the Aśvins; etc. Cf. other texts in my previously quoted article "Ritual as Mirror."

practice of the rite began to hinge on this decisive point, developing it, in course of time, to its ultimate consequences[94]. If it is fire which, with its heat, imparts to the victim the power to rise to immortality, it is on this fire (already divine in itself) and on its power that the whole priestly attention during the liturgical action will be concentrated. It is, in fact, fire which gives value to the whole action inasmuch as it renders it possible and efficacious.

However, since fire exercises its power on the victim itself and not on the offerers or officiants, much less on the Divinity, because it is the victim which is cooked and transformed, the centre of the sacrificial action is consequently displaced. The effect of the sacred activity during the rite is focused on the victim and it is on it that the liturgical attention of the priest, and, consequently, that of the Divinities also, is now turned. Thus the victim assumes the principal role in the ceremony. Not only does it undergo an 'initiation', a 'con-secration', a process, that is to say, implying death and resurrection which (like the courser of *aśvamedha*) ensures that it will go alive to Gods by the shortest route, but it becomes itself the receptacle of the sacred energy and therefore the place where the specific power of the universal Godhead is accumulated. Having itself received life in all its fulness, the victim can, in its turn, extend its immortalized and sacralized glory both to the sacrificer and to the whole cosmos so that they may live strengthened by it.

However, even though it is elevated to the undisputed centre of the whole liturgical action, the victim is not divinized in itself. The victim is transformed, becomes both immortal and an agent of immortality, but it will not simply take the place of the Divinity, thus leaving unaltered the religious scheme generally adopted by the greater part of the world's traditions. The diagram represented above always remains with its Alpha and Omega at the extremities of the line 'S' but now the accent falls on this line 'S', which is stabilized and which becomes the centre of attraction both of Alpha and Omega, both of which are attracted by its sacred Energy. Hence the diagram is now transformed in the following manner :

94. The process, as will be seen, will reach its culmination in the time of the Brāhmaṇas and the Sūtras.

In fact, by attracting the liturgical attention on itself, the victim ends up by *giving value to the sacred Action as such and in itself*. By its being transformed by means of the power which is internal to the cult and operative within the cult itself viz., 'cooking', the victim brings into relief the nāture of the whole liturgical complex. If it is the sacred action itself, which effects the transformation and the immortalization of the victim, it is natural that it tends to become self-sufficient and independent of the whole Ultimate Reality, absorbing in its own sphere of action both men and Gods. Sacrifice becomes a vivifying force independent of any other Agent superior to it, and acts directly first of all on the victim itself and then on the whole universe. Thus it gradually becomes the sole guarantee for the fulfilment of what is asked of it (from the continuation and maintenance of the cosmic order to the granting of progeny and wealth) independently of any eventual intervention by Gods. Thus, the whole sacrificial Action is divinized, by being made to represent the divine activity par excellence, and later on by being absolutized in such a way that it itself becomes cosmic and eternal, the Absolute and Impersonal Godhead itself[95]. The uniqueness of the develoments in the speculative and religious interpretation of the Vedic sacrifice consists precisely in this, as becomes apparent when we compare these developments with what took place in other religions. In other religions, the tendency is

95. Cf. e.g. RV X. 90.16 : *yajñena yajñam ayajanta devās tāni dharmāṇi prathamānyāsan* . . . ("through sacrifice the Gods offered to the sacrifice: these were the first laws . . ."). This verse has been taken again from tradition on various occasions; see e.g. SatBr I.7.3.26 : . . . *yajñe yajñaṃ tanavāma* . . . (". . . we stress sacrifice . .") which will be quoted later in Ch. IV, note 28.

either to divinize the victim itself (as, for example, in Christianity) or to identify it with God (as in Orphism) in such a way that it represents the Divine completely—in which case the Omega of our diagram remains unchanged. For the Brāhmaṇas, on the contrary, the victim always remains a victim and it is the sacrificial Act as such which acquires Absolute Power; it is the Sacred Action which by itself completes and assumes the whole of Reality[96]. This is the essence of immortality to which the various divinities of the Pantheon have recourse to complete, valorize and immortalize their existence. In terms of our diagram : the 'S' does not change place, but rather stabilizes itself and assumes gigantic proportions, attracting to itself, centripetally, not only Alpha but also Omega, thus *ipso facto* emptying the latter of its content (at least of that usually attributed to the Divine as 'Person') : that is why Gods shift their position from Omega into Alpha, becoming themselves performers alongside their position as Receivers[97].

Thus the first and greatest victim, Puruṣa, that is, the Primordial Cosmic Man[98], becomes the basis of the whole creation which originates from the sacrificial dismemberment of his body[99], and later on is transformed into Prajāpati, the Lord of all the creatures which were born of him[100]. Still, it is

96. This pre-eminence of the Cosmic Sacrifice as Divine Reality entitled the Vedic people to be called, rightly, "the people of the Sacrifice" in the same way as the Hebrews are described in the Bible as "the people of Yahweh." Cf. H. AGUILAR, *op. cit.*, p. 57.

97. Cf. below in the Conclusion, pp. 271 ff.

98. We call the human 'greatest' from a 'sentimental' not from a 'liturgical' point of view. In ancient India in fact human sacrifice was not considered to be the 'greatest' one. No mention is made of it in the traditional division (see below Ch. IV, note 18), and in the texts its place is rather secondary to the *aśvamedha* (see below, Ch. V, p. 103 and note 3).

99. Cf. RV X.90.9 : ...*tasmād yajñāt sarvahuta ṛcaḥ sāmāni jajñire chandāṃsi jajñire tasmād yajus tasmād ajāyata* ... ("from this sacrifice integrally offered the *ṛks* and *sāma* were born; the *chandas* were born from this, from this the *yajus* was generated..."). This theme will be taken up again in Ch. III. This way of conceiving the role of the victim does not apply only to man, but to any victim or offering. We refer here to the universalization of the creative power of the victim in the Atharvic hymns quoted in the next chapter.

100. Cf. e.g. SatBr X.2.2.1 : *ekaṃ puruṣam akurvantsa prajāpatir abhavatsa prajā asṛjata* ... ("they make (of him) a Man, he became Prajāpati, he

not he who gives value to the sacred Action by his being an illustrious victim, it is the sacred Action as such which gives him value in his creative function. This is to say that the immolated Puruṣa himself—in the Ṛgveda his is not yet a self-immolation but it is the Gods who 'stretch' him out in sacrifice[101]—has a cosmic importance above all because of the Action which took place in the dismemberment of his body, and not the other way about. Puruṣa *becomes* the Absolute by means of the Action which is performed on him and which, in its turn, is the means by which creation takes place. Only in a second moment—especially in the Brāhmaṇas—is the Cosmic Puruṣa personalized as Lord of Creatures (Prajāpati), presenting himself as the God who receives the sacrificial offering; but even then he does not appear as the divinization of a particular victim but rather as the sublimation of sacrifice as such. 'Prajāpati is Sacrifice' (*prajāpatir yajñas*)[102]. It is his identification with the sacrifice which forms his grandeur and nobility, and not vice versa. This will equally apply to the principal divine figure which appears in the following (Purāṇic) period, namely Viṣṇu, who, as we shall see, will acquire the right to be identified with sacrifice[103] through a proper competition.

### 4. *The Role of Sacred Heat in the Divine World:*

It is important to emphasize, at this point, that the Vedic conception of sacrifice as absolute and self-sufficient Action has nothing of 'magic' about it. First of all, in the Vedic hymns the offering is still addressed to a given Divinity. It is the Divinity which is asked to grant one's own desires, but even when the sacrificial action becomes independent and the focal point of whatever happens in Heaven, on earth and in the entire

generated the creatures . . .).

101. Cf. RV X.90.6: *yat puruṣeṇa haviṣā devā yajñam atanvata* . . . ("with the *purusha* as offering the Gods stretched the sacrifice . . ."). As one can see, the word "stretching" used in the text is taken from the Vedic technical terminology. This hymn will be quoted again in notes 55 and 57 of Ch. III, and also in note 12 of the Conclusion, p. 275.

102. SatBr V.2.1.4; etc.

103. Cf. below Ch. VIII, pp. 220 ff.

universe, sacrifice is never severed from what is considered 'Divine' in the true and most profound meaning of the word. In fact, if it is true that the sacrificial energy which in Vedic theology gives sacrifice its position is so powerful because it derives its force from the fact that it belongs to the whole liturgical and cultic complex, it is no less true that the entire sacrificial apparatus can produce such energy in itself precisely because by its means it is already in contact with the divine world. There is little that man and his ritual action can do if sacrifice is not already in some way connected with that Divine he desires to attain. What, however, specifically differentiates the concept of the Vedic sacrifice, in its religious and speculative development, from that of a sacrifice offered to a Personal God, Absolute Lord, is that, in the latter conception, such a God always remains superior to every sacrificial rite which simply serves to placate, satisfy and render Him well-disposed towards His devotees, whereas in the former conception, the Divinity occupies an inferior place. In the Vedic liturgy, the connection with the Divine takes the form of an identification of Sacrifice with the Divine in an abstract sense, on creative and universal level. Sacrifice is the Divine and the Divine is sacrifice. The elevation of sacrifice to the cosmic level and to universal validity has its repercussions on the individual Divinities whose role, function and power are diminished and yet continue to exist and even to remain the recipients of the sacrifice at least for a certain time.[104]

In the latest hymns of the Ṛgveda, the ṛṣis gradually become aware of the inevitable philosophical change which their liturgy,

104. This pre-eminence of a Divine Action over against a Divine Person has embarrassed many a non-Indian scholar accustomed to a different cultic and religious relationship between the devotee and the Godhead (cf. e.g. the observations of Max Muller, Eggeling, S. Levi, etc. on this point.). Since the norm in this matter is generally taken to be the Christian religion, it will be useful perhaps to recall here that all the arguments given by these scholars to demonstrate the "magic" character of the Vedic sacrifice could equally apply and with equal force to the Christian sacrifice, which however is generally not considered to be "magical". We say this not to invalidate the Christian religion in its main cultic act, but to acknowledge the same faith to the Vedic people. Furthermore, today that a "personal" God is no longer so important for religious Faith, perhaps the pre-eminence of a Divine act can be of help in the deepening of the knowledge of the Absolute.

centred on the symbolic power of heat, is slowly bringing about. In the process of exalting sacrifice to the detriment of the single Divinities the ṛṣi rediscovers the balance between the sacred and sacrifice, precisely in the same sacred heat which had provoked the imbalance. By means of the energy developed by and in his rite, he attains directly to the heart of each Divinity, finding therein the deepest common characteristic of each beyond their various personalities and individual particularities. In this he finds the connection between the act he performs on earth, and the Divine he is attempting to reach. This characteristic or element is the intimate heat of the sacred Fire which, on the one hand, gives the rite its potential to be 'ready' (*śṛta*) to 'reach' (*aśnute*) the other shore and on the other hand reveals itself as the specific attribute of certain Divinities, especially those which are more directly linked to the creative activity. Appellations such as *tapiṣṭha, atapas, saṃtapana,* are predicated of the weapons of Agni[105], of Indra[106] and of the Maruts associated with him[107], while Agni is understandably the *tapiṣṭha* par excellence and it is to him that the following ṛk refers:

*tapā tapiṣṭha tapasā tapasvān*[108].

All these attributes predicated of the heat emitted by fire, are expressed by terms which for the most part are derived from the root *tap.* This word, among the various roots which indicate more or less the same idea and experience of heat, refers, as we have seen, to a special kind of heat which warms slowly but in

105. Cf. e.g. RV IV. 5. 4 : *pra tāṃ agnir babhasat tigmajambhas tapiṣṭhena śociṣā yaḥ surādhāḥ* . . . ("May sharp-toothed Agni, the very liberal, consume with his hottest flames them . . .") (tr. Bloomfield, *Rg-Veda repetitions,* p. 214) ; RV VII.15.13 : . . . *tapiṣṭhair ajaro daha* . . . ("O without age, burn with (your) very hot (flames)").

106. Cf. e.g. RV I.55.1 where *atapaḥ* is perhaps an attribute of Indra, and RV III.30.16 where a stone (*aśan*), a weapon of Indra is said to be *tapiṣṭha*; etc.

107. Cf. e.g. RV VII.59.9 where the Maruts are said *saṃtapana*; etc.

108. RV VI.5.4: "Heat, O you very hot, possessor of heat, with your heat".

depth and, though remaining mostly invisible, penetrates and transforms[109].

This transforming power, however, does not present itself as a 'bridge' (as in other religious traditions) but rather establishes itself as a centre of attraction for them both. So, even before the ṛṣis became aware of the absoluteness of sacrifice as such and elaborated the symbolism of the Sacred Heat of sacrifice, by now concretized into a neutral substantive, *tapas*, we observe it emerge from the bosom of Gods as their divine attribute. It presents itself, beyond their various personalities, as the Unique Centre of the Universe from which everything takes its origin, indeed as the Primordial Principle of the first pre-cosmic principles themselves—those of Night, Ocean and Ṛta the supreme Order.

"*Ṛta* and the True (*satya*) are born of the incandescent *Tapas*; of it is born the Night; of it the vast Ocean"[110].

When the Vedic poets fascinated by the grandeur of the sacrificial action which they are enacting and which has revealed to their understanding the profound depths of this action, ask themselves what is the power underlying its dynamism, a power that incorporated the Divinities[111], they find their answer in that *tapas* which has been experienced by them as the essence of sacrifice and therefore of all Reality, whether divine, human or terrestrial [112], which unfolds from sacrifice. Thus, *tapas*, the principle of transformation, has transformed itself too and become, from the mere sacrificial 'means' which it initially was, the beginning and end of the Real.

However, its transformation does not stop with its apotheosis in the Ṛgveda. Heat resumes its function as a transforming

109. On the etymology and characteristics of *tapas* and *tapati* see Ch. I, pp. 21-22.

110. RV X.190.1 : *ṛtaṃ ca satyaṃ cābhīddhāt tapaso'dhyajāyata | tato rātry ajāyata tataḥ samudro arṇavaḥ||* See my comment on this in U.M. VESCI "Das begriff des Tapas" in *Kairos* III, Salzburg, 1968.

111. Cf. RV X.121.1 etc. regarding the ever-repeated question in the refrain "*to which* (*kasmai*) God shall we give the offering?" (*kasmai devāya haviṣā vidhema*). For the problem involved, see the whole hymn RV X.129.

112. Cf. RV X.129.3 : . . . *tapasas tan mahinā jāyataikam* . . . ("That was born as one for the power of *tapas*").

agent now sublimated out of the ritual while remaining essentially an attribute of what it transforms. *Tapas*, after having been for a short while the universal cosmic principle, soon resumes its place as an energetic element in Sacrifice as Creative principle, to appear still later as an attribute of sacrifice personified, viz. Prajāpati.

CHAPTER THREE

# RITUAL HEAT AS A SOURCE OF ENERGY IN THE ATHARVAVEDA

In the first Veda, as we have seen, cooking is initially nothing but a means, even if very important, of preparing the sacrifice, and the indispensability of its function is asserted more as a fact than as the result of exegetical or other speculation. It is felt that the offering (*havis*) must be prepared or cooked (*śṛta*) to be acceptable and the Divinity invited to partake of it; there is also the idea that cooking is necessarily linked to the preparation of the *havis* so much so that the whole process of preparing every kind of offering, from its preliminaries to cooking proper, is significantly called by the single term '*pakti*' from the root *pac* to cook. Still, the reason for this necessity is adumbrated only in one or two facts and even then in a negative manner, namely as the discomfort and the inconvenience which might be caused by its eventual lack[1].

The exegetical and philosophical development of this small liturgical detail, so full of consequences for the entire speculative conception of the Brāhmaṇic sacrifice, takes place unnoticeably until finally it overtly blossoms all of a sudden into the philosophical hymns of Book X, the last chronologically as well

1. Cf. e.g. the already quoted *atapta taṇūr na... aśnute* of RV IX.83.1 discussed on p. 29, Ch. II, and the texts RV I.162.9 and 16 respectively quoted in notes 47 and 46 of Ch. II.

as kairologically[2], in the apotheosis of the sacred heat now considered as the Universal First Principle.

While the Ṛgvedic pronouncements on sacrifice and on *tapas* seem to take place unexpectedly at the end of the Ṛgvedic Saṃhitā, in the other Vedas the Ṛgvedic intuition of the power of ascension contained in the process of cooking is made more explicit and even expressed in more detailed terms throughout the performance of the rite itself.

Although, for a number of reasons the Atharvaveda has been the last to be included in the definitive Vedic canon, we will not discuss it as the last because it surely contains material which recalls the historical and social conditions depicted in the hymns of the RV rather than those described in the principal schools of the Yajurveda and their Brāhmaṇas. Therefore, we have chosen to treat the Atharvaveda close to the chapter on the Ṛgveda, since both are closely related one to the other[3], but are different from each other in as far as a great part of the Atharvaveda reflects an elaboration with a greater breadth of vision than that of the Ṛgveda. The Atharva, for instance, has certainly taken a decisive step forward in the interpretation of sacred heat, *tapas*.

In fact, what has been only intuited or conjectured from some hints in the Ṛgveda is now, in the Atharva, clearly and con-

2. The terms are taken from the Greek *cronos* and *kairos*. See a comment on their use in R. PANIKKAR, *Religione e religioni*, Brescia (La Morceliana), 1966.

3. According to the present writer the character of the Atharvaveda is very similar to that of the Ṛgveda: both have *mantras* that are mainly to be recited during rituals and sacrifices, and both, especially towards the end, lounge themselves in wonderful religious and cosmological speculations. Perhaps, one of the reasons why the Atharvaveda was not included for a long time in the traditional canon was that since the Atharvaveda was considered to be a duplicate of the Ṛgveda, no necessity was felt to do so. The question which could be asked is how it was that the Atharvic hymns, duly selected, never found a place in the *Ṛk* collection, as the hymns of other families for example the Maṇḍala III of the Viśvāmitras, the VII of the Vasiṣṭha, the VI of Bharadvāja, etc. For a survey of the families (*gotras*) of the Vedic poets see C. KUNHAN RAJA, *Poet-Philosophers of the Ṛgveda,* Madras (Ganesh and Co. Ltd.) 1963, and V.G. RAHURKAR, *The Seers of the Ṛgveda,* Pune (Univ. of Pune), 1964. For a more specific survey of the Atharvic religion see also N.J. SHENDE, *The Religion and Philosobhy of Atharva Veda,* Puna (Bhan. Or. Res. Inst. ) 1952; id., *Kavi and Kāvya in the Atharvaveda,* Pune (Univ. of Pune), 1967.

sciously established. Here the heat of cooking is directly and explicitly connected with what the sacrificer can obtain and even with the upward movement given to the victim itself, which is positively attested. Here the texts which indicate the great part heat has in the preparation of the sacrificial offering are much more numerous than in the Ṛgveda[4] and they now exhibit a greater awareness of the importance of sacred heat developed in and through sacrifice and its liturgical significance is fairly clearly expounded.

1. *Sacred Heat in the Rite*:

Unlike the *ṛṣis* of the hymns previously considered, the Atharvan *ṛṣis* are by now conscious of the link which exists between the heat of sacrifice and sacred energy and do not hesitate to relate the results of sacrifice to the heat which bursts forth from the sacrificial fire.

In a hymn dedicated to the sacrifice of billy-goat (*ajamedha*), after having put a pitcher of water on fire to boil and immersed in it the pieces of the victim, the priest asks the immolators who are in charge of its cooking, to surround it well with burning embers so that the offering when "cooked (*śṛta*) goes to the world of recompense"[5]. When it is heated further (*atapthās*) together with the offering of a hot pudding of grain (*taptāc caror*), it ascends up to the third firmament (*nākam tritīyam*)[6]. The relation between the results of sacrifice and heat is evident, but the *ṛṣi* takes pains to emphasize the propellant power of heat by addressing the victim in these words: "As fire out of the fire have you emerged; conquer and win this effulgent world of light"[7]. A little further on in the same hymn, it

4. The texts concerned are collected in the already quoted book of Ch. BLAIR which serves as background for the present study. We refer also to our study on *The Concept of Tapas* which is still in preparation, but a portion of which has already been published in *La Critica Sociologica*, Roma Nos. 57-58, Primavera-estate 1981, pp. 157-169. Here we quote only the most significant text concerning our topic.

5. AV IX. 5.5 ...*śṛto gacchatu sukṛtām yatra lokaḥ.*

6. AV IX.5.6 ab: *utkrāmātaḥ pari ced atapthās taptāc caror adhi nākam tṛtīyam.* We follow WHITNEY's emendation which reads *atapthās* instead of *ataptas*.

7. AV IX.5.9 cd : *agner agnir adhi saṃ babhūvitha jyotiṣ mantam abhi lokaṃ jayaitam.*

is repeated that it is when cooked that the billy-goat (*ajaḥ pakvaḥ*) offered together with the five rice dishes (the *pañcaudana*) rises to the heavenly world (*svarga loka*) defeating Nirṛti, the Goddess of Darkness, and conquering the worlds illuminated, by Sūrya, the Sun[8]. At the moment, then, of the actual offering when the poet invokes the Divinities so that they receive what is being sent to them[9], or invokes the Universe itself, divinized, and concretely represented by ritual entities made absolute,[10] he is keen to recall once again that the priest 'cooks' (*pacata*) both the billy-goat and the five rice dishes so that "the Quarters may accept it from you(the priest)."[11] On another occasion, the Atharvic *ṛṣi* addresses the billy-goat directly exhorting it to rise to the highest firmament, but he does so only when he is sure that it is well prepared and cooked (*śṛta*).[12]

The same thing happens with other kinds of offerings. With the *odana* can be obtained "the sacrificial word and all the worlds"[13] provided, however, that the cereal-pudding is well-heated by the receptacle (*gharma*) which contains it.[14] In its turn, the *gharma* which contains the milk of the morning offering to the Aśvins, has a very close relation with heat—as its

8. Cf. AV IX.5.18 : *ajah pakvaḥ svarge loke dadhāti pañcaudano nirṛtiṃ bādhamānaḥ| tena lokānt sūryavato jayema ||* ("The goat Pañcaudana, when cooked, transporteth, repelling Nirṛti, to the world of *svarga*; by him may we win worlds which Sūrya brightens.") (tr. Griffith)

9. Cf. e.g. AV XI.6.1 ff. where the Gods invoked are Agni, Indra, Vanaspati, Viṣṇu, Bhaga, Mitra, Varuṇa, Savitṛ, Pūṣan, the Aśvins etc.

10. Cf. e.g. AV XII.1.1 ff. where there is mention of *satya* (truth), *bṛhat* (sacred formula), *brahman, yajña* (sacrifice) etc. as worthy of praise and cult.

11. AV IX.5.37 : *ajaṃ ca pacata pañca caudanān | sarvā diśaḥ saṃmanasaḥ sadhricīḥ sāntar deśāḥ prati gṛhṇantu ta etam ||* ("He cooks the goat and the five cakes. May in accordance the cardinal directions and in agreement united the intermediary points accept it from thee".)

12. Cf. AV IV.14.9 : *śṛtam ajaṃ śṛtayā prorṇuhi tvacā sarvair aṅgaiḥ saṃbhṛtaṃ viśvarūpam | sa uttiṣṭheto abhi nākam uttamaṃ padbhiścaturbhiḥ prati tiṣṭha dikṣu||* (Over a 'cooked' goat lay a 'prepared' skin to robe him 'cooked' in perfect form with ali his members; rise upward to the highest firmament, with their four feet stand firm in the regions".)

13. Cf. AV XI. 3.19 : . . . *odanena yajñavacaḥ sarve lokāḥ samāpyāḥ* . . . ("with *odana* the sacrificial word, all the worlds, have to be won . . .")

14. Cf. AV XI.3.18 : *caruṃ pañcabilamukhaṃ gharmo abhīndhe* . . . ("the cauldron flames around the offering with five open mouths".)

very name, which, as we have seen, means 'heat', indicates. In the hymn which the Atharva Veda dedicates to the cauldron, a vessel very important for *Pravargya*,[15] one can observe a new phase in the cosmicization of the sacred Action in the fact that specific tasks hitherto reserved for the Divinities have transferred to the ritual implements. The ṛṣi is aware of this and stresses it. At a certain moment in the ritual, as we shall have occasion to see later, the cauldron, *gharma*, filled with the milk of the offering, is put on the fire to boil. During the three stages which follow, namely, when the milk first comes in contact with the fire, when it begins to boil and rise and when it starts overflowing—an overflow which is likened to milking—the cauldron, through the increase of its contents ritually *creates* beings and time. This leads the poet to put in relief the transfer to the ritual implement of the creative role traditionally attributed to the Divinity: "it (the *gharma*) milking out the present, the past and the future, discharges all the duties (*vrata*) of Gods".[16]

This is the first hint of the exalted development of *Pravargya* as it appears later in more detail in the Brāhmaṇas. We know, in fact, that during the Brāhmaṇic period the three stages mentioned above have a determining importance in the creation of the worlds which overflow from the sacrifice.[17] In the Brāhmaṇas, however, creation is independent of any intervention on the part of any divine personality. Here, on the contrary, the wonder shown by the Atharvic poet tells us that we are witnessing the moment of transition between two conceptions, one which still assigns to the Divinities creative action, the other which begins already to attribute this action to the ritual *itself*, indeed to the very mechanics of the sacrifice.

## 2. *Divinization and 'Cosmicization' of the Offering:*

The result of this newly acquired conception of a special power obtained in the passage through fire and its heat is that

15. Cf. later on Ch. VIII dedicated to this type of offering.

16. AV IV.11.2 : *bhūtaṃ bhaviṣyad bhuvanā duhānaḥ sarvā devānāṃ carati vratāni* /

17. The motif of the process of creation going through the stages of the boiling *gharma* full of milk is largely developed in the Brāhmaṇas. We shall discuss it in Ch. VIII dedicated to Pravargya.

on the one hand the ritual Act becomes independent and assumes the tasks proper to Gods, while, on the other, the victim is regenerated taking on a new birth which it owes to the sacrificial fire. The billy-goat, for example, is identified with Agni himself and is even called 'light' (*jyotis*) as if to indicate its acquisition of a new luminous nature, due to the effect of the ritual cooking.[18] Thus re-born, it is transferred from this mortal world and, being firmly installed in his newly conquered position, "stands firmly with his four feet in every direction".[19]

Hence not only is all attention now foscussed on the victim in its preparation for the salvific journey to the divine world[20]— but also on it as the centre of the sacrificial Action, rather than on the Divinity. This speculative reflection, moreover, changes aspect when compared to the Ṛgvedic reflection on the same subject. In the Ṛgveda, it is the future of the victim which is taken into consideration; here, on the contrary, it is its *being* itself. It is the victim, and not the sacrifice or even the Divinity, which stands firmly in the firmament, spreading its feet in the four directions. It is installed there and therefore it becomes identified with it. Its transformation, by means of the cooking, has 'cosmicized' it. In the moment of its consecration, every part of the (male-)goat is assimilated to and identified with one or other of the various parts of the *cosmos* in such a way that when the time comes for its dismembering for the final offering, this dismembering will correspond to the unfolding of its sacred energy in the cosmos. Thus, the goat (*aja*), by now one with the ritual action itself which has universalized it,[21] is beyond

18. Cf. AV IX.5.7 : *ajo agnir ajam u jyotir āhurajam* . . . ("the he-goat is Agni, they call the goat light, the goat . . .")

19. AV IV.14.9 d quoted in note 12 of this chapter : *padbhiś caturbhiḥ prati tiṣṭha dikṣu.*

20. Cf. e.g. AV IV.14.5 ff. : *svar yantu yajamānāḥ svasti . . . tena geṣma sukṛtasya lokaṃ svar rārohanto abhi nākam uttamam.* ("may the sacrificers go to heaven in peace; . . . may we go through this (victim) in the world of the blessed, climbing to heaven till the supreme firmament".) The same verse is found in AV XI.1.37 and also with a slight variation, in AV IV.11.6.

21. Cf. AV IX.5.21 : *eṣa vā aparimito yajño yad ajaḥ pañcaudanaḥ* . . . ("truly this incommensurable sacrifice is this goat-*pañcaudana* . .")

the limitations of Time and is "the unborn (*aja*) (which) in the beginning was divided: its breast became the earth, its back the heaven, its middle was the air, its sides the quarters, the hollow of its belly the oceans...".[22] The cosmicization of the immolated animal involves the whole macrocosm by a process of systole and diastole in which every thing is contracted down onto the microcosm of the victim and then expanded out again in every direction to sustain its cosmic existence. To this end the positioning of the goat at the moment of its immolation is very important in order to facilitate the absorption of the energy of the ritual from its every part by the corresponding parts of the macrocosm. Thus the head must be turned towards the East, its right side towards the South, its left side towards the North and so forth, with its backbone facing the Zenith and its belly facing the Nadir.[23]

In its turn, as we have seen, the *gharma*, the receptacle used for *pravargya*, owes to the action of heat its power to appropriate to itself the specific task which belongs to the Divinities, namely, creation.[24] That is to say, by causing the milk to overflow at the culminating moment of the preparation of the offering, that is by "milking it", the cauldron itself, through the thermic energy which is thus developed around it, creates time as present, past and future—and with time also all that flows in it—transferring onto the mechanics of the sacrificial action what before was the specific task of the Divinities.

To say, however, that already by now the Divinities have lost their power is to run too far ahead in time. In the Atharva Veda, Gods are still powerful and important, especially Gods like Indra, Agni, Vāyu and others. The Gods are still invoked

22. AV IX.5.20 : *ajo vā idam agre vyakramata tasyoro iyam abhavad dyauḥ pṛṣṭham | antarikṣam madhyaṃ diśaḥ pārśve samudrau kukṣī ..*

23. Cf. AV IV.14.7 ff. : . .*prācyāṃ diśi śiro ajasya dhehi dakṣiṇāyāṃ diśi dekṣiṇaṃ dhehi pārśvam || 7 || pratīcyāṃ diśi bhasadamasya dhehi ūttarasyāṃ diśy uttaraṃ dhehi pārśvam | ūrdhvāyaṃ diśy ajasyānūkaṃ dhehi diśi dhruvāyāṃ dhehi pājasyamantarikṣe madhyato madhyamasya* ||8| ("Set the goat's head toward the eastern region, and set his right side to the southern quarter; his hinder part turn to the western quarter, and set his left side to the northern region. Set the goat's backbone upmost in the zenith and lay his belly downward in the nadir; set his mid-portion in mid-air between them".) (tr. Criffith.)

24. Cf. previously in note 16.

as those directly responsible for granting that for which the sacrifice is offered to them.[25] Perhaps, we are here in the moment of transit from the Vedic religion, which is still personalistic, to that religion of a 'Brāhmaṇic' kind, in which the sacrificial Action becomes the prototype of cosmic Dynamism. Here the sacrificial Action begins to be universalized, becoming independently a means of obtaining directly what one asks from it. Thus it begins to gradually take the place previously allotted to the Divine. Therefore the praises which were reserved for individual Divinities are now addressed to it. The Atharva, consequently, dedicates entire hymns to the more important ritual implements.[26]

Still this transit takes place only in stages. For example, the *gharma*, to be adequately exalted, needs to be compared with those Gods who are still believed to be among the more powerful and honoured. It is, indeed, because they are believed to be so that they are chosen as terms of comparison and are presented as personifications of the abstract sacrificial vessel which is by now on its way to being universalized. "Born as Indra, brightly glowing among men, the *tapta gharma* goes about....Parjanya is its stream, the Maruts its udders, the sacrifice the milk, the priestly recompense (*dakṣiṇā*) is its milking".[27] Moreover, the cauldron is "Indra by form and Agni by its shoulders, the Lord of creatures (Prajāpati), supreme sovereign".[28] Also the *ucchiṣṭa*, the 'left-over' of the sacrifice, is exalted in the same manner.[29]

Once, however, the process of making sacrifice absolute is set in motion, it is no longer enough to compare the sacrificial

25. Cf. e.g. AV XII.3.32 ff.; 44 and 55 ff. where the oblations are offered to various Gods according to the cardinal directions . . .etc.

26. Cf. e.g. the hymns to the *skamba* (AV X.7), to *odana* (AV XI.3), to the goat (*aja*) of the *ajamedha* (AV IX.5), to the *gharma* (AV IV.11). etc.

27. AV IV.11.3 (ab) and 4 (cd) : *indro jāto manuṣyeṣvantar gharmas taptas carati śośucānaḥ . . ./ . . . parjanyo dhārā maruta ūdho asya yajñaḥ payo dakṣiṇā doho asya . . .*

28. AV IV.11.7 ab : *indro rūpeṇāgnir vahena prajāpatiḥ parameṣṭhī virāt . . .*

29. Cf. AV XI.7.1 ff. : The whole hymn is dedicated to the "rest" of the sacrifice which is compared more or less with the same Divinities with whom the *Gharma* was compared in the just mentioned hymn (notes 27 and 28).

implement with the most high Gods; the *gharma* will soon be raised above everything, will escape its possible domination by men and Gods who are no longer able to *use* it as they please, and it will become the 'Conqueror of all', the 'Sustainer of all' and the 'Maker of all'[30]. It is also the 'cosmic Bull'[31] which sustains the Heaven, the Earth, the Air, the Regions, etc., in a word, the entire Universe[32].

On the other hand, since it is the rite which by itself obtains what is asked of it and since the rite acquires its own power from the heat which transforms the ingredients of the offering enabling them to ascend to the immortal sphere of Reality, the rite becomes itself, perhaps for the first time, the means which the Divinities themselves use to reach "the centre of their immortality" (*amṛtasya nābhi*)[33]. It is logical then that the sacrificer should go along the same route[34]. By so doing he paves the way towards his dependence solely and directly on the rite for his desired aims and for his attainment of immortality and divinization, detaching himself from the necessity of having to ask for graces and favours from the Divinities. Gods, who still seem to him to be charged with their power and whom he still sees being invoked all around him, begin to be for him simple *models* to copy and the guarantors of ritual power. Gods have surely secured their actual status as immortals and blessed beings through the rite which they have meticulously performed,

30. Cf. AV IV.11.5 (cd) : ... *yo viśvajid viśvabhṛd viśvakarmā gharmaṃ no brūta yatamaś catuṣpāt* /("all-winning, all-supporting, all-effecting, which of all quadrupeds tell us is the cauldron?") (tr. Griffith).

31. Cf. AVIV.11.1 & 2 & 7 & 8 & 9 where the cauldron is said to be a 'bull' (*anaḍvān* or *anaḍuhaḥ*) in order to justify the answer : the Bull given at the interrogation stated in the verse 5 of the same hymn (just quoted in note 30).

32. Cf. AV IV.11.1 : *anaḍvān dādhāra pṛthivīm uta dyām anaḍvān dādhārorva 'ntarikṣam . . . pradiṣaḥ . . . bhuvanam* . . . ("the Bull supports the wide-spread earth and heaven, the Bull supports the spacious air . . . the regions . . . the universal world . . .") (tr. Griffith).

33. Cf. AV IV.11.6 (ab) : *yena devāḥ svarāruruhurhitvā śarīram amṛtasya nābhim*/ ("whereby the Gods went up to heaven, the centre (*omphalos*) of life eternal, having left the body".) (tr. Griffith).

34. Cf. AV IV.11.6 cd : *tena geṣma sukṛtasya lokaṃ gharmasya vratena tapasā yaśasyavaḥ* / ("may we go to the world of beatitude with the service of *gharma* and fervour".)

so if man does the same, he too can obtain the same results. This is in fact, as we shall see later, the normal attitude towards Gods found in the two schools of the Yajurveda and in their Brāhmaṇas[35].

Hence, to focus the attention of the ritual on the victim means not only to put in relief the place occupied by the victim as victim (or by the offering as offering) but to centre on it all Reality, whether existent or non-existent, to the extent of subordinating to it any ulterior Divine entity, that is, all the created and uncreated universe, with a directness and audacity much greater than in the Ṛgveda. In fact, in the Ṛgveda the focus was always the sacred Action which very rightly was associated with, equated and assimilated to the Divine, while in the Atharvaveda, the emphasis was laid directly on the victim whose 'entity', before it is transformed into an offering, does not have—and shall never have—high enough ontological status to substitute the Divinity. This is to say that the goat, or the cereal-pudding or the *gharma*, also after they are consecrated, remain ordinary elements, 'things' which belong to the one who offers them, and have as such no ontic *status* of their own. But when they are prepared by means of the heat of the sacred fire, to which they are subjected before they are rendered worthy to be definitely consigned to Agni (the sacrificial messenger), in the Action they are transformed in such a way that there can be no other reality outside them—and yet they are not personalized into any determinate Divine entity. This means that the goat, which previously had to be transformed only to be acceptable to the Divinity who had to receive it, now has become itself (divine) cosmicized, yet it still remains impersonal. This happens not only because nothing which is less than divine is worthy of the Divinity as such (since as darkness cannot subsist in front of light, so nothing which is not divine or divinized can subsist before the Divinity), but also because nothing can exist outside of the Unique Action of which the victim is the Absolute Centre.

35. Cf. e.g. TaittS VI.2.2.7 and SatBr I.7.3.26 which will be discussed later on in Ch. IV, on pp. 96 and 92 respectively and quoted in notes 38 and 28 respectively.

The passage from one conception to the other, made apparent through the 'language' of the ritual has a stringent internal logic. If already as a sacrificial offering presented by man, the immolated goat was the means of sustenance for Gods, the nourishment it provided them had to be adequate to their nature and their being. When later on, due to the change of emphasis in the understanding of the whole sacrificial complex, the focus is shifted from the Divinity to the sacred Action par excellence, the victim, the active recipient of the ritual transformation, must not only partake of the Divine, but concentrate in itself the very prerogatives of that Divine.

Moreover, since on the victim, so transformed into the Divine, falls the responsibility of renewing and sustaining the world, it goes without saying that the world rallies around its microcosm to draw directly from it the needed energy. Every normal offering, whatever it be whether an animal, cereal cooked in milk (*odana*), or the milk itself of the *gharma*—when it is being cooked, is not only transformed into a Divine entity, but gathers into itself the whole universe as its material, spirit and liturgy. The cardinal points, including the Nadir and the Zenith, come to converge, as we have seen, on the sides of the goat; Heaven and Earth on its back and chest respectively; while Truth (*satya*) and the Cosmic Order (*ṛta*) become its eyes, Faith (*śraddhā*) becomes its vital breath (*prāṇa*), and Virāj its head[36]. In the same way, Bṛhaspati is the head of the *odana*, Brahmā its mouth, Heaven and Earth its ears, the sun and the moon its eyes...[37] while the various ingredients of the offering, together with the instruments used for its preparation, are equated with, become or simply *are* the various Divinities (for example, Diti and Aditi)[38] or the various parts of the animal victim which are already symbolically homologized to the entire universe. When the *odana* is being cooked, and therefore being

36. Cf. AV IX.5.21. . . *satyam cartaṃ ca cakṣuṣī viśvaṃ satyaṃ śraddhā prāṇo virāṭ śiraḥ / eṣa vā aparimito yajño yad ajaḥ pañcaudanaḥ //*

37. Cf. AV XI.3.1 ff. : *tasyaudanasya bṛhaspatiḥ śiro brahma mukhaṃ / dyāvāpṛthivī śrotre sūryācandramasavakṣiṇī saptarṣayaḥ prāṇāpānāḥ* . . .

38. Cf. AV XI.3.3 ff. : . . . *cakṣur musalaṃ kāma ulūkhalam // ditiḥ śūrpam aditiḥ* . . . ("vision is the pestle, desire the mortar, Diti is the winnowing basket, *aditi* . . .") (tr. Griffith).

energized in the sacred fire in preparation for its transformation, the *kumbha*, or the receptacle which contains it, is the very Earth which takes this particular form in the same way as Heaven, in this truly cosmic sacrificial action, is the lid[39]. Hence, by this logical series of changes, the cosmic Action, which is performed around the universal grandeur of the victim, becomes the Unique Necessary and the Unique Existent to which all the Divinities turn, they themselves beginning to be more and more dependent on its universal energy. The sacred Action is the Centre around which Gods anxiously assemble, thus losing ever more their specific personalities while anything, which inheres in or comes in contact with sacrifice, becomes a starting point for profound cosmological elaborations[40].

Following the same line of thought, one can go a step further: if sacrifice begins to assume a cosmic character, other more or less abstract realities which owe their origin to sacrifiee, e.g. *dikṣā* (initiation), *bṛhat* and *brahman* (sacred formulae), *ṛta* (the cosmic order), *satya* (truth), etc., become, consequently, cosmic[41]. Above all of these is raised *Brahman* who, as is well known, evolves from a sacred formula to become the Absolute Principle, One without a second[42]. Still, in the Atharvaveda the *Brahman* is still mostly linked to the sacred act of the offering of which it represents the recited formula. But apart from these realities which already in the Ṛgveda[43] have been cosmicized in the very womb of sacrifice, others emerge which owe their origin to the living heat inherent in or absorbed by the victim, or inherent in the ingredients of the sacrificial offering. These new realities figure in the successive Brāhmaṇic speculative and practical field as coadjutors in the act of creation. Among these

39. Cf. AV XI.3.11: *iyam eva pṛthivī kumbhī bhavati rādhyamānasyaudanasya dyaur pidhānam|*

40. Cf. note 26.

41. Cf. AV XII.1.1 ab : *satyaṃ bṛhad ṛtam ugraṃ dīkṣā tapo brahma yajñaḥ pṛthivīm dhārayanti* ("truth, sacred formula, order, rite, consecration, tapas, brahman, sacrifice uphold the earth".)

42. Cf. e.g. J. GONDA, *The Brahman*, Then Agen (Mouton), 1960.

43. Cf. RV IX.113.2 : *ṛtavākena satyena śraddhayā tapasā suta indrāyendo pari srava* ("Thou (O Soma) , pressed with the sacred order's word, with truth, with faith and *tapas*, you run for Indra".)

realities we find also *tapas*, that *tapas* which we have already come across in the Ṛgveda raised to the position of absolute First Principle[44]. In the Atharva, however, it does not soar to those heights, rather it is linked once again to sacrifice which it furnishes with a creative and regenerative power, undergoing a more mature and somehow 'personal' evolution—in that it is more directly connected with the person of the sacrificer or more particularly with the religious man who foments and makes it grow in him. Contrary to the other realities, such as Order and Truth which reveal themselves on a cosmic scale, *tapas* here assumes a subjective tone in that it refers to what the subject, the sacrificer, employs to perform uncommon acts and display supranormal powers. Thus the *brahmacārin*, who prepares the oblation, invests himself with it (that is, in this specific case with the *gharma*) and by means of *tapas*, produced simultaneously both by the *gharma* boiling on the sacred fire and by his personal ascetical effort,[45] he performs a series of supranormal actions primarily those of protecting and maintaining heaven and earth[46].

3. *Prajāpati*:

However, even as cosmic Action, absolute and independent, sacrifice remains always 'something' which is *offered* and therefore needs in its turn to be *received*. In the Atharva Veda, it is true, there are still Gods who are sufficiently powerful to arrogate to themselves this right; however, even here their inadequacy is felt more and more. Consequently Gods often in order to continue to be the masters of sacrifice become the performers as well as the receivers. The logic of things requires that the Receiver be superior to what he receives, otherwise he runs the risk of being crushed by it as indeed the Devas were to be. On the other hand the process of abstraction and of the

44. Cf. RV X.190.1 where the abstract *tapas* becomes the origin of the First Principles of the universe. This verse has been quoted in note 110 of Ch. II.

45. Cf. AV XI.5.5ab : *pūrvo jāto brahmaṇo brahmacārī gharmaṃ* vasānas *tapasodatiṣṭhat* / ("born before the *brahman* the *brahmacārī* dressed in *gharma* rises through the strength of *tapas*".)

46. Cf. AV XI.5.1 ff. and esp. 1,2,8.

divinization of the sacred Action has already been pushed too much ahead to be now arrested. The single Divinities, in their turn, are now about to lose their privileges together with their greatness and individual importance to be grouped ever more in an anonymous collectivity. It is now no longer possible for them to recover in full their importance as it is no longer possible to reduce the importance of Sacrifice which by now has replaced even Divinity in its highest form. Thus already from the end of the Ṛgveda, in order to respond to the new religious needs to bestow a certain amount of personality to the abstract cosmic Action, there began to emerge not only as an epithet but also as a divine personage in himself a new divine figure: Prajāpati, a being on the borderline between speculation and mythic personalization[47]. As his name indicates, he is the Lord of Creatures and they proceed from him. He figures as the personification of sacrifice which gathers into itself the whole universe and recreates it through the dismemberment of himself as victim[48].

Here, in the Atharvaveda, Prajāpati is still a God among other Gods, but his name surfaces with increasing frequency as that of the absolute Supreme Being[49]. There is no speculation about him as there will be in the Brāhmaṇas as to who he is and how he is derived from the sacrificial rite. 'Prajāpati' is used from time to time as an epithet applicable to certain Vedic Gods or cosmic principles[50], as a name of a God who is a God together with and by the same right as the others[51]. It is also

47 For Prajāpati as a mythical and philsophical figure see U.M. VESCI, "Kaḥ, le nome de Dieu comme pronome interrogatif" in *Archivio di Filosofia*, Roma, 1969, pp. 145-154.

48. On Prajāpati, see S. LEVI, *op. cit.* passim; L. SILBURN, *op cit.*, passim; R. PANIKKAR, *Myth, Faith, Hermeneutics, op. cit.*, etc. chapter on the "Original Fault", passim.

49. Prajāpati is a name appearing rather late in the Vedas. He is mentioned only four times in the Ṛgveda, especially in the last *maṇḍala*, with the exception of one passage in the Ninth (RV IX.5.9; X.85.43; X. 169.4; X.121.10). In the Atharvaveda he figures already sixty five times with different shades of meaning. In the Yajurveda he is Supreme Divinity as in the Brāhmaṇas.

50. Cf. e.g. AV IV. 11.7 : already quoted in note 28, and translated in the text on p. 69.

51. Cf. e.g. AV III.15.6 : *tasmin ma indro rucimā dadhātu prajāpatiḥ savitā somo agniḥ* . . .(from here may Indra give me splendour and Prajāpati, Savitṛ, Soma, Agni".)

the name of the 'first-born of *ṛta*' (which is also, at least initially, connected with sacrifice)[52]; of a supreme God who is mentioned alongside other supreme entities, which are either abstract or personifications of sacrifice[53]; of the Creator with a personality of his own, a Supreme Being superior to the other Gods even if not yet definitely their Father and Originator[54]. Prajāpati is a new Deity who emerges only with difficulty in the world of the Gods as no longer side by side with the others but more and more frequently as a Being superior to other beings endowed with the characteristics of the Absolute, midway between a personalized figure and an abstract concept. He appears here for the first time as the Creator above the other Deities who in the first Veda are generally those responsible for the creation and the maintenance of the world.

It is significant that the appearance of Prajāpati coincides with the exaltation of Sacrifice as a means capable of obtaining by its own intrinsic worth results which normally are asked of Gods and their favour as in the *Atharvaveda* is still partly the case. When sacrifice becomes, as it were, self-sufficient, it becomes something desirable in itself both to men as well as to Gods. Thus automatically Gods become dependent on the ritual act, converting themselves more and more into celebrants—as in the immolation of Puruṣa where it is they, the Gods, who collectively, take on themselves the performance of the sacrifice[55] because as receivers they begin to desire so much for this 'gift' that by begging for it they are losing their position as 'Divinities' in the current sense of the term[56]. If it is sacrifice

52. Cf. AV XII.1.61 : ...*prajāpatiḥ prathamajā ṛtasya* ...; etc. The epithet keeps recurring even for more ancient divine figures.

53. Cf. e.g. AV XI.6.11 : *saptarṣīn vā idaṃ brūmo 'po devīh prajāpatiṃ pitṝn yama* ... ("I invoke the seven ṛṣis, this the divine waters, Prajāpati, the ancients, Yama ..."). See also AV IX.7.1; XI.4.12; XI.5.7; XIII. 3.5 ...

54. Cf. e.g. AV II.34.4 : *vāyuṣ ṭān agre pra mumoktu devaḥ prajāpatiḥ prajayā saṃrarāṇaḥ* ("to them at the beginning Vāyu, God, could give liberation, Prajāpati rejoicing in the creatures".) Cf. pertinent texts in S. LEVI *op. cit.*, p. 21 ff.

55. Cf. RV X.90.6 already qouted in note 101 of Ch. II, and recalled in note 12 of the Conclusion.

56. 'Devas' begin to be only used as a category for 'Superior Beings' but which are no longer Supreme.

which transforms and sustains the world by giving it energy to exist; it must obviously be also sacrifice which is responsible for the world's very creation, since the world is born and re-born by the dismemberment of the victim[57]. Gods, therefore, are excluded from this creative process, or rather, they remain 'on this side' of it, that is, they too are the products of Sacrifice as all other existent beings[58], and will give through it their immortality and their position as Gods.

Now the *ṛṣi* and the theologian (*brahmavādin*) who want to inquire into Reality and find its point of origin, can no longer turn to an Indra or a Varuṇa to quench their thirst for knowledge as their predecessors used to do. These Divinities too have acquired their position and, as will be believed later, even their very immortality through sacrifice, and therefore they too belong, in a certain sense, to the created and passing world so they too cannot know that First Principle which the Vedic *ṛṣi* is searching for beyond the supreme cultic Act. Prajāpati is precisely the Being who emerges in answer to the urgent needs of the philosopher, and of the ritualistic man. He is the Creator, the Lord of Creatures, he who, when personified, gathers and makes his the fruits of sacrifice. In the Atharvaveda, he is still on the borderline between a Deity amongst others or an epithet detached from the Divinity, and made to stand independently by himself and the supreme Being connected with sacrifice. The Atharva too, like the Ṛks, is composed of hymns and not of systematic philosophical reflections—even if its hymns are often highly speculative. In these hymns Prajāpati is indeed invoked but is not given a definite character except on certain points and in a vague manner. Still, the emergence of the figure of Prajāpati with ever greater insistence and his gradual imposition on the other figures of the ancient world of Gods, is an indication that at the time when the Atharva

57. Cf. the already quoted RV X.90 and RV I.164, AV IX.5, XI. 3 and also IV. 11. This motif is frequent in the Yajurveda and its Brāhmaṇas.

58. Cf. RV X.129.6 : *ko addhā veda ka iha pra vocat kuta ājātā kuta iyam visṛṣṭiḥ / arvāg devā asya visarjanenā 'thā ko veda yata ābabhūva* ?—("who knows and who can tell us wherefrom this creation is born and is come? The Gods are on this side of creation, so who knows . . .?".)

took its definite form, sacrifice, while retaining the characteristics of the Vedic Divinities to which the collection of hymns is undoubtedly linked, had already risen, in the awareness and in the speculation of its theologians, to assume the status of creative activity, indeed of the first creative being existing in itself. Prajāpati is its concrete symbol, while the hymns of praise to the victims (goat or bull)[59], to the ingredients of the offering (*odana*[60] and *gharma*[61]), even to the *ucchiṣṭa*, the left-over which is the part consumed by the sacrificer and his priests[62], already show to what cosmic and universal height the sacrificial Act has risen—something which seems to have no precedents in the other religions of the world[63].

What seems to be on the way to becoming a definite acquisition in more ancient Vedic times, becomes a precise speculative datum in the Yajurveda and its Brāhmaṇas which are a collection of hymns and exegetical commentaries regarding the performance of the sacrificial celebration. And it is to these that our enquiry will now turn.

59. Cf. AV IX.5 and XX.7.
60. Cf. AV IV. 34 & 35 & XI.3.
61. Cf. AV IV. 11
62. Cf. AV XI.7.
63. A distant resemblance to this can be seen in the Sacrifice of Christ in the Christian religion—although this type of sacrifice is seen more as a redemptive act than a cosmic creative action.

CHAPTER FOUR

# RITUAL HEAT AS A SOURCE OF ENERGY IN THE YAJURVEDA AND IN ITS BRĀHMAṆAS

1. *General Premises Regarding the Effects Obtained by the Sublimation of Ritual Heat*:

If in the Atharvic speculative hymns we witness a transitional period to a rite which, though still performed to please Divinities who are still superior to it, begins to be raised, by the universalization of the material of the offering, to a supreme Entity; in the hymns pertaining to the Adhvaryu, which belong to a later period (with social conditions very different from those portrayed in the Atharvaveda), the transition to the rite becoming completely independent is by now an accomplished fact. In the Yajurvedic hymns sacrifice is by now considered to be the creative First Principle beyond the power of any divine Being. During this period, the ritual Action is the ultimate par excellence; thus, the obtaining of one's desires, of immortality and the very maintenance of the world depend exclusively on the right and perfect performance of sacrifice and no longer on the intervention of any appeased Divinity. This evolution of the ritual, far from being, as is often believed, the decadence of 'pure' religion into 'magic' or into 'empty ritualism'[1], testifies

1. Because of their difficulty of conceiving a ritual which is efficacious in itself independently of a "superior God", many Western scholars in the past century and at the beginning of the present one passed a severely negative judgement on the Brāhmaṇic ritual which they considered either as a barren ritualism or as "magic". Here it would be enough to give one

to a profound interior understanding of the rite. Today it is easier than before to understand, even if not yet to accept, a conception in which the Dynamism of the pure Act is superior to a belief in a 'personal' God. After all, the idea of a God who is principally a 'Person' is no longer so essential to the religious spirit as it used to be previously, not even in the Christian West traditionally dominated by the figure of a Father God[2]. Indeed, the modern world is more inclined to believe in a self-creating nature which obeys its own 'natural' or 'scientific'

---

example out of many. In his *The Religion and Philosophy of the Veda* ... (*op. cit.*, vol II, p. 379) A.B. KEITH writes : "... the Brāhmaṇas ... show beyond possibility of doubt that the whole of the sacrifice was penetrated by conception of magic. Scarcely any rite but can be so adapted as to produce magic ends: the rites are often varied in detail for this very purpose, the mode in which the post is covered with the cord will determine the amount of rain which will fall. ... All we can say with certainty is that *the desire to see magic in everything* was one which was growing in the period of the Brāhmaṇas, which degrade the sacrifice from the position of the appeal to the bounty of heaven to the position of the greatest power on earth, which controls the gods and produces whatever is desired by the priests. ...The position is natural enough; all religions have to contend with magic, and while the higher [ !] religions cast much aside, they cannot be successful in removing all. The Vedic religion had, however, developed no [ ! ] such moral or religious basis as would render it possible to demand the disappearance of magic rites, and thus magic flourished under its aegis in almost a disconcerting degree." (*Italics* ours.) It does not seem to us that such and similar judgements are justified. To characterize a ritual action as "magic", one needs to have a specific conception of the "deity" and of man's relation to it. In the Brāhmaṇas we can witness a gradual but radical change in this conception where the "Deity", man and the sacrificial action form part of a single Total Reality. In such a conception—obviously so foreign to the Western scholars referred to above—the very idea of 'magic' becomes meaningless. We could perhaps add too that such a conception where man, through and in his sacrificial action, is 'at one' with the "Deity" is a such deeper idea than that where man is an importunate beggar always demanding favours for himself from the "Deity". For judgements similar to those of KEITH, see S. LEVI, J, EGGELING (*opera citata*) summarized in H. AGUILAR, *op. cit.*, ch. III.

2. A theistic religion—where the Absolute is 'personalistically' conceived and spoken of—would surely feel the loss of the image of God as "Father" more acutely. This feeling can certainly amount to a religious crisis in the religious tradition as a whole (as well in the individual believer in particular). This obviously applies too to the Indian theistic

laws than in a Creator God. Thus the evolution of sacrifice in India might also appear to be a tantalizing anticipation of themes which have started to enter in modern Western cosmology and theology as well.

In fact, if today the hypothesis of a regulating and creating God has become for many mostly superfluous, a universal Dynamism in which both Man and Divinity (to the extent that this serves the intimate and private life of the devout) participate and to which they contribute, can be an idea which can be made to fall more or less in line with modern exact sciences, whereas the existence of a personal Divinity superior to man and the world remains at most a matter of faith for the individual[3]. According to the Brāhmaṇic idea, Sacrifice, as the unique Act which is absolute and unrepeatable (in its very repetitions), consists in each single ritual act each one of which acquires absolute importance inasmuch as, and above all because, it does not recognize a Divinity superior to it, in much the same way as the cosmic Dynamism is seen today in the totality of its natural laws as *mathematically* measurable without the necessity of having recourse to a basic transcendent Unity, or to a superior God, to explain and account for its 'birth', evolution and maintenance[4]. Hence, the new attitude of the so-called 'modern' world allows the modern scholar to be

traditions, especially when they let themselves be influenced by the vicissitudes in Western cultural society. But these latter could perhaps be helped to recuperate any eventual loss of religious faith in recalling their ancient tradition where Viṣṇu, as Prajāpati, is the *sacrifical Action* par excellence!

3. Cf. R. PANIKKAR, *Il Silenzio del Buddha* (ed. U. M. VESCI), *op. cit.*, p. 256, note 109.

4. We hasten to remark that by making such a comparison we do not subscribe to the idea that the Brāhmaṇic sacrifice is in any way to be considered as an ***exact*** science belonging to a "pre-scientific" age. We want only to bring out a certain parallelism between both attitudes. In fact the Vedic sacrificer treats the sacred world in the same spirit with which the modern scientist treats the material world. Both deal with an 'exterior' reality, which both consider 'objective' governed by certain inherent laws which have to be discovered before man can react to them both in theory and in practice. (And to discover such laws is, in a certain sense, to 'create' them.) Both base themselves on experience of this reality, but whereas for the scientist as scientist the 'real' world is the material one, for the Vedic sacrificer—or for that matter, for any religious believer—the 'real' world is the sacred.

more favourably disposed to evaluate positively the process by which the Brāhmaṇic sacrifice rose to such autonomy than was possible in former days.

At first sight, this state of 'independentization' may seem to have been favourable to the priest engaged as he is in the difficult task of celebrating sacrifice. The fact that he is no longer to turn "with fear and trembling" to a God who has to be propitiated and placated to obtain favours from him, seems to liberate the priest from the preoccupation of rendering himself pleasing to or acceptable to Him and to withdraw himself from the divine capriciousness. What counts now is the impersonal action itself. It is therefore enough to know how to perform it properly to be able to be master of one's life and one's fortune without having to implore grace from anybody, not even of God, exactly as the modern scientist who tries to solve the problems of humanity without having to have recourse to God. To put oneself in a condition not to have to depend on anybody, not even on God, seems to have been one of the greatest aspirations of thinking man[5]. Thus the certitude of being able to solve by himself various problems, which have to do with sacrifice, places the priest in a position to be able finally to dominate the sphere of his own destiny and of the destiny of the *cosmos* which is now in his own hands. In a manner analogous to the feeling the modern scientist has within himself that he can dominate or foretell the behaviour of nature if he but know all its laws, the Brāhmaṇic priest feels that, once he has discovered the way to regulate and increase the power of the sacrifice through an adequate production of thermic energy in the rite, he is in a position to be self-sufficient into providing for the need of himself and of the universe which is entrusted to him. The only thing which is required of him is that he observe certain elementary precautions which are necessary lest he expose himself too much to an excess of energy and so get both psychically as well as physically burnt.

5. From the time when man started, in pre-historic times, to store food, to the time when he began to produce it by tilling the land and breeding animals, to construct water dams and create artificial rain, man's history has been a long struggle to free himself from the whims of Nature and to stop being helplessly passive in front of the "Will" of God.

Far from making matters easier for the Brāhmaṇa priest, however, the new ritual situation proves to be much more complex and unmanageable than the preceding[6]. To put it in the words of a well-known scholar of the last century: "The sacrifice is a difficult operation, and one which, to succeed, does not admit the omission of a single element"[7]. Without the help of a supreme Divinity which, no matter how capricious in its favours, knows also how to be merciful, the task of the priest engaged in an Action without appeal, far from having been facilitated, has become terribly complicated. In fact, a rite which becomes the guarantee of its own success meets with difficulties which are indeed greater than those which it had in former times when the Divinity was at liberty not to grant its favour. Now it is the rite itself which has to overcome the obstacles and it can only do so by itself through the help of its own creative principle: the heat. This new situation has the advantage of liberating the priest from any dependence whatsoever and of freeing him from being subject to the arbitrary acceptance or refusal, by the Gods, of his hymns and his sacrifice; but it also has its disadvantages since the *concentration* of the sacred in the sacrifice is difficult to actuate and sustain.

As a matter of fact, impersonal Action cannot be handled without great effort. To ensure the best results, it is not enough 'to know' theoretically what is to be done—one needs also to have the ability to do it and to remedy every defect or to avoid every mistake: an ability which, on the long run, will prove to be impossible even for the Gods or for the new sacrificial Supreme God, Prajāpati[8]: how much more, therefore, for man. Besides,

6. This is, at least in theory, the problem which confronts man in a modern democracy. Free from the humiliation to have to submit to tyrannical lords who may or may not grant him favours at will, he is now confronted by a more just even if impersonal law—a law which, at least in theory, is "equal for everybody". But without favours, there is no 'mercy'.

7. S. LEVI observes (*op. cit.*, p. 24) : "Le sacrifice est une operation difficile, et, qui, pour reussir, n'admet pas l'omission d'un seul element." ("The sacrifice is a difficult action and to succeed cannot afford to miss a single element.")

8. Cf. e.g. GopBr II.5.9; PancBr VIII.8.14, XXIV.11.2; etc. This topic will be hopefully developed in a separate study. See some passing remarks in one already qouted article, "The role of heat in Vedic sacrifice", p. 415.

it is one thing to offer (worship) to a God, appealing to his benevolence, power and also mercy, and it is another thing to perform an act which has in itself its sole reason for being. In the first case, it is enough to *excite* the divine power to put it in motion and then direct it in one's own favour; in the second case, power has to be *created*. That is to say, in practical terms, that a sacrifice addressed to a Divinity presupposes a Power which is outside it and which already has in itself the possibility of acting and granting what is asked of it; while a sacrifice which is an absolute Action in itself has to be capable of producing this Power by itself. This requires much greater energy, bravery and ability on the part of him who performs it. The conquest of liberty through the rite costs dearly, since independence from a 'master' more powerful than oneself demands substituting oneself for the 'master' and thus to possess as much force and power as he had—and this is not easy.

This is precisely the view which comes across to us in the two major schools of the Yajurveda. From them we come to know how, after having caused the accent to shift from the Divinity to the sacred Action through the universalization of the victim, the priest finds himself, in his turn, involved in a rite which, in the economy of the sacred and the universe, has no other court of appeal than itself. The independence of sacrifice, so to speak, is full of consequences both practical and theoretical. We have just seen the theoretical implications. From a practical point of view, every single ritual acquires a determining and irreplaceable importance. Not only can errors be no longer condoned, errors which now logically have disastrous results on a cosmic level and which can only be remedied by difficult counter-rituals[9], but the cultic action itself becomes more and more complicated. This is not to say that the more ancient rite was intrinsically simpler and that it was only by the passing of time that it gradually became more complicated.

9. Unlike the first Ṛgvedic hymns, in which an invocation to the Aśvins or to Viśvakarman is enough to correct a mistake, Brāhmaṇic literature is replete with expiatory formulas. See e.g. AitBr XXXII entirely devoted to expiations for various mistakes and casual faults, and SatBr XIII.3.3.1 ff. which speaks of the expiations demanded by mistakes committed in the Horse Sacrifice.

Rather, the fact is that, when sacrifice was offered to a Divinity who was superior to the cultic act, the complexity of the liturgical acts was subordinated to the divine Will, their heterogeneity was amalgamated into the unity of the divine figure to which they were directed and their efficacy depended on whether they were pleasing or not to a superior Power. But when this superior Power is attributed to the sacrifice itself, it follows that the value of the sacred Action is equal in each particular rite. Without a God to co-ordinate the various ceremonies and to assign them an order of importance according to his respective necesssity, what happens is that every rite cannot but be given equal importance because, if it is the act itself which is sacred and efficacious, there cannot be an act which has more weight than another. Therefore, since every rite is strictly linked to the one closest to it, the Brāhmaṇic sacrifice is little by little outfitted with a great complexity of actions, all of which are equally important, to such an extent that it ends up by requiring a big specialized personnel to perform it and a whole literature as a guide to fix and explain its intricate rules.

The result of all this was that with the passing of the centuries, really huge sacrifices were conceived entailing a great number not only of victims but also of rites, rules, gestures, meanings, ingredients and priests in a manner nowhere surpassed. All this, as we have said, not out of a debatable taste to "see magic in everything" and to indulge in a ritualism which shows off the virtuosity of the specialists, but out of the necessity to meet the internal exigences of an absolute Act.

The sacerdotal class needed to become more and more specialized and bigger. At least four priests (*ṛtvij*) are needed in the celebration of the more important sacrifices, and each one of them may, in his turn, be assisted by three other helpers, which brings the number of persons attached to a sacrifice to a total of sixteen (or seventeen if we count the *sadasya* who is not always counted in all the traditions)[10]. Each one of them has tasks to perform and hymns to recite. Among these hymns

10. For an adequate description of the role of Vedic and of the Brāhmaṇic priest, see respectively the studies of R.K. POTDAR (*op. cit.*, s.v.) and of G.U. THITE (*op. cit.*, pp. 199 ff.)

those of the Ṛks continue to be of great importance since they are the foundation of the entire mythology and religion[11], but there now arises the need to refine and to amplify the recitation into song and hence the various Ṛks hymns are re-arranged and re-organized into *sāman* whose recitation is entrusted to the Udgātṛ and his assistants (the Ṛks hymns are those of the Hotṛ). Similarly there arises a need for a whole series of new formulae to accompany the gestures, the deeds and the single actions of the sacrifice. These new ritual formulae, often inspired by or completely copied from the Ṛgveda, belong to the Adhvaryu and his assistants, since it is he who busies himself with what has to be materially done during the performance of the sacrifice. These formulae are collected in the Yajurveda which is soon divided into many schools[12]. This division can be explained by the fact that these formulae are related to practical matters and therefore more likely to meet with immediate difficulties which can be solved differently by the various priests during the performance of their duties. Besides, the Yajurveda (studied here in one of its 'white', *śukla*, versions, namely, the Mādhyandina, and in one of its 'black', *kṛṣṇa*, versions, namely, the Taittirīya) is so strictly linked, in its formulae, to the activity which it accompanies that often it cannot be understood unless the rite to which it refers is known. For this reason it needed, from the very beginning, explanations as to how to use the formulae incorporated in it. The Yajurvedic hymns, therefore, were soon provided with exegesis (the Brāhmaṇas) and later also with ritual treatises (the Sūtras—*Śrauta* and

11. Cf. e.g. R. PANIKKAR, *The Vedic Experience*, *op. cit.*, *passim.*

12. The main division is that between the White Yajurveda (*śukla*), and the Black Yajurveda (*kṛṣṇa*). Of these the Black seems to be the more ancient and it came down to us in four recensions : Taittirīya, Kāṭhaka, Maitrāyaṇī, Kapiṣṭhala. The more common recensions of the White—called also Vājasaneya—are the Mādhyandina and the Kāṇva. Most of the Brāhmaṇas whom I know belong to (*śākhā*) Mādhyandina School of the Śukla Yajurveda, which appears to be the most common. In the South of India it seems that it is the *śākhā* Taittirīya of the Kṛṣṇa Yajurveda which is the common. To these have to be added the Śrauta Sūtras, six of which are connected with the Taittirīya School and two with the Maitrāyaṇī of the Kṛṣṇa Yajurveda. Only one belongs to the *śukla* group of the Mādhyandina school namely the Kātyāyana.

*Gṛhya*). Of these, the Vājasaneya school of the 'white' recension has kept the hymns of the Saṃhitā distinct from its Brāhmaṇa (the Śatapatha)[13], while Taittirīya school of the 'black' recension interlaces the sacrificial *mantras* with immediate exegetical commentaries[14]. More or less during this period, the two other collections of hymns, namely the Ṛgveda and the Atharvaveda, were provided with commentaries, both of an exegetical (the Brāhmaṇas) and of a ritual nature (the Sūtras)[15].

13. Namely the Mādhyandina *śākhā* of the Vājasaneya Saṃhitā (abbr. VajSam) with its Brāhmaṇa, the Śatapatha, and its Śrauta Sūtra, the Kātyāyana.

14. This could perhaps reflect the original situation. It was only later, probably under the influence of the *śukla* tradition, that the Taittirīya collection too was divided into two group—or three if the Āraṇyakas are to be included, namely the Saṃhitās and the Brāhmaṇas. Still, even though they were so divided, the *mantras* and the brāhmaṇas remained mixed up. A Purāṇic legend (cf. VisP III. 5. 1-29) gives a strange reason why the two main portions of the Yajurveda were separated—into the "white" and the "black"—and why they became to be so called. According to the legend, Yājñavalkya (the hero of the Śatapatha Brāhmaṇa) was one of the disciples of Vaiśampāyana who, in his turn, was a disciple of Vyāsa. Once, Yājñavalkya earned the displeasure of his master who ordered him to "vomit" the Yajus he had already learnt. The vomited Yajus was then collected by the other co-disciples of Yājñavalkya, who took the form of partridge (tittiri)—hence the name Taittiriya. It was called "black" because of its "uncleanliness". After having been sent away, Yājñavalkya prayed directly to the Sun (Sūrya) that he might be given another Yajus greater than the one he had vomited. Sūrya, pleased with his prayer, granted him the Vājasaneya Saṃhitā with its separate Brāhmaṇa the Śatapatha. Pāṇini, however, who does not seem to have known of this legend (which does not mean that the legend is later than he), simply sees in the name 'Taittiriya' a derivation from the phrase "those who repeat what was said by Tittiri", an ancient Master (*tittiriṇā proktam* : *taittirīyaḥ*, PĀṆINI IV. 3. 102). If this is the case, it is called "black" (*kṛṣṇa*), according to a common explanation, because of its "obscurity', since it contains *mantras* and *brāhmaṇas* all mixed up.

15. These Brāhmaṇas are, respectively, the Aitareya and the Kauṣītaki (and perhaps also the Śāṅkhāyana if this is to be considered different from the Kauṣītaki as against the traditional usage which takes the two to stand for two different names of the same school) for the Ṛgveda, and the Gopatha for the Atharvaveda. For there are Śrauta Sūtras, two for each of the two Vedas. However we shall not be taking them into consideration the numerous Brāhmaṇas and Śrauta Sūtras of the Sāmaveda—except for the Pañcaviṃśa Brāhmaṇa, on one or two occasions.

It is this literature which has handed down to us the complex series of rites in which the Vedic sacrifice is enwrapped, with an abundance of particulars and often of mythological and quasi-philosophical explanations intended to stir up anew religious traditions which begin, with the passing of centuries, to appear strange or at least less understandable. If already from the most ancient times every sacrificial detail was considered to be so important that nothing in the economy of the ritual was allowed to get lost or wasted (not even, as we have seen in the Ṛgvedic *aśvamedha*, the small particles of meat left under the finger-nails of the immolator[16]) such complexity in the ritual was inevitable. Every detail has now become not only important but essential, nothing can be neglected and everything must be not only performed perfectly but also known and interpreted in its most intimate sense.

If Sacred Heat was the energy which caused sacrifice to develop into an independent Action, we should expect there would be elaborated a doctrine which puts in relief this fact, both on the practical level of the performance of sacrifice and on the speculative level of cosmology, in a more explicit and conscious way than it was possible for the two previous collections of hymns.

And this is precisely what happened.

## 2. *In the Rite*:

### (a) *In General*:

By the time of the Brāhmaṇas the necessity of liturgical heat and its effects is explicitly stated. The three functions of this heat, which we postulated on the basis of our initial intuitions we had from studying the original Vedic hymns, are here clearly formulated, thus confirming our interpretation. In the Brāhmaṇas, of the three functions of Sacred Heat namely, purification, transformation, and the bestowal of energy to the victim that it may reach its goal, it is the last which is especially stressed

16. Cf. note 47 of Ch. II.

together with protection from malign spirits, the friends of cold and darkness[17].

Reference to the use of heat is essentially of two kinds: indirect and direct. We have an example of the first kind in the Brāhmaṇic division of the various types of sacrifices in three big groups[18] (of seven each) in all of which, in one way or another, cooking, or at least heating, is included. One of the groups is just called *pākayajña*, 'the sacrifice of the cooked (offering)'. The second group is called *haviryajña*, 'the sacrifice of obtations'— and the 'havis' is 'something' which has to be cooked'[19]. The third group comprises the rites of the pressing

17. Previously this protecting function had no great meaning because protection from demons and from other disruptive forces did not belong to rituals alone, but Agni and other Divinities, who were prayed during rituals for protection.

18. Cf. the traditional division in GopBr I.5.25 : *sapta sutyāḥ sapta ca pākayajñāḥ havir yajñāḥ sapta ta ekaviṃśati / sarve te yajñā aṅgiraso' piyanti nūtanā yān ṛṣayo sṛjanti ye ca sṛṣṭāh purāṇaiḥ/* "seven (sacrifices, of) the Pressing (of Soma) and seven the *pāka* sacrifices and the offering sacrifices (havis) seven; these are twentyone. All these sacrifices the Aṅgiras-s perform; the ṛṣis create them new and these are created through the old (rituals)". On this last sentence a full commentary should be written—something which the present writer hopes one day to do. The separate names for all the sacrifices included in each of these groups are given earlier in the same Gopatha (I.5.23) as follows : "*sāyaṃ prātar homau sthālīpāko navaś ca yaḥ/ baliś ca pitṛyajñaś cāṣṭaka saptamaḥ paśur ity ete pākayajñaḥ*, ("the morning and evening offerings, the *sthālīpāka*, the *bali*, and the sacrifices to the ancestors; the *aṣṭaka* and as seventh the animal sacrifices; these are the *pākayajñas*"). The text continues : *agnyādheyam agnihotraṃ paurṇamāsy amāvāsye/ naveṣṭiś cāturmāsyāni paśubandho'tra saptamaḥ/ ity ete haviryajñāḥ//* ("establishment of fire-altar, agnihotra, the sacrifices for the full and new moon, for the nine asterisms, for the four months, and the animal sacrifices as seventh, these are the *haviryajñas*"), and further on :—*agniṣṭomo'tyagniṣṭoma ukthyāḥ sodaśimāṃses tataḥ / vājapeyo' atirātra cāptoryāmātra saptamaḥ / ity ete sutyāḥ*—(.."all these sacrifices" names with the aptoryāma as seventh, these are sacrifices of the Pressing (of Soma)".) However, another division is given in Ait Ar. II.3.3—*sa eṣa yajñaḥ pañcavidho 'gnihotraṃ darṣapūrṇamasau caturmāsāni paśuḥ somaḥ* . . .—("this very sacrifice is of five parts : *agnihotra*, new and full moon, of the four months, of animals, and of Soma...''). For a detailed description of these sacrifices see in G.U. THITE, *op. cit.*, pp. 104ff.

19. Cf. e.g. SatBr I.2.5.26—*yad vai śuśruma devānāṃ pariṣūtaṃ tad eṣa yajño bhavati yacchṛtāni havīṃṣi klṛptā vedis* ("What we have heard of as produced

of the Soma where, as we have seen,[20] the presence of heat is a condition *sine qua non* for the sacrifice to be efficacious[21]. Even today when, according to the *smṛti*, cooking is not so essential and uncooked grain can be offered in *havana*, all the preliminary ceremonies of the sacrifice still go by the comprehensive name of *pakti* 'cooking'[22].

The second kind of references, the direct ones, consists in straight allusions to heat as the principal cause of the success of a sacrifice, allusions which are in fact numerous, clear and explicit. For example, in the only reference the Ṛgveda makes to *Pravargya*[23], we recall how it was conjectured that the reason why the

---

for the gods that is this sacrifice, that is to say cooked oblations and the prepared altar . . .") (tr. EGGELING)

20. Cf. RV IX.83.1ff. quoted in notes 10 and 20 of Ch. II.

21. We recall here the contrary opinion of Max Muller (*Ancient Sanskrit Literature*, p. 203) quoted by R.L. MITRA in his Introduction to the critical ed. of the GopBr, p. 28 : "although the cooking of rice is a *sine qua non* in these ceremonies, yet some authors are of the opinion that *pāka* here does not mean cooking. It signifies, according to Indian authorities, says Max Muller, 'either *small* or *good*'. That *pāka* is used in the first sense appears from such expressions as *yo matpākataraḥ* 'he who is smaller than we'. But the more likely meaning is *good* or *excellent* or *perfect*; because, as the commentators remark, these ceremonies impart to every man that peculiar fitness without which he would be excluded from the sacrifices, and from all the benefits of his religion". Of course, I take it that the word *pāka* is derived from the root *pac* which means to cook, as is the opinion of R.L.MITRA too. In fact, even in modern Hindi the term *pakkā*, with the meaning of 'perfect', is also found in contexts of 'cooked thing', and not only of food or of 'ripe' but also of any object liable to be perfected by cooking as bricks, solid walls, main roads, as opposed to *kaccā*, 'raw', 'unripe', also used for food, unripe fruit, walls and paths made of earth etc. The same word *pakkā* is then used to mean 'truly' 'perfect' also in a moral sense, as for instance "a *pakkā* hindu", "a proper hindu". This meaning of 'perfection' connected with a root which properly means 'to cook' matches perfectly with the Vedic meaning of the word, and this without supposing a lack of 'common sense'. Actually, for the brāhmaṇas — and therefore for **their** descendants what is *cooked* is truly perfect, or truly perfected. It is through the act of being 'cooked', 'prepared', 'resistant through the right exposure to heat' that both sacrificer and sacrificial objects receive that "peculiar fitness" without which neither could partake in the sacrifice.

22. Cf. Pt. V.R. SHARMA GAUDA, *Yajña Mīmāṃsā*, *op. cit.*, for a summary of the sacrificial texts and their use in the tradition still alive today.

23. Cf. RV V.30.15 quoted in Ch. II, note 12.

*gharma* acquired a great sacral value was precisely the fact that it was heated (*tapta*)[24]. Now, in the detailed description of the rite as handed down to us in the Śatapatha Brāhmaṇa[25], at the climax of the ceremony when the receptacle with its offering is in full boil, we find it affirmed:"... this is what the Adhvaryu, stepping forward, says: the *gharma* is incandescent (*rucitaḥ*). And if it is incandescent, he (i.e. the priest) knows that the *yajamāna* will become better (that is richer); but if it is not incandescent (*arucitaḥ*) he knows that the *yajamāna* will become worse (that is to say, in a worse condition, poorer); and if it is neither incandescent nor non-incandescent (*na rucito nārucitaḥ*) the sacrificer will become neither better nor worse"[26]. The text could not be clearer. The allusions in the Ṛks are taken up and fully developed in the succeeding period when the power to obtain the desired goal is openly connected with the very act of heating, so much so that the well-being of the sacrificer, or his poverty now depends on the quantity of heat which one succeeds in producing by the boiling of the *gharma* or *mahāvīra*.

Again, the cooking of the offerings, besides making them ready to be offered in sacrifice, produces so much energy, by means of the heat innate in the act itself, that it 'thrusts' him who performs it towards the heavenly regions he wants to conquer. In a dispute over which ritual fire is more suitable for the preliminary cooking—now such liturgical subtleties acquire their importance in the understanding of the sacred act—the ritualist who insists that it is the *āhavanīya* (rather than, as is more usual, the *gārhapatya*)[27] offers the following argument which

24. Cf. previously in p. 26 where the passage is discussed.

25. The SatBr dedicates to it the whole *Kāṇḍa* XIV. The whole ritual will be studies in detail in Chap. VIII

26. SatBr XIV.1.3.33 : ... *tad adhvaryur upottiṣṭhannāha rucito gharma iti sa yadi rucitaḥ syācchreyān yajamāno bhaviṣyatīti vidyād atha yady arucitaḥ pāpīyān bhaviṣyatīti vidyād atha yadi naiva rucito nārucito naiva śreyān na pāpīyān bhaviṣyatīti vidyād yathā* ... This text will be quoted later in its proper context in Chap. VIII, note 179.

27. Cf. SatBr I.7.3.27 : *uto gārhapatya 'eva śrapayanti / āhavanīyo va'eṣa na vā'eṣa tasmai yad asminn aśṛtaṃ śrapayeyus* ... ("However, they also cook on the *gārhapatya*, (because) this is the *āhavanīya* but it is not for this, therefore that they should not cook uncooked food on it ...")

for us is significative: "Let them cook the sacrificial food on the *āhavanīya*; since from there, surely, the Gods ascended to Heaven and with it they toiled and worshipped, we too cook the *havis* in this way, we too act thus...the *āhavanīya* is the sacrifice and we will perform the sacrifice in the sacrifice"[28].

Here, though the aim of the author of these verses was not to underline the effect of cooking but simply to indicate on which one of the fires such cooking was to be performed, the need to follow the example of the Gods led the exegete to mention not merely their way of doing things but, more directly and in a descriptive and, at the same time, persuasive way, the result obtained by them. Once again we have here cooking which by itself achieves the first end of sacrifice. This fact exploited by the *ṛṣi* to uphold his point of view against the more usual custom of preparing the offerings on fire taken from the *gārhapatya*[29], confirms our supposition that the energy, required for the proper functioning of sacrifice and which makes it rise up to Heaven, is given precisely by the transforming heat of cooking, as was already the case with the Atharvic goat who drew from the flaming cauldron the power to rise up to the 'third heaven'[30]. Only that, in the latter case, it was only a question of an isolated statement, whereas here the theme of the ascension into Heaven is made an argument in the ritual casuistry Even if the solution of the dispute is finally based more on commonsense than on mere dry ritualism (the text after all concludes by leaving the priest free to cook where he thinks best)[31], it is significant that every liturgical detail, even the smallest, is discussed. It is the act itself which is efficacious

28. SatBr I.7.3.26 : *tad āhuḥ / āhavanīye havīṃṣi śrapayeyur ato vai devā divam upodakrāmaṃseno 'evārccantaḥ śrāmyantaś cerus tasmin havīṃṣi śrapayāma tasmin yajñaṃ tanavāma hā . . . yajña āhavanīyo yajñe yajñaṃ tanavāma hā' iti. //* This text has been already partially quoted in Ch. II, note 95 and will be mentioned again in the Conclusion, note 34 and Ch III, note 35.

29. Cf. SatBr I.7.3.27 : . . . *tasmai vā'eṣa yad asmiṃschṛtaṃ juhuyur ity ato.* . . . ("... therefore this food cooked on it should be offered indeed ...") (continuation of the text quoted in footnote 27)

30. Cf. AV IX.5.6 quoted and discussed in Ch. III, p. 64 and notes 6 and 7.

31. Cf. the end of the first quoted passage. SatBr I.7.3. 27 : ... *ato yatarathā kāmayeta tathā kuryāt //* ("... thus he may do as he likes").

and therefore it has to be weighed and evaluated in all its potentialities. Moreover, if 'climbing' from a fire is taken up for a point of reference in a dispute, it means that it is by now 'obvious'.

So far we have discussed the ascension of the offering into Heaven, i.e. the attainment of the end of the rite. Support for our conjecture regarding the other function which the Vedic people attributed to heat, namely transformation, can be found in a term of comparison which the exegete uses to clarify the effects on the priest or on the sacrificer by his consecration (*mahāvrata*). He compares the priest or the sacrificer to an earthen vessel baked by the heat of his ascetic power (*tapas*, already in the sense of heat obtained by personal effort and abstinence). In fact the text says that the *yajamāna* who is not filled with *tejas* (energy) "would melt as a raw earthen vessel full of or sprinkled with water"[32]. Although this simile is meant to do no more than indicate the sad lot of one who is not adequately prepared for the sacred act he is about to perform, it is still significant in that it brings out the effect of heat in consecration. Both man, who undergoes consecration, and the baked ritual implement, are transformed in such a way that they do not run any more the risk of 'being melted'. Further, this simile seems to us to reflect the surprise of the first *ṛṣis*—which is still alive in their much later descendants—when they saw the changed properties of the clay after its ritual exposure to the sacrificial fire[33]. We are thus led to suppose that the ancients utilized raw clay for their everyday use, while they purified and hardened on the sacred fire only those clay implements which are used for the cult, in the same way as they did with the food which was prepared to be offered to the Divinity and with the sacrificer who was initiated to his office.

Moreover, the transformation effected by the heat, is compared to the attainment of immortality. The baked clay of bricks

32. GopBr I.3.14.: ... *tathā peyurthā 'mapātram udaka āsikte nirmṛjed evam yajamānā nirmṛjyernnuparyyupayanti* ... Cf. also Ch. VII, footnotes 52 and 101.

33. This statement refers especially to the making both of the *ukhā* during *agnicayana* and of the *mahāvīra* during *pravargya*, and they will be explained further on in Chaps. VII and VIII respectively.

and vessels is called 'immortal' (*amṛta*) since on it has been accomplished an irreversible process. Therefore exterior and interior exposure to the sacred fire signifies a certain kind of consecration aimed at assuring immunity from the possible negative effects of contact with the sacred—a contact which is always difficult to sustain. This immunity is attained by a kind of 'hardening', a transformation into the sacred itself without the possibility of falling back. An indirect confirmation that terracotta was used only in the ritual can be found in a much more recent text in Hindu ritual literature which applying sacrificial usages to everyday behaviour even in the most profane situations—as often happens in the course of the centuries—formally forbids eating and drinking in earthen utensils[34].

In any case, all this seen from our point of view seems to confirm the fact that a certain amount of heat in the rite, enough to effect the transformation both of the objects used in the cult and of the person, is necessary for the performance of the sacred ceremony. Without an appropriate amount of heat one cannot obtain either wealth, or interior change, or ascension to the higher worlds.

(b) *Difference in the Amount of Heat amounting to difference of obtainment* :

If it is really the heat which is the major factor responsible for the acquisition of anything through rite, it is but natural that under the guidance of the attentive *brahmavādins* (theologians) a whole liturgy is also developed in which not only

34. Cf. VYĀSA, quoted in *Āhnika-Sūtrāvaliḥ*, Bombay (Nirnaya Sāgar) 1953, No. 409. On this basis one can also explain the unwillingness of many Brāhmaṇas even today to eat from ceramic or glass vessels. These are made of earth. Nevertheless, even in Vārāṇasī, one of the places where there are still many orthodox followers of traditional rules, though one finds it difficult to use vessels of a Western type (like the just mentioned glass and ceramic vessels), small vessels of earth, cooked by fire, are used for drinking outside one's house. The small terracotta-cups, in fact, are thrown away after use but one should be contaminated by using vessels already used by others. According to the explanation of a paṇḍit living in Benares, in this city the rules of Vyāsa are not transgressed because the earthen vessels are baked by fire and therefore are purified. For this kind information we are grateful to Pandit DAROGA TIWARI and Dr. G. BONAZZOLI.

every kind of desire is sought to be fulfilled by means of heat, but also different kinds of desires are sought to be fulfilled by means of different amounts of heat. One is therefore led to think that ultimately the amount of heat obtained in the sacrificial action was considered to be the factor responsible for both the success of sacrifice and for the attainments of various kinds. This is the case in such rites as the *Pravargya* where, as we have just seen, the quantity of heat guarantees the success of sacrifice and in which the very way of presenting the offering to be cooked on the fire is in accord with the result one expects. In the same manner, to every phase of the fire corresponds a different intensity of heat and this did not escape the attention of the Brāhmaṇa who was so keen on perfecting an act on which his own salvation and that of the world by now solely depended. Thus, if the receptacle full of the milk offering is warmed on a small flame, this flame, having relatively less calorific power, will only be able to obtain 'what has been', while if it is put to boil on the white-hot embers, the much intenser heat will obtain 'what must come'. Hence, adds the text, the perceptive Brāhmaṇa "boils the receptacle on the embers; in truth, he obtains what must come, since what must come, is greater than what has been"[35].

Similarly, every oblation offered with a view to obtaining a specific goal will be poured in a specific way, at a specific moment and on a specific form of the fire. If, for example, one wants to obtain a village, the oblation must be poured on the smoke (or, probably, on the still smoking fire), while if one wants to receive the luminosity of *Brahman*, it must be poured on the flame, and if one wants to acquire cattle (the highest form of wealth), it must be poured on the embers[36]. Elsewhere it is the sacrificer's position with respect to the fire at the

35. TaittSam V.1.9.2 : . . . *yad arciṣi pravṛñjyād bhrūtam ava rundhīta yad aṅgāreṣu bhaviṣyad aṅgāreṣu pravṛṇakti bhaviṣyad evāva rundhe bhaviṣyaddhi bhūyo bhūtād* . . .

36. Cf. KausBr II.2 : *dhūmāyantyāṃ grāmakāmasya juhuyājjvalantyāṃ brahmavarcasakāmasya aṅgāreṣu paśukāmasya abhyādhāyeti* . . . ("when it smokes, in it should he offer for one who desires a village; when it flames for one who desired radiance; in the embers for one who desires cattle . . .") (tr. A.B. Keith).

moment of pouring the oblation which is determined by the goal : "He who desires brilliance and splendour must present his offering facing East, since the eastern direction is the brilliance and splendour of *Brahman*; who knows this and faces East will possess *tejas* and *brahmavarcas*; he who wants food, let him go with the offering towards the South, the eater of food and the lord of food is Agni..." Similarly, the officiant must face West for cattle and North for Soma, etc.[37]. We see here that Agni can give food to him who faces in his direction; with his heat he can also grant protection and power to him who asks for them in the rite. His heat is the power of *tapas* which, as we have already seen, is the energy generated internally by the ritual and initiated by the interior power which unifies the Divine and the Human in the specific act of sacrifice. The Devas—mostly looked upon as model because of their perfect way of performing rituals—at the begining of time offered boiling milk to Agni and drank the amount reserved for them as the officiants at the sacrifice, the *ucchiṣṭa*, to clothe themselves with a fiery protection against their rivals, the Asuras, the traditional enemies of light which radiates life-giving heat. In their wake, the *yajamāna* too is invited to perform the same acts and to partake of the same boiling drink to obtain for himself those favours now offered by the rite to whoever knows how to make use of it[38].

37. Ait Br. II. 2 (I.2.8): *yas tejo brahmavarcasam icchet prayājāhutibhiḥ prāṅ sa iyāt / tejo vai brahmavarcasaṃ prācī dik / tejasvī brahmavarcasī bhavati ya evaṃ vidvan prāṅeti yo 'nnādyam icchet prayājāhutibhir dakṣiṇā sa iyād / annādo vā eṣo 'nnapatir yad agniḥ* . . . and so on.

38. Cf TaittSam VI.2.2.6 sq. *devāsurāḥ saṃyattā āsan te devā bibhyato 'gniṃ prāviśan tasmād āhur agniḥ sarvā devatā iti / te 'gniṃ eva varūthaṃ kṛtvā 'surān abhyabhavann agnim iva khalu vā eṣa praviśati yo avāntara āntaradīkṣām upaiti bhrātṛvyābhibhūtyai bhavaty ātmanā parā 'sya.* Cf. Further on Conclusion, note 435. ("The Gods and the Asuras were in conflict. The Gods in fear enter Agni; therefore they say 'Agni is all the Gods'. They /6/ making Agni their protection, overcame the Asuras. Now he as it were enters Agni who undergoes the intermediate consecration . . .") and further on :—*bhrātṛvyo bhavatyām ātmānam eva dīkṣayā pāti prajām avāntaradīkṣaya santarāṃ mekhalāṃ samāyacchate prajā hyātamano' ntaratarā taptavrato bhavati . . . yā te agne rudriyā tanūr ity āha svayaivainad devatayā vratayati sayonitvāya śāntyai //* ("he protects himself by the consecration, his offspring by the intermediate consecration. The girdle he

To sum up, the sacrificial thermic energy is very often explicitly mentioned as the factor responsible for the success of sacrifice and the guarantee of obtaining what one desires. This it does in an abstract way, in accordance with the dry and inflexible 'order of nature'—only the one who succeeds in attaining the required amount of heat gets the results. The power of heat is greater than any other ritual element compared to which every dispute about the liturgy, for example about the best way of offering the sacrifice or the direction to face when presenting the offering, loses its significance. One can always solve a dilemma without fear of error or of obtaining inferior results if one takes recourse to the power of the sacred heat and offers the libation on the most heated part of the fire. In fact "only with an offering on the incandescent fire (*samiddhahoma*) can the oblation be successful (*saṃrddhā*)"[39].

3. *Conclusion* :

The perfection and success of sacrifice rest on raising the heat of fire to incandescence compared to which all other ritual modalities lose their importance. The heat to become the visible expression of the sacred and guarantee of the results obtainable from the sacrificial action, must augment its power and force until it reaches a true and real incandescence. The heat becomes the fulcrum of this sacrificial action and the guarantee of its results and so must be increased in proportion to the external and internal exigences of sacrifice. Here, therefore, the normal heat required for cooking as demanded by the first Vedas,[40] is no longer enough; here we witness a conscious

---

makes tighter, for his offspring are closer to him than himself. He drinks warm milk . . . the dread form, on Agni, he says; verily with his own deity he consumes the hot milk for unity, for atonement.") (tr. A.B. Keith).

39. SatBr I.6.3.39 (fine) . . . *yatro 'eva samiddhatamaṃ manyeta tad āhutīr juhuyāt samiddhahomena hy eva samṛddhā āhutayaḥ* // Here the success of the sacrifice is due to the incandescence of fire, but this seems to be based mostly on etymological grounds : *samiddhatam* (incandescent) and *samiddha homa* (hot offering) which are similar to *samṛddhā* (with success). The text is inserted at the conclusion of a discussion about the ways of offering clarified butter, the portion of Agni.

40. Cf. Ch. BLAIR, *op. cit.*, p. 90.

effort to augment the heat to its extremes, not only in the preparatory preliminaries—such as in the preparatory cooking of the offerings, of the bricks of the altar and other clay utensils, and indeed, in the preparation of the sacrificer himself by means of the *tapas* of his consecration—but also in the final act of sacrifice itself, that is, in the way the actual offering of sacrifice is made. Thus, the texts seem to insist more and more on the need for greater heat. At the same time, parallel to this insistence, arises an abhorrence of the raw. All this leads us to think that from the time of the first Vedas to the time of the Brāhmaṇa of the Yajurveda the heat required for the transformation of offering and the success of sacrifice increased, so much so that the problem arose whether man would be able to bear such heat.[41]

The need for greater heat can be explained by the fact that during the time of the Saṃhitās, the attitude of the poet-priest toward rites was more or less spontaneous so that although he, the poet-priest, was to abide by certain rules intrinsic to the ritual act, he was not as constrained by them since he had not yet begun to reflect on them very consciously. However, during the time when ritual exegesis was taken up in earnest, and perfection in the sacred act became a goal in itself, reflection came very much to the fore. Yet, reflection entails the loss of spontaneity which needs to be compensated with the acquisition of greater energy. In other words, any action, performed without being self-conscious, attains its end directly and immediately, because, by involving no great circumspection, it does not need an excessive expense of energy. If, on the contrary, it is performed in a manner full of reflective awareness in such a way that everything is weighed, controlled, anticipated, and every foreseen effect is consciously related to a cause so that every possible interference can be repelled, the energy, which is required to bring it to its end, will be much

41. Since this study is only concerned with the good and positive effects of heat in Vedic Sacrifice, we cannot discuss here the effects of the lack of the required heat or of its excess effects which are equally, even if differently, damaging. We do so in a summarized form in our already quoted article *The Role of Heat*, Part II and III. We hope to take up the subject again in a longer study in the near future.

greater. Weighing seriously the reasons for and against one's action weighs heavily on the action itself. Especially the reasons against, which have to be resolved in a conscious and painful way. The energy required is proportionally much greater and tends to go on increasing as new difficulties arise. It is significant that now the word mostly used to express the attitude needed to perform a sacrifice is *śrama*, effort.

Here is not the place to stop and consider the possible dangers and deleterious effects which an excess of heat can produce. It suffices at present to point out the positive results of sacrifice when, through its accumulated energy, it succeeds in achieving its own ends, in spite of the many difficulties.

To do this, we shall now study more closely and more systematically the use of ritual heat from this point of view in some of the more significant rites without pretending however to describe these rites in any exhaustive manner. We shall consider in the first place the animal sacrifice (*paśubandha*) which is in all the religions of the world, or nearly all, held to be the sacrifice par excellence. In fact, in the various religions all the other rites which go by the name of 'sacrifice', but which do not involve a blood immolation, must somehow or other 'justify' their name[42]. This we shall do in Chapter Five. Apart from *paśubandha* we shall consider other rites, amongst which we have chosen the kindling of the first fire in the house of the young *yajamāna* (*agnyādhāna*) which is the preliminary rite necessary before any sacrifice could be offered. That will be Chapter Six. Keeping close to the previous topic, we shall then consider in Chapter Seven the construction of the fire altar (*agnicayana*) during the Soma rite because of its importance both cosmological and philosophical which has been attached

42. In academic disputes about the definition of "sacrifice" and the possible extension of the term, scholars agree that the specific character of "sacrifice" is the 'killing' of the victim. Doubts arise when the term is extended so as to include in it other various ways of offering other types of victims. And here the disagreement is great. Cf. e.g. G. van der LEEUW, *op. cit.*, par. 50; A. BRELICH, *Introduzione alla Storia delle Religioni*, *op. cit.*, p. 43 ff.; G. MENSHING, *Religious Sociology* (*op. cit.*, in French tr.); V. MASSUH, *El Rito y lo Sagrado*, *op. cit.*, passis; R. PANIKKAR, *Le mystère du cult dans l'Hindouisme et le Christianisme*, *op. cit.*

to it *ab antiquo*. We shall, however, consider here only the two or three phases of the rite which bear on our subject, such as the baking of the bricks and the preparation and baking of the *ukhā*, the earthen pot used for fire-offering during the construction of firealtar. We then proceed to consider *mahāvīra* in Chapter Eight, the preparation and baking of the earthen vessel used for the *Pravargya*, to bring out certain similarities between these last two implements.

Our aim, as we have said before, is not to reconstruct and present the Vedic rites in all their details and peculiarities, but to bring into relief a religious and speculative process which took its point of departure from a ritual detail in order to follow this process in its main lines of development through a description of some relevant rites serving as examples.

# PART II

# THE CREATIVITY OF RITUAL HEAT IN SOME VEDIC RITES ACCORDING TO THE BRĀHMAṆAS

CHAPTER FIVE

# ANIMAL SACRIFICE (PAŚUYAJÑA or PAŚUBANDHA)

In Vedic India, animal sacrifice, *paśuyajña,* had various forms. As *paśubandha,* where the animal to be immolated is tied to a sacrificial stake, it is included in much greater and complex rituals. It is also, as we have seen, a sacrifice in its own right listed both among *pākayajña* and among *haviryajña*[1]. The great rituals which include various rites, among which is *paśubandha,* are themselves often centred around a greater victim which sometimes is immolated in a manner peculiar to it alone. These are, for instance, the sacrifice of horse (*aśvamedna*)[2], the human sacrifice (*puruṣamedha*)[3] and that of ox

1. See note 18 of Chap. IV.

2. The texts which refer to *aśvamedha* are, besides the already quoted Vedic hymns (RV I. 162 & 163), the VajSam which dedicates to it Adhyāyas XXII to XXIX inclusively and its Brāhmaṇa, **the Śatapatha** which dedicates to it the whole of Kāṇḍa XIII: The Taittirīya School treats of this sacrifice in various places without any order. The AitBr and the KausBr ignore it completely, but their Śrauta Sūtras do treat of it briefly.

3. That *puruṣamedha* is a sacrifice of minor importance, in spite of the fact that the Ṛgvedic hymn X. 90 considers it to be a major one, and that it is perhaps derived from *aśvamedha,* can be inferred from the place reserved for it in the Brāhmaṇas. The Śatapatha dedicates to it the end of Kāṇḍa XIII, as if in an appendix to *aśvamedha.* Similarly the VajSam dedicates to it Adhyāyas XXX to XXXI, that is those coming immediately after the treatment of *aśvamedha* to which many more Adhyāyas are dedicated. *Puruṣamedha* is not treated by the Ṛgvedic Brāhmaṇas; it only refers to it in the legend of Śunaḥ śepa which gives an ambivalent judgement regarding the place held by the human sacrifice. See also Chap. VII, p. 177.

(*gosava*)[4]. Although the principal victim of each of the great rituals is one, the number of secondary victims in a related *paśuyajña* is often great and varies in accordance with the nature of the sacrifice. Thus in *aśvamedha* eleven victims are offered to Soma, seventeen to Prajāpati besides other types of animals which must be symbolically offered "to render the sacrifice complete"[5].

Now, what principally interests us in this context, is to see what effects heat has on the victim. In order to be as clear as possible in our exposition, we shall take *paśubandha* mainly as it appears in one single sacrificial complex. We choose, therefore, as our guiding sacrifice the pressing of Soma, since it is the one in which animal sacrifice of secondary victim is given greater evidence by the texts[6]. Occasionally, we shall refer to the animal sacrifice which accompanies aśvamedha[7], while we shall treat only in passing, the ritual handling and immolation of the more important victim, i.e. the horse[8].

In our description of the role played by fire, we shall have occasion to note the function of ritual heat that was responsible for that peculiar Brāhmaṇic deviation from and modification

4. For more details regarding this sacrifice, which are of smaller interest to us than the others, see G. U. THITE, *op. cit.*, s.v.

5. Cf. e.g. SatBr III. 7. 2. 1 where there is mention of eleven sacrificial poles, plus a twelfth for the animal sacrifice which is to be performed in connection with the Soma, and SatBr XIII. 2. 2. 13 which speaks of the seventeen victims which are needed to complete the horse-sacrifice offered to Prajāpati who is, precisely, represented by the number seventeen or, at least, by a number related to it. see also TaittBr III. 7. 6; JaimBr II. 113 and the various pertinent Sūtras.

6. There is, in fact, a *paśubandha* included in the group of seven sacrifices of the *havis*, which is different in some of its rites from that found in the whole Soma sacrificial complex, but definitely less important than it. This can be inferred from the way the two are treated in the various Brāhmaṇas. For instance, the Śatapatha dedicates to the animal sacrifice of the Soma sacrificial complex all of Kāṇḍa III, while to the animal sacrifice as an independent rite only a couple of short Adhyāyas (XI. 7 & 8). The Ṛgvedic Brāhmaṇas speak of the ceremonies related to the animal sacrifice only in connection with the Soma Sacrifice. See AitBr VI & VII (II. 1 & 2) and KausBr X.

7. As results, for example, from note 41 below and in other similar passages.

8. See pp. 32 ff., Chap. II.

of the more common and more diffused way of considering and interpreting sacrifice.

1. *Circumambulation of Agni* (*paryagni*) :

In *paśuyajña*, fire, the subject of our study, appears for the first time when, after various preliminary rites which do not concern us directly[9], one of the priests, the *hotṛ*, recites, on the invitation of the *adhvaryu*, the hymns concerning the circumambulation of Fire (*paryagni*)[10]. The rite is performed by the *agnīdhra* while the victim is still alive. He takes a firebrand from the sacrificial fire *āhavanīya*, and moves it round the victim as if to protect it by a continuous and uninterrupted line of heat[11]. This ceremony existed already at the time of the Ṛgveda even if in a somewhat different form. It was performed for the benefit of the horse, the principal victim of *aśvamedha*, and for the one goat which had to accompany it as a secondary animal victim. But in the Ṛgveda the circumambulation (*paryaśvam*) was performed by the horse around the fire altar and not the other way about[12]. Its meaning was therefore also probably different. At that time Agni was still an important Deity superior to anything in the entire complex of the sacrificial system. The victim which is despatched to him, or which is despatched by him to other waiting Deities, goes around the fire in its fireplace, to render him homage. In the Brāhmaṇas, on the

9. As, for example, the erection of the sacrificial pole in SatBr III. 7. 3. 1: *paśuśca vai yūpaśca na vā'ṛte yūpāt paśumālabhate*..See also SatBr III. 6.4.1 ff. for the animal sacrifice connected with the Soma; SatBr XIII. 2.2.1 ff., XIII. 2. 3. 1 ff., XIII. 2. 4. 1ff., etc. for the victims connected with *aśvamedha*. This ritual detail is very important and the *yūpa* is so significative that it gave rise to a whole philosophy or to a spiritual development of its own. See, e.g. the hymn to the Skandha in the Atharva Veda X.7, which, however, we cannot examine here. Or the binding of the animal before its immolation, e.g. in SatBr III. 7. 2.3 (*Somayajña*); XIII. 2. 2. 2 (*aśvamedha*), etc.

10. Cf. SatBr III. 8. 1. 6: *athāha paryagnaye' nubrūhīti* ("then he says: recite the circumambulation of Agni."). The verses which are to be recited are taken from RV IV. 15. 1-3.

11. Cf. SatBr III. 8. 1. 6 (continuation of the preceding text):...*ulmukam ādāya agnīt paryagniṃ karoti tad yat paryagnim karoty acohidṛm evainam etad agninā parigṛhṇāti nedenaṃ nāṣṭṛā rakṣāṃsi pramṛśān ity agnir hi rakṣasām apahantā tasmāt paryagniṃ karoti tad yatrainaṃ śrapayanti tad abhi pariharati.*

12. Cf. RV. I. 162. 4a : *trir mānuṣāḥ paryaśvaṃ nayanti*. We refer to our previous discussion on this subject, in Chap. II, pp. 32 ff.

contrary, it is the fire which goes around the victim. The explanation which the exegete feels bound to give—probably to justify this change in the ritual—has recourse to the idea of 'protection' : the uninterrupted line of fire serves to raise a barrier of heat against the malignant spirits (*rakṣases*) of whom Agni is the destroyer *per antonomasia* from very ancient times[13]. The same protection is extended to the place where the victim will be cooked—another very important and therefore vulnerable point[14]. The Ṛgvedic Brāhmaṇas which deal with the same problem insist on this idea of 'protection' and to support it refer to the constant war raging between the Devas and the Asuras. The circumambulation which is threefold, as threefold too was the horse's walk around the fire, builds around the the victim a triple citadel of defence which the Devas built around their sacrifice when they saw their enemies advancing with hostile intentions[15]. The same gesture is therefore re-enacted by the earthly sacrificers to defend their own rite and themselves[16].

However, the Śatapatha Brāhmaṇa gives one to understand—though not in a totally explicit way—that the circumambulation of the fire around the victim has a further use which seems to go beyond that of mere 'protection'. The *Adhvaryu*, as the priest in charge of the material performance of the various sacrificial

13. See the last part of the text quoted in note 12. For a list of pertinent texts, see our already quoted article, "Ritual as mirror reflecting Ṛgvedic Life" and Ch. BLAIR, *op. cit.*

14. Cf. SatBr III. 3. 1. 6 (the last phrase of the text quoted at some length in note 11). See also BharSS VII. 12. 4.

15. Cf. AirBr VII. 1 (II. 2. 11) *tān āprīte paśau pura iva paryagneḥ / yūpaṃ prati purastād upāyaṃste devāḥ pratibhudy āgnimayīḥ puras tripuraṃ paryāsyanta yajñasya cātmanaś ca guptyai / tā eṣām imā agnimayyaḥ puro dīpyamānā bhrājamānā atiṣṭhaṃ //stā asurā anapaghṛsyaivāpādravaṃ/ste 'gninaiva purastād asurarakṣāṃsy-apāghnata.* . . The same idea is expressed more or less in the same words in KausBr X.3 towards the end.

16. Cf. AitBr VII.7 (II. 2. 11) which is the continuation of the text quoted in the preceding note, in which the sacrificer, with the same procedure and the same ritual, repeats the action of Gods and protects himself and his sacrifice with the same three citadels.

rites, has the responsibility to see to their co-ordination and to the eventual legitimacy of the execution of certain acts within the ambit of a liturgical code of a much greater significance,—a code which seems to be defined little by little as the rite develops and becomes firmly established. When the sacrifice becomes independent of a superior divine figure, there arise unforeseen problems. When the sacrifice is dependent on a superior Deity to whom it is offered, the various rites, of which it is composed, find their natural cohesion in the divine power which prescribes them, as we have already seen; when, however, the sacrifice is independent of such a superior Deity, its various rites must find their cohesion in some kind of logical connection inherent in the rites themselves. This connection is not always easy to discover, especially because in the majority of cases, it simply does not exist. Evidently to solve one of the many problems which arise out of the necessity to find an inter-connection between the various rites, the theologian informs us that the circumambulating Agni has not only protected the victim but has also 'swallowed' it in such a way that the fire-brand cannot be put back in the sacred fire from which it has been lifted[17]. In this way the 'swallowing' of the victim by Agni seems to refer also to a form of admittance of the victim into the sacred, or as a kind of 'consecration', a symbolic pre-figuration of that transformation into the Divine which will be later effectively accomplished when the victim itself will be cooked before its final offering. This act of preliminary trans-formation through the swallowing of the animal while still alive by fire serves two functions : on the one hand, it already renders the animal sacred so that when it passes from this world to the other it is already a divine or quasi-divine being, and on the other it tries to solve the important and difficult problem

17. Cf. SatBr III. 8. 1. 8 : ..*yathā vai grasitam evam asyaitad bhavati yad enena paryagniṃ karoti sa yathā grasitam anuhāyācchidya tad anyasmai prayacched evaṃ tat tasmād etasyaivolmukasyāṅgārānnimṛdya tasminn enaṃ śrapayeyuḥ* || But, on the other hand, cf. ApSS VII. 15. 3 and perhaps too BharSS VII. 12. 7, where it is said that the firebrand after the triple deambulation, must be put down and then carried three times again, in the opposite direction, before it is finally put back in the *āhavanīya*. Thus, the firebrand, in a certain sense undoes the performed action and can be laid inside it intact once again.

of how to overcome the intitial raw state of the offering. The 'swallowing' of the victim by the fire directs our attention on another difficulty—ignored for the time being in our study—with which the Vedic priest has to reckon when he comes to systematize the rules which govern sacrifice, namely, the contact with what is yet raw.

Since the rite whereby the victim is admitted to the sacred is, as it were, a pre-immolation, it allows a full series of liturgical subtleties with respect to various complications arising from the incompatibility of certain Brāhmaṇical ritual forms required for the *completeness* of the sacrifice and the demands of the liturgical 'rules' which cannot be broken, not even because of local needs. Thus, the movement of the fire around the victim, by its symbolic 'swallowing' becomes itself a symbol of immolation and can therefore replace that very immolation in those circumstances where it is required by the Brāhmaṇic rite, although expressly forbidden by the 'general rules'. Contingencies of this sort are not rarely to be found in the Brāhmaṇas. An example is *paśubandha* itself, when linked to some liturgical complexes of much greater importance, as for example, the *aśvamedha* or the *somayajña*. Here amongst the animals called to be immolated with the horse or Soma, some are rightly 'quietened' while others as for example, wild animals[18] or animals which are still vigorously fertile[19] are not at all fit for

18. For the *aśvamedha*, cf. SatBr XIII. 2. 4. 1 : *prajāpatir akāmayata ubhau lokāvabhijayeyaṃ devalokaṃ ca manuṣyalokaṃ ceti sa etān paśūn apaśyad grāmyāṃś cāraṇyāṃś ca tān ālabhata tair imau lokāvavārunddha grāmyair eva paśubhir imaṃ lokam avārunddhāraṇyair amum ayaṃ vai loko manuṣyaloko 'thāsau devaloko yad grāmyān paśūn ālabhata 'imam eva tair lokaṃ yajamāno 'varundhe yad āraṇyān amuṃ taiḥ* //

("Prajāpati desired: I want to conquer both worlds, the world of the gods and the world of men; he sees these victims, the tame and the wild; he took hold of them and through them he possessed these worlds, through the tame animals he possessed this world, with the wild that. In fact, this is the world of men, that is the world of the gods. Thus when the sacrificer takes hold of the tame animals, he possesses, through them, this world, and when (he takes hold of) the wild, he (possesses), through them, the other.") Wild animals, which do not belong to the sphere of human culture, serve, in *aśvamedha*, to complete the domesticated world produced by man with that other sphere of Reality which is beyond it.

19. In the case of *paśubandha* of Somayajña, however, the 'forbidden'

such an immolation. They must be bound like the rest to their respective sacrificial stakes to comply with local demands (otherwise the sacrifice cannot be considered to be complete), but they cannot share the same fate as the rest of the victims, otherwise a much greater 'law' would be transgressed, namely, the 'order of ritual nature'. Normally, a sacrificial victim must be one which man himself has reared; in other words, it must belong to the human sphere as the product of his labours,—although at the same time it must not be 'contaminated' by participating in human work. It is precisely here that the difference lies between a sacrifice and the offering of first fruits. While the latter presupposes a cultural and religious background where the means of sustenance are considered to come from a world which already exists independently of human labour, sacrifice is the cultic form more typical of a culture of a productive economy where man is aware that what he possesses belongs to him by right because it is fruit of his own effort, work and personal inventiveness. What he offers in sacrifice represents him wholly and in all respects is identified with him. It must therefore be a product of his labours—of his agriculture or his cattle-rearing. The victim to be immolated cannot be but a domestic animal[20]. The wild animal, on the other hand, cannot according to the 'sacrificial code', be immolated and offered since it does not belong to man and his labour. To capture a wild animal is to somehow violate a world which is alien to man and which pertains to the '*numinous*'. It has no value in a ritual of this type since it is not a 'human offering', so much so that it would not need a 'consecration', if it should be offered, because it is a creature which already belongs to the Divinity.

---

animal is the adult male already capable of procreating. This must be offered to Tvaṣṭṛ. Cf. SatBr III. 7. 2. 8 : *atha patnībhyaḥ patnīyūpam ucchrayanti / sarvat vāya nveva patnīrūpa ucchrīyate tat twāṣṭraṃ paśum ālabhate tvaṣṭā vai sitkaṃ reto vikaroti tad eṣa evaitat sitkaṃ reto vikaroti muṣkaro bhavaty eṣa vai prajanayitā yan muṣkaras tasmān muṣkaro bhavati taṃ na saṃsthāpayet paryagnikṛtam evotsṛjet sa yat saṃsthāpayet prajāyai hāntam iyāt tat prajām utsṛjati tasmān na saṃsthāpayet*.... ) /

It is a male animal which is required for the *yūpa* offered to the female consorts of the Devas, but its immolation would go against the more general rules of sacrifice.

20. Cf. W. BURKERT, *op. cit.*

Now, all this furnishes us with a further proof with regard to the efficacy of fire and of its heat, whose presence is already enough to symbolize a whole sacrificial process. When in the course of the development of Brāhmaṇic sacrifice, internal exigencies begin to clash with some of the rules of nature governing the sacrifice[21], the power of heat can help to find a solution in the difficulty. Thus it has happened with the rite of the circumambulation of Agni as conducted by the assistant of the *adhvaryu*[22]. This rite, which has come to symbolize the immolation of the victim, is used at the place of the true immolation when Brāhmaṇic development of sacrifice introduces on the altar animals which, strictly speaking, cannot serve as victims. The sacrifice now apotheosized by Brāhmaṇic speculation into an identification with cosmic creative action must be able to reach out to all the spheres of the universe and not only to the human cultural sphere. But how is one to represent on the altar the 'other world'? The most direct way of doing this is to include wild animals also in the sacrifice. If the domestic animals which live in contact with man and his world can represent him and his sphere of life and action, the wild animals which live in that part of nature which is not yet subjugated to the needs of man, can obviously represent the world of the 'numinous', of the beyond, of what is imponderable and unmanageable[23]. But, as

21. On this point, we refer to what we have already said in the Introduction and to the following note 23. See also Chap. VII, note 24.

22. See the last part of SatBr III. 7. 2. 8 quoted in note 19 and for *aśvamedha* SatBr XIII. 2. 4. 3 which is the conclusion of the text quoted in note 18 : ..*paryagnikṛtān evotsṛjanti*...

23. And it is in this that, at least to the present writer, lies the difference between the sacrifice, strictly so-called, and the offering of first fruits particularly that prevalent among nomad and non-agricultural peoples. The idea behind the latter is principally that of a de-consecration while that behind the former is that of a consecration or, simply, of a sacralization. This is to say that the cultural and religious background of the sacrifice is a vision of the world in which everything is already given, independently of human labour, and of which man takes possession by means of harvesting, hunting (or fishing). Thus, anything which surrounds man does not belong to him but to the 'Deity', to the Lord of the animals, from whom he takes things for his own use. To be able, therefore, to consume his portion, he must first 'de-sacralize' it and restore the first fruits to their legitimate owner. On the contrary, in the context of a productive economy, man is conscious of the fact that anything which

we have seen, wild animals cannot be immolated without transgressing the 'general order'. Thus, although the inclusion of wild animals in the sacrificial complex serves to symbolize the non-human world in order that the entire universe might be fully represented—as expressed by the previously stated desire of the Supreme Lord to win an appropriate place for himself on all the levels of the cosmic Act[24]—yet, on the other hand, this would not be legitimate : the sacrificial rite as such precludes it. Obviously the *brahmavādin* cannot know of this very rule, however, he does perceive it, so much so that he speaks of violation and profanation of the sacrifice (*yajñaveśasa*) [25] when the above considerations lead him to bring to the altar a type of victim which cannot be officially immolated. He comes out of this impasse by performing a symbolic immolation, by means of the circumambulating fire, of these 'pseudovictims' and then letting them go free. In this way, the application of sacred Heat, whose transforming capacity enables it to act as a substitute for the actual immolation allows the priest to perform his rite without transgressing the 'general rules' and at the same time without failing to meet the Vedic demands. All this, however, is for him neither a simple matter nor immediately evident, so much so that the Brāhmaṇic theologian finds himself obliged to look for plausible excuses why it is impossible that his theory be materially implemented in its entirety.[26]

---

he possesses belongs to him by right since it has been produced by his own labour. But since this belongs to him, it belongs to this world of his, and if man wants to offer it in sacrifice, it needs first to be 'consecrated' and thus rendered worthy of being offered. It must be made 'sacred' to be able to be absorbed by the Deity without rendering it profane, to come in contact with the Transcendent without this stopping being such.

24. Cf. SatBr XIII, 2. 4. 1 already quoted in note 18.

25. Cf. SatBr XIII. 2. 4. 3 : *tad āhuḥ / apaśur vā eṣa yad āraṇyo naitasya hotavyaṃ yajjuhuyātkṣipraṃ yajamānam araṇyaṃ mṛtaṃ hareyur araṇyabhāgā hy āraṇyāḥ paśavo yanna juhuyād yajñaveśasaṃ syād iti paryagni*. . It is to be noted, however, that even today a sacrifice is performed, during a great festival, in which the sphere of wild animals (lions, elephants, etc.) is included. Wild animals are regularly immolated and then thrown into the sea. This happens in the island of Bali. This phenomenon, which goes counter to the universal rules which govern the sacrifice needs to by studied separately to bring out clearly its internal and external motivations.

26. It is interesting to note that the *Vedic brahmavādin*, obviously without

What has been said of the wild animal applies equally well to the male domestic animal which is fully potent and which is offered to the Goddesses (the divine spouses of the Gods). The 'general rule' seems to require that the victim be always a young male animal (usually two years old), not yet capable of reproduction and "which has never worked" (a phrase which also applies to other animals related with the sacred). If this could not be the case it has to be motivated and/or adequately dealt with.[27] Hence even here the Brāhmaṇic priest must stir midway between the demands of the rite to please the female Deities with a fully potent male animal and the 'general rule' which forbids its immolation. Hence here again the circumambulation of the fire with its symbolical 'swallowing' of the victim, serves to 'immolate' the victim dedicated to Tvaṣṭṛ while leaving it alive.

The triple movement of the fire around the victim serves a function which is consonant with the general character of sacred heat : it consecrates and prepares the victim in all respects even to the extent of taking the place of an actual immolation[28].

---

knowing anything about the modern theories of sacrifice and without being able to compare and contrast his rites with others more or less similar to or dissimilar from his, must have felt that he had to relate the offering of tame animals to the advantages of 'civil' life, and the improper offering of wild animals to its disadvantages, to the trespassing by the wild elements of nature on domestic life. Thus the improper offering of wild animals could only cause insecurity. Cf. SatBr XIII. 2. 4. 2 :

*sa yad grāmyaiḥ saṃsthāpayet | samadhvānaḥ krāmeyuḥ samantikaṃ grāmayor grāmāntau syātāṃ na 'ṛkṣīkāḥ puruṣavyāghrāḥ parimoṣiṇa āvyādhiny astaskarā araṇveṣvājāyeranyadāraṇyair vyadhvānaḥ krāmeyur vidūraṃ grāmayor grāmāntau syātāmṛkṣīkāḥ puruṣavyāghrāḥ parimoṣiṇa āvyādhin | yastaskarā araṇyeṣvājāyeran.*

27. The sacrifice of ox in ancient Greece is an exception which must have had a mythological reason. See, for example, A. M. DI NOLA, *Antropologia religiose*, Firenze, (Vallecchi), 1974, pp. 202 ff. Even the phrase used by the Rabbi of Nazareth to specify the kind of colt which had to carry him to his messianic triumph in Jerusalem ("on which no one has ever sat" cf. Mk XI. 2 and Lk XIX. 30) may be understood in this sense. Matthew and John do not report the phrase.

28. Cf. the last parts of SatBr III. 7. 2. 8 and of XIII. 2. 4. 1 quoted already in notes 19 and 18 respectively. It would be interesting to relate this interpretation of the initial rite of sacrifice with the still prevalent custom of carrying the fire three times around the funeral pyre before this is set on fire. The significance of this custom is by now lost to the greater number of people who perform this gesture or who have it performed for them. Is it meant to protect

It can, however, also count in an opposite sense, that is, to express the fact that immolation has taken place where there was no animal to kill. Such is the case where the circumambulation of fire is performed around the cereal cake, the vegetable offering which is offered together with the animal and in certain cases can take its place[29].

2. *The Torch* :

When the ceremony of the circumambulation of Agni is over, the firebrand is broken near the sacrificial stake and the same priest, the *agnīdhra* takes another one (probably from the same fire as before) and proceeds towards the place of immolation followed by the victim. Whilst he does so, he must think : "Agni will repel the malign spirits in front"[30], thus assigning to the fire its primary function which is protection against bad spirits loving the 'cold'. As he walks towards the place where the victim is to be 'pacified'[31], immediately followed by the

---

the corpse from the malign spirits at the extreme moment of its existence? Or does it still perhaps retain a reference, by now lost, to the consecration of the body as a (last) sacrificial victim?

29. Cf. SatBr I. 2. 2. 13 where it is affirmed that that the cake must be given the circumambulation of Agni as protection against the Rakṣas-s: *taṃ paryagniṃ karoti / acchidram evainam etad agninā parigṛhṇāti nedenaṃ nāṣṭrā rakṣāṃsi pramṛśān ity agnir hi rakṣasām apahantā tasmāt paryagniṃ karoti//* And a little further on it is added that the *puroḍāśa* is the substitute for the victim:..*paśur ha vā'eṣa ālabhyate yat puroḍāśaḥ //* This affirmation is followed by the list of the various victims which are replaced from time to time by less and less important animals even, finally, by cereal offerings. See, however, our own interpretation of this topic later on in the section dedicated to the *paśupuroḍāśa.*

30. Cf. SatBr III. 8. 1. 9 : ...*agnim evaitad purastāt karoty agniḥ purastān nāṣṭrā rakṣāṃsy apaghnan nety athā bhayenā nāṣṭreṇa paśuṃ nayanti...*

31. We too avoid using the word 'to kill' to indicate the immolation and the suppression of the victim so that we retain the spirit of the Scriptures which we are commenting since these explicitly forbid the usage of such a word. Cf. SatBr III. 8. 1. 10 : *tad anvevārabheta na vā'etaṃ mṛtyave nayanti yaṃ yajñāya nayanti tasmād...* On this point see also SatBr III. 7. 1. 15 where the terms used are *anvaganniti* which means "to go behind" and *saṃjña* which really means "to accept". With these terms, the intention is to bring out not only the peaceful nature of the passing over of the victim but above all willingness of the victim to go and meet its destiny: *tann āha jahi mārayeti mānuṣaṃ hi tat saṃjñapayān vagann iti taddhi devatrā sa yad āha anvagann ity etar hi hy eṣu devān anugacchati tasmād āhānvaganniti //* Indeed, this willingness is so important that consent and

victim, the victim is guided by another priest who touches it with the point of the two spits which will serve to roast its interiors. This latter priest is followed by the *Adhvaryu* who, in his turn, is followed by the sacrificer, all in direct contact with one another[32]. This procession, in which physical contact is very important, establishes a close union between the victim and its sacrificer through the mediation of the other priests. This union is a kind of identification, made 'in a mysterious way", between the one who offers and his offering, so that he may receive its benefits.

Thus, identifying himself with the animal through the mediation of his priests, the sacrificer hopes to transfer to himself the apotheosis to which the victim is destined. This apotheosis, however, cannot be obtained except at the price of death. It is for this reason that certain priests, who realized the danger implied in this identification with the victim on its way to meet its death, seek to avoid this risky contact, prefering to forego the important resultant benefits rather than face the moment of trial[33]. Others, however according to the Śatapatha Brāhmaṇa, want to maintain the identification and react against this fear, but can do no better than repeat with the Ṛgveda that the victim will not die and hence that *yajamāna* need not fear[34].

---

approval are also asked from its parents, brothers and even its companions in the fold. Cf. AitBr VI. 6 (II. 1. 6: *anvenaṃ mātā manyatāmanu pitānu bhrātā sagarbhyo 'nu sakhā sayūthya iti janitrair evainaṃ tat samanumatam ālabhante* || See also ManSS VII.3. 3. We cannot, however, delay on this point which is extremely important to understand the psychology of sacrifice.

32. Cf. SatBr III. 8. 1. 9 : ..*taṃ vapāśrapaṇībhyāṃ pratiprasthā tānvārabhate pratiprasthātāram adhvaryur adhvaryuṃ yajamānaḥ* || See also BharSS VII. 12. 3 ff.; ManSS I. 8. 3. 22 ff., etc.

33. Cf. SatBr III. 8. 1. 10 : *tad āhuḥ | naiṣa yajamānenānvārabhyo mṛtyave hy etaṃ nayanti tasmān nānvārabheteti*... See also BharSS VII. 12. 12 where the Adhvaryu with a formula separates the Breath of the sacrificer from that of the victim lest they should be too united in the same destiny. Also ManSS I.8. 3. 31.

34. Cf. SatBr III. 8. 1. 10 (continuation of the text quoted in the preceding note) : *tad anvevārabheta na vā 'etaṃ mṛtyave nayanti yaṃ yajñāya nayanti tasmād anvevārabheta*...And the phrase which the theologian adds to justify the desire of the yajamāna to withdraw from that contact which leads to death, is characteristic of the general brāhmaṇic conception of the sacrifice. The text continues:..*yajñādu haivātmānam antariyād yan nānvārabheta tasmād anvevāra-*

But the *Brahmavādin* of the Ṛgveda sees the importance of the obligatory passage through death and he in no way minimizes it but rather faces it as, for that matter, the victim itself has to do in spite of the many assurances given to it that it will not die. Thus, the Aitareya Brāhmaṇa which limited the function of the circumambulating firebrand to a mere chasing away of demons, contrary to the Śatapatha Brāhmaṇa, assigns to Agni which precedes the procession the important task of opening the way to Heaven and explains this task with a myth. When the goat was proceeding at the head of the procession to meet the Gods, who were anxiously waiting for it, all of a sudden it saw Death in front of it and was afraid. It therefore stopped and refused to proceed. The Gods, seeing their expectations being deluded by the legitimate hesitation of the victim about to be sacrificed, began to entice it to come forward promising it Heaven if it had the courage to proceed beyond Death. The goat let itself be convinced but to overcome its persistent fear, asked that one of the Gods precede it on its way to the great trial. This God was none other than Agni who, under the form of a firebrand, went to the head of the procession and guided both the victim and its sacrificer towards heaven.[35]

Here again, heat appears as the power which reveals its character as a protector against demons, as guide and propellant force through the passage towards transformation. The animal enters into a direct relationship with Agni, a relationship which is extended to the sacrificer by virtue of his touching it. This identification, merely alluded to in the Brāhmaṇa of the Śukla Yajurveda, is clearly stated in the Aitareya : "the sacrificer is truly, essentially this victim"[36]. It is also stated there that the torch is the divine guide of both, the victim and its sacrificer,

---

*bheta*...See also BharSS VII. 12. 6 where during the circumambulation of Agni is recited the verse found in TaittSam III. 1. 4. 1. 2 wishing the victim to go alive to the Gods.

35. Cf. AitBr VI. 6 (II. 1. 6): *prāsmā agniṃ bharateti / paśur vai nīyamānaḥ sa mṛtyuṃ prāpaśyat / sa devānnānnvakāmayataitum / taṃ devā abruvannehi svargaṃ vai tvā lokaṃ gamayiṣyama iti / sa tathety abravīt tasya vai me yuṣmākamekaḥ purastād aitviti / tatheti tasyāgniḥ purastād ait / so'gnim anu prācyavata / tasmād āhur āgneyo vāva sarvaḥ paśur agniṃ hi so 'nu prācyavateti / tasmād vasyāgniṃ purastād dharanti //*

36. AitBr. VII. 1 (II. 2. 11) : *yajamāno vā eṣa nidānena yat paśuḥ.*

and the guarantee of their salvation through the passage through Death which needs to be traversed in order to obtain immortality in the supreme world : "With this light the sacrificer goes to the celestial world having light in front of him"[37]—this is what the *tedophoros* (torch-bearer) should think whilst approaching the place of immolation.

3. *Blood* :

When the victim is finally 'pacified', the next important ritual concerns its blood. In all the religions of the world where sacrifice is practiced, the blood poured out in sacrifice is the most sacred element in it. 'The blood', in the words of a scholar at the beginning of the century, "is essentially the living part and either can be treated as efficacious (as in the Greek purification ritual by blood) or as too full of divinity through contact with the god for the use of the sacrificer"[38]. However in Vedic India blood is treated in a rather disconcerting way : it is the first portion of the victim to be extracted and is assigned to the *rakṣas-s* as their portion (as if it were not a 'portion' at all). In this way they are excluded from receiving the benefits of the true and real sacrifice[39], while the formula which accompanies this 'pre-offering' aims at driving them away[40].

37. AitBr VII. 1 (II. 2. 11) : ...*anena jyotiṣā yajamānaḥ purojyotiḥ svargaṃ lokam eṣyatīti | tena jyotiṣā yajamānaḥ purojyotiḥ svargaṃ lokameti ||*

38. Cf. A. B. KEITH, in the Introduction to his translation of TaittSam (vol. I, p. CVII). This comment is correct as far as the qualities attributed by the majority of religions to the blood are concerned, but it seems strange if it is meant to explain how the blood was treated in brāhmaṇical India—as we shall see later.

39. Cf. SatBr III. 8. 2. 14 ff. : *sa yatrācchyati| yata etat lohitam utpatati tad ubhayato'nakti rakṣasāṃ bhāgosīti rakṣasāṃ hy eṣa bhāgo yadasṛk || tadu pāsyābhi tiṣṭhati | idam ahaṃ rakṣo'bhitiṣṭhāmīdam ahaṃ rakṣo'vabādha'idam ahaṃ rakṣo 'dhamaṃ tamo nayāmīti tad yajñenaivaitannāṣṭrā rakṣaṃsyavabādhate*..See also AitBr VI. 7 (II. 2. 7) *asnā rakṣaḥ saṃsṛjatād ity āha | tuṣair vai phalīkaraṇair deva havir yajñebhyo rakṣaṃsi nirabhajann asnā mahāyajñāt | sa yad asnā rakṣaḥ saṃsṛjatādityāha rakṣāṃsy eva tat svena bhāgadheyena yajñān niravadayate ||* Also BaudhSS (ed. Dandekar, P. 819): BharSS VII. 14. 10; ManSS I. 8. 4. 1 ff.

40. Cf. the formula of the White Yajur, VajSam VI. 16 : *svadhite maiṇaṃ, hiṃsīḥ | rakṣasāṃ bhāgo 'si nirastaṃ rakṣa*....and that of the Black Yajur, TaittSam I. 3. 9. 2 : *rakṣasāṃ bhāgo'sīdam ahaṃ rakṣo'dhamaṃ tamo nayāmi*...

In Vedic India, the blood, far from representing the vivifying part of the sacrificial offering and being offered to the Gods as something which belongs to them by right, is thrown at the demons as a weapon of death and destruction. Only the blood of the horse, the major victim of *aśvamedha*[41], has a different way to be offered. It is claimed as oblation by the Gods who choose it as their portion in order to defeat the demons. And because it remains as portion to the Devas, the horse's blood as oblation is offered not only on a different shrub but also on a different part of the altar : the blood of the horse on its Northern part, and the blood of the accompanying victims on the Southern[42]. Even then, the blood is not the sacrificial element pre-eminently pleasing to the Gods as our author states[43], because the oblation in a sense retains its 'demonic' character since in all its three successive phases it is practically offered to Rudra[44], the Vedic God who is the one who has all along remained on the border-line between the 'demonic' and the 'divine'. The reasons for this strange behaviour accorded to blood as oblation can for the time being be left aside since they would lead us too far beyond the scope of our study. Suffice it to say that we cannot see any other plausible way to account for it than the fact that blood cannot be cooked, and so cannot be adequately transformed. One can easily understand how the *rakṣas-s* who are so much at home with the raw and the cold would desire it.[45]

4. *Omentum* (*vapā*) :

The next ritual in which heat and cooking are important is

41. Cf. SatBr XIII. 3. 4. 2 : *te* (*devān*) *'bruyan / agnayaḥ sviṣṭakṛto 'śvasya vayamuddhāram uddharāmahai tenāsurān abhibhaviṣyām iti.*

42. Cf. SatBr XIII. 5. 3. 8 : *nānyeṣāṃ paśūnāṃ tadanyā avadyanti/ avadyanty aśvasya dakṣiṇato 'nyeṣāṃ paśūnām avadyanty uttarato 'śvasya plakṣa śākhāsvanyeṣāṃ paśūnām avadyanti vetasaśākhāsvaśvasya //* Cf also Panc Br xxi.4.13.

43. See the continuation of the text quoted in note 38.

44. Cf. SatBr XIII. 3. 4. 3-5 where *agni viśvakṛta* is clearly and three times identified with Rudra.

45. All of this part is concerned with the brāhmaṇic ritual procedure when there is a lack of heat. This topic is treated in our already quoted article, "The Role of Heat..." and will hopefully be taken up again in a separate study. This is the reason why we are not dealing with it here.

that of the offering of the *omentum*, the membrane which envelops the intestine. The history of this offering goes back to the remotest antiquity tracing its origin most probably from the pre-historic use of people, living on fruit-gathering and hunting, of setting aside (as an offering ?) the long bones of the animal caught in the hunt covered with fat and the interstine membrane for the regeneration and preservation of the same[46]. This usage continued, and later found expression in the sacrifice where the *omentum* was an offering specifically reserved for the Gods. However as religions became more and more organized and the Divine assumed absolute rights over the faithful, the division of the parts of the victim began to seem incongruous. Having lost its original significance as a means of regeneration, the *omentum* began to be regarded simply as the part of the animal which is discarded as uneatable. Hence a contradiction arose between the 'traditional' (i.e. pre-cultural) demands and the new human consciousness demanding that the best part of everything be offered to the Gods. To offer the *omentum* seemed at times a deceit or to be selfish. Thus some religions have felt the need to justify in their myths the importance of this offering.

An example of this can be found in the Promethean myth which makes Zeus himself, through the cunning of Titanus, responsible for choosing that part of the victim[47]. Also in ancient India, the extraction of the *omentum* and the rites which are performed on it, and indeed the disputes about it, all testify to its traditional importance[48]. On the other hand, the new consciousness finds expression in the fact that, as we shall presently see, greater significance is given to the *havis* which is rightly considered the best part of the victim to eat.

46. See, for example, W. BURKERT, *op. cit.*

47. See, for example, *Theog.*, pp. 535 ff. and our remark in Chap. II, p. 47 notes, 83-84.

48. For the disputes on the normal rite of *paśubandha* included in the group of the Soma sacrifices, see, e.g. SatBr III. 8. 2. 18 ff., AitBr VI. 6 (II. 1. 6), VII. 2-4 (II. 2. 11-14) and KausBr X. 5. For the disputes on the *vapā* of the animal sacrifice of Vājapeya, see SatBr V. 1. 3-4 (in its entirety but especially V. 1. 3. 4-6 and V. 1. 4. 12). The *vapā* is also disputed in connection with the offering of other collateral sacrificial victims of *aśvamedha* —see SatBr XIII. 5. 3. 1-7.

In any case, the privileged status which the *omentum* enjoyed from remotest antiquity permits the attentive Brāhmaṇic ritualist to make use of it for his own liturgical ends in spite of the fact that its status is now superseded by that of the *havis*. We have already seen[49] that from very ancient times the sacrifice had to be a complete action without break or omission. However there are many libations to perform, the *medha* or the *rasa* can try always to escape, parts of the offering may fall to the ground...; there are, in short, an infinite number of contingencies which could prevent the victim reaching its goal intact. Thus for the priest who is faced with the performance of such rites which are so demanding, so complex and elusive, it is always better to try to complete sacrifice on every occasion even before the final conclusion. The offering of the *omentum* is one such rite. The *omentum*, in fact, was considered to be the best offering. Inspired by the idea that from time immemorial the *omentum* stood for the complete offering, the priest tried to take advantage of this idea and attempted to identify in a conscious way the part with the whole[50], in such a manner that by performing this libation before any other offering of the animal, he may be sure to have already offered "a sacrifice with the complete victim, in its entirety, even though the libations are many"[51]. Thus there are no longer irreparable risks. If, in the course of the sacred act, anything came to be missing—as could often happen—the priest, in the name of the sacrificer, is already assured that the sacrifice is somehow complete precisely since the *omentum*, that portion which both because of its traditional status and because of its having been the first to be extracted, can be rightly considered the part most adapted to assume the role of the whole. In this way, the *omentum*, retains its privileged position.

Nearly all the Brāhmaṇic texts which mention the animal sacrifice dwell upon the subject of the extraction of the

49. See Chap. II, pp. 33 ff.

50. Cf. AitBr VII. 3 (the end) (II. 2. 13) : *te viduriyān vāva kila paśur yāvatī vapeti / sa etāvān eva paśur yāvatī vapā //*

51. AitBr VII. 3 (II. 2. 13), continuation of the text quoted in the preceding note: *bhūyasībhir hāsyāhutibhir iṣṭaṃ bhavati kevalena hāsya paśuneṣṭaṃ bhavati ya evaṃ veda //*

*omentum*,[52] and also the Sūtras speak about it at some length.[53] Often there are disputes as to which Deity the *omentum* is due, or as to order of precedence in which the *omentum* of the secondary victims, in the larger and more complex sacrifices, has to be offered. For example, Indra claimed for himself the *omentum* of the special victim dedicated to the Maruts[54]—perhaps to assert by this his lordship over them. Therefore, some priests thought that because of the importance assumed by this offering it must be the first to be consigned to the fire without waiting its turn[55]. Others, however, do not accept this claim prefering that everything be done in accordance with the rules and that each *omentum* be offered following the normal order of the preparation and offering of the many victims[56]. These speculations and others of the same kind[57] have their importance for us not

52. A detailed description of how the *vapā* is to be treated in the animal sacrifice of Agniṣṭoma is given in SatBr III. 3. 2. 18 ff., AitBr VI. 6 (II. 1. 6), VII. 2 (II. 2. 11-14) and KausBr X. 5. These texts will be quoted almost in their entirety later on when we shall come to deal with the subject. A description of how it is to be treated in the other animal sacrifices of Vājapeya and Aśvamedha is given in SatBr V. 1. 3-4 (esp. V. 1. 3. 4-6 and V. 1. 4. 12) and SatBr XIII. 5. 3. 1.5 respectively.

53. Cf. e.g. BharSS VII. 15. 1 ff.; VII. 16. 1 ff.; BaudhSS (pp. 819 ff.); ManSS I.8. 4. 11 ff.; etc.

54. i.e. the spotted sterile cow in SatBr V. 1. 3. 4 in the Vājapeya :*tasyā āvṛt || yatra hotā māhendraṃ graham anuśaṃsati tad asyai vapayā pracareyur eṣa vā'-indrasya niṣkevalyo graho yan māhendro*.. ("the course of procedure thereof is:when the Hotṛ recites after the Mahendra libation, then let them proceed with (the offering) of her omentum, for that Mahendra is Indra's special libation..")

55. Cf. SatBr V. 1. 3. 4 (end) : *indro vai yajamānas tan madyata evaitad yajamāne vīryaṃ dadhāti tasmād asyā'atra vapayā pracareyuḥ* || ("..now the sacrificer is Indra thus he thereby puts strength into the sacrificer in the middle (of the sacrifice); that is why they should proceed with her omentum at that particular time.") (tr. EGGELING).

56. Cf. SatBr V. 1. 3. 6 : *tadu tathā na kuryāt | hvalati vā 'eṣa yo yajñapathādetyeti vā 'eṣa yajñapathādya evaṃ karoti tasmād yatraivetareṣāṃ paśūnāṃ vapābhiḥ pracaranti tad evaitasyai vapayā pracareyur*....

57. Cf. SatBr V. 1. 3. 12-14 for a discussion about the *omentum* of the victims dedicated to Prajāpati in the Vājapeya. Some want it to be offered immediately after the recitation of the Vāmadevya while others want the order of the offerings according to the victims to be respected: *teṣām āvṛt | yatra maitrāvaruṇo vāmadevyam anuśaṃsati tad eṣāṃ vapābhiḥ pracareyuḥ prajānaṃ vai vāmadevyaṃ praja, nanaṃ prajāpatiḥ prājāpatyā ete tasmād eṣāṃ atra vapābhir pracareyuḥ* ||12||.... || *tadu tathā na kuryāt | hvalati vā eṣa yo yajñapathādetyeti vā 'eṣa yajñapathādya evaṃ*

directly for their subject-matter but because they indicate that the *omentum* is a part of the animal worthy of note, whose offering cannot be made arbitrarily. Yet, among them we may take note of one dispute which seems to be rather significative. In this dispute, those who, as we have seen, are for making a special offering of the fat of the spotted sterile cow before its turn, are also for cooking the offering in two distinct parts. Why, then, this distinction in cooking, which as such is an *unicum* in Vedic ritual ? The reason can only be that, since one of these two parts is destined to the Gods, and the other is evidently destined to be consumed by the sacrificer and his priests[58], the two cannot be prepared in the same cooking because of the sacrality of the offering. This can be inferred from the fact that those priests who are against the two cookings, do not approve as well of the idea of eating a part as sacred as the *omentum*[59]. In their opinion to do so would mean to want to push a little too far the divinization of man—even if this is the more or less consciously declared goal of any sacrifice in India. Thus because the orthodox do not accept communion with the 'left-over'—the *ucchiṣṭa*—of the *omentum*, then for them a division in the cooking becomes evidently superfluous, and this confirms our supposition.

This fact is of interest for us because it brings out even more clearly the sacred energy which is attributed to this important ritual act. We know[60] that the sacrificer has no right to any specific portion of the sacrificial victim; all that is due to him is the *ucchiṣṭa*, namely what remains of the offering already made. This *ucchiṣṭa* can be taken from any or almost any part worthy to be offered as a libation. Strictly speaking, there

*karoti tasmād yatraivetareṣāṃ paśūnāṃ vapābhiḥ pracaranti tad evaiteṣāṃ vapābhiḥ pracareyur yatraivetareṣāṃ paśūnāṃ havirbhiḥ pracaranti..* //14/ See also SatBar XIII. 5. 3. 1-6 for a discussion about the opportune moment to offer the *omentum* of the secondary victims of *aśvamedha*. There a list is given of the ritualists together with their opinions. The last to be mentioned is Yājñavalkya.

58. Cf. SatBr V. 1. 3. 5 : *dvedhāvadānāni śrapayanti / tato 'rdhānāṃ juhvām upastīrya dvir dvir avadyati sakṛd abhighārayati..atha yad etaiḥ pracarati tena daivīṃ viśam ujjayaty athārdhāni d mānuṣyai viśa 'upaharati teno mānuṣīṃ viśam ujjayati* //

59. Cf SatBr V. 1. 3. 6:.. *ekadhāvadānāni śrapayanti na mānuṣyai viśa 'upaharanti* //

60. see what we have said earlier in Chap. I, p. 17.

would normally be no place for a 'separate cooking' since there is no 'separate portion'—as the more traditionalists in fact affirm. Therefore, if such a need is felt for the *omentum* that means that the innovators, in spite of their audacity, did not dare to take the *ucchiṣṭa* of the *omentum*, but *thought* it better to separate during the cooking the part destined for human consumption from that to be offered to the Divine.

Is it therefore the cooking which renders the *omentum* so sacred? Or it is the case that, since the *omentum* was already considered to be sacred in itself from pre-historic times, the *brahmavādins* are led to consider that, once the *omentum* is cooked, man is not allowed to partake of it? Or, on the contrary, that it is precisely in a separate cooking that man looks for strength when he approaches what is normally not due to him? In any case, the fact remains that, at the moment when man may dare usurp the portion which is mostly reserved for the Divinity, he does not dare do so with portion which is cooked together with the portion offered to the Divinity.

We come now to the description of the rites performed in connection with the cooking of the *omentum*[61]. As soon as the animal fat membrane is extracted, it is wrapped around two special spits (*vāpaśrapaṇis*) made of a particular kind of wood[62]. While this is done, the formulae which are recited identify these two spits with the primordial cosmic couple and so addressing the fat they say : "May you envelop Heaven and Earth with ghee".[63] In these spits is found the sap of the sacrifice which escaped in primordial times when the Gods "stretched out" the first victim,[64] and so there is the need to

61. In this respect we shall follow above all the description of the animal sacrifice with the Pressing of Soma. Cf SatBr III. 8. 2. 1 ff. The other rites of other sacrificial complexes are not so substantially different.

62. That is, the wood called *kārṣmarya* of which we give more details in note 65 below.

63. SatBr III. 8. 2. 16. The formula is taken from TaittSam I. 3. 9. 2 : *ghṛtena dyāvāpṛthivī prorṇuvāthām iti*. :.See also BharSS VII. 14. 13.

64. Cf. SatBr III. 8. 2. 17 : *kārṣmaryamayyau vapāśrapaṇyau bhavataḥ| yatra vai devā agre paśum ālebhire tad udīcaḥ kṛṣyamāṇasyāvāṅ medhaḥ papāta sa eṣa vanaspatir ajāyata tad yat kṛṣyamāṇasyāvāṅ patat tasmāt kārṣmaryas tenaivainam etan medhena samardhayati kṛtsnaṃ karoti tasmāt kārṣmaryamayyau vapāśrapaṇyau bhavataḥ ||*

restore it. There is always the fear of losing the essential part of the victim its *rasa*, sap, or essence (*medha*), which invariably tends to escape from both the Gods and men who imitate them[65]. The door for such an escape is generally the cut which is made on that part of the victim which has to be offered. And each time the sap is believed to be gathered up again and inserted, once more, in the sacrifice through the use of the last ingredient to be used in the sacrifice, where it is believed to have taken refuge. In this particular case, the sap which escaped from the sacrificial victim, to the detriment of the entire cosmos, is restored to heaven and earth through the use of the wood of the spits where the sap is said to have taken refuge[66]. Even though this idea of an escaping 'essence' to be gathered up again and re-integrated in the sacrifice may seem strange, the vision which is unfolded here of the sacrifice has a deep and wide significance. Here we are confronted by an act which involves a whole cosmic dynamism in an exchange of energies, which, though auto-sufficient, has nothing of 'magic' about it in the strict and pejorative sense of the word[67].

To return to the *omentum*. As soon as the priest has finished enveloping the spits with it and is about to approach the fire to cook it, he is faced with a new problem—a problem which, judging from the texts of the two groups of the Saṃhitās described earlier,[68] does not seem to have been noticed at the time. We have seen that the blood which flows out first is offered to the Rakṣas-s because it is *raw* and the spirits of evil

65. See preceding note. See also SatBr I. 2. 3. 6 where in the sequence of animals which from time to time are substituted one for the other it is the *medha* which escapes and takes refuge in the successive animal. The same thing is said also in AitBr VI. 8 (II. 1. 8). see also SatBr III. 8. 3. 12. This idea is very common and it is usually the reason given to justify the use of an utensil or a sacred object, namely, that in it has sought refuge, either immediately or mediately through other animals, the *medha* of the sacrificial victim. The sacred object is the last one in which has taken refuge the *medha*. See below note 130.

66. Cf. SatBr III. 8. 2. 16 (continuation of the text quoted in note 64): ...*tad ime dyāvāpṛthivī' ūrjā rasena bhājayaty anayor ūrjaṃ rasaṃ dadhāti te rasavatyā 'upajīvanīye 'imāḥ prajā upajīvanti* || (In the *kāṇva* version '*rasa*' is replaced by '*medha*'.)

67. See what we have got to say on 'magic' in Chap. IV, note 1.

68. See Chaps. II and III.

are attracted to what is theirs : the raw and the cold[69]. Now it is clear that the *omentum*, when it is extracted, is still raw and hence cannot be put in contact with the sacrificial fire[70]. The problem is solved, however, by making use of the firebrand which served to accompany the victim to the place of its 'pacification'[71] and which has remained lit for the occasion[72]. According to others, one must, instead, light near the immolator a new fire altogether—which is, therefore, considered in a sense 'profane'[73]. The use of this fire, called *paśuśrapaṇa*, is to render the *omentum* "cooked already there"[74] thus solving for the priest two otherwise insoluble difficulties : that of approaching the altar with its sacred offerings and sacred fires "with an element which is still raw" and that of placing on the sacred fire itself something which is still 'raw', or profane, which thus would contaminate it. In fact, according to the Kāṇva version, the priest while putting the fat on the fire of the immolator must think : "(I do this) lest I should cook it on the *āhavanīya* uncooked"[75]. This 'abhorrence of the raw' inevitably develops in a ritual context where everything is centralized on the energizing effects

69. See above Chap. IV, fn 41.

70. As we have previously noted, we are leaving the negative effects of the lack of the required heat or of its excess for a separate study. In the meantime we refer to some relevant texts in our article "The role of ritual heat in the Vedic Sacrifice", *art. cit.*

71. See above fn. 31.

72. Cf BharSS VII. 12.13 where it is stated that the Agnīdhra, after having performed the circumambulation of the victim with the firebrand and accompanied it to its place of departure, must break the firebrand while facing north. In the following verse (v. 14) it is also stated that the lit coal, left on the north side of the place of immolation, becomes the fire of the immolator. See the same idea expressed in ManSS I.8. 3.28.

73. Cf. BharSS VII. 12. 15 where other possibilities are given of how to establish the fire of the immolator. Besides using the burning cinders of the firebrand with which one had performed the circumambulation of the victim, one can, optionally, either take it again from the *gārhapatya*, or produce it by friction with two pieces of wood.

74. SatBr III. 8. 2. 18 : *tatho hāsyātrāpi śṛtā bhavati*. . .The passage is inserted as follows: *tāṃ parivāsayati*/ *tāṃ paśuśrapaṇe pratapati tatho hāsyātrāpi*. . ."fumigates it (perfuming it); warms it on (the fire) *paśuśrapaṇa* (which cooks the raw animal) and thus it becomes cooked just there."

75. This version is found in the translation of J. EGGELING, S.B.E., vol. XXVI, part II, p. 195, note 1.

of cooking and of heating in general. The problem of dealing with the raw emerges as soon as one affirms the necessity of cooking. Thus the Śrauta Sūtras for this first heating recommended the formula : "the Rakṣas-s are burnt, the malign spirits are burnt"[76]. It is in the first heating that the evil forces attached to the raw and the cold are *attached* and dispersed.

After this first cooking, which actually amounts only to an intitial warming of the victim, the priests approach the *āhavanīya*[77] where the *adhvaryu* heats the *omentum* facing North after having gone around the fire from the South to propitiate it[78]. Here another precaution is taken: as the priests approach with the *omentum* to go and cook it on the *āhavanīya*, they take care not to pass across the middle of the sacrificial platform lest they risk bringing what is not yet perfectly cooked in contact with the rest of the altar and with the other food ready to be offered[79]. Here, the *brahmavādin* is carried by two considerations: the fear of contaminating the sacrifice with the not-yet cooked and the fear of stepping out of the sacrificial ground[80]. Anything which takes place during the sacrifice must, by definition, take place within the confines of the sacrificial grourd which

76. Cf. BharSS VII. 15. 1 : *śāmitre vapāṃ pratitapati / pratyuṣṭaṃ rakṣaḥ pratyuṣṭā arātayaḥ iti //* Cf. also ManSS I. 8. 4. 20. The formula, however, is found only in the Śrauta Sūtras and only they add the imprecation against the Rakṣas-s and the enemy during the first boiling of the *omentum*. It is not found in the Brāhmaṇas, nor are the formulas to be found in the ritual sequence given by the yajurvedic mantras. (See VajSam VI. 16 and TaittSam I. 3. 9.2 where the missing formula should have been found between 'k' and 'l'.)

77. Cf. SatBr III. 8. 2. 18 :...*punar ulmukam agnīdādatte te jaghanena cātvālaṃ yanti ta'āyanty āgacchanty āhavanīyam...*

78. Cf SatBr III. 8. 2. 19 : *athottaratastiṣṭhan vapāṃ pratapati / atyeṣyan vā'eṣo 'gniṃ bhavati dakṣiṇataḥ parītya śrapayiṣyaṃstasmā 'evaitan nihnute tatho hainam eṣo'tiyantam agnir na hinasti tasmād uttaratastiṣṭhan vapāṃ pratapati //*

Cf. ManSS I. 2. 4. 23 where it is the Pratiprasthātṛ who cooks the *omentum*, sitting down on the south side of the Āhavanīya. See also BharSS VII. 15. 3 ff.

79. Cf. SatBr III. 8. 2. 20 *tām antareṇa yūpaṃ cāgniṃ ca haranti / tad yat samayā na haranti yenānyāni havīṃṣi haranti nedaśṛtayā samayā yajñāṃ prasajāma iti yadu bāhyena na haranty agreṇa yūpaṃ bahirdhā ha yajñāt kuryus tasmād antareṇa yūpaṃ cāgniṃ ca haranti dakṣiṇataḥ parītya pratiprasthātā śrapayati //* Cf. also BharSS VII. 15. 6; ManSS I. 8. 4. 22; etc.

80. Cf. the preceding note. The altar is the universe and one cannot step out of it !

represents, indeed *is* the entire universe[81]. Nothing can therefore be consciously taken out of it; anything which for some reason or other quits it is lost for ever and falls into the 'profane', that is the 'non-sacred', which is 'non-world,' a 'nothing'. However, what interests us here is the possible contamination by contact with the 'uncooked'. The clause which states that one cannot pass with any object across the middle of the altar seems to refer almost exclusively, or at least principally, to raw food because, since there are cases of cooked food being subjected to the same prohibition (for example, the heart of the victim as we shall see later), the Brāhmaṇa wonders why and feels the needs to give an explanation[82].

When the preliminary cooking and the cooking on the two fires is over, the actual offering begins[83]. The offering too has its own preliminaries. First Vāyu is called upon to participate in the offering by placing the tip of a blade of grass under the *omentum*[84], and then Agni. To Agni, the carrier of the offerings to the other Deities is allotted a more sophisticated offering: a spoonful of melted butter is poured onto the *omentum* as soon as this is cooked so that the drops fall into the fire as the offering are made more potent by their initial contact with it. The invocatory verses pronounced during the libation are addressed to Agni that he may perform his task as carrier of the offerings

81. Cf. fn. 80 and also SatBr III. 7. 2. 1 where the altar is likened to the earth whose breadth it has: *yāvatī vai vedis tāvatī*. See also, e.g. SatBr IX. 2. 1. 20 where it is *agnicayana* which is likened to these worlds: *ime vai lokā eṣo 'gnir...* For *agnicayana* we refer to Chapter VII.

82. Cf. SatBr III. 8. 3. 10 : *tad yat samayā na haranti yenānyāni havīṃṣi haranti śṛtaṃ santaṃ nedaṅgaśo*...As one can see, an explanation is sought for the anomaly of the fact that the heart "although cooked" cannot be carried through the middle of the altar. We shall see the reason why later.

83. We recall that we are talking of whole sacrificial complexes where the secondary offerings are many, as for example, Somayajña with its eleven secondary offerings, the sacrifice offered to Prajāpati with seventeen, *Aśvamedha* with even more, etc.

84. Cf. SatBr III. 8. 2. 18 : *sa etat tṛaṇam adhvaryur āhavanīye prāsyati vāyo veḥ stokānāṃ iti stokānāṃ haiṣa samit* // The same is said in BharSS VII. 15. 7. while BaudhSS XXIV. 36 (S.K, ed. DANDEKAR, 2, p. 819) points out that the oblation to Vāyu is laid on the grass so that the *omentum* is heated on the grass itself: *etyā 'havanīyasyā 'ntam eṣvaṅgāreṣu vapāyai pratitapyamānāyai barhiṣo' gram upāsyati*..

and make plants fertile[85]. The Brāhmaṇa which always seeks a more profound explanation than that given by the Sūtras and looks for reasons to justify each parts of the rite, is careful to explain that these drops of liquid fat poured on and strengthened by the other offering of fat (the *omentum*) which is still boiling or almost cooked are meant to add, as it were, heat to heat 'a cooking to a cooking' (thus acquiring double energy)[86]. Thus, doubly energized, the offering has the power to bring down rain[87]. The Brāhmaṇa seems to suggests that because this is not the usual fruit of the sacrifice it needs a greater quantity of energy to realize it.

At this point the *omentum* is finally cooked and the priest in charge, the *pratiprasthātṛ*, must announce the fact[88]. This announcement, and the confirmation that the offering is ready once it has been completely cooked, is rarely omitted—which fact indicates that the offering's transformation by the sacred fire is a necessity and cannot be allowed to happen secretly but must be openly proclaimed. Only after this announcement is made is the offering finally gathered by a special spoon and prepared to be libated. This preparation includes a fresh sprinking of the *omentum* with melted butter—an act which gives rise to endless ritual discussion[89] which leads to the placing of two pieçes of gold above and under the whole portion of *vapā*[90]. Gold, an eminent symbol of vitality is here used to symboli-

85. Cf. BharSS VII. 15. 8; See also BaudhSS XXIV. 36 (p. 819), etc.

86. Cf. SatBr III. 8. 2. 21 : ...*tatho hāsyaite stokāḥ śṛtāḥ svāhākṛtā āhutayod bhūtvāgniṃ prāpnuvanti* //

87. Cf. SatBr III. 8. 2. 22 :...*tad yad āgneyī stokebhyo'nvāhetaḥ pradānā vai vṛṣṭirito hyagnir vṛṣṭiṃ vanute sa etaiḥ stokair etāntstokān vanute ta 'ete stokā varṣanti tasmād*....

88. Cf. SatBr III. 8. 2. 23 : *athāha pratiprasthātā śṛta pracareti* /

89. That between Yājñavalkya and Caraka Adhvaryu regarding which should come first, the basting of the *varā* or of the ghee. Here too the central issue of the dispute regards the possibility of anointing something which "is not cooked". On this subject see also SatBr III. 8. 2. 24-25 which, for reasons already given, we have to leave out of our present discussion reserving it for a separate study.

90. Cf. SatBr III. 8. 2. 26 : *athājyam upastṛṇīte / atha hiraṇyaśakalam avadadhāty atha vapām avadyannāha...atha hiraṇyaśakalam avadadhāty athopariṣṭād dvirājyasyābhighārayati* // See also BharSS VII. 16. 3. ManSS I. 8. 4. 32, etc.

cally restore the victim to life before its definitive oblation[91]: "The reason why there is a piece of gold on both sides", the Brāhmaṇa explains "is this, (namely that) when they offer the victim in the fire they slay it; and gold means immortal life. Hence it (the victim) rests in immortal life. And so it rises from hence, and so it lives; for this reason there is a piece of gold on both sides"[92]. Moreover, the offering needs to be composed of five parts in order to be complete,[93] and the gold added to it sees that this completeness be there. A Sūtra adds that if no gold is available the priest can replace it with ghee[94]. Gold, as a guarantor and restorer of immortal life, is often met with in the sacrifice. The sacrifice, in fact, is closely linked to death, and every offering (and not only in the obvious blood sacrifice) must in some way undergo its own immolation. However the victim, we have seen, must still be alive to be able to accom-

91. The addition of gold is common to many brāhmaṇic rites and serves to assure immortality. See, e.g. the text quoted in the following note, and also SatBr VII. 5.2.8 where the gold put in the heads of the victims offered in sacrifice for the construction of the altar (about which we shall speak in Chap. VII) serves to reinfuse in the victims the vital air (*prāṇa*) which had come out of them when they were immolated : *athaiṣu hiraṇyaśakalān pratyasyati / prāṇa vai hiraṇyam atha vā'etebhyaḥ paśubhyaḥ saṃjñapyamānebhya eva prāṇā utkrāmanti tad yaddhiraṇyaśakalān pratyasyati prāṇān evaiṣvetad dadhāti //* See also SatBr V. 3. 5. 15 where gold intertwined in a filter serves to purify and vivify the water used for the consecration of the king; or SatBr XII. 5. 2. 6 where gold serves for the immortalization of the dead *agnihotrin*, etc. Still, in spite of its properties, gold cannot replace the heads of the sacrificial victims for *agniciti* —as we shall see in Chap. VII, p. 181 and note 40.

92. SatBr III. 8. 2. 27 : *tad yad hiraṇyaśakalāvabhito bhavataḥ / ghnanti vā 'etat paśuṃ yad agnau juhvatyamṛtam āyur hiraṇyaṃ tad amṛta 'āyuṣī pratitiṣṭhati tathāta udeti tathā saṃjīvati tasmāddhiraṇyaśakalāvabhito bhavata [āśrāvyāhāgnīṣomābhyāṃ chāgasya vapāṃ medhaḥ preṣyeti na prasthitam ity āha prasute prasthitam iti vaṣatkṛte juhoti]*

93. Cf. BharSS VII. 16. 4-5 : *sā pañcāvattā bhavati / yady api caturvattī yajamānaḥ pañcāvattaiva vapā bhavati //* For the importance of the number five to render the offerings "complete", see later on in Chap. VI, note 30, and in Chap. VII, note 12.

94. Cf. BharSS VII. 16. 6 : *yadi hiraṇyam na syādājyāt pratyavadyet/* See also BaudhSS XXIV. 36 (SK, p. 820) where gold is recommended by Śālīki and fat by Baudhāyana himself. Also AitBr VII. 4 (I. 2. 14) where it is said that if no gold is available, two layers of ghee at the beginning of the offering can be used instead, for "'in fact ghee is immortal [ambrosia] and gold is immortal [ambrosia], therefore.." : *amṛtaṃ vā ājyam amṛtaṃ hiraṇyam tatra sa..*

plish fruitfully its divine and cosmic mission. While in the Saṃhitās the problem is solved by assuring the victim (for example, the horse) that it will not die[95], here the priest adapts the rite itself to the formula and without leaving anything to his imagination or to the whim of the Gods (who are now impotent before the power of the rite), ensures the revitalization of the victim himself by what he thinks to be the most appropriate means[96].

At this point the entire oblation, after another assurance that it is completely cooked, is poured with the verse *vaṣaṭ* into the fire while a prayer is offered to Agni that he do his duty as *hotṛ* of consigning to all the waiting Gods this first offering of the animal sacrifice[97]. The prayer is first addressed to Indra and Agni[98], or to Soma and Agni[99], and then to all the Gods together[100]. Immediately after the offering is thrown into the fire, the

95. Cf. RV I. 162. 21 already discussed in Chap. II, p. 37 and quoted, in part, in note 50.

96. The necessity of infusing life again in the killed animal is very acutely felt—as can be gathered from the many formulas and rites for the purpose which are found all throughout the text regarding the animal sacrifice. These rites, spread all over, accompany many different ritual actions. Cf. e.g., SatBr III. 8. 2. 4 ff. which describes the rite of purification of the killed animal, performed by the principal wife of the sacrificer in virtue of her procreative nature : *atha paśoḥ prāṇān adbhiḥ patny upaspṛśati / tad yad adbhiḥ prāṇān upaspṛśati jīvaṃ vai devānāṃ havir amṛtam amṛtānāṃ athaitat paśuṃ ghnanti yat saṃjñāpayanti yad viśāsaty āpo vai prāṇās tad asminn etān prāṇān dadhāti tathaitaj jīvam eva devānāṃ havir bhavati amṛtam amṛtānām //4// atha yat patny upaspṛśati / yoṣā vai patnī yoṣāyai vā imāḥ prajāḥ prajāyante tad enam etasyai yoṣāyai prajananti tasmāt patnī upaspṛśati//5//* See also SatBr III. 8. 2. 27 (quoted above in note 90) where gold is added to the *omentum*, and SatBr III. 8. 3. 8 where the heart of the dead animal is anointed so that life might be re-infused into it after it has suffered and been deprived of it : *sa hṛdayam eva agre 'bhighārayati / ātmā vai mano hṛdayaṃ prāṇaḥ pṛṣadājyam ātmany evaitan manasi prāṇaṃ dadhāti tathaitaj jīvam eva devānāṃ havir bhavaty amṛtam amṛtānām //*

97. Cf. SatBr III. 8. 2. 23 : ..*svāhākṛtibhyaḥ preṣyeti vaṣaṭkṛte juhoti.*

98. Cf. BharSS VII. 16. 1 : *indrāgnibhyāṃ chāgasya vapāyā medaso 'nubrūhi iti...* (repeated in v. 7); see also ManSS I. 8. 4. 33 ff.; etc.

99. Cf. SatBr III. 8. 2. 26 : ...*vapām avadyannāhāgnīṣomābhyāṃ chāgasya vapāyai medaso 'nubrūhīty atha....*

100. Cf. BharSS VII. 16. 9 : *tata uttaraṃ parivapyaṃ juhoti devebhyaḥ svāhā iti.* See also ManSS I. 8. 4. 35; etc.

spits too which had served to gather the *omentum* when it was extracted from the animal and to cook it, are thrown into the same fire with appropriate *mantras*[101]. This offering of the fat membrane is particularly pregnant with 'sacrality' and hence extremely powerful. Even those objects which come into the close contact with it have to be destroyed lest they should endanger the 'everyday world'. Their destruction too has to be, as it were, 'sacralized' and turned into a regular offering with *mantra, svāhā* and dedication (to the son of the Maruts, Ūrdhvanābhasa). After this last rite of 'reposition', the Sūtras conclude this part of the sacrifice with gifts to the *adhvaryu*[102] and go on to describe the other sacrificial rites which still need to be performed[103].

It would seem, therefore, that surrounding the least eatable part of the victim with a geater 'sacrality' than others did not cause the *sūtrakāras* any concern. Anyway the Sūtras are not concerned with problems of this kind. Such problems concern the Brāhmaṇas, and these do seem in a sense alarmed by the status enjoyed by the *omentum.* Its role and importance seem to the Brāhmaṇa exegetes strange and difficult to explain, in a world where the better part of the sacrificial victim tends to be

101. Cf. SatBr III. 8. 2. 28 : *hutvā vapāṃ samīcyau / vapāśrapaṇyau kṛtvānuprāsyati svāhā kṛte 'ūndhvanabhasaṃ mārūtaṃ gacchataṁ iti nedime 'amnyā sato yābhyāṃ vapāṁ aśiśrapāmeti //* See also BharSS VII. 16. 10; ManSS I. 8. 4. 38; etc. It is clear that, unlike the heart the *vapā* does not seem to be considered capable of suffering. In fact, the heart is the organ where the suffering of living beings is but concentrated, but this is not necessarily the case with the fat which envelops the kidneys. That the *vapā* is not considered to suffer when it is pierced with the spits and put into the fire is shown from the fact that these spits *are* laid 'to repose' in the fire when the ceremony is over. They are in fact sacred enough to be burnt after use but uncontaminated by suffering so that the sacred fire can receive them. The spits which have been used to pierce the heart and to save it from suffering—see below., note 142—cannot be similarly burnt even though the sacrality of the rite would have demanded it (cf. SatBr III. 8. 5. 9). The sacred fire refuses to participate in any manner in this suffering.

102. Cf. BharSS VII. 16. 14 : *hutāyāṃ vapāyāṃ varaṃ dadāti kanyāmalaṃkṛtāmanadvāhaṃ tisro vā vatsatarīḥ.* ("When the *vapā* has been offered, he must give a present: an adorned virgin or a draught-ox or three horses.")

103. Cf. BharSS VII.17.1 which goes on immediately to speak of the preliminaries of the next rite, the *paśupuroḍāśa* and its offering, without delaying too long on the rites regarding the *omentum* and without looking for explanations.

regarded as the more eatable. The schools of interpretation are, therefore, divided between the necessity of remaining loyal to the tradition which held the *omentum* in high esteem—now no longer understandable[104]—and the necessity of relegating it to a less important position because of its 'inedibility'.

The Aitareya Brāhmaṇa, though it is contemporaneous with or even later than the Brāhmaṇas of the Yajus, remains in a certain sense 'archaic' and traditional when it comes to comment upon the rites. Thus it respects the idea of the pre-eminence and grandeur of this offering and tries to explain it by having recourse to a divine example. When the Gods stretched out the sacrificial offering for the first time, their intention was to find the way which led to heaven and to be assured of immortality. The rites they used for this purpose were the normal ones of *yajña*, *śrama* and *tapas*; but no sooner had they extracted *omentum* than their desires were immediately appeased and they found the way to heaven. Hence soon after they had offered this part of the sacrificial victim, they abandoned everything and without bothering to finish what they had started, they departed to the world above. The aim of the sacrifice was achieved and consequently its continuation seemed superfluous. The obvious conclusion drawn by the priestly exegete who continues the work of the Gods for his own salvation and that of the whole cosmos, is that the *vapā* has the power by itself to be a complete sacrificial offering. The Brāhmaṇa continues that this is what was immediately understood by the *ṛṣis* who were watching the Gods to extort from them the secret of their success. Seeing the sacrificial victim left in its place but without its entrails and without the *omentum*, they understood at once that the

104. The present writer hopes one day to publish a separate study in which it will be shown how the sacrifice—and more generally, many cultic actions—consists of rites which surpass the coordinates of time and space in which they are, on a practical level, inserted. The different cultures, in fact, receive them from a time which preceded their respective history. These rites, therefore, are felt to be in a sense 'traditional', that is, belonging to a tradition with which these cultures have not as yet broken all links. Still these cultures interpret them in accordance with their own new cultural requirements and hence these rites are in a certain sense too an adaptation of 'alien' elements which pertain to a different way of life. See on this topic, e.g. G. MENSCHING, *op. cit.*

victim was in fact the *omentum* (*sa etāvān eva paśur yāvatī vapā*)[105]. The equivalence is quickly made: not only is the *omentum* ambrosia (*amṛta*) as much as is ghee and Soma, but even more so because of its strange behaviour at the fire; it becomes liquid. As 'Immortal' offering,[106] therefore it can, in its turn, be a guarantor of immortality both to the Gods and to the sacrificer. Here we see again how the tradition attaches importance to the way the different parts of the victim do react to the fire and to cooking which determines their relative worth. The blood which cannot be cooked (since it coagulates and stinks), is practically excluded from being an offering and is assigned to the Demons; the *omentum*, on the contrary, which can be cooked and changes its smell into pleasant fragrance[107], although it melts and disappears into the form of an incorporeal liquid, is accepted and exalted in accord with the general rule. In fact its behaviour at the fire is indeed strange. The *vapā* first turns red and then white. The Ṛgvedic exegete dwells on this peculiarity. The *omenum* can be likened to the fertilizing human seed, *retas*[108]: both are white and both are liquids and disappear. When it disappears, the *omentum* becomes 'incorporeal' just as the human seed is 'incorporeal[109]. The human seed gives life, it is responsible for life, and the *omentum* is also the seed of life and so an appropriate symbol for the elixir of immortality... and hence, as well as the entire sacrifice. It is at this point, that the Vedic exegete inserts the clause in which he identifies the *omentum* with the whole victim. Both the victim and its *omentum* are complete as sacrificial offerings and the Devas might as well offer the *omentum* alone, neglecting to do all the rest[110].

105. AitBr VII. 3 (II. 2. 13).

106. Cf AitBr VII. 4 (II. 2. 14): *sā vā eṣāmṛtāhutir eva yad vapāhutir amṛtāhutiragnyāhutirajyāhutiramṛtāhutiḥ somāhutiḥ* /

107. We have seen earlier (pp. 33 ff.) that one of the reasons which led the first ṛṣis to consider cooking as a potent means of transformation was perhaps the ability of fire to change the smell of food. In any case, the fact is that this ability of fire is very much insisted upon by the texts which deal with *aśvamedha*.

108. Cf. AitBr VII. 4 (II. 2. 14) : *sā vā eṣā reta eva yad.*

109. Cf. AitBr VII. 4 (II. 2. 14) : *etā vā aśarīrā ahutayaḥ.*

110. Cf. AitBr VII. 3 (II. 2. 13) quoted already in notes 50 and 51 of this chapter.

In fact the Gods interrupted their sacrifice after having offered the *omentum* since they had already obtained what they desired. This does not mean, however, that the priest does the same: he continues to the end with the ceremony which he has begun but is by now assured that his offering is already complete.

Unlike the Aitareya Brāhmaṇa, the Śatapatha, after having given the *vapā* its due importance in the ritual and having performed meticulously all the rites commanded by the complexity of the first offering, does not resign itself to conceding to it a pre-eminent role. But when it seeks to give a plausible meaning to the rite in question, it again surprises us. According to it, the offering which should be the most pleasing to the Gods is the part which is the most edible, namely the *havis*. Consequently, it does not seem convinced of the importance attributed to the *vapā* and thus it looks for an explanation which is more consonant with the way of thinking prevalent in its time. The explanation allows us to see deeply into the change in the conception of the Divine which was brought about by the development of the sacrifice. We read that: "the reason why they make an oblation with the *vapā* (*tad yad vapayā caranti*) is that the Deity to whom the victim is taken is pleased with the offering of the fat (*etena medhena*) and thus pleased, *it patiently waits for the havis to be cooked* (*havīṃṣi śrapyamāṇāni*)"[111].

With this one remark, a whole tradition is swept away not only concerning the specific offering which in all, or nearly all religions has been considered to be eminently due to the Deity, but also concerning the relation of man to his God. Whatever may be the order of precedence or importance of the offerings—to which we shall return presently—what is immediately striking is the place held by the Deities in the sacrifice. If one remembers the care with which the first *ṛṣis* sought to make their sacrifices acceptable to their great Vedic Gods with appropriate praises and invocations to attract their benevolent attention; or if one remembers the caution not to invoke Indra too early before the victim is completely cooked; and now compares it with the new necessity to hold at bay the impatient Gods, one cannot

111. Cf. SatBr III. 8. 2. 29 : *tad yad vapayā caranti / yasyai vai devatāyai paśum ālabhante tām evaitad devatām etena medhena prīṇāti saiṣā devataitena medhena prītā śāntottarāṇī havīṃṣi śrapyamāṇāny uparamati tasmād vapayā caranti.*

help noticing a difference between the earlier and later conceptions of Deity. Even though Indra does not like waiting after having been invoked[112], he must all the same be induced to come—which implies that he may not come at all[113]. Here, on the contrary, the situation is so changed that the sacrificer must somehow defend himself against the divine guests who are so intrusive that they can invade his house almost before he has decided to perform a sacrifice[114], and once they are in the house, are so impatient that they are unwilling to take the necessary time until the most enticing offerings (the *havis*) are cooked[115]. In this context the *omentum* is depreciated as being a mere 'snack' to calm down and restrain the greedy Devas including those still important and mentioned by name. Is this the counterpart of the myth of Prometheus intended to justify the incongruity and inadequacy of the distribution of the parts of the victim? This question will perhaps have to remain without an answer. Perhaps it never had one. Hence we shall not attempt to give one ourselves.

Or is it instead the case that the *omentum*, which always behaves a little differently from the rest of the flesh when it is cooked, has had, on a minor scale, the same difficulties as the blood is having its value justly recognized? The *omentum* needs to be cooked in a special way, it must be first roasted to make it lose its evident 'rawness', then smeared with ghee to increase its heat and productivity and, finally, to have gold added to it to make it 'complete'. It is true that gold is added because it restores the life which was lost in the act of immolation, but it is equally true that gold is full of energy. It is called upon to restore life not only

112. See p. 26 and the text quoted in Chap. II, notes 8 and 9.

113. The God may in fact desert the house of the *yajamāna* at any moment if he is more pleased with the praises and offerings of his rival. The God is in no way anxious to receive the portion of the sacrifice which is his due; it is rather a privilege for the one who offers to see his offerings accepted by the Deity. For some texts regarding frequent rivalries between bards to win the divine favour and the Deity's benevolent acceptance of their sacrifices, see our article "Ritual as mirror reflecting Ṛgvedic life", *art. cit.*

114. Cf. SatBr I. 1. 1. 7 (quoted in the Conclusion, note 3) which speaks of the position held by the 'Divine' and the 'Deities' following the ritual change which occurred in the Yajurveda and its Brāhmaṇas.

115. See the Conclusion.

where this was lost in slaughter, but also and especially where it was lost by being cold and raw. The *vapā* is the first to be extracted after the first incision of the victim; on it gather, immediately after the blood, the destructive powers of coldness of the raw, of death visibly observed. The energy which it accumulates from the fire is enough only to break the resistance of its inertia, after which its very solidity melts as it liquifies like *retas* and disappears no sooner than it is poured on the fire as an oblation. Thus the *vapā* remains a pre-offering capable only of making the Deities well disposed and of helping them to wait more patiently until all the preparatory rites necessary for the final offering of the principal victim are performed.

The old Vedic idea of calling the Gods only when the milk is warm[116] or when the *havis* is cooked[117] was because the Gods appreciated the offering only when it was adequately prepared and ready for consumption. The Gods were more pleased with a warm than cold offering. Here it is the other way around. The cooking does not merely serve to make the offering edible and so acceptable, for the Gods are anyway always ready to launch themselves at what is their due whether cooked or not. Is it that the priest still fears lest they might still after all prefer their part well cooked and warm and get angry when in their haste they realize that they are not served as they should have been? Or is it by chance that the priest is aware that even though the Gods will ravenously throw themselves onto the food without waiting for it to be cooked, there are certain ritual acts which cannot be omitted for any reason whatever without the rite losing its efficacy?

### 5. *The Sacrificial Cake* (*paśupuroḍāśa*):

Let us proceed with our analysis of the sacrifice. Once the offering of the *omentum* is over the priest prepares to perform another rite which, though not as important, is as full of meaning. This rite is the offering of the sacrificial cake *paśupuroḍāśa* (or *paśupuroḷāśa*, according to the Aitareya Brāhmaṇa). The sacrificial cake is to be made and baked while the animal

116. Cf. RV V. 30. 15 already quoted in Chap. II, note 12.
117. Cf. RV X.179. 1 ff. already quoted and discussed in Chap. II, p. 26 and notes 8 and 9.

entrails are dissected and cooked, and offered immediately after the *omentum* (*vapā*)[118]. This offering can never be omitted from any animal sacrifice. The cake must be placed on eleven fragments of pottery in honour of the various Deities to which the eleven victims are dedicated. It is cut and offered piece by piece at the cardinal points[119]. The first divine name mentioned while it is cut is that of Indra-Agni[120]. Every part is smeared with butter at each cut, both on the side of the cut portion and on the side of the rest of cake [121]. Is this meant to infuse energy where it is lost because of the incision and separation of the parts of the cake?

While the cake is being prepared and its parts deposited in the proper pot, the attention of the priest is turned to the immolator and he directs him in cutting the animal's entrails at the same time[122]. It is a complementary offering which completes the entire animal sacrifice, but takes little time in itself and so the Sūtras to not trouble themselves much about it. Even so it does attract the attention of the priest who in explaining its meaning finds occasion for reflection.

It seems that within the sacrificial economy typical to various religions, a non-animal food offering is a necessary element in any

118. Actually the precise moment when the cake is to be offered varies from school to school and is a matter of dispute. See, e.g. AitBr VI. 9 (I. 2. 9) which seems to favour the view that its preparation and offering should be made before that of the *omentum*. SatBr III. 8. 3. 2 clearly holds that they should be made after, as we shall soon have the occasion to see. Similarly, BharSS IV. 8 and VII. 17. 1-4, and ManSS I. 8. 5. 1 are inclined to hold that they should be made after.

119. Cf. e.g. BaudhSS IV. 9; etc.

120. Cf. BaudhSS IV. 9 : *indrāgnibhyāṃ puroḍāśasyā 'vadīyamānasyā 'niubrūhi.* See also BharSS VII. 17. 11.

121. Cf. BaudhSS IV. 9 according to which, however, the cut portion, of the cake facing north, unlike the remaining portion facing west, is not to be smeared.

122. There seems to be a pretty close connection between the preparation and offering of the cake on the one hand and the extracting and cooking of the interiors of the animal on the other. See the Śrautic texts referred to in note 118 above where the two actions are consciously connected and performed more or less at the same time.

animal offering in order for it to be complete[123]. If we are to believe the many theories about the origin of the sacrifice which trace it to the offering of the first fruits by peoples who lived by hunting food-gathering, the offering of the first animal had to be complemented by the first food either gathered or cultivated.[124] The Vedic tradition affirms that the two offerings are contemporaneous and complementary, but it does not see how this connection is brought about. For Vedic theologians this combination is not self-evident, since it belongs to more 'general' sacrificial rules than their own. Therefore, it needs an explanation. Thus, one of the most plausible reasons they could find is the identification of the rice cake with the whole of the animal. "The victim which is slaughtered, this is the *puroḍāśa*."[125] How is this identification made? It is by finding a correspondence between every part of the rice and every part of the animal: "The chaff is the hairs, the bran is the skin, the bright side is the blood, the ground grain is the flesh, the more solid grain is the bones"[126]. It was then but a short step to consider the cake as containing the essence not only of the victim which is actually being offered but also that of all the victims. Thus we read that "he who offers a sacrifice with this *puroḍāśa*, offers the essence of all the animals"[127].

The Vedic priest does not see any reason why there should be any need to offer a rice cake, right in the middle of a sacrificial offering as important as that of the *omentum*. The Brāhmaṇa exegetes in their attempt to explain the need for this offering, see in the cake a concentration of the essence, or sap, of the entire victim,

123. We could recall here a classical example taken from a sacrifice of another religious tradition—the Hebraic—where side by side with the animal offering there are unfailingly to be found bread (often unleavened) and sour herbs, which seem to be a necessary element of the sacrifice.

124. For a very succint compendium of the various theories, see A. BRELICH, *Introduzione alla Storia delle Religioni, op. cit.*, pp. 43 ff., and his dealing with the subject of the offering of first fruits, pp. 45 ff. See also some of the papers read at the Geneva Conference of the History of Religions, held in 1980 whose acts are being prepared for publication.

125. AitBr VI. 9 (I. 2. 9) : *sa vā eṣa paśur evālabhyate yat puroḍāśaḥ |*

126. AitBr VI. 9 (I. 2. 9)...*tasya yāni kiṃśārūṇi tāni romāṇi | ye tuṣāḥ sā tvag ye phalīkaraṇāṣtadasṛg || yat piṣṭaṃ kiknasāstanmāṃsaṃ | yat kiñcitkaṃ sāraṃ tad asthi |...*

127. AitBr VI. 9 (I. 2. 9) : *sarveṣāṃ vā eṣa paśūnāṃ medhena yajate yaḥ puroḍāśena yajate |*

which, as we have seen, is always liable to be lost. This additional offering is justified in that it completes the sacrifice although at first sight it did not seem to need it. "With that same essence" comments the Śatapatha Brāhmaṇa, "he (the priest) now completes the victim and makes it whole"[128]. A myth dramatically describes how the essence, or sap of all the main animal victims, after having passed from one to another, eventually sank into the soil and sprang up as rice from which, precisely, the cake is made.[129] It is true, the sequence, described in the myth, of the animals in order of importance and ending in the vegetable kingdom, could in a certain sense, be understood as a first step towards the effective substitution of the victims (deprived in turn of their vital essence) leading finally to the realization of the main human (philosophical and 'mystical') aspiration of getting rid of bloody sacrifice through any substitution whatsoever. According to a myth recorded in the Brāhmaṇas the essence of the victim flowed down through a graded series of animals until it finally flowed down into the earth and sprang up again as the grain with which the cake is made. Some have seen in this myth a justification for the abolishing of the bloody sacrifice and substitution of the victim with the *puroḍāśa*. However this does not seem to

128. SatBr. III.8. 3. 1 : *etan medhena samardhayati kṛtsnaṃ karoti*. The whole passage is : *yad devatyaḥ paśur bhavati / tad devatyaṃ puroḍāśam anunirvapati tad yat puroḍāśam anunirvapati sarveṣām vā 'eṣa paśūnāṃ medho yad vrīhiyavau tenaivainam etan medhena samardhayati kṛtsnaṃ karoti tasmāt puroḍaśamanunirvapati /*

129. Cf. AitBr VI. 8 (I. 2. 8) and also SatBr I. 2. 3. 6 ff. Both texts, with a slight difference between them, are in substantial agreement that at first the Gods immolated man as victim but his essence (*medha*) escaped and entered the horse. So then they immolated the horse but again its essence escaped and entered the ox and so on and so forth with the ram, the goat, till finally the essence of the last animal escaped and entered the earth from which it sprang up as rice and barley of which the pudding is made. The AitBr (*loc. cit.*) completes the picture by listing the names of the more or less fantastic animals into which the various victims, once deprived of their *medha*, were changed. This idea of the *medha* (or *rasa*) escaping from the sacrificial victim is found frequently in the Brāhmaṇas and persists in subsequent literature from the Upaniṣads on. See, e.g. SatBr XI. 8.3.5 ff. where many victims are mentioned whose essence escaped till finally the horse, as representative of the sun, willingly offers itself for the *aśvamedha*, thus bringing the sequence of flights to an end. See also n. 65 above.

have been the case[130]. We do not deny, of course, that the identification of the rice cake with the entire animal, and with all the victims in general, did serve as a good argument for this final substitution when, by its internal evolution (whose principles we shall see later), the bloody sacrifice tended to be surmounted and replaced first by symbolic offerings and then by meditation[131]. But this does not seem to us to have been the case with the offering of the rice cake during the course of the normal sacrifice. At most the ritual presence of the cake may have rendered it easier to find a practical substitute for the bloody sacrifice when this became necessary. Even so, this idea was certainly not implied in the necessity of the offering of the rice cake, nor can this offering be interpreted as a step in a transition between one conception of the sacrifice to the other[132]. In fact, in the Brāhmaṇa rite the rice cake does not *replace* the victim but *completes* it. It serves as one of the many means to concentrate the essence of the sacrificial victim which always seeks to escape. It has the same, or nearly the same, function, *mutatis mutandis*, as that of the gold, ghee, purificatory water, etc., that is, of any ingredient which in one way or another is used to purify, heal, make whole again the wound suffered by the sacrificial victim. The rice cake is added to the victim but it does not replace it. Moreover, according to the Śatapatha Brāhmaṇa, this complementary rite is performed in connection with and immediately after the offering of the *omentum*; and the reason it gives is that since it is performed half-way through the ceremony and since the *omentum* is extracted from the middle of the animal, the priest "from the middle completes the victim by means of that sacrificial essence and makes it whole. It is for this that he proceeds with the offering of the cake immediately after the offering of the *vapā*, and the exegete

130. This is the usual interpretation normally given both by traditional commentaries and by modern erudite Indologists. For a compendium of these interpretations, see G. U. THITE, *op. cit.*, pp. 145 ff.

131. For example, the opening sacrifice in BṛhadĀrUp I. 1. 1 which is only meditated. See our remarks on this manner of going beyond the sacrifice in our article "The role of ritual heat in Vedic Sacrifice", *art. cit.*

132. This is supported both by a certain internal exegesis and by the greater number of scholars. See the compendium, already referred to, in G. U. THITE, *op. cit.*, pp. 145 ff.

continues and says, "The relation of this (cake to the animal offering) is the same everywhere: the cake is prepared after the victim"[133]. It is clear then that the rice cake requires and presupposes the animal victim but does not replace it.

However, this is not the only interpretation given to account for the offering of the rice cake in the Brāhmaṇic bloody sacrifice. By presenting it as the complement and completion of the animal sacrifice, the Aitareya Brāhmaṇa links itself to its own Saṃhitā. When it comes to comment on the *mantras* referring to the "lost parts" of the victim, namely those which have evaded the transformation and the accumulation of energy wrought by cooking, the exegete of this Veda makes use of the presence of the cake to identify it with these parts and thus to re-integrate them into the whole. Attention then naturally turns to those parts of the animal victim which have not been cooked either because they cannot be cooked, such as the hooves, the harness, etc., or because of unexpected accidental causes, such as their having been eated up by flies[134]. The cake which is represented as gathering into itself the essence of the animal victim is the most suitable for this purpose[135]. The reasoning there is simple: if the cake in any case gathers into itself the energy which escaped from the various victims in the act of immolation, then those parts of the victim which were lost either because they could not be cooked or due to accidental causes could also be represented by the same. Thus

133. Cf. SatBr III. 8. 3. 2 : *atha yad vapayā pracarya | etena puroḍāśena pracarati madhyato vā 'imāṃ vapām utkhidanti madhyata evainam etena medhena samardhavati kṛtsnaṃ karoti tasmād vapayā pracaryaitena puroḍāśen pṛacaraty eṣa nvevaitasya bandhur yatra kva caiṣa paśuṃ puroḍāśo 'nunirupyate ||* Here the text states its position with regard to the moment when the offering is to be made—a subject of controversy as we have seen (see note 118). If the cake is to be offered after *omentum*, and in connection with it, it is clear that it is not meant to replace it.

134. Cf. RV I. 162. quoted in Chap. II, note 47 and discussed on p. 35.

135. Cf AirBr VII. 1 (I. 2. 11) : ...*tad āhuḥ | yad eṣa havir eva yat paśur athāsya bahvapaiti lomāni tvagasṛk kuṣṭhikāḥ śaphā viṣāṇe skandati piśitaṃ kenāsya tad āpūryata iti || yad evaitat paśau puroḷāśam anunirvapanti tenaivāsya tad āpūryate || paśubhyo vai medhā udakrāmaṃstau vrīhiścaiva yavaśca bhūtāvajāyetām | tad yat paśau puroḷāśaṃ anunirvapanti samedhena naḥ paśuneṣṭam asat kevalena naḥ paśuneṣṭam asad iti...*

the Vedic priest can really affirm that the *puroḍāśa* completes the sacrifice[136]. It remains to be seen whether the offering of the *paśupuroḍāśa* can be considered to have formed part of the Vedic rite from the very beginning or to have been introduced in a subsequent ritual phase. This is not so important as far as we are concerned. One could argue either way since the manifest need to justify its part in the rite could be accounted for either by its introduction in a subsequent phase of development of the rite or —and this seems to us more probable—by the fact that, though it formed part of the rite from the very beginning, it needed no such justification or explanation at a time when there was yet no coherent reflection on the sacrifice.

### 6. *The Cooked Offering* (*havis*) :

While the rice cake is being offered, the immolator is busy removing the internal organs of the animal, from a cut in its middle, and in cutting its external limbs according to the explicit command of the *pratiprasthātṛ*.[137] He begins from the heart, the tongue and goes on to the liver, the kidneys, the sternum, the sexual organs, etc.[138] These have then to be boiled in an earthen pot[139]. All this procedure is supervised in its minutest details by various priests who command its execution, while the offering of the *paśupuroḍāśa* is being performed[140]. All these parts of the animal are considered as *havis* and each one is to be cut and offered in a specific way. The heart is handled with greater care and circumspection : it is not put directly in the pot but has first to be pierced by the priest with a spit, after which the priest hands it over to the immolator to be cooked and further prepa-

136. Cf. AitBr VII. 1 (I. 2. 11) which is a continuation of the text quoted in the preceding note : *samedhena hāsya paśuneṣṭaṃ bhavati kevalena hāsya paśuneṣṭaṃ bhavati ya evam veda* // The text then goes on to reserve this kind of offering only "to him who knows". But this is a suggestion of a philosophical nature apt to lead one to go beyond the blood sacrifice, which however has not been decisively effective in the latter's eventual replacement by this ritual detail.

137. Cf. BaudSS IV. 8 (ed. SK, vol. I, part II, pp. 831 ff.)

138. Cf. e.g. BharSS VII. 17. 6.

139. Cf. BharSS VII. 17.7.

140. Cf. BharSS VII.17.10

red[141]. This piercing is an important liturgical act and full of symbolic meaning. The spit with which the heart is pierced and later put on the fire to be cooked is disposed of in a special manner once the offering is made. It cannot be burnt as are the spits which are used to cook the *vapā*, nor can it be buried in the earth or thrown into water; the way out of this difficulty is to place it on the border between the two[142]. The reason for this difficulty can be understood in terms of the negative effects of heat—an analysis of which we are omitting in this study. Here we shall content ourselves with one explanation explicitly given in the Brāhmaṇa of the *adhvaryu*. The Brāhmaṇa states that after the heart has been cooked separately, it cannot be brought to the *āhavanīya*, where it is to be offered, by traversing the altar where the other fires and the rest of the *havis* are found. It has to be brought along the border of the fire-platform. The same thing is applied to the *omentum*, but the reason for carrying it along the side of the altar was the fact that it was not fully cooked. This is not the case with the heart since when it is carried towards the *āhavanīya*, it is completely cooked (*śṛta*). The reason must be sought elsewhere. The heart has been cut and mishandled and so leaks, rents, and clefts have been formed on it. These could have the adverse effect of emptying the sacrificial victim—in view of the fact that the *medha* is always ready to escape at the first opportunity through any cut which may be made in it. This could, in a sense, reduce the sacrificial victim to its previous 'raw' state by draining it out of the energy infused

141. Cf. BaudhSS IV. 9 (SK vol. I, part II, p. 834) which gives this opinion of Baudhāyana on the matter. However the matter is debated in this Sūtra itself and also in others. See BharSS VII. 17. 8 where it is the immolator himself who does the piercing without having to act through the mediation of the priest.

142. Cf. SatBr III. 8. 5. 9 : *atha hṛdayaśulaṃ prayacchati | tan na pṛthivyāṃ parāsyen nāpsu sa yat pṛthivyām parāsyedoṣadhīśca vanaspatīṃścaiṣā śuk praviśed yad apsu parāśyed apa eṣā śuk praviśet tasmān na pṛthivyāṃ nāpsu ||* ("the immolator returns the spit; let him not put it on the earth, not in the water, because if he were to put it on the earth , its heat [or, pain, *śuk* ] would enter the plants and trees; and if he were to put it in the water, its heat [*pain* ] would enter the water. Therefore not on the earth, not in the water.") The solution, given a little later in the text, is : " [let him put it ] where the dry and the wet meet." : *apa evabhyaveti*. (This passage has already been referred to above in note 101.)

into it by the cooking. But the text adds another reason, perhaps deeper and full of ulterior meaning : the heart is the centre of life of any being and in it is amassed the anguish and the pain of injury and death. The heart is pierced with the spit to remove the pain from the heart and transfer it to the spit so that the heart may be freed from it and so rendered edible[143]. For the same reason, the heart is to be smeared with ghee and offered together with pieces of gold[144]. Ghee and gold, as we have already seen, symbolize life and are directly connected to Agni whom they often represent; both the one and the other restore life and ease pain.

In the meantime the rest of the *havis* consisting of the entrails, tongue, sternum, thighs, legs, hoofs, etc., all cut in a pre-established manner, is put in a special cauldron for a final boiling. This task is entrusted to the immolator under the supervision of the priests and it is the immolator, therefore, who pledges himself to its success. The priest assures himself of this by asking the immolator three times whether the *havis* is cooked, to which the latter must reply directly and without useless elaborations, according to the instructions given to him[145]. The answer must

143. Cf. SatBr III. 8. 5. 8 : *atha hṛdayaśūlenāvabhṛthaṃ yanti / paśorha vā 'ālabhyamānasya hṛdayaṃ śuk samabhyavaiti hṛdayādhṛdayaśūlam atha yacchurtasya paritṛndanti tad alaṃ juṣaṃ tasmādu paritṛdyaiva śulākuryāt tattriḥ pracyute paśau hṛdayaṃ pravṛhyottamam pratyavadadhāti //*

All these texts merit to be studied more in depth—something which we hope to do on some future occasion.

144. Cf. BaudhSS IV. 10 (SK vol. I, part II, p. 835) for the way one should smear with ghee the various cooked parts of the victim, including its interiors, its bones and especially its heart which, as we have seen, has certain special characteristics because of its peculiar nature. See also SatBr III. 8. 3. 8 which gives, besides, the reason why the heart should be so smeared, namely that breath and immortality be infused into it (this being in accordance with the usage discussed above in note 94.) Also SatBr III.8.3.13 where it is said that gold is put in the spoon used for the offering. Similarly BharSS VII. 8. 11. (On the use of gold, see above notes 89, 90, 92 and 94.)

145. SatBr III. 7. 3. 4, informs us that the priest, before he proceeds to ask the ritual questions, instructs the immolator on the correct manner of answering one of the questions which seems to be vital in this context : *yattvā pṛcchācchṛtaṃ havīḥ śamitār iti śṛtam ity eva brūtānna śṛtam bhagavo na śṛtaṃ hīti* ("when anybody asks you: 'Is the havis cooked, O immolator ?', answer only: 'Yes, it is cooked' and not: 'It is cooked, O Lord' or 'Yes, it is really cooked".")

be simple and to the point : "Yes, it is cooked"[146]. The question is repeated three times while the priest approaches the place where the offering is to be cooked and may or may not be followed by the quiet repetition of a *mantra*[147]. The priest must ask the question because he must make sure that the ritual is performed as it should be, since "the *havis* must be cooked; for not uncooked must be the gods' food"[148]. There is 'fault' (*enas*) if the required condition is unfulfilled : "and again why he asks : 'I will perform with cooked (food)' so he thinks; and if that sacrificial food be uncooked, it is yet cooked food for the Gods, and is cooked as regards the Sacrificer; and the Adhvaryu is guiltless; on the slaughterer that guilt lies."[149]

That is to say that, by asking to the immolator the assurance of the right preparation and cooking of the offering, this one is considered in any case as cooked with respect to the sacrifice; and the *yajamāna* is free of guilt. The guilt belongs to the one who has given the wrong information.

Ritual cooking has by now become so obligatory that to omit to perform it meticulously is to be guilty of a 'fault' (*enas*). Aware of this, the *adhvaryu* is not ready to assume responsibility for seeing to it that the food is properly cooked but lays it on the immolator (*śamitar*) who, in any case, is already responsible for the killing of the victim. Moreover, it is the immolator who should know whether the *havis* is cooked or not[150]. As he could not taste the food to see if it was cooked (nor does any Indian even today in his own home[151]), he must learn with practice to know when

146. *śṛtam iti* (SatBr III. 8. 3. 5)

147. Cf. BaudhSS IV. 10 & XX. 29 (SK vol. I, part II, p. 834)

148. SatBr III. 8. 3. 6 : ...*śṛtaṃ vai devānāṃ havīr nāśṛtaṃ*...

149. SatBr III. 8. 3. 7 : *tad yat pṛcchati | śṛtena pracarāṇīti tad yady aśṛtaṃ bhavati śṛtam eva devānāṃ havir bhavati śṛtaṃ yajamānasyānenā adhvaryur bhavati śamitari tad eno bhavati*...(tr. EGGELING)

150. Cf. SatBr III. 8. 3. 6 : ...*śamitā vai tad veda yadi śṛtaṃ vā bhavatyaśṛtaṃ vā* ||

151. Even today, in India, one should not taste the food while it is being cooked. That would be a great lack of respect towards others since in that case, the food becomes 'a left-over' (*ucchiṣṭa*) and hence entirely contaminated. If, as we have said before, the *ucchiṣṭa* is the 'edible' part of the sacrificial victim, this is because it is the part 'sanctified' by its contact with the Divine. A common man, however, (not the guru nor the priest in the exercise of his functions), contaminates the food when he touches it with his mouth and does not sanctify it.

the food is ready by exterior signs. The fault therefore, if there is one, falls on the expert (who is usually, but not always, the immolator)[152]. The immolator has just discharged an unpleasant duty, the immolation of the sacrificial victim, for which he could already be at fault[153]. Hence, if, here is to be yet another fault, it is better that it be made to lie on him. It is, therefore, important that someone other than the *Adhvaryu* assumes the responsibility of announcing that the offering is transformed so that in case the information given proves to be mistaken, the *Adhvaryu* remains faultless in the eyes of the Gods, of the sacrificer and of the sacrificial victim itself. Moreover, he can prove his sincerity in thinking that the cooking was perfectly done since he has sought information three times and is thus "free from fault".

When everything is ready and the sacrificial victim is completely cooked, smeared with ghee and covered with gold in order to heal and complete it, the priest invites the *hotṛ* to recite the appropriate formulae to inform the Gods that the offering is ready. Here a new problem arises with the sacrifice, which seemed not acknowledged in the Ṛgvedic hymns. Even if the priest in the Brāhmaṇic period has an advantage over his predecessor in that he does not need to take great pains to propitiate the Gods and to urge them to come to the offering due to them, he is, however, faced with another kind of difficulty : the impatience and avidity of the Gods who are eager to come before they are called and who want to be the first to be mentioned by name. This means that a difficulty remains, only this time it is the opposite of the one there was before, If the *ṛṣi* had to take the trouble to show himself worthy of receiving the divine guests, the Brāhmaṇic priest has the trouble of first staying their impatience and then of not displeasing his exigent guests all of whom

152. Cf. e.g. BharSS VII. 22. 15 where a case is foreseen in which the immolator belongs to a different caste.

153. Here, however, the fault is not yet indissolubly linked to the act in itself as will be the case later on when the Indian spirituality will have gone beyond the blood sacrifice, but to the skill or its lack with which the act is performed. There is above all the fear lest pain be caused—something which has to be avoided as much as possible. See e.g. SatBr III. 8. 2. 1 ff. which mentions the various rites of expiation which are necessary to diminish the suffered pain.

want to be the first to be invoked. In fact, as the Śatapatha Brāhmaṇa explains, "All the deities draw near to the victim while it is immolated, thinking, 'My name he will choose, my name he will choose !'"[154]. Therefore what is the Brāhmaṇic priest to do to avoid showing preferences and thus inevitably causing jealousy among them, if he obviously cannot pronounce more than one name at a time ? In response to this problem the same Brāhmaṇa continues : "they (the Deities), having their minds (*manas*) fixed upon (*ota*) the victim, are collectively satisfied by a hymn which pleases their minds"[155]. The hymn referred to is a Ṛgvedic hymn addressed to Agni there called *manotā*[156] So, by addressing the *manotā* Deity (Agni), the Brāhmaṇic priest addresses at the same time all the Deities whose minds are fixed upon the victim !

The exegete of the Aitareya Brāhmaṇa, however, seeks another explanation for the use of this hymn. Faithful to the letter of the hymn, he cannot forget the fact that the hymn is, after all, addressed to Agni alone whereas all the Deities are desirous of the victim and all of them are involved in the sacrificial action. So he too plays on the etymological meaning of the word *manotā,* but unlike his colleague of the Yajur who sees in it a reference to *manas* and hence refers it to the collectivity of all the Deities, he sees in Agni, the *manotā* Deity, a universalization of all of them. He argues that Agni, the Word, the Sacrificial Cow, are all united in the term *manotā*, and that Agni, to whom the hymn is directed, is all in all, hence to address Agni is to address all the Deities[157] !

The change in the understanding of the reciprocal relation between the Sacrifice and the Deities, is evident in these two

154. SatBr III. 8. 3. 12 : *tad yan manotāyai haviṣo 'nuvāca āha sarvā hà vai devatāḥ paśum ālabhyamānam upasaṃgacchante mama nāma grahīṣyati mama nāma grahīṣyatīti...*

155. SatBr III. 8. 3. 14 *..sarvāsāṃ hi devatānāṃ haviḥ paśustāsāṃ sarvāsāṃ devatānāṃ paśau manāṃsyotāni bhavanti tāny evaitat prīṇāti tatho hāmoghāya davatānāṃ manāṃsyupasaṃgatāni bhavanti tasmān manotāyai haviṣo'nuvāvca āha ||*

156. The hymn is given in RV I. 1-13 where Agni is called by the name *manotā*. Cf. J. EGGELING comments in his translation of SatBr III. 3. 3. 14 (*op. cit.*, p. 203, note 4).

See also SatBr I. 1. 2. 18 quoted in the Conclusion, note 4.

157. Cf. AitBr VI. 10 (I. 2. 10).

ways of explaining the same hymn. We shall return to this topic in the Conclusion where we shall try to isolate, the 'religious' and 'metaphysical' reactions to this change of attitude.

Finally, the *paśuyajña* ends with the ritual disposal of the implements used during the course of the sacrificial celebration.[158]

After the performance of the *paśubandha*, there follows the performance of the other rites normally included in all the great sacrificial ceremonies of the Soma Pressing.

158. We do not consider them here because most of them reveal the characteristics of excess of heat accumulated during the course of the rites. It therefore falls into another category with respect of our present topic, the 'right amount of heat' in rituals.

CHAPTER SIX

# THE FIRST KINDLING OF THE SACRIFICIAL FIRE BY THE HEAD OF THE FAMILY (AGNYĀDHĀNA or AGNYĀDHEYA)

The order we have followed in our exposition of the rites gives precedence to *paśubandha* because of the important place it has in some religions, even though in Brāhmaṇic India it is at most ancillary to other greater ritual complexes and is not considered to be one of the more important sacrifices or, even, essential. Even so it is considered to be such in nearly all the religions of the world, in this ritual phase; it is for this reason that it has assumed for us such importance. Even the most orthodox Vedic tradition seems to approve of a choice of precedence which is based on the importance of the rite rather than on the order in which the rite is to be performed. Thus the Śatapatha Brāhmaṇa for example, prefers to give precedence to *darśapūrṇamāsa* over *agnyādhāna* because it considers the former more important than the latter even though the latter is to be performed first. Consequently we too will discuss *agnyādhāna* after having treated *paśubandha* because of its lesser importance for us, even though according to the sequence it should have come before.

This rite is connected with the erection of fire-places by the sacrificer and with its kindling at the moment of his first sacrifice; which means that this rite, directly connected with fire which is the principal source of the sacred heat we are studying, is for us, as it is for the sacrificer, the first requisite, as it were, for the diffusion of the ritual energy which is born of the sacred fire. Moreover one of the principal effects of the sacrificial heat is linked to the erection of a special fire-place during the long and complex rite of the offering of Soma[1]. To understand the peculiarity of this rite it is necessary to see how it differs from the erection of the more ordinary fire-places which serve the *vajamāna* for any type of sacrifice he may offer throughout his life.[2]

When a young male member of a family belonging to one of the three higher castes[3] reaches adulthood and has married, he is in position to erect his own fireplaces and personally assume his religious and sacrificial obligations. Ancient authorities are divided as to when it is opportune for this new member of society to become independent. Some think that the son must wait till the death of his father or at least his retirement from active life —while others disagree[4]. Moreover the choice of the most propitious time for the initiation ceremony is of special importance and one to which particular attention is given. All the texts which concern themselves with the matter begin, generally speaking, by giving advice about the choice of the most suitable time in accordance with the seasons, the phases of the moon, the position of the stars, etc., appropriate to a particular caste.[5] To understand the importance of this rite it is necessary to bear in mind how difficult it was to kindle a fire in ancient times, both in physical terms and from the point of view of the ritual. Fire has this sacred character in all cultures.[6] Since its emergence is often

1. See later on, Ch. VII, first few pp.

2. In ancient India the primacy of kings and princes, vassals, *rājā* and *mahārājā* and the like, was shown and maintained through the celebration of big sacrifices like the *rājasūya*, *vājapeya*, and other Soma sacrifices, also the *aśvamedha*, each according to the degree of the king's power. Cf. two major Epic works of India's tradition: the Mahābhārata and the Rāmāyaṇa where there are many examples. History tells us that the actual performance of these took place at least up to the Muslim times. In order to be able to perform any one of these rites the establishing of one's own fires is the first ceremony a sacrificer had to do.

3. Cf. e.g. BharSS V.2.9 where it appears that often it is a matter of discussion to which caste a potential *yajamāna* has to belong.

4. Cf. BharSS V. 2.10.

5. Cf. e.g. SatBr II.1.2.1 ff.; BharSS V.1.7 ff.; APSS V.3.4 ff.; and, or the connection of the castes with the seasons, SatBr II.1.3.5ff.; BharSS V.2.1ff.

6. Cf. e.g. the Vesta Temple in Rome and the importance of the hearth in ancient Roman and Greek houses, and the like. Even today the ancient

fraught with danger, nearly all the various cultures of the world have sought to surround with rites and protective measures their primary necessity to keep a fire permanently alight privately at home and sometimes even publically in a state owned locality. Moreover from the necessity of keeping it permanently alight there arises a parallel necessity of its periodical renewal so as to keep it always fresh and its energy always pure. This need is felt even today in the desacralized Western world and survives in a rite performed during the Christian Easter Vigil in which a candle is lit from a consecrated fire symbolizing Christ, the light of the world. The extinction of the old fire and the kindling of of the new is one of the features of the rite which passed over to Christianity from more ancient religions. Even if it is interpreted in the light of the Christain myth, namely that of Christ's death and resurrection the idea behind it remains closely linked to that of having a public fire which must be purified and renewed at least once a year. It is still the custom in many countries even today to light great bonfires once a year to celebrate some feast.[7]

With greater reason, therefore, the kindling of the sacred fire and keeping it alight had a particularly important role to play in ancient India. In Vedic India, however, where personal religion far outweighed public religion in importance, the fire, its kindling and maintenance, assumes a markedly personal character. From the moment a young head of a family considers himself capable of assuming responsibility for his own household and of celebrating the prescribed rites in his own name and in that of his family, the first thing he has to do is to erect his own fireplaces with which he enters into a deep personal relationship. Thus when he prepares to kindle the fires for the first time he must undergo two special initiation restraints of behaviour (*vrata*) during an initial preparatory period and at the time of

---

tradition of a permanent public fire still persists, although its meaning is radically changed. For instance the use of fire on the grave of the unknown soldier or the eternal lamps burning on altars (in Christian churches) and those burning in front of sacred images or on tombs.

7. Cf. e.g. in the modern Italy alone, as an example of 'Western' cultures, the fires of S. John in Toscana; those of S. Anne in Marche, of the Madonna on the Soratte Mountain and the like. In North India and the West the fires for Holikā are kindled for the full moon of the spring equinox.

the kindling. The erection of the fireplaces is likened to the building of the body of the sacrificer.

It is generally prepared and lit far away from the house[8], preferably in a secluded place where the land slopes down towards the East, near to a source of water such as a river or a well. After the ceremony is over, the *gārhapatya* fire is taken to light other new fires constructed in accordance with the requirements of the rite which the sacrificer intends to perform. Each of the various types of sacrificial rites requires that the fireplaces be arranged in a special way and be of various shapes. For example the arrangement of the altar for the *paśuyajña* is different from that for the *cāturmāsya*, or for the *agniṣṭoma* or for any other kind of sacrifice.

The ceremony of *agnyādhāna*, the erection of the sacrificer's own fireplaces, is usually performed only once during his life. It is always the same fire which is brought from the *gārhapatya* to the other fireplaces erected for the various sacrifices which the *yajamāna* will have to perform in his capacity as *paterfamilias*[9]. There are cases, however, when the ceremony can be repeated with certain modifications. This would happen when some kind of disaster has rendered the fires impure which makes it necessary to light them again. Or, it may happen that after having lit the fires and proceeded with his normal everyday rites, the sacrificer does not prosper or meets with bad luck; this means that the fires have not been propitious to him and that it is better for him to extinguish them and replace them with better ones[10].

The texts which speak of this ceremony are above all those belonging to the *adhvaryu* who is the one in charge of the greater part of the material construction of the fireplaces. These texts

8. In order to avoid possible confusions, it is as well to remember that in Vedic India the fire which has to be kindled is the sacred one, whose specific place is the altar, where it is two-fold or threefold (see previously Ch. I, p. 16 ff.).

9. We have to bear in mind that we are talking about times when those who performed sacrifices as sacrificers were the numerous *rājās* of the country. Nevertheless the smaller rites like the *agnihotra* and the *darśapūrṇamāsa* were performed by all the representatives of the three main castes who had the right to enkindling their sacred fires.

10. Cf. the rules for the repetition of the *agnyādhāna* in SatBr II. 2. 3.1 ff.

are the Brāhmaṇas and Sūtras of the Yajurveda which we are studying here in the Mādhyandina version of the Śatapatha Brāhmaṇa, and in the Taittirīya version of the *Kṛṣṇa* School.[11]

Normally there are at most two fires to be established: the *gārhapatya*, which is usually used to cook the offerings, and the *āhavanīya* , which is used to receive the oblation. At times, but not necessarily, to these is added a third, the *anvāhāryapacana*, (called also *dakṣiṇāgni* because it is constructed, in the form of a half-moon, to the South, *dakṣiṇa*, of the *gārhapatya*). Besides, there can be two fires, the *sabhya* and the *āvasathya*, to the North and North-East respectively of the *āhavanīya*.

The ceremony of the *agnyādhāna* normally requires two days: the first day to collect the material and to perform the preliminary rites, the second to construct the fireplace and to light the fires.

1. *Gathering of the Material* (*sambhāra*) :

The first thing the new sacrificer has to do when he is ready to light his own fires is to gather the material for the construction of the fireplaces. Such material, technically called *sambhāra* (literally, "what is gathered"), has a symbolic value and varies according to the different schools and traditions. The school of the *Śukla* Yajurveda prescribes five things: water for the ceremonial washing of the ground chosen for the occasion, a piece of gold, salt, soil taken from a cavity dug by a mole or a rat, and finally some pebbles.[12] The explanation for the choice of these objects is given by the *Śukla* School in the following way: Water is woman and therefore mother; it is fertile and represents any kind of sustenance especially food. To wash the ground of the fireplaces with it is to render it fecund and to ensure permanently a good provision of food in the house of the *yajamāna*, so that his family will always be prosperous. Moreover, water being feminine, it can be coupled with the fire which will be later lit, so they will ensure productivity[13]. "It is for this that he (the

11. Cf. BharSS V. 1. 1 ff. which follows the Taittirīya School and KatySS IV. 8. 1 ff. commenting foot by foot on SatB II. 1. 1.1 ff.

12. Cf. SatBr II. 1. 1. 1 ff. For the variations of the Taittirīya school see later notes 20 and 31 ff.

13. Cf. SatBr II. 1.1.3 sq. *athādbhir abhyukṣati* / *eṣa vā apāṃ sambhāro yad*

*adhvaryu*) carries water"[14]. The gold, being a seed of immortality, is, according to the myth, the result of the coupling of the Waters with Agni; it is Agni's seed which is resplendent as light emanating from the flame. Gold serves to furnish the sacrificer with the divine seed[15]. The salt represents the savour of the earth and, by association, what the Vedic people consider to be its best produce, that is, cattle. The salt, therefore, strengthens the *vajamāna's* expectations as to the wealth he hopes to receive from his fires[16]. The soil taken from the cavity of a mole or rat symbolizes the connection of the fireplace with the centre of the earth, with its profundity. It represents the very medulla of the earth and the essence of its splendour[17]. Finally, the pebbles symbolize a support. In fact, when all materials have been collected and bound in a black antelope's skin, the pebbles serve to fix such a skin and to prepare it to be hanged with hooks at the end of the first day. Thus, they are supposed also to give stability and support not only to the black antelope's skin itself but to the whole earth. The reason for this is to be found in the myth of the original fluctuation of the earth. When the earth which originally was as mobile "as a lotus leaf" arrived in its fluctuations, near the Devas, these, in order to have a firm support for their sacrifice, snatched it away from their rivals, the Asuras, and fixed it down with rope and pegs as tight as "the skin of an animal". Only when the earth was thus solidly fixed, in fact, could the two principal fireplaces be constructed[18]. The pebbles, therefore,

---

*adbhir abhyukṣati tad yad apaḥ sambharaty annaṃ vā 'āpo 'nnaṃ hi vā 'āpas tasmād yademaṃ lokam āpa āgacchanty athehānnādyaṃ jāyate..*//3//..*vṛṣāgnir mithunenaivainam etat prajananena....*

14. SatBr II. 1.1.4 (end) ..*tasmād apaḥ sambharati.*

15. Cf. SatBr II. 1. 1. 5 *atha hiraṇyaṃ sambharati / agnirha vā 'apo 'bhidadhyau mithunyābhiḥ syām iti tāḥ sambabhūva tāsu retaḥ prāsiñcat tad hiraṇyam abhavat tasmād etad agnisaṃkāśam agner hi retas tasmād....*

16. Cf. SatBr II. 1. 1. 6 *asau ha vai dyaur aṣyai pṛthivyā etān paśūn pradadau tasmāt....paśavo hy evaite sākṣād eva tat paśubhirevainam etat samardhayati....tam anayor dyāvāpṛthivyo rasaṃ manyante....etad dyāvāpṛthivyo rasena samardhayati tasmād....*

17. Cf. SatBr II. 1. 1. 7 *atha ākhu karīṣaṃ sambharati / ākhavo ha vā'asyai pṛthivyai rasaṃ vidus tasmāt te 'dho'dha imāṃ pṛthivīṃ carantaḥ pīviṣṭhā asyai hi rasaṃ vidus te yatra te'syai pṛthivyai rasaṃ vidus tata utkiranti tad asyā'evainam etat pṛthivyai rasena samardhayati tasmād...*

18. Cf. SatBr II. 1. 1. 8 ff. *atha śarkarāḥ sambharati / ... sā heyaṃ pṛthivyalelāyadyathā puṣkaraparṇam evaṃ tāṃ ha sma vātaḥ saṃvahati sopaiva....*//8// *tad dhocuḥ hantemāṃ pratiṣṭhām....agnī 'ādadhāmahai....*

placed all around the black antelope's skin, serve to strengthen and stabilize the universe as the proper ground on wnich will be celebrated the cosmic sacrifice.[19] The corresponding myth of the fixing of the earth, as found in the Taittirīya version, contains some elements of most ancient cosmogonies. In the beginning —as in many 'beginnings' of the mythologies of the world —there were only the waters and a lotus-leaf floating on them. Prajāpati, wanting to provide a solid and fixed basis for the earth so that he could offer his sacrifice, thought that he could find such basis under the waters whence had sprung the stem of the leaf. Taking the form of a wild boar (*varāha*), the Creator dived to the bottom of the waters and brought with him to the surface a piece of earth which he spread on the lotus-leaf and then fixed this by placing pebbles all around it[20]. The myth of the creation of the earth from a piece of mud brought up from the bottom of the primordial Ocean is known to many mythologies of the European and American world and exists even today in the folklore of the Baltic and Slavic peoples.[21] In the Brāhmaṇas, where the myth is still in its unitarian form, the one who dives to the bottom of the waters is the Creator himself and for this purpose he takes the form of an animal. Elsewhere, on the other hand, it is, so to say, the stand-in figure of the God, who in the form of a bird, is entrusted by the Creator with the task of fishing out the earth from the bottom of the primordial Ocean. This stand-in figure in the middle East or Eastern Europe, under the influence of the Iranian dualism, nearly always appears as the God's antagonist, and, in the legends influenced by the Christian tradition, is often called Satan[22]. In India, however, the myth is still in its 'original' state, if we can so express ourselves. There is no dualism involved, and no problem arises as to

19. Cf. SàtBr II.1.1, 10 *tad yathā saṅkubhiścarma vihanyāt | evam imāṃ pratiṣṭhāṃ śarkarābhiḥ paryavṛmhanta seyaṃ dhruvāśithilā pratiṣṭhā tasyām dhruvāyām-aśithilāyām agni ādadhata tato'syai sapatnān ṇirabhajan ||*

20. Cf. TaittBr I. 1. 3. 5 and comment in J. GONDA, *Aspects of Early Visnuism*, Delhi (Motilal Banarsidass), 2nd ed. 1969 (1st 1954), p. 129 ff.

21. Cf. M. ELIADE, *De Zalmoxis à Gengis-Khan. Études comparatives sur les religions et le forklore de la Dacie et de l'Europe Centrale*, Paris (Payot) 1970, Ch. III.

22. Cf. M. ELIADE, op. cit., p. 74 (It. ed.)

how evil entered into a 'perfect extension' of the earth;[23] therefore there is no demonic stand-in. Prajāpati needs only to *fix* a solid basis for his cosmic sacrifice and therefore for his fires. Since all he has in front of him is an unstable lotus-leaf and he needs a stable base for his sacrificial action, the Creator goes in search of such a base. He intuits the fact that it lies in the depth, under the stem on which the leaf rests. Thus it follows that the stability sought after is to be found in the depths, unreachable under the immensity of the primaeval waters.

The parallel version of the myth given by the *Śukla* School does not mention waters and, therefore, any dive or immersion of any kind, but it agrees with the previous version in saying that the earth was mobile "*as* a lotus-leaf". The common element in both is that the earth shifts and so connot offer a firm and secure ground on which to lay the foundation for a relationship between the profane World and the divine, that is, it cannot afford to be a place on which to lay the *pivot* around which revolves the cosmic-divine action par excellencé: the sacrifice. Where there are no waters, the earth is immediately fixed with pebbles and is 'stretched' as the black antelope's skin is stretched. Where there are waters, the earth must first itself be 'created', by being fished out and brought to the surface, before it can be 'stretched' and fixed with pebbles. To this end, unlike many myths of other religions, Prajāpati does not seek the help of anybody else but plunges into the deep himself directly. He succeeds straight away and the Brāhmaṇic

23. Cf. M. ELIADE, op. cit., Ch. III 11 cc. The earth created by God was originally—at least in the mind of the Creator—a plain, flat and without obstacles. The existence of valleys, mountains, lakes and marshes (all obstacles for nomadic shepherds) is due either to the intervention of Satan who, more or less intentionally disturbed the work of the Creator; or is due to the inability of God himself to keep it within the sky's limits. In the first case the Devil, after sinking to the bottom of universal sea in order to fetch the necessary earth to create the world, hides some portions of it in his mouth in order to produce a second creation; in the second case God is compelled to accept the advice of a rabbit to wrinkle it into mountains and valleys. For Prajāpati this problem does not exist. In any case the mountains are not felt to be obstacles in India. As for the evil—an unavoidable fact of human experience—it has an origin independent from the act of immersion and we shall find it at the end of the ritual vicissitudes of our study. Cf. the last part of my already quoted article *The Role of Heat...*

myth does not need to add anything else, although in similar myths there are usually at least two first unfruitful attempts[24]. The antiquity of the myth which is perhaps greater than that centered on Prajāpati himself[25], imposes on the supreme God to assume an animal form in the performance of his task. The form which is usual in other myths is that of a bird. In these myths certain diving birds take it on themselves—or are given the charge by God—to go in search of the earth. In the Brāhmaṇic tradition, however, even though on a similar occasion also connected with the sacrifice, Prajāpati is said to be a bird and is even so represented[26], he appears as a boar in this myth. Although this animal is strictly speaking, not associated with water, it has symbolical meaning as an animal who digs the soil with its snout as if it were a plough. Prajāpati, then, plunges into the water in this very form which is a form that normally is assumed for penetrating into the womb of the earth. The figure of the wild boar begins to take its mythical shape in the Brāhmaṇas, and it seems to be connected with the sacrifice[27]. Here it represents Prajāpati in one of his creative acts, but in later classical Hinduism it remains tied to the figure of Viṣṇu as his third *avatāra*. Viṣṇu is the God of the more recent *trimūrti*, which has retained the closest ties with the cosmic sacrifice: he, like Prajāpati, *is* the sacrifice[28].

This myth, then, brings out once again the Vedic feeling that from the very beginning the earth is constantly moving and fluctuating. But this will not do when this very earth is called upon to support the sacrifice. In this case the earth should be held firm and not be allowed to be like "a lotus-leaf" floating on the waves or blown by the wind. This too is, therefore, a

24. Cf. M. ELIADE, op. cit., p. 76 ff. especially p. 77 (It. ed.) where the three immersions are prescribed at the begininng, therefore independent of the negative result of the precedng two. In another version, however, the failed immersions are eight, and only at the ninth does the Devil succeed in bringing to the surface the earth needed for creation.

25. Cf. M. ELIADE op. cit., p. 73 and 105 f. (It ed.)

26. Cf. further on in ch. VII where *agnicayana* is discussed.

27. Cf. e.g. TaittSam IV. 2. 4. 2 f. where Viṣṇu or *varāha* is the sacrifice that runs away and is conquered back by Indra; etc.

28. Cf. SatBr V. 2. 3. 6 : *yo vai viṣṇuḥ sa yajño*...and his right over the sacrifice comes to him—as we shall see—through a ritual victory over sacrifice itself.

necessity directly derived from offering the sacrifice. The sacrifice is a potent, stable and weighty action: it cannot fluctuate. The point at which the divine world —the macrocosm—enters into contact with the microcosm must be similarly stable. "This is the reason why the priest collects pebbles", concludes the text[29].

The material has been thus collected and the collected objects "are five because quintuple is the sacrifice, quintuple is (its) victim as five are the seasons of the year"[30]. According to the Taittirīya School of the *Kṛṣṇa* Yajurveda, the objects to be collected are fourteen, seven from the earth and seven from the vegetable kingdom. Added to the list as found in the tradition which we have just examined are for the first group: sand, soil of an anthill or termitary, and mud from a dried puddle—because it is from there that Prajāpati brought up the earth after plunging into the primordial Ocean. In this list water is omitted since this is considered to be an element required for normal washing. For the second group, seven types of wood are to be gathered to nourish the fire. These are : one piece of *aśvattha*, one of *udumbara*,two pieces of *palāśa*, one of *śāmī*, one of *vikaṅkata*, and one piece of wood which has been hit by lightning—though there is a controversy with regard to the latter, possibly for the reason that it is considered dangerous because of the cosmic power which it has absorbed through the lightning.[31]

2. *Preparation of the Fireplaces and Preliminary Rites* :

When everything is gathered and bound in a bundle made of the antelope's skin, is hanged in a safe place at a short dis-

29. SatBr II. 1. 1. 11 (end) *tasmāccharkarāḥ sambharati* //

30. SatBr II. 1. 1. 12 *tān vā'etān / pañca sambhārānt sambharati pāṅktaḥ paśuḥ pañcartavaḥ saṃvatsarasya* //

Note the fluctuating number of the seasons. In some places they appear to be four, five or six according to the ritual exigencies of the moment. The same number five, as already seen, symbolizes to the complete sacrificial offering (cf. BharSS VII. 16. 4 quoted in note 93 Ch. V) and to the *agnicayana* (in SatBr VI. 1. 2. 17 f.) as we shall see in Ch. VII, fn. 12.

31. Cf. TaittBr I. 2. 1. 1-7 and BharSS V. 1.5 including the controversy on the dangerousness of the last piece of wood. Heat added to heat may be very dangerous, especially if one of the two types of heat is a cosmic one. Nevertheless, if one knows how to handle it, it can be very powerful.

tance from the place chosen and prepared for the kindling of the new fires, one is ready to begin with the rite proper. The *adhvaryu* is the one in charge of the material part of the work to be done. It is he who takes the measurements fixing the distances between the fireplaces according to the orientation and the lay of the land. He divides the space into two with a line running from West to East and then sweeps and cleans well the side chosen on which to erect the *gārhapatya* which must be *circular*, and digs out the pit. The fireplaces which must be constructed, as we have said, are generally two, sometimes with a third added, the *anvāhāryapacana* or *dakṣiṇāgni* and more rarely two others linked with the *āhavanīya*, namely, the *sabhya* and the *āvasathya*. The order in which the two principal fireplaces are to be constructed varies according to the caste to which the *yajamāna* belongs and to the specific purpose for which they are to be used. Precedence is normally given to the *gārhapatya*. Starting from this the prescribed distances are then measured to where the *āhavanīya* would be constructed and to where the other fireplaces. The rules which determine the distances between the fireplaces vary according to the caste to which the sacrificer belongs since they have got to agree with the verses of the *mantra* that every person has to pronounce according to his caste: eight paces for the Brāhmaṇa who recites the eightfold *gāyatrī*, eleven paces for the Kṣatriya who recites the *tṛṣṭubh* of eleven *padas*, and twelve paces for the Vaiśya who recites the *jagatī* with twelve *padas*.[32]

When the pits for the construction of the two principal fireplaces are dug out, the *yajamāna* starts to observe a vow (*vrata*) and for this purpose, his priest i.e., the *adhvaryu*, and the supervisor of the sacrifice, the *brahman*, go in solemn procession to the house of a Vaiśya according to the texts, (or according to modern usage to the house of a Brāhmaṇa who is well-known and of goods reputation) to take a fire-brand from his *gārhapatya* and bring it, again in solemn procession, to the spot where the new *gārhapatya* has been just dug out[33]. On this provisional fire

32. Cf. SatBr I. 7. 3.23 ff. for the *Śukla* version and BharSS V. 2.13 ff. for the *Kṛṣṇa* one.

33. Cf. BaudhSS in SK vol. I, part I, p. 14, par. 7. I have integrated the passage with information coming from the living tradition of the *paṇḍits*. Cf. also

is cooked the *brahmaudana*, a rice mush, which must then be divided into four equal parts and distributed by the future *yajamāna* to be eaten by the four principal priests who are participating in the erection of the fireplaces[34]. This provisional fire may remain lit for a whole year, or only for twelve, four, three days, or even for only one day, depending on the duration of the *vrata*[35]. The practice of eating the *brahmaudana* is not, however, supported by the Śatapatha Brāhmaṇa[36] which while taking note of it in other schools, does not favour it. The Brāhmaṇa, on the authority of Bhāllabeya, objects that, since this fire is only provisional, nothing should be fed into it to keep it alight because this would amount to a consecration which is unacceptable in the case of a provisional fire.[37] Hence it would be better not to cook anything on it and have the Brāhmaṇas fed from the domestic fire. According to the Sūtras, however, the rite of the *brahmaudana* is important and it must be performed at least once, at the end of the *vrata* of the *yajamāna* while he still has his provisional fire.

During his *vrata* the new *yajamāna* must make a vow not to eat meat, not to have sexual intercourse with any woman, not to sit on high stools and not to sleep[38]. Finally, on the eve of the day when the fireplaces have to be erected, the *yajamāna* ends his period of *vrata* by observing, together with his wife, the prescribed fast and by keeping vigil the whole night playing the *viṇa* and watching over the provisional fire lest it should die out[39]. The fast and the vigil are explained by the texts both as a form of *tapas* to strengthen the *yajamāna* and as a way of paying honour to the Deities who are present at the ceremony and of thus fulfilling one's duties of host in their regard.

---

KatyaSS IV. 7.14f. where the kindling of an independent fire is prescribed, or its collection from a house of a Vaiśya is recommended. The oral tradition speaks however of the house of a Brāhmaṇa.

34. Cf. BaudhSS ib. p. 15; BharSS V. 3. 2ff. both giving great importance to the *brahmaudana*.

35. Cf. BhrSS V. 2. 26 for the *Kṛṣṇa* recension, and KatySS IV. 8. 9 for the *Śukla*.

36. Cf. SatBr II.1. 4.4.

37. Cf. SatBr II. 1.4.6.

38. Cf. BharSS V. 3.21 sq.

39. Cf. BharSS V. 4. 2 ff.

In fact, as we have already seen in case of the *paśuyajña*, the Deities are by now so dependent on the sacrifice and so desirous of eating the sacrificial victim that, as soon as they guess the intention of the *yajamāna* to offer a sacrifice, they hurry to his house even from the night before. Their arrival will forbid him to take any food without serving his guests first and to sleep in their presence while they obviously remain awake[40]. However, the Śatapatha Brāhmaṇa is not so rigid in this respect, at least with what regards the young *yajamāna* on the occasion of his first kindling of the fire. In fact, while they certainly prescribe these rules similar to those of any other *vrata* observed during a sacrifice, the authorities of the Śukla Yajurveda are more indulgent with the young man who is preparing himself to have his own fire but who does not actually have it yet "since the observance of the vow is not necessary on the part of him who has not yet performed the *agnyādheya*. So long as he has not yet established his own fire, in fact, he is only a man and can therefore eat (or sleep)[41] if he so desires"[42].

With this sentence the Brāhmaṇa authorities testify once again to the transformation wrought by the sacrifice on him who offers it. Before any initiation, the one who submits to it is not yet transformed and therefore still belongs to the old order, here too, before and during the ceremony of the first kindling of his fires, the neo-sacrificer is not yet transformed but still belongs to the old order, the human order with its weaknesses and deficiencies. He is still a man (*manuṣya*) and it does not matter whether he conforms himself or not to behaviour which is proper to another level of life. At the same time they also testify that, after the fires are kindled and installed in his sacrificial house the *yajamāna* will no longer be at liberty to behave in accordance with his frail human

40. Cf. SatBr II. 1. 4.2 ff & 7.

41. Cf. SatBr II. 1. 4. 7

42. SatBr III. 1. 4.2...*kāmam eva naktam aśnīyānno hānāhitāgner vratacaryāsti mānuṣo hy evaiṣa tāvad bhavati yāvadanāhitāgnis tasmād....*

This rather loose attitude to the rules seems to be a characteristic of this Brāhmaṇa, because it is rather indulgent towards the *yajamāna* also in such initiatic rites as those which appear in the *agnicayana* (see below in Ch. VII). The *śrauta* texts which impose them, consider such rites to be a proper *dīkṣā*, while the Śatapatha Brāhmaṇa, by denying them this status, can easily exempt the sacrificer from maintaining these vows.

nature since by then he would have divested himself of his condition of *manuṣya* to put on another nature. He will put on this new condition in due time when with the recital of some special *mantras* all the preliminary rites will have been performed, that is when the more immediate preparations for the kindling of the new fire are about to begin.

3. *Kindling of the Sacred Fire* :

At the break of dawn, on the day chosen for the final preparation of the fireplaces and the long-awaited kindling of the fire, the *adhvaryu* starts warming on the provisional fire two pieces of (*aśvattha*) wood taken from an *aśvattha* tree on which a *śāmī* tree is grown. These two are the fire sticks, named the *araṇis*, which are called the parents of Agni, because it is through their rubbing together that fire is produced. The priest hands them over to the sacrificer who recites *mantras* over them. These *mantras* ask blessings from Agni who is about to be born and at the same time commence the transformation of the sacrificer. "Come on my ten fingers; come to me with *ṛta*, fullness of life, splendour (*varca*) so that by living for many years, I may be able to offer for a long time the sacrifice of the new noon and the full moon"[43]. Taking a vow to keep silence during the time necessary to churn the fire, the *yajamāna* prays and says: "From falsehood, I approach the truth (*anṛta*...*satya*); from the human, I approach the divine; I keep in the divine word"[44]. Finally, when the sun rises and its light touches the top of the trees, the fire is produced by friction. This is done by the *yajamāna* himself, at first together with his wife and assisted by the *adhvaryu*, then by himself.

Today it might seem absurd to surround with so many precautions and so much symbolism an act which is really quite simple. Still the production of fire in this way is not easy and runs the risk of failure. Fire is the only natural element which is not found in nature ready-made but has to be got at. It is true that all peoples at a certain stage of culture have had first to discover it

43. TaittBr I. 2. 1. 14 *ārohataṃ daśataṃ śakvarīr mama / ṛtenāgna āyuṣā varcasā saha / jyogjīvanta uttarām uttarāṃ samām / darśamahaṃ pūrṇamāsaṃ yajñaṃ yathā yajai* / Cf. anche BharSS V. 4. 8.

44. TaittBr I. 2. 1. 15 *anṛtāt satyam upaimi / mānuṣād daivam upaimi / daivīṃ vācaṃ yacchāmi* / Cf. also BharSS V. 4. 9; BaudhSS. II. 15.

and then to learn how to maintain it and eventually learn how to produce it. It is also true that the ways they discovered to produce it turned out to be practically the same everywhere—that is, by percussion of two stones, or by the friction of two pieces of wood. And yet, nowhere has the production of fire assumed such a cultic significance, so important and dramatic at the same time, as in Vedic culture. The Vedic people were evidently more sensitive to the fire and its heat in a 'visceral' way, so to say, than most of the other peoples, so much so that as far as we know, in no other mythology is such a high divine status accorded to Fire. Moreover, for such a speculative mind as the Brāhmaṇic, so attentive to everything which happens in nature and so sensitive to the least emotion connected with any new birth, the process of kindling fire appeared pregnant with symbolism and hidden meaning. The author of these lines once assisted at such a birth of a sacred fire. The sudden appearance of smoke coming from a piece of dry wood stirs up such emotion that it defies description. To be present at this event, in appropriate circumstances, is to experience something of a theophany. Agni is born unexpectedly, preceded by the appearance of smoke and of a black burnt mark which like a small eye made of embers, indicates the place where the God will soon appear. As soon as it is born, then, Agni is placed by the *yajamāna* and the *adhvaryu* in a cradle made of soft combustible material and rocked to and fro for it to catch as much air as possible. This practice is the practice which prevails now-a-days because the breath is considered to be impure. In the past, however, the *yajamāna* used to breath on it reciting a *mantra* while breathing in and another one while breathing out[45]. The Taittirīya School stresses even further the mediatory function of the newly-born fire between the human and the divine. As the *yajamāna* receives the newly lit fire, he is made to pray: "I take in myself, from the beginning, this fire so that I may have an abundance of wealth, good offspring and good health; I take in myself offspring, in myself splendour so that I remain unharmed in my person and become rich in brave heroes. This Agni, O Fathers,

45. Cf. KatyaSS IV. 8. 26 f. and also BharSS V. 6. 4.

who immortal has entered in us mortals, we receive in ourselves so that he may not leave and abandon us''[46].

At this point, according to the Taittirīya School, the *adhvaryu* prepares the *gārhapatya* fireplace with a third part of the material previously collected, pronouncing a formula with every object he deposits there. Then the new fire, protected by the horse which has assisted at its kindling as a defence against the Rakṣas-s and other eventual external disturbance, is solemnly deposited in the new fireplace with the formula '*bhūr bhuvaḥ*' or some other formula, depending on the caste to which the *yajamāna* belongs or on the injunctions of the various Schools. Here however, the formula of the *vyāhṛtis* remains incomplete, since the *gārhapatya* is only the first of the fireplaces. The formula will be completed only when the fire is deposited finally and definitively also in the second fireplace, the *āhavanīya*[47].

When the first of the fires is well lit, a part of it is then carried towards the principal fireplace, the *āhavanīya*, which is to the East of the sacrificial area. Then once again a procession is formed which is again guided by the horse and followed by the *yajamāna* and the *adhvaryu*. The latter carries the fire in his hands, while formulae are pronounced propitiating Agni and asking Him to remain and enjoy the offerings[48]. Here the sacrificer is instructed that, while going from one fireplace to another, he must make sure of walking in such a way as to have the wind blowing in his favour, so that the smoke and heat of the fire, considered to be the *ātman*, power and *rasa* of it, are blown towards him, thus imbuing him with their essence. The fire is in fact the breath of the sacrificer and therefore is intimately connected with him and represents him. If, while on its way, it inclined towards the sacrificer and filled him, that means that the divine element has accepted

46. TaittSam V. 7. 9.1 *mayi gṛhṇāmy agre agniṃ rāyaspoṣāya suprajāstvāya suvīryāya / mayi prajāṃ mayi varco dadhāmy ariṣṭāḥ syāma tanuvā suvīrāḥ/ yo no agniḥ pitaro hṛtsvantar amartyo martyām āviveśa / tam ātman pari gṛhṇīmahe vayaṃ mā so asmām avahāya parā gāt* Cf also BharSS V. 4. 11.

47. The laying of the new fire occurs only in these two main fire-places: the *gārhapatya* and the *āhavanīya*. If a third fire, the *Dakṣiṇāgni*, is required, this one does not receive the new fire, but the one which served for cooking the *brahmaudana* and was preserved for this reason.

48. Cf. BharSS V. 8. 1. ff.

its communion with the sacrificer and hence it will penetrate him, strengthening his vital power. If, on the contary, the fire inclined in the opposite direction, that means that it has not accepted this communion and the *yajamāna* may lose his breath and the fruits of the sacrifice if somebody should wish it[49]. In the latter case, the result would not be either the death or the immediate physical weakness of the sacrificer, but as the Śatapatha Brāhmaṇa maintains, if the *yajamāna* is not strengthened by his fire, he only remains internally weak and therefore exposed to the effects of *eventual* maledictions. According to the ritualistic authorities, the inclination of the fire in the opposite direction, during the procession from the *gārhapatya* to the *āhavanīya* does not necessarily mean that the sacrificer is deprived of the benefits of the sacrifice which he will offer on it, or necessarily cause his enemies to lay curses on him. More realistically the 'negative' transfer of the fire could simply mean that it will be inefficacious in affording extra protection *in case* someone would wish him ill and say: "may the sacrifice (or breath) leave him". But even if this curse will positively take place—and this is surely not implied—the *yajamāna* not favoured by his fire, is only exposed to the *risk* that this wish be fulfilled. If he is instead enwrapped in the smoke and heat of the fire during the procession, and if he is able to inhale them, such a possible curse would in all probability remain sterile.

Wheh at last the procession arrives at the *āhavanīya*, the horse, according to the Śukla Yajurveda School, marks with his footprint on a piece of gold placed at the centre of the fireplace, the exact place where the fire will be placed as soon as it is brought there[50]. According to the Taittirīya School, however, to let such

49. Cf. SatBr II. 1. 4.19 f. *taṃ vai tathaiva hareyuḥ / yathainam eṣa pratyaṅṅupācared eṣa vai yajño yad agniḥ pratyaṅ haivainaṃ yajñaḥ praviśati taṃ kṣipre yajña upanamaty atha yasmāt parāṅ bhavati paraṅu haivāsmād yajño bhavati sa yo hainaṃ tatrānuvyāharet parāhṅāsmād yajño 'bhudit īśvaro ha yat tathaiva ṣyat //19// eṣa u vai prāṇaḥ / taṃ vai tathaiva*....Cf also. KatyaSS IV. 9. 11.

The Taittirīya School, however, does not seem to consider such details. It requires that the fire, when taken from the Gārhapatya to be brought towards East (the direction of the Āhavanīya), it should be not raised above the mouth of the Adhvaryu who carries it. Cf. BharSS V. 7. 13.

50. Cf. SatBr II. 1. 4.23 : *athāśvam ākramayati*.

a thing happen would be like opening the gate of the cowshed and losing all one's cattle. It argues that, since the horse represents, in a certain sense, the cattle but is also Rudra himself, if he leaves his footprint on the place where the sacrifice is to be offered, he will have the right to reclaim for himself, in the name of Rudra, every head of cattle acquired by means of the sacrifice[51]. Better then not to let Rudra make him claim and to see to it that the horse make his footprint *near* but not *on* the fireplace and certainly not, in any case, on the exact spot where the fire is to be placed. According to the Śatapatha Brāhmaṇa, on the other hand, the horse represents strength and virility and hence to put the fire where the horse has left the imprint of his energy means to put it on a solid base, endowed with power[52].

The fire is eventually placed at the centre of the fireplace (on or near the footprint of the horse)[53]. First the priest touches the proper place with the fire twice in silence and then he places it there a third and final time with the now completed formula *bhūr bhuvaḥ svaḥ* by means of which the sacrificer is said to conquer the three worlds[54]. The placing of the fire in silence is, according to the Śukla School, an additional way of taking possession of the sacrificial place and of fixing it firmly[55].

Then follow the ceremonies for the other fires, where these are necessary, with fire taken from the *āhavanīya* to light the *sabhya* and the *āvasthya*, and fire taken from the provisional *brahmaudana* to light the *anvāhāryapacana* or *dakṣiṇāgni*. When all the fireplaces

51. Cf. TaittBr I. 1. 5. 9 *paśur vā eṣaḥ / yad aśvaḥ / eṣa rudraḥ //8// yad agniḥ/ yad aśvasya pade'gnim ādadhyāt / rudrāya paśūn apidadhyāt, apaśur yajamānaḥ syāt / yannā' 'kramayet / anavaruddhā asya paśavaḥ syuḥ / pārśvata ākramayet / yathā' 'hitasyāgner aṅgārā abhyavavarteran / avaruddhā asya paśavo bhavanti / na rudrāyāpidadhāti / ti //*

52. Cf. SatBr II. 1. 4. 24 *tam aśvasya pada'ādhatte / vīryaṃ vā 'aśvo vīrya 'evainam etad ādhatte tasmād....*

53. Although if we may give some of the variants in the ritual, we do not intend to look for a general rite behind them, ora rite that can unite all of them. Such a 'mixed' rite does not exist, and never existed. We want only to show how, since ancient times, there were many solutions for one and the same rite, and how every school had its procedures.

54. Cf. SatBr II. 1. 4.25 *sa vai tūṣṇīm evāgra 'upaspṛśati / atho dyacchaty atho paspṛśati bhūr bhuvaḥ svar ity eva tṛtīyenādadhāti....*

55. Cf. SatBr II. 1. 4. 27 *sa yat tūṣṇīm upaspṛśati / tad asyāṃ pratiṣṭhāyām pratiṣṭhanti so 'syām pratiṣṭhita adhatte tathā na vyathate....*

are ready and their fires well lit, there begins a whole series of offerings with which the *yajamāna* establishes himself as sacrificer, qualified to start his career as head of a family—a career which ends only with his death or, after the lapse of at least thirty years with his retirement from active life. The most common sacrifices of his career are the *darśapūrṇamāsa* and the *agnihotra*. But occasionally he may have to offer sacrifices of greater importance, such as the soma sacrifice about a detail of which we shall apeak in the following chapter.

## CHAPTER SEVEN

# CONSTRUCTION OF THE FIRE-ALTAR (AGNICAYANA or AGNICITI)

When the sacrificer has established his own fires in such a way that they become part of himself, he is ready to begin his great sacrificial adventure which will last, as we have just said, till the end of his active life. Normally this cultic activity includes, as we have said, the *agnihotra* (to be offered daily, morning and evening, usually for twenty or thirty years) and nearly so often the *cāturmāsya* or, more commonly, the *darśapūrṇamāsa*, the sacrifice of the New Moon and the Full Moon. If the sacrificer belongs to a social class which permits it—if, for example, he belongs to a royal family, or if he is a man of means and power—he may, on occassion, offer more engaging sacrifices like the *rājasūya*, the *aśvamedha*, and the Soma Sacrifice in any of its seven forms. Among these the *vājapeya* is of such importance that it gives the one who celebrates it the right of bearing its name as the widespread surname 'Bajpeyi' (= *vājapeyin*) testifies today. In what follows, however, we shall not treat of any of the sacrificial complexes mentioned here, but we shall limit ourselves to presenting two ritual details connected with all the ceremonies of the Soma Sacrifice. The first of the two, treated in this chapter keeps us within the general subject regarding the construction of the sacred fire-altar, that is the *agnicayana*. And the second—which will be treated in the next chapter—has to do with the rite of the *pravargya*, a pre-offering within the whole Soma Sacrifice complex, and later included as 'head' in all sacrifices.

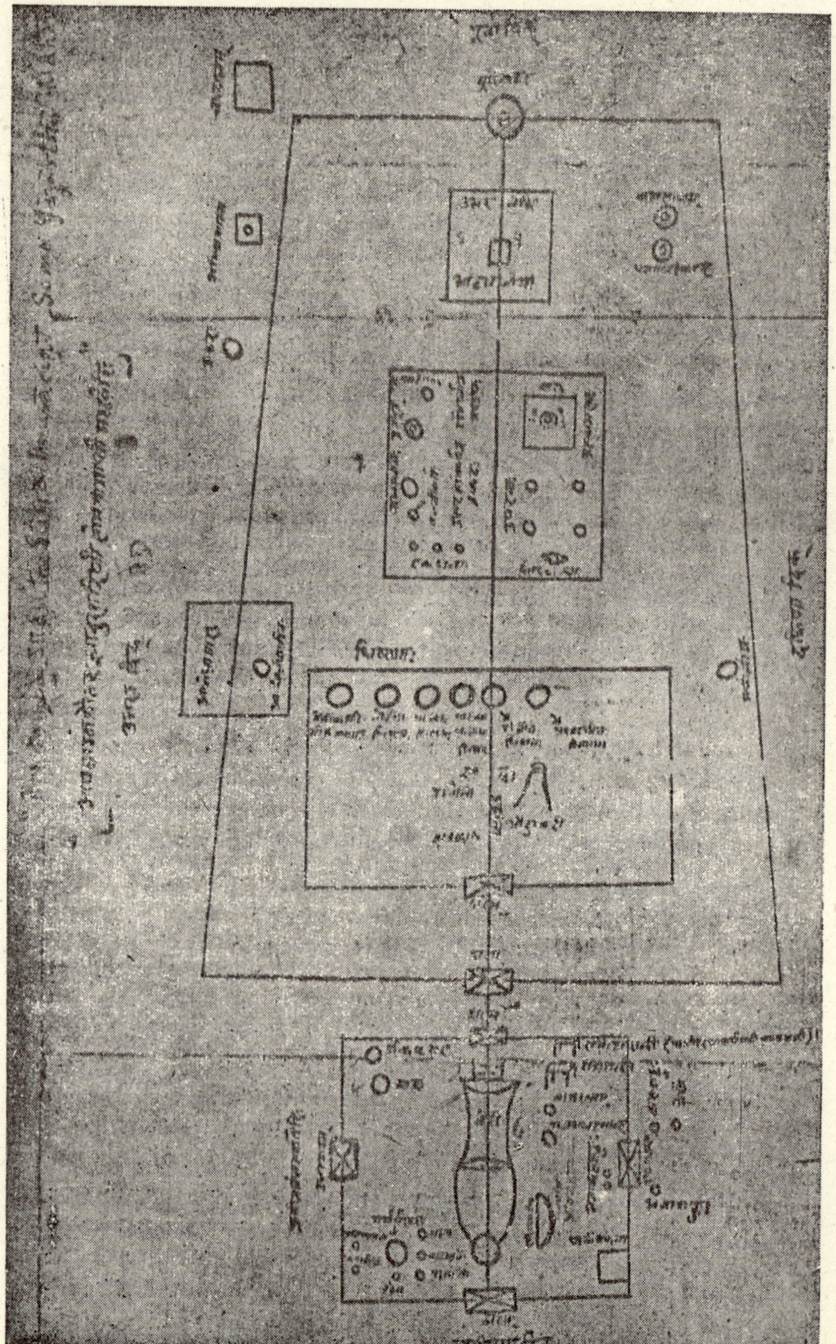

The *agnicayana* is an optional construction of an altar to the East of the *āhavanīya*, in a specific part of the *uttaravedi* during a *somayajña*. If the *yajamāna*, after having established his own fires, decides to perform one of the libation rites of the Soma, he proceeds, first of all, to construct the usual fire-altars in the form required for the intended sacrifice[1] and on them he deposits the fire of his *gārhapatya*. Then, as the rites of this ceremony (i.e. the animal sacrifice, the acquisition of the Soma plant, the various libations in the morning and evening, the rite of the *pravargya*. etc.) are going on, there comes a time when it will be necessary to construct, besides the normal *vedi*, another altár, the *mahāvedi* (See Fig. I). This is constructed to the East of the usual fire-altar. The first *vedi* is surrounded by its usual fire-altars: the *gārhapatya* round, the *āhavanīya* square, the *anvāhāryapacana* (or *dakṣiṇa*) a half-moon, and near them the throne on which will be installed King Soma. Then, further East, is the *mahāvedi*, with the fire-altars of the various priests, and further away the *uttaravedi* with its centre, the *uttaranābhi*. It is not our intention, however, to delay on these details, even though they are very interesting. We shall restrict ourselves only to the *uttaravedi* with its *uttaranābhi*. This is a new altar which, at a certain moment during the ceremony, solemnly receives the fire from the *āhavanīya*, thus becoming, from that moment onwards, the new *āhavanīya* for the rest of the ceremony. The old *āhavanīya* becomes, in its turn, the new *gārhapatya* (retaining its square form), while the old *gārhapatya* (now called 'old', *purāṇa*) is for the time being neglected[2]. It would seem that the solemnity of the rite requires a more potent *āhavanīya* than the ordinary one. Besides, on the *uttaravedi*, to be more precise on the *uttaranābhi*, are deposited, as on an island, the implements of the *pravargya* sacrifice when this is over[3]. After the 'deposition' ceremony—if this is to

1. It is worth remembering that in Brāhmaṇic India, as still today, every sacrificial complex entails a different collocation of altars and fireplaces according to the internal exigencies of sacrifice.

2. Cf. e.g. BaudhSS VI. 24; KatyaSS VIII. 3. 20; etc. Cf. a description of this in W. CALAND & V. HENRY, *L'Agniṣṭoma*, op. cit., p. 79.

3. Cf. below, in Ch. VIII, dedicated to the *pravargya*. Many of the closing ceremonies, however, especially those concerning these rites full as they are of extraordinary sacred heat, have been left out of the present book. They will

be performed—the sacrificer may, if he so wishes, construct on this *uttaravedi*, at his second or third offering of the Soma, a fire-altar which is much more elaborate than the other previous ones and whose construction itself (*agnicayana*) is full of cultic and cosmologico-philosophical symbolism[4]. It is the construction of this special fire-altar which now engages our attention. We shall not, however, describe the entire rite but discuss only some points which are more directly related to our general topic. We shall then discuss: 1. The role of the 'foundation sacrifice' and its meaning in the construction of the fire-altar and of the *ukhā* (the vessel containing the provisional fire); 2. The way the *ukhā* is made and baked, and 3. The use of the *ukhā* and of the *ukhyagni* during the 'initiatory' time preceding the actual *agnicayana*.

The text which treats of the subject most extensively is the Śatapatha, the Brāhmaṇa of the *Śukla* Yajurveda, dedicating to it no fewer than five *kāṇḍas*, that is, practically a third of the whole book. The principal authority on which the presentation and the commentary of this rite are based, is the sage Śāṇḍilya (whereas for the rest of the Brāhmaṇa, the greatest authority is Yājñavalkya). Śāṇḍilya comments on and explains the *mantras* used in the rite as found in the Vājasaneyi Saṃhitā, from about the eleventh to the eighteenth *kāṇḍa*. The same description of this rite is found in the Kātyāyana Śrauta Sūtra from the sixteenth to the eighteenth *adhyāya*. The Taittirīya School also concerns itself with this very important rite. However, this ritual, as it appears in the Taittirīya Saṃhitā (the *mantras* in the fourth *kāṇḍa* and its *Brāhmaṇas* in the fifth), is less developed and less detailed. Hence, not to burden our description with too many variants, we prefer to follow mostly the Mādhyandina School of the Śukla Yajurveda and only occasionally turn to the Taittirīya. Another reason for our preference is that this relates Prajāpati to the procedure followed in the making of certain bricks, which fact bears on the topic of our study.

be tackled in a subsequent essay. The closing ceremonies of these rituals so full of 'sacrality' prescribe many precautions against the damage arising from an excess of heat and of sacrality.

4. Cf. J. EGGELING, *The Śatapatha Brāhmaṇa*, *op. cit.*; see vol. XLIII, Intr. pt IV, p. XIII, who defines this ritual as "..the practical devotional expression of certain dominant speculative theories of the time".

The erection of this special altar, which aims to be permanent —although the permanence seems alien to Vedic constructions, implies both, a deeper cosmological symbolism and a spiritualization of the relationship of the sacrificer with the supreme God, Prajāpati. The *agnicayana* is the body of the God,—and hence of the *yajamāna* which is to remain in concrete form in the world. Therefore, the sacrificer, according to an injunction laid down by the texts, should be his own *adhvaryu* because, given the difficulties and the cosmological symbolism in the construction of the altar (which is Prajāpati himself) in such a task no one can act *in the name of another*[5]. The *adhvaryu* in so doing would help with his own body to build up the body of another person. In fact in this rite is carried on a triple identification: that of Agni (i.e. the Altar), of Prajāpati and of the *yajamāna*. Thus, it is the performer of the sacrifice himself who undergoes metamorphosis and so becomes identified with the Divinity and this identification he must achieve by himself. He has, therefore, to act for himself.

This injunction, however, should limit the possibility of constructing the *agnicayana* during the ceremony of the Soma Pressing, to only Brāhmaṇas as yajamāna. But in reality, the same Śatapatha Brāhmaṇa lays down rules to be observed in case the *yajamāna* happens to be *kṣatriya*[6] or of another caste, thus implicitly accepting that the original injunction need not always be observed to the letter.

### 1. *The 'Foundation Sacrifice' and Baking of the Brick 'Earth'* :

The *agnicayana* is a superstructure of baked bricks, built on the *uttaravedi*, more precisely on the *uttaranābhi*. It has the shape of a bird in flight, stylistically represented with spread wings, a body, a tail and facing East with its beak jutting out. Its measurements are those of the sacrificer himself or their multiples.[7]

5. Cf. KatyaSS XVI. 6. 14 which refers to SatBr IX. 5. 2. 12 and ff.

6. Cf. e.g. SatBr VI. 6. 3. 12-15; cf. also SatBr IX. 3. 4. 1 and ff. where the initiatory note of the *agnicayana* seems to refer to a king (cf. J. EGGELING, *Śatapatha Brāhmaṇa, op. cit.*, see, pt IV, Intr. p. XXVI) and also KatyaSS XVI. 4. 41 f.

7. Cf. e.g. SatBr VI. 5. 3. 2; KatyaSS XVI. 3. 21; etc.

It is constructed only at the second or third offering of Soma by a given sacrificer, but as we said before, it remains optional (except in the case in which the sacrifice is a *mahāvrata*).[8] This means that its construction must, on the one hand, be important enough to be justified, yet on the other hand, it could not be of such relevance that its omission could compromise the efficacy of the Soma rite.

The rite, as we have said, is long and complicated. It is performed during the course of the *agniṣṭoma*, or of other offerings of the Soma, both before and after the plant is obtained, and after the conclusion of another ancillary rite—that of the *pravargya*[9]. Generally it requires a whole year, during which the *yajamāna* undergoes a special *dīkṣā*, without however interrupting his other duties as a sacrificer of the Soma.

The *agnicayana* starts with the solemn *pūrṇamāsa* sacrifice, preferably in the month of Phālguna (about the middle of February)[10]. Five victims are immolated[11], as five will be the layers of the firealtar, five the seasons and five the components of the body of Prajāpati[12], who is the altar about to be built. The five victims, the heads of which are embedded in the base of the

8. For this reason and because of its complexity some scholars (see e.g. A. B. KEITH, *The Religion and Philosophy of the Veda and Upaniṣads*, op. cit., p. 354, pt. III, ch. XX) thought this rite was not frequently performed. Nevertheless, its erection by a *yajamāna* gave him the right to erect also a *loṣṭacayana* (or *loṣṭaciti*) on his bones after his cremation.
This was probably a sufficent reason by itself to suppose that its performance was not too rare after all. Even today, whenever there is a Soma ceremony to be performed, the *agnicayana* is present, regardless of its difficulties. For the description of the *Loṣṭaciti* cf BaudhSS XVII. 30 & BaudhPrMed. I. 14-16 and ib. 11. 3 for the limitation mentioned above (SK op. cit., vol. I. pt II, p. 1049). Cf. on the *Agnicayana* **a study published by F. STAAL** *The Agnicayana* (Motilal Banarsidass).

9. Cf. below Ch. VIII.

10. Cf. SatBr VI. 2. 2.18 and KatyaSS XVI. 1. 5.

11. Cf. SatBr VI. 1.2 ff. describing the myth and KatyaSS XVI. 1.5 ff. for the ritual prescriptions.

12. Cf. SatBr VI. 1. 2. 17 sqq. *tad etā vā asya tāḥ | pañca tanvo vyasraṃsanta loma tvaṅ māṃsam asthi majjā tā evaitāḥ pañca citayas tad yat pañca citīś cinotyetābhir evainaṃ tat tanūbhiś cinoti yaccinoti tasmāc citayaḥ||17|| sa yaḥ sa prajāpatirvyasraṃsata | saṃvatsaraḥ so'tha yā astyaitāḥ pañca tanvo vyasraṃsantar tavaste pañca vā 'ṛtavaḥ pancaitāś citayas tad yat pañca citīś cinoty ṛtubhir evainaṃ tac cinoti yac cinoti*

firealtar, are the five victims of the great principal sacrifices : that is, man, the horse, a young bull, the ram and the goat[13]. The man, who must be either a *vaiśya* or a *kṣatriya*[14], is not different from any of the other victims, nor has he any special part to play[15].

However, to have five victims which are all central to their respective sacrifices is not normal in a single Vedic *yajña*. It is true that in a sacrificial complex there can be many secondary victims but these are indeed secondary and surround the main one, which remains alone. Moreover, here the victims are treated differently from the way generally imposed by Vedic liturgical rules. These rules usually prescribe the dismemberment of the immolated victims, their cooking and their offering as *vapā* and *havis*. Here, instead, only the cutting of their heads is required so they can be embedded in the altar. The complete ritual of the offering of *vapā* and *havis* is performed only with the last victim, the goat, which is the most important one since it cannot be left out even if the rite is simplified[16]. The bodies of the other victims are 'thrown away', instead, in marsh from which the clay for the *sambhāras* of the bricks and of the *ukhā* will be taken[17].

None of these procedures have counterparts in other Vedic rituals and therefore need to be explained by a myth of their own. An analysis of this myth gives us an idea of the effort made by priests and exegetes to amalgamate in their own religious tradition rituals which seem to have been alien to it.

*tasmāc citayaḥ //18//. . . . atha yā asya tā ṛtavaḥ pañca tanvo vyasraṃsanta diśas tāḥ pañca yai diśaḥ pañcaitāś citayas tad yat pañca citīś cinoti digbhir evainaṃ tac cinoti. .* . ./19 Cf. also SatBr VI. 2. 1. 15 f.; VI. 3. 1. 2.

For the importance of the number five see also ch. VI, p. 157 and especially the text quoted in note 30, and also Ch. V, note 93.

13. SatBr VI. 2. 1. 2 ff. esp. 6 and 16-19 for the order of immolation; cf also KatyaSS XVI. 1. 8 ff.

14. Cf. KatyaSS XVI. 1. 17 *vaiśyaḥ puruṣo rājanyo vā* /

15. At most he is treated with special care and regard, as having a longer rope tightening him, or a special place where he is "quieted". Cf. SatBr VI. 2. 1. 16-19 & KatyaSS XVI. 1. 9-14.

16. Cf. SatBr VI. 2. 1. 29 (end) and VI. 2. 2.1 ff. esp. 7 ff. KatyaSS XVI. 1. 15 & 36.

17. Cf. SatBr VI. 2. 1.7 & KatyaSS XVI. 1.19.

(a) *The Myth* :

The myth which introduces and explains the necessity of the fivefold sacrifice in the *agnicayana* is complex, proceeding by means of elaborated reflections made by Prajāpati himself which perhaps mirror the perplexity of the liturgist who found himself obliged to include it in the Soma sacrifice. The general features of the myth lead us to think that important though it may be because of cosmological doctrine, this rite must have been only with difficulty accepted into Vedic culture.

In the Śatapatha Brāhmaṇa the myth opens with a majestic vision of a time when only the not-being existed : "Om, the not-being here at the beginning was"—(*om, asad vā idam agra āsīt*)[18]. This Non-being then concretized itself in the seven *ṛṣis* who, in their turn, become the seven *puruṣas*. But they soon become aware that, being many, they could no longer create. They had, therefore, to concentrate their life-sap (*rasa*) in the top part of their bodies, the head, to form in this way only one *puruṣa* who becomes Prajāpati in performing his creative act[19].

The 'beginning of times' is here described differently than elsewhere in the same Brāhmaṇa. Normally the sequence is from the One to the many and not vice-versa. The idea behind the collecting of the *rasa* in the head is a way of justifying the alien ritual of embedding just the heads in foundations of the altar. There is, however, something even more important to justify, that is, the necessity of having a fixed altar. Thus, the myth continues by explaining that Prajāpati creates by means of his self-immolation, and that, being half mortal, he risks at the end of every creative (and sacrificial) act to be dissolved in his own creation[20]. Now, the most obvious way for him to avoid this fate is to build for himself a body which will defy the passage of time. And what else could the body of one who has identified himself with the cosmic Sacrifice be except an altar ? However, the altar

18. SatBr VI. 1. 1.1.

19. Cf. SatBr VI. 1. 1.2 ff.

20. Cf. SatBr VI. 1. 1. 1 ff. The narration of this 'myth' continues for about two *Adhyāyas*. See also SatBr. X. 4. 2. 2. Cf. exposition and comments of this famous myth in S. LEVI, op. cit., p. 24 ff; L. SILBURN, *Instante et cause*, op. cit.; R. PANIKKAR, *Myth, Faith, Hermeneutics*, op. cit., ch. 5 and also the Conclusion of this book.

is normally neither fixed nor durable, while the Creator is looking for a durable body as a means of overcoming his constant fear of becoming exhausted in every sacred action. How to proceed then to make an altar durable and 'immortal' ? The myth tries to explain this.

The myth tells us that, to realize his project, Prajāpati wants to re-absorb in himself the energy, splendour, and brilliance that he has bestowed on his first born—Agni. Thus the Creator goes after him. But, guessing his father's intentions, Agni escapes from him and goes to hide himself in the five victims which he 'sees' (*paś*) [21] in front of him. However, Prajāpati too, pursuing, sees the 'victims' (*paśu*) in front of him and, realizing that it is in them that lies the hidden form of him whom he wants to absorb again, takes hold of them to immolate and embed them[22] in the altar. The myth seeks to explain not only why the Creator needs to have an immortal body, but also why this body requires a founding sacrifice of five primary victims. The very necessity of an explanation indicates that the ritual was considered 'abnormal'. The addition of secondary victims in the *paśuyajña* linked to the *aśvamedha,* for instance, or the normal offering of victims in connection with the various Soma rites, needs no explicative myths. At most the Brāhmaṇas indicated their function. Here, however, the myth dwells upon the way Prajāpati felt the need to take hold of the victims and immolate them. No such need was felt on the occasion of the first kindling of the fires of the sacrificer even though the fixing of the fireplaces required that the earth be first held firm[23]. Whereas in the case of the kindling of the fires importance is given to the very act of kindling the sacrificial fire which is 'mobile', in the case of the building of this fire-altar we witness, perhaps for the first time, the erection of a construction made to last, indeed as the myth would have it, to last for ever.

21. Cf. SatBrVI. 2.1.2f.

*sa (agni) etān pañca paśūn apaśyat | puruṣam aśvaṃ gām avim ajamṃ yad apaśyat tasmād ete paśavaḥ ||2|| sa etān pañca paśūn prāviśat | sa ete pañca paśavo 'bhavat..||3||*

22. Cf. SatBr VI. 2. 1. 4 f.

*sa (prajāpatiḥ) etān peñca paśūn apaśyat....||4|| sa aikṣata | ima vā'agnir imān evātmānam abhisaṃskara vai....).*

23. Cf. above in Ch. VI, p. 153.

(b) *The Foundation Sacrifice* :

The 'general syntax' of the liturgy[24] prescribes that stable constructions should be strengthened at their foundation by sacrifices with victims prevalently human. In the myth, Prajāpati, and with him the Brāhmaṇic priest, perceive this need. Does the myth lead us back to a time when a sacrifice performed at the foundation of an edifice entered to form part of the Vedic cult? The priest, who wants to keep his Deity present in a form which can be maintained visible and 'immortal' even after the sacrifice is over, must fortify this form with those requisites necessary for it to stand for a long time. He can do this only by means of an extra quantity of sacred energy. The religious and ritual 'language' in 'general' tells that that 'something' which furnishes this extra sacred energy and therefore permanent stability to the construction is the blood of an immolated victim whose body, or part of it, is embedded in it. And here lies the explanation for the actions of the Brāhmaṇa priest (and of Prajāpati himself) when he constructs this strong and durable fireplace without, of course, bothering with the blood which has already been discarded from the start because of internal exigences[25]. Since the tradition of offering a sacrifice at the founding of an edifice most probably did not exist in Vedic culture, the reason which is contrived for justifying the presence of the victims could not be expressed according to this line but is sought for in that way of thinking in symbols which sees things as standing for other things : Prajāpati 'sees' in the victims Agni.

24. We recall here that the "syntax" of the rituals is, as all syntaxes, a product of reflection on some data. It is, therefore, not introduced here as a conscious motif of the ritualistic activity of the ancient Vedic people, but as the result of a comparison of rituals made under the aegis of Historico-religious Studies. We call 'general' the ritual rules common to many religions and reconstructed on the basis of concrete data taken from the various religions of the world. Yet, the brāhmaṇic priests have the feelings of the existence of such rules, even if unconsciously. Theirs is, perhaps, an attempt of adapting external 'rules', valid amongst surrounding people, into their own internal religious framework. Possibly, even if the sacrifice of foundation is not found in the Vedic structure, it was well represented amongst the autochthon population, as attested by the presence of foundation sacrifices even in modern India. Cf. the same discussion on a grammar or syntax of rituals in p. 2 of Introduction and of Ch. V, p. 110 f.

25. Cf. above Ch. V, par. c, p. 116.

Here we may add another observation. The victims, which are normally immolated in the *paśuyajñas* ancillary to the great sacrifices, never include all the five great sacrificial species, and certainly not man. At most, man can be the principal victim of a *puruṣamedha*, as the horse is of an *aśvamedha* and the cow or the ox of a *gosava*. The great victims are not offered in ancillary rites. However, according to the language of the sacrifice, the best victim for such a foundation sacrifice is a man[26]. In India, however, human saerifice was rare and of less importance than the others[27]. It is reasonable to suppose that, as the foundation sacrifice had to include at least one of the principal victims, the Brāhmaṇas thought more desirable, for the greater efficacy of the sacred act to include all the victims of the great sacrifices, indeed all the sacrificial victims in descending order of importance[28]. At this point the Brāhmaṇic narrative, in order to justify the presence and the role of all these victims (of which only one is to be offered integrally), has to suggest a reason which is valid in the context of its own cult. Even so, it is certainly an anomaly in the Vedic cult to immolate all the five principal victims in an ancillary ceremony of a ceremony which is itself ancillary. This explains why the myth portrays the flight of Agni and of its being 'seen' by Prajāpati in the victims.

But there is more. The foundation sacrifice follows its own rules not only in the choice of victims but also in the way it treats them. Here again the treatment accorded to the victims has no precedent in the various animal sacrifices we have analyzed so far. The essential part of the animal sacrice is the offering of the *vapā* and of the *havis* of the victims.[29] But in the foundation sacrifice the fate reserved for them is that they be embedded in the base

26. The main victim of foundation sacrifices was almost all over the world a human being (a man, a child or a virgin). Where it was replaced, it was either with 'another' animal, or rather with the shadow of a man. Cf. J. G. FRAZFER, *The Golden Bough*, abridged edition, London (MacMillan) reprinted 1961 (or 1922), p. 252 f. In modern India, the rare cases of human sacrifices are most often foundation sacrifices for houses, dams, bridges.

27. Cf. above note 3, at the beginning of Ch. V.

28. Cf. e.g. the series of main victims and their descending degree of excellence in AitBr VI. 8 (I. 2. 8) and SatBr I. 2. 3.6 quoted in note 130, Ch. V.

29. Cf. KatyaSS XVI. 1. 15 and Ch. V, p. 117 ff; p. 141 ff.

of the construction which is to be fortified. Thus as soon as Prajāpati of our myth gets hold of the victims and immolates them, he is immediately faced with another technical problem which he is to solve in a way which is more consonant with the 'general' tradition of the sacrifice in general throughout the world than with his own, the Vedic. Prajāpati, and his priests, must justify in their own eyes the fact that it is not necessary for the great victims, except the goat, to be cooked and offered on the fire as *havis*, but rather that their heads be embedded in the base of the construction in accordance with the 'general' rules governing the foundation sacrifiee. But to be valid, the justification must spring from the 'particular' rules of their own tradition. Thus Prajāpati, referring to the cosmogony of his tradition, realizes that the splendour of Agni, which he wants to incorporate in himself, is concentrated precisely in the heads of the immolated animals : "He considered, 'those glories upon which I have set my mind are contained in the heads : well then, I will only put on the heads.' He cut off the heads and put them on himself, that is, the firealtar"[30]. But, from a traditional point of view, the action thus described is not complete; so the myth continues, hesitantly in a way more in line with tradition : "The remaining trunks he then let float on the water, and brought the sacrifice to its completion by means of (the offering of) the he-goat (alone and in its entirety, that is, with its *vapā* and *havis*)"[31].

Everything then should run smoothly. The rules of the 'general' tradition would have been well adapted to those of the 'particular' Vedic tradition and the two types of sacrifice have been integrated into a new rite which has been rendered necessary by this new kind of sacrificial construction. However, the way the narrative continues shows that this adaptation has not been as satisfactory as one would have thought. We read that "though he performed the animal sacrifice, Prajāpati saw that he had not yet reached the end of Agni"[32], that is, he saw that he had not yet

30. SatBr VI. 2. 1.7 : *ṣa aikṣata / yā vai śrīrabhyadhyāsiṣamimāstaḥ śīrṣasu hanta śīrṣāṇy evopadadhā iti..sa śīrṣāṇy evotkṛtyopādhat*..which refers to SatBr VI. 1. 1. 4 where it is said how the splendour of the body is found on the head.

31. SatBr VI. 2. 1. 7..*tāthetarāṇi kusindhāny apsu prāplāvayadajena yajñaṃ samasthāpayannenme yajño vikṛṣṭo'sad tyātmā*....Cf. also KatyaSS XVI. 1.19.

32. SatBr VI. 2. 1.7 : ..*vai yajño nemne'yamātmā vikṛṣṭo asad ity etena paśuneṣṭvā tat prajāpatir apaśyad yathaitasyāgner antaṃ na paryait //*

exhausted the whole potential of Agni in the fireplace. Merely the incorporation of the animals into the fireplace is not enough, either for the Deity or for the poet-priest, for a complete and satisfactory construction of the fireplace-body of the Lord of creatures. The heads of the victims, even though they contain the complete *rasa* of Agni and in them is concentrated the whole essence of the immolated animals, are not sufficient to give to Prajāpati, and to his priests, that sense of completion which they are seeking. The foundation-sacrifice may perhaps be able to sustain and strengthen a construction built in accordance with the 'general' rule, but the heads alone, though they are very important, cannot either guarantee immortality or, and above all, assure that Prajāpati will assume that brilliance of Agni which he (Prajāpati) was seeking to concretize as the visible form of his epiphany on earth during the Soma sacrifice. The Father of the Gods once again overcomes this difficulty by further reflection inspired by the 'general' world sacrificial tradition : since, according to the 'general' world sacrificial tradition, it is the blood which guarantees the stability of the construction, Prajāpati returns to the place where he has left the carcasses to putrefy with the idea of incorporating into himself those parts which he has discarded when he thought they were useless. Once on the spot, however, he does not consider it necessary any longer to gather the animal carcasses by now emptied of their blood and of their *rasa*, and prefers, since he has still to build an altar, to gather the clay and the water on which the carcasses have settled and with them makes a square brick,[33] representing the earth[34], to be embedded

33. The earth is often represented as square because it has the four corners as the four directions. Some other times however it is the sky which is square because of the directions. Cf. G.DUMEZIL, *La Religion romaine archarique*, Paris (Payot), 1966, pt. II, ch. 2, pp. 307 ff.

34. Cf. SatBr VI. 2. 1. 8 : *sa aikṣata | yam imam ātmānam apsu prāpiplavam tam anvicchānīti tam anvaicchat tad yad eṣām apsu praviddhānāṃ pratyatiṣṭhat tā apaḥ samabharad atha yad asyāṃ tāṃ mṛdaṃ tad udhayaṃ sambhṛtya mṛdaṃ cāpaś ceṣṭakām akarottasmād etad ubhayam iṣṭakā bhavati mṛccāpaśca ||* ("he considered 'I must search for that body which I let float on the water'. He searched for it; and what (part) of those (bodies) cast into the water had settled therein, that water he gathered; and what (had settled) in this earth, that clay (he gathered). And having gathered both that clay and water, he made a brick; hence a brick consists of these two, clay and water.") (tr. J. EGGELING).

in the base of the construction which thus reaches the coveted completion. Thus brick is formed of the essence of all the victims.

(c) *Making the Brick 'Earth'* :

The introduction into the myth, of the idea that the brick made by Prajāpati contains the essence of the bodies of the five animals seems to indicate the introduction into the liturgy of a rite as an after-thought, that is, when the Father of the Gods realizes that with the heads alone "he has not reached the end of Agni".[35] In the actual rite, however, the presence of the bodies of the immolated animals in the clay is mainly a manner to consider the *sambhāra* complete, since actually the *sambhāra* cannot be said to be completed without the clay which serves as concrete proof that the rite has taken place. The Śatapatha Brāhmaṇa even rejects the *sambhāra* as invalid if it does not include the bodies of the animals and goes as far as to forbid all or nearly all attempts to replace them by something else in the offering. The tendency in India, dating from the most ancient times, to avoid as much as possible any animal sacrifice, set in motion at a very early date the search for substitutes which were as valid but which did not require the sacrifice of a life. Thus, some theoreticians, knowing that they could not do without them, had them embedded in the base of the construction, bypassing the action prescribed to procure them, namely the sacrifice. For this purpose, they suggested that the heads be obtained, for example, from carcasses of animals which died of natural causes[36], or even that they be replaced by their golden or earthen images[37]. But the Śatapatha Brāhmaṇa, while it does mention these alternatives as suggested by others, condemns them strongly, thus implying that both, the heads of the animals embedded in the base of the construction and their carcasses whose essence impregnated the clay and the water, were irreplaceable elements of this rite—especially the heads. According to this school, what is really important is the sacrifice which vivifies and energizes both

35. *agner antam na paryait*, end of the text quoted above at note 32.

36. Cf. SatBr VI. 2. 1. 37, commented by Sāyaṇa, who suggests to buy or beg them, and KatyaSS XVI. 1. 32.

37. Cf. KatyaSS XVI. 1.33-35 and note 43 of this chapter.

the heads and the clay used in the making of the bricks. Without the sacrifice, not only are the heads deprived of their vivifying and fortifying energy, but there would be no animal bodies to energize the *sambhāra*. It is adamant in this respect : "Now some, having in that way (i.e. without the sacrifice) obtained the heads, put them on (the firealtar), thinking, 'Either way [i.e. either consecrated by the sacrifice or not, as Sāyaṇa says ] they are animals (victims)'. But (by so doing), they become mortal corpses (*martyāḥ kuṇapāḥ*) because their heads are not propitiated"[38]. Ritual slaughter makes the victim satisfied (*prita*) much more than mere profane killing or even a natural death. The Brāhmaṇa goes on to warn that : "in this way, indeed, they put them (the victims) on (the firealtar) for the son of Aṣāḍhā and Suśromatā and he immediately died"[39].

Even the other alternative, of replacing the victims by their golden images is, according to the Mādhyandina School, to be discarded. Its words of condemnation are no less strong than before : "some, moreover, make gold ones [i.e. images of the heads in gold], saying, 'These are immortal (*amṛteṣṭakā*) bricks'. But indeed they are 'immoral' (*anṛteṣṭakā*) bricks' and no heads of victims"[40]. Finally earthen images (*mṛṇmayānyu*) too are rejected since he who has proposed such an alternative does not understand either the theoretical or the practical rules which govern the sacrifice[41]. This authority insists that the immolation of all the five victims as far as possible is the best. In the end, however it too is obliged to permit another alternative, thus perhaps accepting a practice already in use and difficult to suppress, namely, the immolation of the goats alone, "But nowadays only these two (goat victims) are slaughtered, one for Prajāpati and one for Vāyu"[42].

38. SatBr VI.2.1. 37 : ..*ity evaitāni paśuśīrṣāṇi vittvopadadhaty ubhayenaite paśava iti te ha te martyāḥ kuṇapāḥ sambhavaty anāprītāni hi tāni*....

39. SatBr VI. 2. 1. 37 (cont.) : ..*taddha tathāṣāḍheḥ Sauśromateyasyopadadhuḥ sa ha kṣipra'eva tato mamāra* //

40. SatBr VI.2.1.38 : *hiraṇmayānyu haike kurvanti / amṛteṣṭakā iti vadantastā ha tā anṛteṣṭakā na hi tāni paśuśīrṣāṇi*.. On the vivifying power of gold see above ch. V, note 91.

41. Cf. SatBr VI.2.1.39 : ..*yo vā eteṣāmāvṛtaṃ ca brāhmaṇaṃ ca na vidyāt*....

42. SatBr VI.2.1.39 (end) : ..*athaitar hīmau dvāveva ālabhyete prājāpatyaś*

It seems, therefore, that one cannot do away with the immolation. Even today, when the Vedic priest shrinks more than ever from any animal sacrifice, there is still no other way out despite the many proposals already made in antiquity, than this last concession made by the Śukla School.[43]

To conclude, then, the stability which Prajāpati seeks for the construction of an altar as his own immortal body must be obtained and ratified by the irreplaceable foundation-sacrifice in its sanguinary form. This sacrifice is potent as a sacred action in itself, for the luminosity which it spreads on the altar through the incorporation of the heads of the victims, and for the completion it gives to the whole sacrificial complex through the energy with which the bodies of the animals impregnate the clay and water of the *sambhāra* used in the manufacture of the brick representing the Earth.

(d) *Baking the Brick* :

Once the heads of the victims have been embedded in the base of the fireplace, the next ritual act, according to the myth, is the putting in place of the brick, made of clay and water, which as we have seen, also ensures the completion of the firealtar. And here there should be no further problems since the brick has been lawfully obtained and is impregnated with the essence of at least one victim, if not of all the five[44]. But as a matter of fact, it is not so. Prajāpati's reflections, when he is about to put in place the brick, show that once again the Creator himself, together with his priests who fulfil his plans on earth, finds himself obliged to resolve a conflict between what he is doing and the internal exigencies of Vedic sacrifice. If the brick made of clay and water is placed in the base of the firealtar in its crude form, it will not have the power to guarantee either immortality

*ca vāyavyaś ca*..Cf SatBr VI.2.2. which gives the reasons for this double immolation, while ib. vv. 2 & 6 give the reasons for their dedication to Prajāpati and Vāyu. Cf. KatyaSS XVI. 1.30.

43. The immolation of a he-goat is performed today whenever a Soma sacrifice is offered with the building of the *agnicayana* in the form of a *śyena* (bird). But the usage of the five heads of different material such as earth or gold is now the usual custom. Information from a *paṇḍit* of Puna.

44. Cf. SatBr VI.2.1.39 : ..*sa etāneva pañca paśūn ālabheta*..("let him immolate all these five victims").

or stability. On the contrary, in spite of its being the receptacle of the sacrificial power derived from the *sambhāra*, it is considered to be a harbinger of death. Prajāpati, in fact, "considered: 'If I incorporate this brick (as it is) into my *ātman* (into my sacrificial body)[45], a mortal corpse (*martyaḥ kuṇapaḥ*), not freed from evil (*anapahatapāpmā*)[46] I shall remain".[47] The dilemma is indeed strange, and strange it must have appeared to those who felt the need to express it in these terms through the mouth of the Creator ! The brick is necessary for the completion of the construction of the firealtar and for Prajāpati to "reach the end of Agni", but at the same time it is the harbinger of death. It is already 'propitiated'—unlike the heads of animals obtained without the sacrifice[48]—it contains whatever it should contain and, with it, all the potentialities of Agni (as Deity and as fire-place) are fulfilled. Still, according to the Vedic tradition and in the eyes of the Creator himself, all this is not enough to overcome death. The brick is still mortal. In fact it does not yet possess that internal strength which was expected from it because in spite of the presence in it of the *rasa* of animal victims, it is still liable to disintegrate into its primary components. Without this internal strength, it can revert to its former state and extend this reversibility, and hence its mortality, also to the altar, that is to say to Prajāpati himself.

Here again, the 'general' rule cannot be validly applied to this 'particular' context. The solution of the dilemma is sought for and found in the only possible and valid way, that is, the tradition itself. To continue, in fact, to have recourse to 'general' rules, no matter how perfect they may be in themselves, is not sufficient to re-establish an equilibrium between what is demanded by the very nature of things and its particular effect within the ambit of a given culture[49]. Prajāpati, however,

45. Sāyaṇa explains, *in hoc loco*, *ātman* as *śarīra*, and *śarīra* as "sacrificial body".

46. *anapahata* is an epithet referring usually to the dead, *pitṛs*, to distinguish them from the Devas, who are 'free'.

47. SatBr VI. 2.1.9 *sa aikṣata / yadi vā idam ittham eva sadātmānam abhisaṃskariṣye mārtyaḥ kuṇapo'napahatapāpmā bhaviṣyāmi.... /*

48. See above, pp. 180-181 with the notes 36-38.

49. This is a lesson that modern India should learn while adapting itself to modern life.

shows that he does not have as a point of reference, other foundation-sacrifices or other kinds of stable constructions, internal to his own cultic tradition, to let himself be inspired by it. Among a nomad people, as were the ancient Vedics, there were probably no buildings intended to be permanently stable, and the faithful upholders of this tradition never thought of their buildings as permanent constructions, not even at a later stage when they turned to agriculture and a more sedentary way of life, and small kings and landowners built palaces or large buildings to live in[50]. In any case, the only thing which was truly 'stable' in his tradition to which Prajāpati could refer was the sacrifice as such and its offering of the *havis*. In this religious culture, the *havis* is the only thing which was believed to be really immortal and therefore stable in its effects. The paradox is here complete for him who does not share from within this way of looking at things: what is truly 'immortal' and therefore really *stable* is something which is *transitory* by nature because it forms part of an action—and an action is by its very nature an event which is impermanent, transient, always in movement and fleeting—and of an action which is, moreover, destined to make its object disappear in the fire !

The *havis* is a source of inspiration for Prajāpati and his priests and this not only because it is immortal as is the immortality to which they aspire but, and above all, because it has *attained* its immortality by means of a specific action. The Creator, then, needs to do nothing else but to repeat the same action which made *havis* 'immortal', to this still mortal brick, so that it too may undergo the same transformation, and, once it, as brick, has become immortal, it may extend its immortality to Prajāpati's body and consequently, to the whole cosmos—including the *yajamāna*. Hence the Creator decides, "well then, I will bake it on the fire", and his priests comment, "So saying, he baked it on the fire and thereby made it immortal. In fact, the *havis* which

50. One could ask here what kind of material was used for building houses. Possibly even royal palaces were made of raw bricks, since excavations show that buildings of cooked bricks apart from altars are rare. It could also be the case that, whatever the material, 'profane' buildings were not considered 'permanent'.

is cooked on the fire becomes indeed immortal. Hence they bake the bricks on fire and thereby make them immortal".[51] The fire thoroughly and profoundly transforms anything which is entrusted to it, so it gives the bricks baked in it hardness and stability rendering them insoluable in water. The brick, rendered thus 'immortal' on the fire, can for the first time defy the rain and the inclemency of the weather without danger of melting away. The same thing, as we have seen, is said by another Brāhmaṇa of the properties acquired by the baked clay of a vessel, and its newly acquired death-defying property is taken as an illustration of the effect *dīkṣā* can have on the body and spirit of him who submits himself to it[52]. The underlying reason is the same: the passage through fire hardens the mortal matter both materially and spiritually, transforming it into a substance which can withstand the disintegrating and dissolving action of death. 'Immortality' (*amṛta*) defines here its own contours. It is not necessarily an affirmation of 'life' but rather a negation of 'death', an overcoming of death—in our case an interior 'strengthening', a radical change of the material qualities which from 'corruptible'—that is 'decomposable', 'breakable'—become 'incorruptible', 'undissolvable' and 'unbreakable'.

What is more important for us, however, is not so much the comparison just drawn between the baking of the clay and the *dīkṣā*, but how the Brāhamṇa tradition derived the necessity of baking the bricks from the necessity of cooking the *havis* before it can be offered in honour of the Deities. We have seen that from the most accient times, the *ṛṣis* of the Ṛgveda were led to the idea of transforming their offerings by cooking by a process which imposed itself from within their own tradition. The peculiarity, therefore, so characteristic of Brāhmaṇism, of having to transform the offerings before they are rendered fit to be offered or poured again into Agni, must have evolved gradually from the very beginning out of a hermeneutic from within the

51. SatBr VI. 2.1.9 (continuation of the text quoted in footnote 47) : ..*hantaitad agninā pacānīti tad agnināpacat tad enad amṛtam akarod etad vai havir amṛtaṃ bhavati yad agninā pacanti tasmād agnineṣṭakāḥ pacanty amṛtā evaināś tat kurvanti* //

52. Cf. GopBr I. 3. 14, previously quoted in note 32 ch. IV, and further in fn. 102 Ch. VII.

tradition itself until it finally transformed not only the offerings but the rite of which they formed part and the cosmogony itself which was its basis and ultimate justification. Here we see how this idea also imposed itself on the construction of a Vedic altar; as the *havis*, so too the bricks are rendered 'immortal' by means of their passage through the fire. Semantically too, it is the 'sacrificial' offering (*iṣṭa*) which becomes really 'brick' (*iṣṭaka*) hard enough to defy the onslaught of Time. In a subsequent version of the construction of this altar of Agni as the body of the Father, exhausted in his creative work, or, in the expression of a modern author, "dead because he has created"[53], the Gods called to his succour, re-construct his body by means of sacrificial offerings (*havis*) rendered firm and stable with the help of Agni. It is these very offerings (*iṣṭa*) which as such form the bricks (*iṣṭaka*) of the immortal body of the Altar. "The Devas put him together again (that is, they healed him) by means of the oblation (*āhutibhir*) on the fire. And the oblation they offered, itself became a baked brick (*pakveṣṭakā*) and entered him. And because they are produced from the offering (*iṣṭāt*), therefore they are (called) bricks (*iṣṭakāḥ*)." "And hence" repeats the priestly commentator with greater emphasis, "they (i.e. the *Devas* and later the priests) bake the bricks on the fire for by so doing they make an oblation"[54].

Thus the two principal actions described in the myth which serve as model for the construction of the *agnicayana* on the second *āhavanīya* of the *uttaravedi*, that is, both the one attributed to Prajāpati himself and the one attributed to the Devas, his sons, while they reconstitute his body, are directly inspired by the sacrificial offering, the *havis*. But they are inspired in a different way. In the case of Prajāpati, the bricks are baked as the *havis* is and it is because they are thus baked on the fire that they are durable. In the case of the Devas, on the other hand, it is the offering itself (*āhuti*) which is poured into the fire and is converted into a brick fit for the divine body of the altar. We observe here a phenomenon common in the sphere of religion, namely that an

53. "mort d'avoir créé" R. PANIKKAR : *La faute originante*, art. cit.

54. SatBr VI. 1. 2.22 *taṃ devā agnāv āhutibhir abhiṣajyan / te yāṃ yām āhutim ajuhavuḥ sā sainaṃ pakveṣṭakā bhūtvāpyapadyata tad yad iṣṭāt samabhavaṃs tasmād iṣṭakās tasmād agnineṣṭakāḥ pacanty āhutīr evainās tat kurvanti //*

action, which is inspired by another, becomes, in its turn a source of inspiration for still other actions.

This leads us back to the central theme of our study, that is, the essential role heat has in the Vedic liturgical action, so essential that its absence invalidates the rites which, in other religions, would still be perfectly efficacious without it. Here as was also the case in earlier times, the myth reminds us that the necessity of cooking the offerings does not arise from the rite directly but from the realization of the inadequacy of the offering if not cooked. Thus Prajāpati, setting about to construct for himself a stable altar in order to give his body an immortal form, does not immediately bake the bricks but comes to that decision after some thought about the foundation-sacrifice. His thoughts continue along two overlapping paths: the embedding of the heads of the sacrificial victims in the base of the firealtar, and the presence of the essence of their bodies in the clay and water moulded into a brick. The necessity of cooking the offerings comes, as it were, in a third moment, that is, with the realization of the imperfection of all that has gone before, and is applied to the baking of the brick under the influence of what goes on in the sacrifice: "And hence they bake the bricks on the fire, for by so doing they make an oblation"[55]; "he baked it on the fire and thereby made it immortal. In fact, the *havis* which is cooked becomes indeed immortal"[56]. The offering, therefore, is immortal because it has passed through the fire, and in their turn, the bricks, having also passed through the fire, are immortal because they become *havis*. Here cultic motifs intersect and are superimposed in their common quest for immortality.

After the fashioning and baking of the first symbolic brick, the *yajamāna* proceeds, during the period of *vrata*, to collect other clay to fashion the other bricks to be used in the construction of the fireplace. These bricks made during this time are many—their number reaching and surpassing the ten thousand mark. Every brick, or group of bricks, has its own specific shape and name[57] and is manufactured while certain *mantras* are recited, till

55. SatBr VI.1.2.22 quoted in the previous note 54.
56. SatBr VI. 2. 1. 9 quoted previously in note 51.
57. Cf. SatBr VII. 4. 1. 1 ff. and the entire Kāṇḍa VIII.

they finally find their place in the whole body of the construction. Shape, name and *mantra* serve to give the brick, or group of bricks, its proper identity enabling it to support a whole cosmic symbolism and to actualize a whole series of identifications between the micro- and macrocosm.

Besides clay bricks and water, various other objects, representing the various provinces of nature, form a part of the construction. Since the fireplace is Prajāpati who is the Lord of creation before, during and after his act of producing the worlds and their creatures, and it is symbol, therefore, of all the universe, it must contain within itself all the elements necessary to represent everything which can be found in nature. Therefore, besides earth and water, it must contain within itself elements representing the animal kingdom (the heads of the five victims or their substitute) and the vegetable kingdom. Man (essentially the *yajamāna*) is not represented in actual fact by the head of the human victim, but by a small golden figure which, together with a disc symbolizing the sun, is embedded in the first layer of the construction[58]. Various kinds of grass and of grain represent the vegetable kingdom and these together with ample aspersions of ghee (*ghṛta*) are said to supply abundant food to the whole universe, to the earth, to humanity and to the sacrificer[59]. The golden image gets ritual nourishment, *prāṇa* and sacred energy through an aperture made in some perforated bricks in the first, third and fifth layers of the construction. In front of it is also embedded a tortoise (*kūrma*) which is a cosmogonic symbol and a symbol of life. When the construction is finished fire, taken from the *gārhapatya* and the *āhavanīya*, is installed. Before that is done, there are various offerings to be made with the recital of various *mantras*, particularly the *śatarudrīya*, which is accompanied by a continuous libation.[60]

(e) *Agnicayana, half mūrti and half altar* :

The attainment of immortality is man's most deeply felt aspiration. The material body must one day yield to decay and to an earthly end, the desire for survival after death is realized both

58. Cf. SatBr VII. 4. 1. 15 ff.
59. Cf. SatBr VII. 4. 1. 32 ff.
60. Cf. VajSam XVI.

through the continuation of one's lineage and by leaving vestiges of one's passage through life. The presence of monumental edifices and grandiose tombs of the world attests to this desire for survival after death. In India *agnicayana* seems to be a first timid attempt of the kind. As we have seen, Prajāpati exhausted by the sacrifice was in danger of death and so the Devas, his sons, constructed for him a body made of baked bricks imbued with the vitality of the sacrifice, which can resist decay and the ravages of weather and time. This body, which belongs at the same time to the *yajamāna*, can in its turn remain as a lasting vestige of the latter after his bodily death.

Still, in a religious culture which, generally speaking, does not seek to leave lasting traces of itself, the construction of a permanent structure is indicative of a new mentality. Moreover, besides the idea that one can leave behind after death something of oneself, we notice here a new need—on the level of cultured religion and not merely on that of popular religion—for a real and concrete presence of the Deity in the form of an effigy[61]. This may seem perhaps to be a 'compensation' for the growing philosophical tendency to universalize the Divine—a tendency which can be clearly sensed in the more and more abstract figure of Prajāpati. Thus, while, on the one hand, the Divine loses more and more its theoretical contours to gradually disappear into an interrogative pronoun[62], the cultic requirements, on the other hand, feel the need for an ever more concrete representation of It. Here theory and practice seem to balance each other to offer the faithful an equilibrium between his religious belief and ritual practice. When the ancient Vedic people had a very concrete idea of their Deities (as can be seen from the hymns which are dedicated to them), their cult was not in need of effigies—unlike the cult of

61. The other Vedic altars and fireplaces do not have a shape recalling any *mūrti*. The fire-places have geometrical abstract forms and the *vedi*, although thought to be feminine in shape so that it could form a couple with the grass (*veda*) over it, responds more to cultic exigencies than to an attempt to 'anthropomorphize' the cult. The other supposed *mūrti* in Vedic times, that of the *mahāvīra* of *pravargya*, is an interpretation of J.A. B. van BUITENEN which we do not support. See further in Ch. VIII.

62. Cf. my quoted article "Kaḥ, le nomme de Dieu.."

the Indian autochthonous peoples as we know from archeological excavations. As soon as theological reflection runs the risk of rendering the Supreme God too abstract and universal, this God demands an effigy as his "immortal body" so that he may remain present among men in a concrete and palpable way. That is to say, when theory becomes aware that the universalization of the Sacred Action is rendering It too abstract not to risk losing itself into ever more vague impersonal actions, and at the same time becomes aware that the price of the Sacrifice is Death brought about by the periodical dismemberment of the victim and the exhaustion of the Sacrifice itself, practice seeks to obviate this danger by having Prajāpati ask for the construction or reconstruction of a concrete, lasting and immortal body. Hence the erection of the firealtar by a special procedure and in a prominent place of the whole sacrificial area: on the *uttaranābhi* of the *uttaravedi*. It is built in such a way as if to be a *mūrti*, that is an 'image' of the Divine, while remaining faithful to its primary function, namely, that of being an *altar*[63].

To concretize the Divine in a centre of cultic activity rather than in a statue is to achieve a valid compromise between the need for a visible, permanent form of God and that of salvation which can only be achieved by means of the transitory ritual. The image of Prajāpati, more than representing the features of a personal God, must be able to be, by its very nature, the image of an *Action*. The firealtar respects both the requirements of a concrete exteriorization of the Divine Person to adore and of a spiritual interiorization of the salvation sought for by the individual *yajamāna*. One must not forget that the fireplace (*agniciti*) represents both Prajāpati and the sacrificer himself through the Mediator Agni, while its form, that of a bird in flight[64], represents the transitoriness of the whole ritual complex. But once the

63. Cf. an interpretation of the *mūrti* in P. CARACCHI, "The presence of the Divine in the mūrti according to the Purāṇas" in *Purāṇas*, XXIV, 2 (July, 1982) pp. 261 ff., All India Kashiraj Trust, Vārāṇasī.

64. It is interesting to note that, although the *mūrti* of Prajāpati is here in the form of a bird, *śyena*, as in many myths and tales about the creation of the earth (cf note 21 of Ch. VI), in the corresponding Indian myth of fixation of earth which mentions the dive of Prajāpati to the bottom of primordial waters as he does so after assuming the shape of a boar, *varāha*. Cf. Ch. VI, note 20.

'idol', the exteriorization of the Divine, somehow succeeded in penetrating the dynamic Vedic sacrifice, the road was laid wide open for the shift of responsibility for the attainment of salvation from oneself and one's personal efforts to Gods, who manifest, as it were, in their visible and palpable form before the devotee and release him. And this is a great risk for a religion which stored great value in a personal salvation gained through one's own efforts. In vain the Upaniṣadic sages, who are also the champions of the Brāhmaṇic rituals, warn as much as they can against the danger of remitting once again into the hands of the Gods—and Gods now concretized in an exterior form—what they fought to gain through their rituals alone. By praying to an external *mūrti*, man is again surrendering himself to an external Agent, and this, for them, would mean indeed that the denaturalization of Vedic religion is near at hand.

But the sages, to prevent this happening perhaps reacted too drastically, favouring a spiritual interiorization of the sacrifice to the undue detriment of the external rite inasmuch as they want to do completely or almost completely away with visible worship which they deemed too concrete. They hoped to attain immortality solely through meditation. Interiorization, however, when pushed to its extremes, without the support of an exterior ritual, can, in the long run, lead to a situation which is no less critical and difficult than the exaggerated concretization of the exterior cult. The risk of going to either extremes is present in every religious tradition. On the one hand, the natural tendency to externalize the Divine risks leading the individual to abandon personal effort in the quest for immortality and to entrust it exclusively to some exterior Mercy. On the other hand, the fascinating attraction of a pure spirituality stripped of rules runs the risk of dissolving away man and the Divine into a vague abstraction. There should be no deep split between the two : disincaration of the Divine into an abstract absolutism can, in fact, be as dangerous as its incarnation into an 'idolatrous' religion.

Cf. a description of such *śyena altar* in G.R. SHARMA, *The Excavation at Kausambi*, 1957-1959, *Defence in the syenaciti*, Allahabad 1960, by the book review in "East and West" Rome, March 1962.

### 2. *Making and Baking the Ukhā* :

We now pass on to another part of the ceremony of *agnicayana*, important for us because of the effects of heat implied in the rite.

So far we have seen how the *havis* is transformed by cooking, so too the bricks of the firealtar. We shall now examine the treatment accorded to the receptacle made of clay and water in which the sacred fire is put while the making of *agnicayana* is going on : the *ukhā*.

#### (a) *Gathering of the Material* :

When the *yajamāna* together with his priests had gone in procession, preceded by some cultically significative animals such as a horse, a donkey and a goat, to collect the clay and bring the water to make bricks, he had put some of this material into a square hole dug in front of the *āhavanīya*, of which he would, when the time comes, make the *ukhā*, the earthen pot in which the sacrificial fire is to be kept.[65] "Thus, when the time has come to make this important pot the *adhvaryu* goes again in procession to pick up the clay left in the hole and, according to the *Śukla* School, before he does so, he makes the horse used in the procession leave an imprint with its hoof, and makes an offering on it.[66] After this rite, intended to impart to the clay strength and protection, the clay is collected in a bag made of the skin of a black antelope, on which is placed a lotus leaf, and carried, on the back of the animals, to a place near the Northern gate of the *āhavanīya*. There the bag is opened and the clay prepared to be kneaded[67]. However, the clay does not have all it needs to make it sufficiently hard to be turned into a pot, so that other things are added to it to give it the required hardness and solidity. First of all, it is sprinkled with water in which was boiled either resin or the rind of the *palāśa* plant, and then again with the foam resulting from this decoction[68]. Finally, the paste thus made

65. The making and baking of the *ukhā* is treated in SatBr VI. 3.2.1 ff. till SatBr VI. 5.4.17 and by KatyaSS XVI.2.1 ff. till XVI.4.45.

66. Cf. KatyaSS XVI.2.1 ff corresponding to SatBr VI. 3.2.1 for the extraction of the clay and for the other details SatBr VI. 5.1.1. For the oblation to be made on the horse's spur cf. KatyaSS XVI. 2.2.

67. Cf SatBr VI. 5.4.16 ff. and KatyaSS XVI.3.14 f.

68. Cf. SatBr VI. 5.1.1-3 where various justifications are also given and KatyaSS XVI.3.16 f for the procedure.

is strengthened with goat's hair (*ajalomāni*)[69] and with three kinds of powder: sand, stone dust and rust.[70] All this is kneaded and the ingredients added while appropriate *mantras* are recited.

When the paste is ready—with the help of special Deities invoked for the purpose[71]—it is consigned into the hands of the Goddess Aditi, the mother of the Gods, representing the earth. Only she, the Great Mother, can give the supreme blessing and the required firmness to the clay which is to hold Agni in its womb—and which for this reason is called the "womb for Agni"[72]. From this paste, the first wife of the sacrificer cuts a piece big enough for her to make the brick called *aṣāḍhā* (invincible)[73]. This brick measures a foot in length and breadth and is marked with three lines[74]. It is the first to be made because it represents the earth and the earth was believed to be created before the other worlds[75]. The *yajamāna*, in his turn, takes from the paste that quantity which is enough for him to make the *ukhā*, reciting a verse which calls the pot about to be made "the head of *Makha*", that is to say "the head of sacrifice"[76].

(b) *Making the Ukhā* :

The making of the *ukhā* is a delicate affair dense with symbolism. The *ukhā* is called to represent the three worlds and hence

69. Cf. SatBr VI. 5.1.4.

70. Cf. SatBr VI. 5.1.6 : *athaitat trayaṃ piṣṭaṃ bhavati / śarkarāś māyorasas tena saṃsṛjati sthemne...*

71. Cf. SatBr VI. 5.1.9 f.; the quoted verses are in VajSam XI. 55 f.

72. SatBr VI. 5.2.21 : *...mṛṇmayī hy eṣā yonir agneḥ...*

73. Cf. SatBr VI. 5.3.1: *tasyā etasyā aṣāḍhāṃ pūrvāṃ karoti / ...etasyā eva mṛdaḥ karoty eṣāṃ hy eva lokānām iyaṃ mahiṣī karoti mahiṣī hīyaṃ tad yaiva prathamā vittā sā mahiṣī //*

74. Cf. SatBr VI. 5.3.2, and KatyaSS XVI.3.22.

75. Cf. SatBr VI. 5.3.1 quoted above at footnote 74.

76. Cf. SatBr VI.5.2.1 (and KatyaSS XVI.3.23) : *atha mṛtpiṇḍaam apādatte / yāvantaṃ nidhaye 'laṃ manyate makhasya śiro'sīti yajño vai makhas tasyaitacchira āhavanīyo vai yajñasya śira āhavanīyam u vā etaṃ cesyan bhavati tasmād āha makhasya śiro'sīti //*

("He then takes a lump of clay, as much as he thinks sufficient for the bottom part, with 'Makha's head thou art'—Makha doubtless is the sacrifice, and this is its head; for the āhavanīya fire is the head of the sacrifice and that Āhavanīya (fire-altar) he is now about to build: hence he says 'Makha's head thou art'. ") (tr. EGGELING)

the whole universe; initially however it is still a piece of profane clay. Its transformation into a true and proper microcosm is entrusted to the *mantras* which are recited over it at every stage of its moulding. Thus it is transformed into the earthly world when its base is finished, into the atmospheric world when its middle part is strengthened and into the celestial world when the finishing touches are given to its neck. Each part is confided to one of three distinct groups of Deities into which the Vedic Pantheon is divided : namely, the Vasus, the Rudras and the Ādityas. Each group presides over one of the three worlds: the Vasus over the terrestrial world, the Rudras over the atmospheric, and the Ādityas over the celestial. Each group in turn takes charge of making and, therefore of blessing, their respective part of the pot. By their blessing, each group ensures abundance of wealth, in terms of offspring, treasures, cattle, virility and clansmen for the sacrificer[77]. The metres of the *mantras* used are the *gāyatrī* for the terrestrial world, the *triṣṭubh* for the atmospheric and the *jagatī* for the celestial[78].

When the three parts are ready and form one pot, the *yajamāna* encircles it with a horizontal band at the top and further strengthens it with four vertical bands, running down from top to bottom, as its supports, so that "the upper part of it becomes firm by means of the horizontal band and the lower part of it by means of these (vertical bands)"[79]. It could be that these vertical bands serve as four legs, which make it like the *gharma* of the Atharva Veda which is likened to a bull because of its four supports.[80]

77. Cf. SatBr VI. 5.2.3. *dhruvāsīti sthirāsīty etad atho pratiṣṭhitāsīti pṛthivyasīti pṛthivī hy eṣa nidhirdhārayā mayi prajāṃ rāyaspoṣaṃ gaupatyaṃ suvīryaṃ sajātān yajamānāyety etad vai vasava imaṃ lokaṃ kṛtvā tasmin netāmāśisamāśāsata tathaivaitad yajamāna imaṃ lokaṃ...*

This verse is repeated with the same formulas in verse 4 for the Rudras and in verse 5 for the Āditya in the atmosphere and in the sky respectively. See for the usage of these *mantras* KatyaSS XVI. 3.26-28.

78. Cf. SatBr VI. 5.2.3-5.

79. SatBr VI. 5.2.15...*tad yad ata ūrdhvaṃ tad etayā tiraścyā dṛḍham atha yad ato 'rvāk tad etābhiḥ* //

80. Cf. above ch. III, p. 69 ff. and fn. 31.

Every single implement and every single action in the making of the *ukhā* is accompanied by the recital of verses which complete every stage of the identification between the *ukhā* as microcosm and the macrocosm. Thus the *ukhā* becomes, to all intents and purposes, the three worlds into which the universe is divided : the terrestrial, the atmospheric and the celestial, with the four cardinal points as its fourth dimension[81]. There is therefore no need, the Brāhmaṇa of the *Śukla* Yajurveda clearly affirms, to make three *ukhās* as some ritualists suggest, following the example of the *mahāvīra* in the *pravargya*.[82]

The *ukhā* is already triple and complete in itself. To duplicate or triplicate it, the Śatapatha Brāhmaṇa argues, is not only useless but also dangerous because in the sacrifice it is very important to maintain the right measure in everything.

When the *ukhā* is finally ready and identified with the three worlds, the three presiding Deities—Agni (the Fire) who presides over the terrestrial world, Vāyu (the wind) who presides over the atmospheric world and Āditya (the Sun) who presides over the celestial world—are further represented by three bricks, called *viśvajyotis* ("all-light" or "light of all", that is of universe) which the *yajamāna* sets about to make as soon as he finishes making the *ukhā*[83]. Thus, together with the brick made by the first wife of the sacrificer and these three bricks, the *ukhā* takes on itself a new symbolism. It symbolizes the self, the *ātman*, of the sacrificer himself, completed by the *aṣāḍhā* brick representing his voice—that is the word which is in the body of the sacrificer[84]—and by the three *viśvajyotis* bricks representing, besides the three above-mentioned Deities, desired offspring[85].

81. Cf. SatBr VI.5.2.22 *tā haike tisraḥ kurvanti | trayo vā'ime lokā ime lokā ukhā iti vadanto....sātha yad etac caturthuṃ yajur diśo....*

82. Cf. SatBr VI.5.2.22 : *tā haike tisraḥ kurvanti | trayo vā 'ime lokā ime lokā ukhā iti vadanto atho anyo'nyasyai prāyaścittyai yadītarā bhetsyate 'thetarasyāṃ bhariṣyāmo yadītarāthetarasyām iti na tathā kuryād....*See further in ch. VIII, p. 237, and fn. 87 the importance of *mahāvīra* in *pravargya* for such attempted repetition in the *ukhā*. Today, however, the usage of preparing three *ukhās*, for the sake of substitution in case the first will break, has prevailed.

83. Cf. SatBr VI.5.3.3 *atha viśvajyotiṣaḥ karoty etā devatā agniṃ vāyum ādityam etā hy eva devatā viśvaṃjyotis tā etasyā eva mṛdaḥ karoty ebhyas tal lokebhya etān devān nirmimīte yajamānaḥ karoti....*

84. Cf. SatBr VI.5.3.4 : *..ātmaivokhā vāg aṣāḍhā tāṃ pūrvāṃ karoti purastād dhīyam ātmano vāk tām etasyā eva mṛdaḥ karoty ātmano hy eveyaṃ vāṅ mahiṣī karoti...*

85. Cf. SatBr VI.5.3.5 *athokhāṃ karoti | ātmānaṃ tat karoty atha viśvajyotiṣaḥ karoti prajā vai viśvajyotiḥ prajā hy eva viśvaṃ jyotiḥ prajananam evaitat karoti...*

Once again, the microcosm and the macrocosm intersect and meet in the ritual implements. Once again the symbolized cosmos and the symbolizing clay enter into an intricate relationship, each playing the part of the other. In the middle stands the concrete human reality of the sacrificer. In order to identify the sacrificer with the universe even more, the bricks are made to be as long as his foot[86] and the *ukhā* one or five hand spans long (depending on whether his *sambhāra* contains only one or all five of the prescribed victims)[87]. Man and the universe are once again intimately linked in such a way as to lead them to their destined identification.

(c) *The Putting of the Ukhā into the Furnace* :

Finally, when everything is ready, the texts move on to prescribe the ways of putting the *ukhā* into the furnace—without, however, having to proceed through those thinkings which Prajāpati had to make when he had to find a way of baking the bricks of immortality. The difference in the myth though not in the rite, in the two cases gives us to understand that the baking of the *ukhā* enters the general pattern, which was not the case with the bricks. In fact, as regards the *ukhā*, the priest is in no doubt whatever that what he has to do, after he has made it, is to expose it, and its accompanying bricks, to the strengthening power of the fire. At most, he has to face other practical difficulties—as we shall see presently—but he does not find himself obliged to justify its baking or to impose it from outside by some kind of comparison. Prajāpati, on the contrary, before according to his square brick the treatment due to the *havis*, had to ponder and reason considerably. This confirms our view that Prajāpati performed, so to say, an 'imported' rite of which the baking of the brick was a conscious adaptation, assigning to it the energetic effects normally assigned to blood. Here, on the contrary, while baking the *ukhā* without further ado, the priest feels that he is acting in the spirit of his own ritual tradition.

The *ukhā* will be used to receive the fire and to retain it during the time needed to perform *agnicayana*, so that it has to be prepared

86. Cf. SatBr VI.5.3.2 and KatyaSS XVI. 3. 22 *yajamāna padam*...
87. Cf. SatBr VI. 5. 2. 8-10 and KatyaSS XVI. 3. 24 f.

and strengthened by an initial contact with the intense heat to which it will later have to be exposed. Translated into the language of the ritual, the baking of the pot, which is its first contact both with physical fire on the material plane and Agni the God-fire on the spiritual, is equal to an initiation (*dīkṣā*) into a new phase of its existence as baked clay and sacred vessel. This initiation is necessary before it can enter into close contact with the Sacred—the Fire-God in person. This initiation is at the same time a conservation. The clay baked into a pot has absorbed part of the divine energy of the fire and incorporated it into itself. It has become sacred along with and by virtue of the ritual power of the sacred heat. It has absorbed it and so become 'con-secrated', that is become 'sacred along with the sacred' In order to enter into contact with the Sacred without danger, the profane must somehow already participate in its sacrality —otherwise either the Sacred will burn and destroy it, or the profane profanate the Sacred.

Once filled with the energy of the consecration, the *ukhā* becomes dangerous as anything else which has to do with the Sacred. If it is to represent the entire sacrifice, that is the universe as Cosmic Act, and so replace the ritual implements all charged with the energy of Sacred heat, then it requires a big quantity of energy which, in its turn, requires special protection by the Deities themselves who are preparing the *ukhā* and the bricks to partake of their sacrality. Hence the baking of the *ukhā* is formally entrusted to the sons of Aditi so that they may bless and protect it in its difficult passage.[88] Indeed, the whole process of putting the earthen implements into the furnace is marked with fear lest some mishap should befall the *ukhā* and the bricks, or the furnace should fail to reach the right temperature—a lack of heat being as damaging to the result as excess.

(d) *The Fumigation of the Ukhā* :

Before one can perform the sublime and dangerous operation

88. Cf. SatBr VI. 5.1. 21 *putrebhyaḥ prāyacchad aditiḥ śrapayān ity etad va 'enām aditiḥ kṛtvā devebhyaḥ putrebhyaḥ śrapaṇāya prāyacchat tathaivainām ayam etat kṛtvā devebhyāḥ śrapaṇāya prāyacchati.*

of exposing the *ukhā* to the immense power of sacred heat, the cult prescribes another preliminary rite : the fumigation of the *ukhā*. The purpose of the rite is to infuse vital breath (*prāṇa*) into the implements and is performed, according to the Sūtras, on the *dakṣiṇāgni* (or with a firebrand lit from it or, again, with a fire lit by another friction)[89], using a special fuel made of seven balls of horse dung over each one of which a special formula is recited[90]. The smoke, which is scented, is considered to be the vital breath (*prāṇa*) and is supposed to strengthen the *ukhā* for the baking. At the same time *prāṇa* is infused into the sacrifice through the *ukhā* which is thought to be its head[91]. From another point of view, this fumigation might also have been the concrete and perhaps still unconscious, answer ('unconscious' because not clearly expressed in all its hidden implications, as Brāhmaṇic answers of this kind often are) which the priest has for preventing the 'raw'—that is whatever is still inert, immature, earthly or mortal—from coming into direct contact with Agni. Thus also the material used as fuel acquires an important meaning. It has to be horse dung because the child of the Sun, can give the smoke the necessary power to overcome the resistance of the 'raw' and exhale a truly efficacious *prāṇa;* but, on the other hand, being only dung, that is food which for the most part has been emptied of its vital content, it cannot overcharge the sacred fire with vital energy nor generate an excess of heat, an excess which can be extremely dangerous[92].

(e) *Baking* :

When all the preliminaries are over, then comes the actual baking of the *ukhā* as well as of the bricks which are to go with it. The furnace is prepared in a hole, dug in the ground and filled

89. Cf. KaytaSS XVI. 4.13.

90. Cf. KatyaSS XVI. 4.8.

91. Cf. SatBr VI.5.3.8 *athainām dhūpayati / sthemne nvevātho karmaṇaḥ prakṛtatāyai yady eva dhūpayati śīra etad yajñasya yad ukhā prāṇo dhūmaḥ śirṣaṃs tat prāṇaṃ dadhāti.*

92. Cf. SatBr VI.5.3.9 f. A discussion of this point, about the effects of both lack and excess of heat, will have to be left aside for another book. Cf. a similar case in ch. VIII, p. 244 for the *mahāvīra*'s fumigation.

with fuel. Here too protective action is taken against the *rakṣas-s*, the spirits of evil, which stubbornly insist on enjoying the fruits of the ritual without knowing how to put them to profit. The baking has also to be protected against the (by now) usual (and disturbing) possibility of violence breaking from the side of the Gods who are involved in the sacred action. Hence the hole is dug in the ground because the Earth cannot harm the fire which will be placed in it. Then, Aditi is invoked because, she being Earth, will not do damage either to herself or to her own son, Agni[93].

When the furnace is ready and filled with the appropriate fuel, the first to be carefully placed at the bottom are the *aṣāḍhā* bricks those which were the first to be made. This is done 'in silence' (*tūṣṇīm*); also in silence are placed the *viśvajyotis* bricks laid on the *ukhā* positioned in the furnace upside down.[94] Silence serves a special function in the rite. That the most important bricks are placed in the furnace in silence is very significant. Silence is sacred to Prajāpati. It reaches up to that part of the universe which is infinite and therefore ungraspable by any uttered formula no matter how full of meaning this might be[95]. The *ukhā*, on the contrary, is put in its place of trial with the recital of *mantras* invoking the protection of the Goddesses, the consorts of the Gods, since it was they who; at the beginning of time, placed the primordial *ukhā* onto the lap of the earth[96]. Other Goddesses are then invoked with similar *mantras*; these are the *Dhiṣaṇās*, known for their power to grant prosperity and ful-

93. Cf SatBr VI.5.4.1 f. *athainam asyāṃ khanati / etad vai devā abibheyur yad vai na imam iha rakṣāṃsi nāṣṭrā na hanyur iti...// taṃ vā adityā khanati/ iyaṃ vā'ditir no vā'ātmātmānaṃ hinasty ahiṃsāyai*....Cf. the *mantra* in VajSam XI.61, and also in SatBr VI.5.4.3.

94. Cf. SatBr VI.5.4.3 f. ..*atha pacanam avadhāyāṣāḍhām avadadhāti tūṣṇīm eva tāṃ hi pūrvāṃ karoti //3// athokhām avadadhāti...atha viśvajyotiṣo 'vadadhāti*....

95. On silence in the brāhmaṇic rituals cf. R. PANIKKAR, with the collaboration of U. M. Vesci, *Il silenzio del Buddha*, op. cit., pt III, ch. 3 a. p. 430 (pro man.), notes 372-397. A silence to 'take possession' of a thing has been seen in ch. VI, notes 54 and 55 of this book. This note is recalled again in note 25 of the Conclusion.

96. Cf. SatBr VI.5.4.4..*devānāṃ tvā patnīr devīr viśvadevyāvatīḥ pṛthivyāḥ sadhasthe' aṅgirasvad dadhat ūkha iti devānāṃ haitāṃ agre patnīr devīr viśvadevyāvatīḥ pṛthivyāḥ sadhasthe 'ṅgirasvad dadhus tābhir evaināṃ etad dadhāti*....

fil desires. They protect and assist the *ukhā* when the fire is lit in the cavity of the furnace[97]. These Deities also represent speech, the Word (*vāc*), so that both silence and the word are present at the delicate moment of transformation. While the *ukhā* is being baked, these and other Goddesses continue to be invoked all the time, sometimes collectively and sometimes individually, so that they may continue to assist and protect its delicate, difficult and even painful passage[98]. Word and silence alternate. Silence touches the undefinable and reduces it in an incorporeal way to the measure of the sacrifice—which, we recall is like the altar measured according to the proportions of a man[99] —and the Word, in its turn, defines concretely and incorporates in the sacrifice all that goes on in the world. Just as the terrestrial world is ruled by time and develops in time, the Word, spoken in the measure of the metre, represents, delimits and concretizes such time on the altar, in all its diverse forms and products even identifying it with Agni. The word, in fact, is time, and time is Agni which shines in diverse forms. So the text explains: "thus he (i.e. the sacrificer) digs with one (formula), he sets down (the firepot) with one, he kindles with one, he heats with one, he bakes with two, whence twice in the year is food ripened. These (formulas) amount to six as six are the seasons of the year. And the year is Agni". And the text, following its ritual logic, concludes: "As great as Agni is, as great as his measure is, so great does this become"[100].

The clay's passage through the fire is for it a new kind of initiation (*dīkṣā*), or perhaps a kind of ordeal which it has to undergo to be consecrated, to be internally transformed, to pass from being profane matter to divine state. After being fumigat-

97. Cf. SatBr VI. 5.4.5 ff. *dhiṣaṇās tvā devīḥ | viśvadevyāvatīḥ pṛthivyāḥ sadhasthe 'aṅgirasvad abhīndhatām ukha'iti....||5||...viśvadevyāvatīḥ pṛthivyāḥ sadhasthe aṅgirasvacchrapayenūkha'iti...|| 6|| gnāstvā devīḥ |...pacantūkha'iti...||* etc.

98. Cf. SatBr VI. 5.4. 6-8. Cf. my article "The Role of Ritual Heat in Vedic Sacrifice", cit., pt III, for the place.

99. Cf. notes 87 and 88 above.

100. SatBr VI.5.4.9 : *sa vai khanaty ekena | avadadhāty ekenābhīndha 'ekena śrapayaty ekena dvābhyāṃ pacati tasmād dviḥ saṃvatsarasyānnaṃ pacyate tāni ṣaṭ sampadyante ṣaḍṛtavaḥ saṃvatsaraḥ saṃvatsaro'gnir yāvān agnir yāyatyasya mātrā tāvat tad bhavati ||*

ed, the passage through the fire completes the infusion of life, a life of a higher order, an order which is 'supranatural'. The clay, whose change of properties in passing through the fire surprised the Atharvic *ṛṣi*, also served as a term of comparison in explaining the effectiveness of initiation (*dīkṣā*) on whoever submits himself to it[101]. Baked clay is 'immortal'—as Prajāpati will realize later when he comes to make his brick[102]. Neither water, nor wind, nor excessive heat can make the clay, once it is baked, revert to what it was before. It is an irreversible process. It is the immortality which the contact with the Sacred confers on him who exposes himself to It at the right time, for the right motive—and with the due caution lest he should be burnt to ashes !

Through the same act whereby the sacred object acquires its sacrality and immortality, it concentrates in itself the whole universe of which it becomes a symbol. It is at the moment when it is baked that the *ukhā* actually *becomes* the three worlds to which it was likened when it was being prepared, and that the bricks are transformed into their respective Deities, each one of whom presides over its own part of the cosmos (the terrestrial, the atmospheric and the celestial) with the *aṣāḍhā* as the divine Word[103].

This process, precisely because it is so important and decisive, seems to be fraught with dangers, judging by the *mantras* which are recited while the *ukhā* and the bricks are being baked, and by the devices which are used continuously and with increasing earnestness during the whole process, starting from the fumigation, continuing through the digging of the furnace and becoming more and more frequent in the *mantras* which are intended to protect the actual moment of transformation. This protection continues, moreover, to be requested in the final and delicate phase when new fuel is added, and even while and after the *ukhā*

101. Cf. GopBr I. 3.14 quoted previously in ch. IV, note 32, and ch. VII, note 52.

102. Cf. fn. 51 above. We use the future because, although we have already spoken about the erection of the *agnicayana* and its making, actually the formation and baking of the *ukhā* comes first in the ritual.

103. Cf. SatBr VI.5.3.3-5 already mentioned in notes 84, 85 and 86.

and the bricks are taken out of the furnace. The protector of these difficult and delicate moments is Mitra, in his role as 'Friend' [104]. It is to him that the *ukhā* is solemnly entrusted as soon as it is taken out of the furnace, so that he may give it the final touch and see to it that the whole process proves to be a success[105]. Then it is greeted with verses intended to strengthen it further : " 'Having risen, do thou become great', for these worlds, having risen, are great; 'and stand up steadfast !', that is, 'stand thou up firm and fixed !' "[106].

After all this, the *ukhā* is even further strengthened when its interior is washed with goat's milk. To receive this milk of fertility is for the *ukhā* another way of being protected because as it is argued, the goat came out of the head of Prajāpati: it is, therefore, Prajāpati himself and Prajāpati is Agni, and so Agni will not be able, either now or later, to harm the *ukhā*, otherwise he would harm himself[107]. The milk is also a vital element, and as such, it is the breath, the *prāṇa*, which is infused in the sacrifice through the *ukhā* as soon as it is cooked, the *ukhā* which is its head[108]. The infusion of *prāṇa*, therefore, takes place both immediately before and immediately after the *ukhā* is baked, that is, transformed. This implies that the transformation by itself does not necessarily infuse lasting life even if it can transfer the object from one sphere of Reality to another; and that, once this 'divine' sphere of Reality is reached, also the *prāṇa* infused at the beginning of the whole process is by itself not enough to confer

104. Cf SatBr VI.5.4.10 *atha mitrasya carṣanīdhṛta iti / maitreṇa yajuṣopanyācarati yāvatkiyac copanyācarati na vai mitraṃ kañcana hinasti na mitraṃ kaś cana hinasti tatho haiṣa etāṃ na hinasti no'etam eṣā tāṃ divaivopavaped divod vapedaharhy āgneyam //*

105. Cf. SatBar VI.5.4.14 *tāṃ parigṛhya nidadhāti / mitraitāṃ ta'ukhāṃ paridadāmy abhittyā 'eṣā mā bhedity....*

106. SatBr VI. 5.4.13 *athainām udyacchati/ utthāya bṛhatī bhavety utthāya hīme lokā bṛhanta udu tiṣṭha dhruvā tvam ity udu tiṣṭha sthirā tvaṃ pratiṣṭhitety etat*....The verses are taken from Vaj Sam. XI. 64.

107. Cf. SatBr VI.5.4.16 *ajāyai payasācchṛṇatti / prajāpater vai śokādajāḥ samabhavan prajāpatir agnir no vā'ātmātmānaṃ hinasty ahiṃsāyai....*

108. Cf. SatBr VI.5.4.15 *athainām ācchṛṇatti / sthemne nvenātho karmaṇaḥ prakṛtatāyai yad vevācchṛṇatti śira etad yajñasya yad ukhā prāṇaḥ payaḥ śīrṣaṃs tat prāṇaṃ dadhāty atho yoṣā vā ukhā yoṣāyāṃ tat payo dadhāti tasmād yoṣāyāṃ payaḥ...*

enough vitality on the object for it to approach the Sacred. For this, the object needs to be still further strengthened and to inhale more vital breath—which is done by means of the potent goat's milk. Thus, the last act to which the *ukhā*, now ready, baked and cleansed of ashes, is subjected is a fresh infusion of life, for which are invoked the Deities who, significantly, are the same as those who presided over its fumigation[109].

The *ukhā* is now ready for use. Then, the *yajamāna* and his *adhvaryu* are free to devote themselves to the task of making the other bricks needed for the construction of the fireplace and of which we have already spoken.

We conclude this section with a quote from the Śatapatha Brāhmaṇa in which the etymology of the word '*ukhā*' is given : "This is called *ukhā* because the Devas, by means of these rites (*karman*) and in this way, dug out (*udakhan*) these worlds, and inasmuch as they so dug, it (i.e. the pot representing these worlds) is called '*ukthā*', from which comes '*ukhā*' its mysterious form by which it is called by the Devas, for the Devas love the mysterious"[110].

### 3. *The Use of the Ukhā During the Initiatory Period* (*dīkṣā*) :

The *ukhā*, which was surrounded with so much care when it was being made and transformed in the furnace, has an important part to play in the various initiatory ceremonies to which the *yajamāna* must submit himself before he can undertake the performance of a rite as engaging as the *agnicayana*.[111] We shall deal only with the features of this special *dikṣā* which relate to the use of the *ukhā*, leaving out all the rest. We are not trying to make a complete reconstruction of a rite or even to give an accurate description of it. It may happen that some particular point which we put here in relief because of its special significance for our

109. Cf. SatBr VI. 5.4.16 ff. with VajSam XI 65 and KatyaSS XVI.4.23.

110. SatBr VI.7.1.23 *sā yad ukhā nāma / etad vai devā etena karmaṇaitayāvṛtemāṃ lokān udakhan anyad udakhanaṃs tasmād utkhotkhā ha vai tāṃ ukhety ācakṣate paro'kṣaṃ paro'kṣakāmā hi devāḥ //*

111. The texts regarding the *dīkṣā* for *agnicayana* are SatBr VI.6.1.1 ff. till the end of the VI *kāṇḍa*; KatyaSS XVI.5 and XVI. 6 .

study, may in reality be marginal and of little importance to the economy of the whole rite of which it forms part. *Vice versa*, the more imposing aspect of the rite as a whole may here be passed over in silence if it contains little of interest for our study. Our remarks presuppose a preliminary comprehensive knowledge of the rite in question derived from other sources. Having said this, which is valid for all the rites dealt with in this book, let us now return to our theme.

(a) *The Transfer of the Fire* :

The proper use of the *ukhā* is to contain the fire which is taken from the *āhavanīya* to enable the *yajamāna* or the *adhvaryu* to build on it the Agni, the Fire Altar, with solid bricks, during the year of his initiation.

We will now proceed to describe the placing of the fire in the *ukhā*. This is not an easy operation, but for that matter, no rite which has to do with fire is easy. Since the *ukhā* is not a fireplace to which Agni can be transferred from another fireplace by means of a firebrand directly—as is the case when it is transferred to the *āhavanīya* from the *gārhapatya*—a rite is necessary for the flame to pass from the stable fireplace to the mobile one. For this purpose the *ukhā* is filled with dry hemp and *muñja* herb, finely minced and smeared with clarified butter, while *mantras* are recited. This highly inflammable material is conceived to be a placenta filling the *ukhā* which is now compared to a womb (*yoni*) and is treated as if it were bait to attract the child Agni to come and hang on to it. The transfer of the fire to the *ukhā* is considered to be a birth. The *ukhā* is the pregnant mother-to-be, ready to conceive after having been inseminated by the child Agni himself. This transfer is fraught with dangers; so *mantras* have to be recited while the fuel is placed in the *ukhā* to protect the womb and the fire which will be born from it. When dealing with Agni, especially at the moment when he arises, there is always a certain amount of ritual fear.

When the mother-to-be is ready and sufficiently equipped for the child to come and cling to her womb with ease she, the *ukhā*, is placed ceremoniously on the *āhavanīya* by the *yajamāna* who must be standing and facing North-East. The North-East (*iśāna*) is the direction, in which Prajāpati faced when he set creation in motion[112], where the gates of *svarga* are[113] and where men and Gods dwell together[114]. The *yajamāna* must face the North-East while he performs this rite so as to give greater power to the two worlds—the earthly and the heavenly—that they may penetrate one another. Moreover a standing position helps to give the *yajamāna* that robustness necessary for his identification with the worlds represented by the *ukhā* : "Standing he puts the *ukhā* on the fire (i.e. of the *āhavanīya*) for the *ukhā* is these worlds and these worlds stand. And, moreover, whilst standing one is strongest (*vīryavattamaḥ*) [115]. One could ask here whether this robustness is needed by the *yajamāna* alone or whether it is also needed by the *ukhā* at the moment when it is about to pass another test : that of becoming a mother to come into a more direct and intimate contact with the fire than when in the furnace. The 'mother' needs strength at this moment and so *mantras* are recited while she is put in the fire and they invoke strength for her, a strength which is granted by the *mantras* themselves : " Break not ! Suffer no injury ", they say[116]; again, " O mother, bear up bravely " which is explained as meaning that the *ukhā* is called 'mother' because it is female[117], and that she needs courage and strength to bring to a happy end the 'work' (*kariṣyantau*) which she and Agni are called upon to accomplish[118]. The number of the verses has its own symbolism which serves to stress once again the

112. Cf. SatBr VI.6. 2.2 *udaṅ prāṅ tiṣṭhan| udaṅvai prāṅ tiṣṭhan prajāpatiḥ prajā asṛjata ||*

113. Cf. SatBr VI.6.2.4 *yad vevodaṅ prāṅ tiṣṭhan | etasyāṃ ha diśi svargasya lokasya dvāraṃ tasmād....*

114. Cf. SatBr VI.6.2.3 *...eṣā hobhay eṣāṃ devamanuṣyāṇāṃ digyad udīcī prācī ||*

115. SatBr VI. 6.2.1 *tāṃ tiṣṭhan pravṛṇakti | ime vai lokā ukhā ti ṣṭhantīva vā'ime lokā atho tiṣṭhan vai vīryavattaraḥ ||*

116. SatBr VI. 6.2.5 : *mā su bhitthā mā su riṣa iti |*

117. SatBr VI.6.2.5 (cont.) | *...amba dhṛṣṇu vīryasva sviti yoṣā vā 'ukhāmbeti vai yoṣāyā 'āmantraṇaṃ sviva....*

118. Cf. SatBr VI.6.2.5 (end) *...vīrayasvāgniś cedaṃ kariṣyatha ityagniśca hy etat kariṣyantau bhavataḥ ||* Cf. the same request of courage made to the "mother" clay of the *mahāvīra* of *pravargya* taken from the same *yajus* (VajSam XI. 68) in ch. VIII, fn. 165. The topic of the emerging of "pain" and "suffering" in sacrifice will be tackled in a separated study.

identification of everything in the ritual with the all, of the sacrificer with Agni, of the various Deities with one another and with Agni, of the firealtar itself with the year and its seasons etc.[119].

After the *ukhā* is placed on the *āhavanīya* with the required precautions and suitable *mantras*, the fire is stirred so that the flames lap the sides of the *ukhā* and envelop it from the outside up to the brim which is said to be just as a man who embraces a woman to warm her, penetrate her and impregnate her with his seed. When the flames touch the highly inflammable fuel placed inside it the fire cannot help spreading to it and is as if it were born again in a womb impregnated by itself, the parent fire signifying the continuity between the Agni of the *āhavanīya* and the Agni of the *ukhā* (*ukhyagni*). This is the reason why the ritual authorities of the Śatapatha reject as unlawful the hastening of the process of combustion, if it is slow, by inserting in the *ukhā* a lit firebrand or a piece of live charcoal : seed they say cannot enter a womb already solid with the bones of the child to be born[120]. Solid fuel consisting of thirteen pieces of different kinds of wood is added but only immediately after the flames have entered the maternal womb, the first piece to help the embryo grow and the others to gradually give it further strength [121]. Naturally, every piece of wood of this new fuel has a specific meaning which is given and explained as every piece is put in the *ukhā* accompanied by the recital of its *mantras*[122]. The first five pieces are of different kinds, the other eight are of *palāśa* wood[123]. Their length is a handspan of Viṣṇu which is the measure of an embryo—and this is so because it is only in his own measure that Viṣṇu can impart growth and food[124]. Finally,

119. Cf. SatBr VI.6.2.7 *dvābhyāṃ pravṛṇakti | dvipād yajamāno yajamāno'-gnir yāvān agnir yāvaty asya mātrā....*

120. Cf. SatBr VI.6.2.9 *yadi citam arcir ārohaty aṅgārān evāvapanty ubhayenaiṣo'gnir iti na tathā kuryād asthanvānvāva paśur jāyate'tha taṃ nāgra evāsthanvantam iva nyṛṣanti reta ivaiva dadhati reta u 'etad anasthikaṃ yad arcis tasmād....*

121. Cf. SatBr VI.6.2.10 ff.

122. Cf. SatBr. VI.6.2.11 ff. and VI.6.3.1. ff.

123. Cf. KatyaSS XVI.4.35-40 on top of those already quoted in the preceding note.

124. Cf. SatBr VI.6.2.12 (and VI.6.3.17): ...*prādeśa mātro vai garbho viṣṇur ātmasamitām evāsminn etat saṃbhūtiṃ dadhāti ||*

the comprehensive number thirteen too has a symbolic meaning, even though in certain well determined cases, it can be reduced to twelve or even eleven[125]. It serves to signify the basic unity of time, that is, the year, to which both Agni and Prajāpati are identified : "Thirteen months are a year, and the year is Agni; as great as Agni is, as great his measure is, by so much food does he (i.e. Agni) gratify him (i.e. the sacrificer)"[126]

Here once again the unity of time is inserted into the spatial unity which is being created. Prajāpati and Agni, in fact, who are the sacrificial Deities par excellence, symbolize too, in all the rites which are linked to them and especially in *agnicayana*, the time cycle which the sacrifice redeems and perpetuates. They do so by their identification with the standard measure of one complete revolution of the sun through its various seasons and its various months. So, if it takes *agnicayana* a year to be performed, and if it contains as many layers of bricks as the year has seasons, the *ukhā* can represent the year no less. In fact, it too represents Agni since it is in it that Agni is kept during the period of the sacrificer's *dīkṣā*. If it cannot do so by the number of its layers (which, obviously, it does not have), it does so by the number of kindling-sticks which are one by one inserted into it.

All this reasoning forms part of that rigorous ritual logic which certainly does not obey the rules of philosophical logic but which is no less coherent in its own way. Hence the *ukhā* is identified with the unity of time, that is with the year, both by the duration of its use in the course of the Soma sacrifice, and

125. Cf. SatBr VI.6.3.13 f. and KatyaSS XVI.4.41-43 where the sticks are twelve for a *kṣatriya*, thirteen (with the addition of two more than normal) for a *purohita* (Brāhmaṇa) or simply eleven if the *yajamāna* is neither of the two. This shows that priests could act as *adhvaryus* also in the name of others. SatBr VI.6.3.12 specifies that eleven sticks are put into the fire of a 'common person' "because eleven is an incomplete number and he who is neither *purohita* nor *kṣatriya* is incomplete" (*tad yad ekādaśa asarvaṃ tad yad akṣatriyo vāpurohito vā*).

126. SatBr VI. 6. 3.16 *tās trayodaśa sampadyante / trayodaśa māsāḥ saṃvatsaraḥ saṃvatsaro'gnir yāvān agnir yāvanty asya mātrā tāvataivainam etad annena prīṇāti //*

the number of kindling-sticks which it consumes as offerings made to it. All these are in fact offered to it one by one and with an accompanying *mantra* explaining its name, function and the matter of which it is made and concluding by pronouncing the sacrificial formula '*svāhā*', thus making of it a true and real offering[127].

(b) *The Use of the Ukhā during the Dīkṣā* :

At this point the fire of *āhavanīya* is transferred to the *ukhā* and this is ready to be used in the other rites which have to be performed during the *dīkṣā* of the sacrificer and during the time when the other bricks needed for the firealtar are made and baked. This means that the *ukhā* is now ready to receive the offerings previously destined to the *āhavanīya*[128].

The fire thus kindled in its new mobile dwelling-place must be kept alive day after day throughout the whole year of *dīkṣā*[129] —a year which is employed in the preparation of the bricks of the firealtar and in the performance of the other rites of the Soma sacrifice[130]. During this period only the bricks are prepared. The actual work of constructing the altar can only begin after this year is over[131].

During this year a series of rites is to be performed which help and hasten as much as possible the absorption by the *yajamāna* of the splendour of his sacrificial fire. The aim is to bring about a kind of symbiosis or mutual penetration of the sacrificer and his sacred fire leading to their sacrificial identification. This identification will last throughout the rest of the life of the sacrificer and its effects will reach out even beyond his death. This

127. Cf. SatBr VI. 6. 3. 17 and KatyaSS XVI. 4. 44.

128. This can be inferred from the fact that SatBr VI. 6. 1. 22 is against the usage of other ritualists of offering for the *dīkṣā* in the *ukhyagni* (as in KatyaSS XVI. 4. 45). It wants the offerings be made on the *āhavanīya* before this fire enters the *ukhā*. In this way the fire of the *āhavanīya* will enter the *ukhā*, becoming the *ukhyagni*, already powerful with the offerings.

129. Cf. SatBr VI.1.3.20

130. As inferred by KatyaSS XVI. 6.7 : *somā'virodhena vā tat prādhānyāt* ("the Dīkṣā rites for the building of the fire-altar should be performed without any conflict with the rites of the Soma sacrifice"). (tr. H. RANADE)

131. Cf. KatyaSS XVI.5.26.

explains why this year-long *dikṣā* can only be taken once in a life-time and can even be omitted in such cases as when the *yajamāna* has kept the *ukhyagni* alive for a whole year for some previous occasion[132], or if he has already performed for a whole year some other Soma sacrifice or the *agnihotra*[133], or if he has already experienced a kind of initiation by being exceptionally born after thirteen months of gestation rather than the usual ten[134]. To maintain this time unit is indispensable, but once the sacrificer has, in one way or another, been through it and been fortified by it, its repetition is no longer necessary. In these cases, then, the construction of *agnicayana* may start immediately after the kindling of the *ukhyagni*. Let us go back now to those rites which the *yajamāna* has to perform during the period of his initiation and begin from the time when the *ukhyagni* is installed in its 'womb'[135]. When his 'portable fire' is ready, the sacrificer puts it on himself, so to say. To do so, he must take certain precautions not to be prematurely burnt by his intimate closeness to the fire. To this end, he hangs around his neck, while pronouncing as usual a suitable *mantra*[136], a golden disk which symbolizes the sun attached as a pendant to a necklace made of twenty beads—and which will later be embedded in the base of the *agnicayana* about to be built[137]. This disk is identified with the sun[138] and with truth (*satya*)[139]. By putting it on himself, the sacrificer indentifies himself with it and absorbs its power and strength. Thus he identifies himself with the sun and so acquires its power, by wearing an object made of a metal which represents this, and therefore, the fire of the three worlds. This act is a preliminary necessary safeguard for him to continue

132. Cf. KatyaSS XVI.6.9 referring to SatBr IX.5.1.65

133. Cf. KatyaSS XVI.6.10 and 11.

134. Cf. KatyaSS XVI. 6.12. KatyaSS XVI.6.13 gives the alternative in this last case to having a *dīkṣā* of six months instead of that of one year.

135. Cf. above p. 206 of this chapter and the corresponding text.

136. The *mantra* is taken from VajSam XII. 1 as prescribed in KatyaSS XVI. 5.1.

137. Cf. KatyaSS XVI.5.1 and SatBr VI.7.2.1.

138. Cf. SatBr VI.7.2.1.

139. Cf. SatBr VI.7.1.1.

with the other rites. What is required of him, on this occasion, is that he enter in an intimate and deep relationship with his fire, that he handle it, raise or lower it, carry it on him, in a way that the two get used one to the other, become friends and eventually identified with one another. However, the sacrificer, man that he is, even if consecrated and strengthened by the various rites which he has already performed as *paterfamilias*[140] and by the rites of the *dīkṣā* which he has gone through so far, is not as yet strong enough to bear such intimate contact with the sacrificial fire concentrated in the *ukhā*. The golden disk placed in front of the more sensitive, and hence more vulnerable part of the body, that is, the zone immediately beneath the navel[141], serves as a kind of protection and as a source of strength to the *yajamāna* at a time when the rites of the *dīkṣā* are deepening his identification with his sacrificial fire and therefore with the sacrifice in its entirety[142].

Thus protected and strengthened, the sacrificer who in the meantime has prepared a special seat (*āsandī*) on which to put the flaming *ukhā*[143], lifts the *ukhā* by means of two pads made of entwined straw smeared with clay lest they should catch fire[144] and puts it on the seat with the proper *mantras*[145]. Again he lifts it up from there by means of a kind of netting made of six entwined strings of reed-grass which is tied in such a way as to enable him to hang it from his neck and rest it on that part of his body covered and protected by the golden disk. After having thus lifted it up, he turns towards the East and raises it above his head, as high up as his arms can reach, and then lowers it to the level of his waist, as low as the length of

140. It should be remembered that the *agnicayana* and its *dīkṣā* were performed after the first Soma sacrifice.

141. Cf. SatBr VI.7.1.8-11 where various reasons are given for the choice of this position of the golden disc. Anyway this is a very vulnerable and important spot for *yoga* and other types of bodily asceticism.

142. Cf. SatBr VI.7.1.3-5.

143. Cf. SatBr VI.7.1.12ff. where there is the description of the seat *āsandī*, its shape, its material, its measurements etc. This seat is, significantly, higher than the throne of Soma.

144. Cf. SatBr VI.7.1.15 f. and 26.

145. Cf. KatySS XVI.5.3-5 with the *mantra* taken from VajSam XII.2.

the string around his neck allows. By this gesture, the *yajamāna* places his fire in heaven, identifying it with the sun and at the same time giving the sun the energy it needs to be kept and sustained in its heavenly rounds. By lowering it, he ensures that the rite turns to his advantage so that it will not only be profitable for the cosmos but also for him.[146]

Of course, no one today believes that meteorological and astronomical phenomena are governed by ritual acts. Surely the sun rises and sets even without the potent gestures of the Vedic rite. Yet, according to those who believe in it, this rite is capable of capturing the energy which is manifest in the universe and in its dynamics, and of reproducing it in a concentrated manner in the sacred act of the rite to strengthen man and his *cosmos*.

(c) *The Rite of the Steps of Viṣṇu* (*viṣṇukramāḥ*) *and other Rites* :

By these rites performed on the *ukhā* which is thus further energized by its identification with the sun, the *yajamāna* completely assumes in himself the provisional fire, absorbing its heat and energy through his umbilical zone protected and strengthened by the golden disk. Thus, he has acquired sacred power and is made one with the Divine. He is thus ready to perform another rite which, because of its power and significance, has had a great deal of influence on later mythology. The *yajamāna*, identified with the three worlds and with the irradiating energy of the sun, carrying the *ukhyagni* which is he himself and at the same time the entire universe, takes three steps while reciting four mantras. These are the three steps of Viṣṇu (*viṣṇukrama*)[147] which have found such deep echo in later Hindu tradition. However, their ritual performance in the Brāhmaṇas has a different meaning from the one found in Purāṇic literature. While in the latter the three steps are normally taken by an *avatāra* of Viṣṇu, namely Vāmana in the form of a dwarf, with which the Supreme God conquers, or re-conquers, the three worlds from the dominion of the Demon Bali, here in the Brāhmaṇas, they

146. Cf. SatBr VI.7.2.9 with reference to VI.7.1.8.

147. Cf. SatBr VI.6.4.1 and especially VI.7.2.10 with KatyaSS XVI. 5.11 ff.

have an eminently creative significance and attest to the realized identification of the *yajamāna* with his fire. "These Devas, as the being (*bhūtva*) of Viṣṇu, strode on these worlds....Now, this same Viṣṇu is this sacrifice; and he who is this sacrifice is indeed this same Agni who is in the *ukhā*. Into it the Devas changed themselves (i.e. made themselves like it) and strode through these worlds. So also this *yajamāna*, having made himself as it (i.e. Agni), strides through these worlds"[148]. The sacrificer is now totally one with his Agni, and therefore he is also, in a certain sense, Viṣṇu himself. Hence following in the footsteps of the Deities who by virtue of the very identification creatively strode through the worlds, the sacrificer, turned towards the North-East[149], re-enacts this divine action and thus obtains the objects of his desires, such as offspring, freedom from his enemies [150], ascension into heaven[151], identification with Parjanya[152] and the like[153].

After having taken these ritual steps with the flaming *ukhā* in his hand, the sacrificer performs on the *ukhā* itself the *vātsapra* rite which consists in the recitation of certain Ṛgvedic verses taken from the Yajurveda[154]. This rite is complementary to the preceding one inasmuch as it is intended to infuse life in what has been created[155]. For every action performed in the first rite there is a corrresponding action in the second. This correspondence symbolizes, respectively, the infusion of the life-breath

148. SatBr VI.7.2.10 f. ..*etad vai devā viṣṇur bhūtvemāṃ lokān akramanta... //10// sa yaḥ sa viṣṇur yajñaḥ saḥ / sa yaḥ sa yajño'yam eva sa yo'yam agnir ukhāyām etam eva tad devā ātmānaṃ kṛtvemāṃl lokān akramanta tathaivaitad yajamāna etam evātmānaṃ kṛtvemāṃl lokān kramate //11//*.

149. Cf. SatBr VI.7.2.12. For the meaning of the direction North-East see above] notes 113-115.

150. Cf. SatBr VI.7.2.13.

151. Cf. SatBr VI.7.2.14 ff.

152. Cf. SatBr VI.7.3.1ff.

153. Cf. SatBr VI.7.1.1 ff. for the whole *adhyāya* which describes the *dīkṣā* and what it can obtain.

154. Cf. VajSam XII.18-29 referring to RV X.45. 1ff. and explained by SatBr VI.7.4.1 ff.

155. Cf. SatBr VI.7.4.1 (end)...*athaivaitad yajamāno viṣṇukramaiḥ prajāḥ sṛṣṭvā tābhyo vātsapreṇāyuṣyaṃ karoti //*

(*prāṇa*) into matter, the placing of the Deities at the head of their respective worlds, and the positioning of the luminaries according to the various times of the year. In fact, "as by the steps of Viṣṇu (*viṣṇukrama*) Prajāpati created this world, by the *vātsapra* (he created) Agni (the fire); as by the steps of Viṣṇu he created the air, by the *vātsapra* he created Vāyu (the wind); as by the steps of Viṣṇu he created the sky, by the *vātsapra* he created Āditya (the sun); as by the steps of Viṣṇu he created the quarters, by the *vātsapra* he created the moon..."[156] and so on. This correspondence is applied to the various divisions of time, its months, fortnights, days and nights etc. Hence the two rites are to be performed alternately. Theoretically, the *viṣṇukrama* should be performed during the first half of the year when they create the worlds and the *vātsapra* during the second when they create the corresponding Deities[157]. In practice, however, except for the first day of the *dikṣā* and the day after it is completed, they are performed on alternate days. On the two days mentioned, both rites are performed—so that "he (i.e. the sacrificer) encloses the universe on both sides, between the day and the night when he is about to create and when he has created it"[158]. It is interesting to note how the accompanying *mantras* make it clear that the rites of the renewal of creation, performed on the *ukhā*, are not a mere commemoration of what once took place at the beginning of time—"*in illo tempore*"—but give birth to a new creation here and now : "This is the reason why the *viṣṇukrama* and the *vātsapra* are performed : by them he (i.e. the sacrificer) creates all this"[159]

Another rite which the *yajamāna* must perform with the sacrificial fire while it is still mobile in the *ukhā*, is to take it for a

156. SatBr VI.7.4.7 : ..*viṣṇukramair vai prajāpatir imaṃ lokam asṛjata vātsaprenāgniṃ viṣṇukramair vai prajāpatir antarikṣam asṛjata vātsapreṇa vāyum viṣṇukramair vai prajāpatir divam asṛjata vātspreṇādityaṃ viṣṇukramair prajāpatir diśo'sṛjata vātsapreṇa candramasaṃ*....etc.

157. Cf. SatBr VI.7.4.11 f. with the corresponding note of J. EGGELING, *in h. l.*, p. 287 (SBE, vol. XLI, pt. III).

158. SatBr VI.7.4.12 ..*athaivaitad yajamāna idaṃ sarvam prajanayiṣyaṃśca prajanayitvā cāhorātrābhyam ubhayataḥ parigṛhṇāti* ||

159. SatBr VI.7.4.7 (end of the text of note 157) *tad yad viṣṇukramavātsapre bhavata etad eva tena sarvaṃ sṛjate* ||

drive in a chariot for a short time[160]. This too is a rite which must be performed daily throughout the whole year of the *dikśā*, when the fire, therefore, has still no fixed abode.

In the evening, at sunset, the ashes accumulated during the day, in the performance of the rites of the day, are gathered with care[161] and new fuel is added for the night. This process is repeated very early in the morning at sunrise[162]. This is done every night and every morning throughout the initiatory period to ensure a prosperous and unending succession of days and years in the family of the sacrificer.

There are many more things which could be said about this important rite but we must now pass on to *pravargya*, another optional rite, which is performed for three days while the preliminary rites of the second or third Soma sacrifice of a *yajamāna* are going on. We will deal with *pravargya* now, in spite of the fact that it is performed before *agnicayana*, to bring out the similarities between its ritual vessel, the *mahāvīra*, and the *ukhā* described in this chapter.

160. Cf. SatBr VI.8.1.1 ff.
161. Cf. SatBr VI.6.4.1.
162. Cf. SatBr VI.6.4.2 (end) & 3.

CHAPTER EIGHT

# RITUAL HEAT IN THE PRAVARGYA

Besides the *ukhā*, we find in the Brāhmaṇas another ritual vessel, whose material, way of being made and baking, resemble very closely those of the *ukhā*. The similarities between the two are such that they can easily lead one to think that they must have influenced one another. This vessel is the *mahāvīra*, the chief implement of the *pravargya* rite[1].

We have already had several occasions to refer to this rite found since the Ṛgveda, and it is important from our own point of view because of the central and decisive role heat plays in it—particularly that which is localized in the *mahāvira* or, as it is also called, *gharma* meaning, as we have seen, 'heat'. The *pravargya*, like the *agnicayana*, is an ancillary rite in the Soma sacrifice, and like it too, cannot be performed during the first sacrifice of a new *yajamāna*. He has to wait for his second or third *Somayajña*. Though in practice, the *Pravargya* is well inserted within the whole complex of the Soma sacrifice and occupies a well determined place related to the *upasad* (another offering of milk with verses), it appears to be an autonomous whole and gives the impression of having been originally an

1. Cf. J.A.B. van BUITENEN, *The Pravargya*, Poona (Deccan College), 1968 (op. cit.). Although this is a good monograph based on the ritual texts some of the interpretations cannot be accepted fully. Cf. also G.U. THITE; op. cit., p. 125 ff. and R. N. DANDEKAR, SK, op. cit., vol. II, pt. I pp. 18 ff. and 166 ff. for the Śrautic texts, and W. CALAND & V. HENRY, op. cit., vol. I, par. 128 f.

independent rite which only subsequently was inserted into the more complex ceremony of *somayajña*.

This impression is confirmed by the status attributed to it by the liturgical texts which prescribe its rules and *mantras*. There it appears as forming one whole and it is discussed after the exposition of *agniṣṭoma*, whereas it is hardly even mentioned at the place where it should be. It is mentioned by practically all the four Vedas and their Brāhmaṇas and Śrauta Sūtras and at its performance priests of all the four types of *mantras* take part.[2] Since the heavier part of the rite is performed by adhvaryu, it is his Saṃhitās, with their exegetical and ritual literature which treat of it in greater depth and with an abundance of details,—the Brāhmaṇas commenting on the *mantras* recited by the priests, and the Sūtras prescribing and explaining, as usual, the ritual rules to be observed[3].

The place assigned to *Pravargya* in this literature is indicative of the great respect and circumspection with which, at least in theory, it was treated. It was rated as a 'mystery'; one Sūtra calls it '*āraṇyaka*' (belonging to the forest)[4]. This reference to the forest, traditional place for meditation and spiritual retreat, gives it that mysterious, mystical, character of the teachings imparted there.[5] It is surely not by chance that the Taittirīya School deals with the *mantras* and the *Brāhmaṇas* of *Pravargya* in the section devoted to the *Āraṇyakas*, a place which can be compared with that given to *Pravargya* by the Śatapatha Brāhmaṇa

2. Cf. AitBr I.18-22 (I, 4.2-5) and KausBr VIII. 3-7 which are dedicated to the description and commentary of *Pravargya*; and also GopBr II.2. 6 summarizing the quoted AitBr. The three of them mostly comment upon the *ṛks* formulas recited in the rite. Śatapatha Brāhmaṇa and Taittirīya Āraṇyaka have a detailed narration of *Pravargya* in Kāṇḍa XIV and in Kāṇḍa IV respectively.

3. Cf. a selection of the texts in SK, vol. II, pt. I, p. 18 ff. and 166 ff. and in J.A.B. van BUITENEN, *The Pravargaya*, passim. The first of them takes as its basic text Baudhāyana Śrauta Sūtra (BaudhSS) while the second follows the Āpastamba SS (ApSS). We add the Bhāradvāja Śrauta Sūtra (BharSS) and Mānava SS (ManSS).

4. Cf. ManSS IV.8.1.

5. Cf. J.A.B. van BUITENEN, op. cit., p. 1.

which deals with it immediately before the *Bṛhadāraṇyakopaniṣad*, and with that given to its *mantras* by the Vājasaneya Saṃhitā as immediately before the *Iśopaniṣad*[6]. *Pravargya*, while remaining essentially a rite, touches a high point of spirituality—and hence its mysterious, mystical character. This fact makes of it a kind of bridge between the ritual aspect of Brāhmaṇic religion and its more spiritual, philosophico-mystical aspect—something which can be very well said of the Āraṇyakas.

Another feature of this rite which enhances its mysterious and mystical nature is its secrecy. The whole rite, from its very start, is surrounded with the greatest discretion, both when the implements are prepared—something which is done behind closed doors, often in an interior enclosure—or when its meaning is being explained. Moreover, it requires a special initiation with special provisions for study, so that not all priests can participate in it. To be taught the 'mystery', the novice must be a man of proved competence, already versed in the Vedas, and interiorly pure, without sin. Hence, a master who possesses this kind of knowledge must be careful to whom he imparts it and can accept as his disciple only someone with whom he is closely acquainted, or who is a member of his own family or is very dear to him, otherwise he will incur the wrath of Indra[7]. This injunction also indicates that this secret knowledge is so full of meaning that often not even the officiating priests themselves are fully aware of its extent.

In actual fact the *pravargya* is a relatively simple rite. The secrecy which Indra demands would not be of interest to us, were it not that, apart from this, the rite is unusual also in the large quantity of heat required to make the *mahāvīra*, and in the ritual offering. This heat is also an index of its sacredness, hence the safeguards with which the rite is surrounded including the secrecy which shrouds many of its features as well as all the precautions which surround every concentration of the Sacred to protect it, lest anyone should approach it indiscriminately.

6. Cf. VajSam XXXVII-XXXIX. IsaUp. is the XL. Cf. also A.B. KEITH, *The Veda of the Black Yajus School entitled Taittirīya Saṃhitā*, op. cit., p. CXXIV.

7. Cf. SatBr XIV.1.1.26 quoted below, in notes 33, 59, 60, 63 of this chapter.

We notice, however, that the secrecy with which this knowledge is kept and the special initiation spoken of by the texts concern only the officiating priests and not the *yajamāna* who perhaps participates in the rite only when the preliminary rites and the kindling of the sacred fire are over. This is something rare and is in itself already an indication that *pravargya* goes well beyond the limits of a Vedic normal rite.

1. *The History of Pravargya* :

The whole *pravargya* complex has two distinct parts : the preparation of the earthen implements, especially *mahāvīra*, and the rites which are performed on the latter as soon as it is taken out of the furnace. These include the offering of hot milk to the Aśvins, and repeated in the evening and so for three consecutive days preceding *upasad*[8]. It comes to a solemn end at the noon of the third day before the start of the other more engaging ceremonies of *somayajña*, such as the animal sacrifice offered to Agni-Soma, the possible construction of *angniciti*, the pressing of Soma, etc. At its conclusion, the ritual implements used in the rite, especially the earthen ones, and particularly *mahāvīra*, are carried in procession to the *uttaravedi*, arranged in the form of a man and 'buried' there. Or else they are taken to an island and after a last rite of farewell, are abandoned.

One cannot help noticing a contrast between the simplicity of the actual offering of hot milk, and the relative complexity of the other rites having to do with the preparation, use and disposal of the ritual implements, particularly of *mahāvīra*. This led some to think that *pravargya* is a fusion of what originally were two distinct rites: the normal offering of hot milk to the Aśvins, already present in the Ṛgveda, and a perhaps non-*śrautic* rite which consisted in the preparation, unction, adoration and disposal of a ritual vessel, or perhaps of an earthen figure more or less in the form of a man. The word '*mahāvīra*' itself (lit. 'great hero') retains the connection between the ritual vessel and this human figure. In any case, the second supposedly independent rite could have been the first recognizable ins-

8. Cf. W. CALAND & V. HENRY, op. cit. par 51, 67, 72, 73, 76, 77.

tance of a *pūjā* made to a *mūrti*, that is a ritual offered to an image of the Deity[9]. The idea of seeing in the second part of *pravargya*, a *pūjā* made to a *mūrti* is certainly an interesting suggestion and worth taking into consideration provided, however, that it is not pushed too far. In fact, the 'two' distinct rites, which this theory is obliged to postulate, do not seem to be as distinct as one could easily be led to believe. Moreover, the 'two' parts of *Pravargya* may have already formed one whole in Ṛgvedic times even though, probably, in a different way from that fixed by the Brāhmaṇas, and Sūtras[10]. Moreover, the fact that a ritual implement is exalted to the rank of a great Deity while still being treated as a mere offering, pertains to that very process of divinization and cosmicization which, as we have seen, forms part of the evolution of the ritual proper to the Brāhmaṇic sacrifice and, therefore, is no sure indication that the two rites have been inadequately fused.

On the contrary, *pravargya*, as a unit, was originally a morning offering to the Aśvins and perhaps only at a later stage in the Indian tradition was it officially incorporated into the ceremony of the Pressing of Soma. Indeed, to judge by the myth which

9. Cf. J.A.B. van BUITENEN, op. cit., p. 23 ff. "..Not only does the name Mahāvīra demonstrate that the artifact is thought of as a *person*, also the shape of the moulded clay artifact, however, inchoate, is recognizably human..." Nevertheless, to justify his idea the Author has to suppose a fusion of 'two' different rites; "One cannot fail to recognize in the scene and the litany the dramatic evocation of a theistic sentiment, directed (...) to a concrete God in the icon here and now (...). But immediately after this both intimate and spectacular worship of the image, the nature of the rite changes abruptly. (...) The recitation of the Hotar (...) already announces that the mahāvīra is just a vessel and the God Gharma of an instant ago a sweet milk draught for the Aśvins (...). From the above exposition the conclusion emerges that in the Pravargya we have basically the coalescence of two distinct rites. The first, not necessarily the oldest, is the ceremony of the actual shaping, baking, anointing, adoring and disposing of an icon in which the Great God is immanent; the ceremony itself reminds us of typical "Hindu" rites ...). The other is an old Ṛgvedic and Atharvavedic rite (...) offered to the Aśvins" (p. 26 f.). We will see later the reasons why we cannot accept this theory. Anyway that a Great God can become a sweet draught for offering is something which ennobles the sacrifice rather than diminishes it.

10. Cf. in the previous chapters II and III p. 27 note 12 and pp. 65-66 with notes 14,16.

presents it to us, this incorporation did not take place without opposition on the part of the more traditionalist. The myth, is very significant in this respect. The way it is articulated is somewhat strange—as many sophisticated myths are—and is pregnant with motifs susceptible of various interpretations. So let us delay a little to describe it in its entirety before we attempt to interpret it in the light of the successive phases of the corresponding rite.

(a) *The Myth* :

The myth, as it is presented in the Śatapatha Brāhmaṇa, starts with the session (*satra*) for a *somayajña* held at Kurukṣetra on a night of full moon, by a select group of Deities including Indra, Agni, Viṣṇu, Soma, Makha, Viśvedeva, but not—and this is said explicity—the Aśvins[11]. All these Deities are connected, in one way or another, with *pravargya*[12]—also, and especially, the absent Aśvins, the heavenly twins, who were its first beneficiaries.[13]

After the usual preparations, the Devas desire a deeper knowledge of the sacrifice they are about to perform. So, they enter into a contest among themselves to see who will succeed in being the first to attain the end of the sacrifice. The means to be used are the usual religious ones : *tapas*, *yajña*, faith and asceticism[14]. The palm of victory will be luminous glory to be then shared by the rest of the group[15]. The winner is Viṣṇu, a

11. Cf. SatBr XIV.1. 1.1 : *devā ha vai satraṃ niṣeduḥ | agnir indraḥ somo makho viṣṇur viśve devā anyatraivāśvibhyām ||*

12. Agni is the Receiver of the first Pressing in the morning because he is the Sacrificial God par excellence; Indra is the Receiver of the second Pressing, at midday, because he reconquered it from Viṣṇu (see below), Viṣṇu is the Receiver together with the others of the following *upasad*, because he conquered the sacrifice first. Soma is present because it is in his Pressing that the *Pravargya* is offered; and *Makha* is there because it is the sacrifice's head. The Aśvins, who are so drastically and explicitly excluded, are the Receivers of the *Pravargya* itself.

13. Cf. above ch. II, p. 26 ff.

14. Cf. Sat Br XIV.1.1.4 *te hocuḥ | yo naḥ śrameṇa tapasā śraddhayā yajñenāhutibhir yajñasyodṛcaṃ purvo'vagacchāt....*

15. Cf. SatBr XIV. 1.1.4 (end) : .. *sa naḥ śreṣṭho'sattad u naḥ sarveṣāṃ saheti tatheti ||*

Deity relatively new to the Pantheon, who begins to acquire prominence precisely because of this victory,[16] for which he became the sacrifice.[17] But Viṣṇu is puffed up by his triumph which sets him on his way to becoming the Supreme God, and forgetting the agreement to share his glory with the rest of the group, he takes up his bow and three arrows for self-defence and withdraws to a place apart, waiting and at the same time resting, erect and with his head reclined on the end of the bow. The other Deities, defeated, sit around him, keeping a respectful distance from him, not daring to reclaim their share of the glory[18]. Then, some ants (*varmī*), of the *upadīkā* species, offer to help them to recover the lost sacrifice in return for the gift of finding food and water even in the desert.[19] The Deities agree. So the ants secretly approach Viṣṇu and start gnawing away at the bowstring. Finally it snaps, and the end of the bow on which Viṣṇu is confindently resting his head, is suddenly cut loose and severs his head clean off[20]. With a '*ghṛn*' sound, the head falls and becomes the sun[21], while the rest of the sacrificial body of the Deity lies stretched out (*pra-vṛj*) pointing towards the East.[22] Hence the names '*gharma*' and '*pravargya*'. Viṣṇu, still resplendent even though decapitated is admired by the Deities and finally recognized to be the 'Great Hero'; hence the name '*mahāvīra*'[23].

Again the Deities enter into a contest to take possession of the beheaded yet glorious sacrificial body of Viṣṇu. The winner this time is Indra who reaches him first and stretching himself out on him, limb on limb, takes on himself the glory of Viṣṇu.[24]

16. Cf. SatBr XIV. 1.1.5 : ..*tad viṣṇuḥ prathamaḥ prāpa* ("Viṣṇu reached it first in fulness".)

17. Cf. SatBr XIV.1.1.6 : ..*sa yaḥ sa viṣṇur yajñaḥ saḥ* quoted again below in note 43 of this ch.

18. Cf. SatBr XIV.1.1.7.

19. Cf. SatBr XIV. 1.1.8.

20. Cf. SatBr XIV, 1.1.9 : ..*viṣṇoḥ śiraḥ pracicchidatuḥ* / mentioned again in note 54 below.

21. Cf. SatBr XIV, 1, 1.10 : ..*tad patitvāsāvādityo'bhavad.*

22. Cf. SatBr XIV.1.1.10.

23. Cf. SatBr XIV. 1.1.11 commented below on p. 238 with note 91.

24. Cf. SatBr XIV. 1.1.12.

Makha does the same and is, in his turn, taken on by Indra. Hence the latter's Vedic name of 'Maghavat' which is explained as being the exoteric form of Makhavat (possessing Makha)[25]. The Deities, then, now in possession of the sacrifice through Indra, their leader, proceed to toil round it (*śram*) and enjoy the headless body as it is[26]. Indeed, it seems that they take their delight precisely because it is headless. They divide it into three distinct parts : the morning-pressing, the midday-pressing and the afternoon-pressing which they then share among themselves in accordance with their needs. To the Vasus and Agni is offered, with the *gāyatri*, the morning one; to the Rudras and Indra, with the *triṣṭubh*, the midday one; to the Ādityas and Viśvedeva, with the *jagatī*, the evening one[27].

While the Deities go on, thus satisfied, with their 'headless sacrifice' (*apaśirṣṇā yajñena*), there appears on the scene a *ṛṣi* of the Atharvan family, Dadhyañc Atharvan, who having spied on the Deities from afar, now knows about the mystery of the sacrificial decapitation[28]. He knows too how to put the head back on the Soma sacrifice and offers to demonstrate it to the Deities. These, however, there and then turn him down. What is more, far from permitting him restore the head to the sacrifice, Indra forbids the *ṛṣi* from divulging the secret for otherwise he would cut off his head[29]. Indra is overheard by the Aśvins who, we recall, were absent from the *somayajña* and understanding that Dadhyañc Atharvan knew a great liturgical secret went to him and insistently begged him to disclose to them the secret of how to make the sacrificial body whole again. The *ṛṣi* hesitates for he fears the anger of Indra, now the Lord of the Gods. But the ingenious Aśvins devise a stratagem by means of which they replace the *ṛṣi*'s head with that of a

25. Cf. SatBr XIV. 1. 1. 13.

26. Cf. SatBr XIV. 1. 1. 17 (end)

27. Cf. SatBr XIV. 1. 1. 15-17 (see previously note 12).

28. Cf. SatBr XIV. 1. 1. 18 : *dadhyaṅ ha vā 'ātharvaṇaḥ etaṃ śukram etaṃ yajñaṃ vidāñcakāra yathā yathaitad yajñasya śiraḥ pratidhīyate yathaiṣa kṛtsno yajño bhavati* //

29. Cf SatBr XIV. 1. 1.19 : ..*sa hendreṇokta āsa / etaṃ cedan yasmā 'anubrūyās tata eva te śiraśchindyām iti* //

horse[30] so that when Indra, enraged at the transgression of his command, makes good his threat and cuts off the talking head, they, the heavenly doctors, can easily return him his original head.[31] When Indra sees that the secret is now out, he accepts in his own name and in that of the other Gods, even though reluctantly, the re-incorporation of the 'head' in the Soma sacrifice by means of the *pravargya* rite. Still, he demands that the *yajamāna* should not perform this rite until at least his second or third sacrifice of Soma under penalty of having himself and his possessions burnt to ashes[32]. He also lays down severe conditions for the eventual selection of disciples to be initiated into this secret knowledge.[33]

(*b*) *The Interpretation*[34] :

Even though the myth does not directly concern us, it is significant enough to have it narrated in such detail. It seems to refer to the time when *pravargya*—a simple morning offering to the Aśvins—was incorporated into the whole complex of the Soma sacrifice offered to other Gods. It also reflects the resistance to it on the part of the traditionalists who maintained that it was possible to continue performing the Soma sacrifice as they had always done, without any addition of any sort. They had always regarded the rite of the three

30. Cf. SatBr XIV, 1, 1, 23.

31. Cf. SatBr XIV. 1. 1. 25. The talking head of a horse is a Ṛgvedic topic (cf. RV I.116. 12) mentioned again in the Upaniṣads (cf. e.g. BrUp II. 5. 16 ff).

32. Cf. SatBr XIV. 2.2.45 : *taṃ yat prathamayajñe pravṛñjyāt / eṣo 'sya taptaḥ śuśucānaḥ prajāñ ca paśūnś ca pradahed atho āhuḥ pramāyuko yajamānaḥ*.... ("and were he to perform the pravargya at the first Soma-sacrifice, that (Mahāvīra) of his when heated and ablaze, would burn up his family and cattle and also his life....") (tr. EGGELING). In ib. 44, it is suggested the idea of the performance to be postponed to the second of third Soma sacrifice of a *yajamāna*. The implications of this important passage are left for another occasion.

33. Cf. SatBr XIV.1.1.26. See it again in note 7 and notes 59, 60 and 63 where the text will be quoted *in extenso*.

34. We give here an interpretation that can be considered different from our line of research, and which will be explained in the following volume on this topic. By not insisting here on the concentration of heat and sacrality we do not deny it; we will only give here a different point of view not in contrast with the other.

Soma-pressings perfectly complete in itself without needing any 'head' to be joined to it. Moreover, the inclusion in a rite already so potent by itself, of still another rite which is as potent as *pravargya*, could give rise—as in fact happened—to an excess of sacred power causing problems within the performance of the rite[35].

It is but natural that, in a world where it is believed that the sacred energy of the rite must be maintained in equilibrium, there should be feared a danger in fusing two rites, each one of which is already full by itself of sacred energy. But if one wants, in spite of this, to have the two together, it is essential that this equilibrium is not disturbed. Thus, the innovators take recourse to a stratagem and present *pravargya* as the head of Soma sacrifice. But, in so doing they implicitly suggested that the Soma sacrifice was itself without head and in need to have one. Hence, the myth of the **falling** of the head of Viṣṇu with the consequent restoration of it in the form of *pravargya*. In fact, there would have normally been no reason to consider any *somayajña* which is perfectly complete in itself, as lacking anything, let alone a head ! On the theoretical level, the explanation as to how the principal sacrifice came to be deprived of its head is, therefore, left to the myth. To the explanation given by the myth, there is added another: *agniṣṭoma* (or any other kind of Soma Sacrifice) normally consisting of three principal pressings. Since the sacrifice is thus divisible by three, it was not difficult for the masters of liturgy to present it as incomplete because the number three itself is incomplete, lacking as it does 'the fourth'. This 'fourth' is the element which is more subtle, spiritual and 'mysterious' than the other three and is none other than *pravargya*[36].

The idea however that the sacrifice lacked a head was not immediately accepted. The myth itself tells us that the Gods

35. Excess of heat and sacrality will be the topic of the second volume of this research.

36. Often in Indian speculations the number three is completed by a fourth one, remaining subtle and impalpable. Cf. e.g. the final nasalization of the sacred syllable AUM or the fourth status (*turīyā*) of Upaniṣadic realization (cf. e.g. MandUp).

were engaged in the Soma sacrifice in its 'normal' form and satisfied with it as it was, even though, according to the myth, it was "without a head". The fact that the Gods are said to still persist in celebrating the Soma sacrifice in the traditional way even though it is 'incomplete', and seek to suppress the knowledge of "how to restore the head to the whole of the sacrifice"[37], records the opposition encountered by those who wanted to introduce the new rite. However, the innovation did take place through a compromise which could at least retain the idea that, even without the addition of a new head, the sacrifice was once complete: *pravargya* can be added only after the *yajamāna* has offered his second or third Soma Sacrifice.[38]

Another thing which is of interest in the myth is the explicit mention of Kurukṣetra[39]. Whether the place was really that in actual fact or not, is of no importance here, but its explicit mention could perhaps be an indication that the myth wants to link this innovation in the Soma Sacrifice to that great movement of ritual and doctrinal renewal for which Kurukṣetra is so dear to both the Vedic and Epic Indian tradition[40]. At this point it is interesting to note how a 'learned myth' can reveal not only the actual state of affairs which gave rise to it but also all the doctrine which serves it as support. It is significant that it is during a sacrificial session held there that the Gods, mostly the traditional ones, spontaneously feel the need to acquire a 'deeper knowledge' of what they are about to do. In this sense, the Gods associate themselves with the sentiments of a society whose religion had reached the limit of exteriorization and now feels the need both for a re-systematization of its religious patrimony and for deeper understanding of its significance on an inner and spiritual level beyond the normal ritual requirements. The Gods, significantly, want to know more just in Kurukṣetra

37. Cf. SatBr XIV. 1. 1. 17-19 (mentioned above in notes 26, 28 and 29).

38. Cf. SatBr XIV. 2.2. 44 already hinted at in note 32 and KausBr VIII. 3.

39. Cf. SatBr XIV. 1.1.2 : *teṣāṃ kurukṣetraṃ devayajanamāsa* /....

40. Cf. the importance of Kurukṣetra in Vedic literature and especially in the Purāṇas in G. BONAZZOLI, "Places of Purāṇic Recitation according to the Purāṇa-s", *Purāṇa*, XXIII, 1 (Jan., 1981), Varanasi (All-India Kashiraj Trust), pp. 48-61.

where the Indian tradition says that Vyāsa undertook the monumental work of systematizing the Vedas and the Mahābhārata.[41]

Another indication of the 'actuality'[42] of the myth is that, in the divine contest, the winner is a 'new Deity', namely Viṣṇu who up to that time has not held any prominent place but who precisely because of his victory and his identification with the Cosmic Sacrifice, begins to soar high in the Vedic Pantheon. "Indeed Viṣṇu, he himself (becomes) this sacrifice"[43]. Thus the myth presents pictorically what is already known from another source, namely, that the wind of reform which is blowing over Brāhmaṇic India has brought in its wake a 'mysterious' understanding of the sacrifice and its effects. The first concrete result is the realization that it is possible for one who possesses such an understanding to become identified with the Sacrifice itself. The possessor of this knowledge is, in the myth, Viṣṇu, who becomes, by the fact that he came to know the cosmic Dynamism at its highest form, the Supreme Deity above all the other Gods. Indeed, Viṣṇu goes on to become the Highest God in the 'Vaiṣṇavite' Pantheon and in the new Brāhmaṇism which is known today by the name of Hinduism. The 'wise man' can also identify himself with the sacrifice and by so doing transcend Death, the common fate allotted to the other members of his species.

The myth's purpose is not only to teach this deeper saving knowledge. Its principal purpose is to justify a liturgical reform and especially to explain how it is that a sacrificial session, which, up to then, was considered complete, all of a sudden finds itself obliged to admit that it is "without a head". At the same time, the myth points out the danger in which spiritual exaltation, unless adequately controlled, can put him who experiences it. Viṣṇu was the only one among the Gods who was capable of reaching to the depths of the sacrifice and identifying

41. Cf. G. BONAZZOLI "The Dynamic Canon of the Purāṇa-s", *Purāṇa*, XXI, 2 (July, 1979), Varanasi (All India Kashirāj Trust), pp. 116-166.

42. By 'actuality' we mean the contemporaneity of the event with its account in the myth.

43. SatBr XIV. 1. 1. 6 quoted in note 17.

himself with it, but "was unable to sustain its glory"[44] just as many of the new ascetics were unable to do.[45] Viṣṇu became proud and decided to keep the knowledge he acquired all to himself. This is a dramatic way of expressing another consequence of the interiorization of the ritual, namely the realization that true knowledge cannot easily be communicated since it lies hidden in the depths of a live experience. Viṣṇu has won for himself "the depths of the sacrifice" with his personal effort, which, even if he wanted, he could not pass on to the others. Direct knowledge of the Truth is now a personal experience which one needs to acquire for oneself and make one's own. Thus in the second divine contest when the Gods rushed to the fallen Viṣṇu to extort the secret from him and understand the sacrifice[46], the victory did not entail a 'mystical' identification with the sacrifice, since Indra's knowledge was only, as if it were, second-hand—directly of Viṣṇu himself but only indirectly of the sacrifice[47].

This 'learned myth', however, besides exposing the consequences of the interiorization of the ritual and of a deepened personal knowledge of the sacrifice, covers also the changes in the liturgy. In other words, it moves on two levels simultaneously, the 'mystical' and the 'liturgical'. This is the reason why it continues to present the Gods as engaged in the Soma sacrifice even though they have reached, won for themselves and assimilated, a more profound understanding of it. After having divided among themselves the traditional offerings, in the way prescribed by the rite itself, they are perfectly satisfied since they do not consider the supposed lack of anything else to be decisive[48]. This is what was probably happening also at the human level in the great Soma Sacrifice celebrated at Kurukṣetra at the time. It was being performed, most likely, in the traditional manner, with the *upasad* in the first three days and

44. SatBr XIV. 1.1. 6 ..*taddhedaṃ yaśo viṣṇur na śaśāka saṃyantuṃ*..

45. Cf. SatBr XIV. 1. 1.6 (end) ..*tad idam apyetar hi naiva sarva iva yaśaḥ śaknoti saṃyantuṃ* // ("and so even now not every one can control that (love of) glory of his".) (tr. EGGELING).

46. Cf. SatBr XIV. 1.1.12 quoted in note 24.

47. See also in Conclusion, p. 280 with note 31ff.

48. Cf. e.g. J.A.B. van BUITENEN, op. cit., p. 16 ff.

the three pressings and libations of Soma three times a day. No need was felt for any additions to the ritual.

This great sacrifice at Kurukṣetra, remembered in different ways by all the later traditions as a point of transition between the preceding age and *kaliyuga*, besides having unified in a systematic way the traditional cultural and religious patrimony of the Vedas was also a theatre of liturgical innovations. Thus it is not unlikely that on that occasion there was inserted into the complex of *somayajña* also the offering of the *gharma* in honour of the Aśvins by some group of dissident ṛṣis. The story is narrated only briefly in the Śatapatha and is not found in the other Brāhmaṇas. It is also variously interpreted [49]. We cannot exclude the possibility that the fusion of the rites was an attempt to reconcile two rival groups. It is not unreasonable to see in the ṛṣi Dadhyañc Atharvan of the myth the mediator in this dispute who offers Indra the possibility of reconciling the 'dissident' group by inserting the latter's rite in the main *Somayajña* under the title of "the head of Makha." But the mediation was a difficult affair. At first, the traditionalists, through Indra their spokesman, refuse. Indra, at least at first, not only refuses to incorporate the *gharma* rite but even forbids the very idea to be made known. He threatens to have the head of whoever divulges it cut off. This drastic punishment—which in the Upaniṣads and elsewhere becomes the penalty of defeat in philosophical disputes—has a profound ritual import and already serves to give in outline the new level to which a dispute of this kind is going to be shifted. The traditionalists are convinced that what they are performing is a complete sacrifice with no missing 'head'. If, therefore, the innovators want to add a new 'head' as charged with sacred heat and full of mystical significance as is *pravargya*—so powerful in fact that it is capable of assimilating and identifying the priest with sun—this will evidently lead to a dangerous excess, which can only be balanced by the loss of the head either of the one who performs the combined sacrifice or of the sacrifice itself. The Gods—and the traditionalists—seek to avoid this but they are finally obliged to yield. The very existence of the myth is proof of that. The

49. Cf. SatBr XIV.1.1.18 ff. quoted previously in notes 29-31.

myth, in fact, is narrated by those who by now have succeeded in imposing the fusion of the two rites, so that the Gods ( that is the conservatives) are already aware that theirs is a sacrifice without a head, without sap and intrinsic sweetness (*madhu*), and yet continue to delight in it as it is and do not want to admit defeat to the innovators. Nonetheless the bringing together of these rites had its advantages, especially at a time when, as we have seen, it was necessary to generate much more sacred heat than in previous times when a greater faith and the immediacy of the sacred action were enough to surmount the difficulties presented by the opacity of the sacrificial matter which had to be transformed[50]. Hence the idea of fusing the two rites, after the initial resistance to it was finally accepted with a pledge on the part of the priest to respect, as much as possible, the injunctions of secrecy given by Indra.

Here however a new difficulty arises. *Pravargya* is performed in honour of the Aśvins[51] who, as we have seen, are explicitly said to be absent from the Soma sacrificial session[52]. It is to them, and in secret, that the sweet (*madhu*) doctrine about the 'restoration' of the head to the sacrifice, is taught, which may mean that it was the task of the mediating *ṛṣi* to teach the representatives of the devotees of the Aśvins themselves about the advantages and the way of this fusion. After having convinced the Gods that their own *satra* was incomplete, the mediating *ṛṣi* has to explain also to the Aśvins that the *gharma* of their rite is not the only one to represent the sun (known already from antiquity as "the *gharma* of the Aśvins")[53], but also the head of Viṣṇu cut off by the bow has the same claim. He then equates the two rites representing the sun and present them as the same 'head' which has to be "healed"[54]. The *ṛṣi* in fact knew that this was a doctrine that the Aśvins, being the physicians of the Gods, could undoubtedly value. Both factions have to see that there is a

50. See above in Ch. IV, p. 97 ff.

51. Cf. RV VII. 70.2.

52. Cf. SatBr XIV.1.1.1 (quoted in note 12) and ib. XIV. 1. 1. 15-17 (note 27) whee the Aśvins are not mentioned.

53. Cf. AV XI. 5.

54. Cf. SatBr XIV.1.1.9 (note 20 and 21).

sound basis for the proposed fusion (even if artificial) and at the same time that they have to be satisfied with this way of reconciling their differences. This fusion could produce much greater sacred energy, provided one knew how to confine it within certain limits and thus diminish its perils.

The imparting to the Aśvins of the secret doctrine of the integration of *Pravargya* into the body of one of the most important Brāhmaṇic rites is, moreover, the imparting of the same doctrine, with its recondite meanings, to the priest whose task it is to perform *pravargya* together with *upasad* of *agniṣṭoma*. This doctrine has, however, to be imparted in secret and surrounded with many precautions. A concentration of energy is extremely dangerous and only those who are spiritually strong—that is, strengthened for the purpose—can bear it.

We shall now pass on to see in some detail some of the more salient features relevant to our study, and begin with a preliminary of the rite, namely the initiation and instruction into its secret doctrine.

2. *The Intermediate Initiation* (*avāntaradīkṣā*)[55]:

The texts speak of two distinct *avāntaradīkṣās* in the Soma sacrifice, each one of which is linked in one way or another with *pravargya*. The first is a simple initiation which the *yajamāna* and his wife must undergo to welcome the arrival of Soma and perform *pravargya*. It consists in the repetition of certain formulas and in retaining the power of the hymns of *yajus* by tightly fastening the belt and closing hard the fists[56]. At this time the water is boiled on *gārhapatya* which will be used during *pravargya* which follows. Immediately after this initiatory rite some Sūtras prescribe certain rites to be performed on the Soma plant with some of the hot water just mentioned, after which one

55. The *avāntaradīkṣā* is dealt with in BaudhSS VI. 3-5 (SK vol. II, pt. I, p. 67 ff.) and ib. IX. 19 f. (SK, vol. II, pt I, p. 18 ff.). Cf. for a complete exposition from the ApSS integrated with variants from other Śrauta Sūtra J.A.B. van BUITENEN, op. cit., appendix I, p. 137ff., which is the basis of our reconstruction.

56. Cf. KatyaSS VIII. 2. 4. f; ManSS II.2. 1.6-8; BaudhSS VI.19; etc. Cf. also, besides J.A.B. van BUITENEN loc cit., W. CALAND & V. HENRY op. cit., p. 66.

proceeds to the offering of *pravargya* if this is to be performed.[57] This *avāntaradīkṣā*, therefore, does not seem to be directly linked to *pravargya* as such, but is rather a further consecration, added as an 'intermediate' (*avāntara*) initiation, meant to purify and strengthen the sacrificer at the moment when he is about to come into a more direct contact with Soma. When *pravargya* was later introduced, this *avāntaradīkṣā* was probably considered to be a sufficient purification and a powerful enough *vrata* even for *pravargya*. Still, this initiation clearly forms part of the Soma sacrifice complex and is undergone in any case, even when *pravargya* is not performed[58].

However, when the texts of the Yajurveda School speak of *pravargya* they generally mention at the end of their exposition, another *dīkṣā* which, though also called '*avāntaradīkṣā*' and though including the recitation of some of the formulas and the performance of some of the rites proper to the preceding initiation, is much more complex and seems to be completely independent of the *agniṣṭoma* sacrificial complex[59]. It requires a whole year although there is no hint in the Soma rites of such a long waiting period. Moreover, from what we can make out from the Sūtras, this kind of initiation is optional and required only for one who wishes to acquire a deep knowledge of the 'mysteries' in their most hidden meaning. This is perhaps the reason why the one who has to undergo the initiation is not the *yajamāna* as one would expect, but usually the officiating priest. It is the *adhvaryu* who, if he so desires, may ask a competent master to disclose to him the inner meaning of the rite he may be called upon to perform. We must admit, however, that this restriction is less clear in the rules prescribed by the Śatapatha Brāhmaṇa[60].

57. Cf. KatyaSS VIII.2.6-13 mentioning Pravargya in v. 14 and ManSS II.2.1.9 ff. with the mentioning of *Pravargya* also in v. 14.

58. Cf. W. CALAND & V. HENRY op. cit., p. 66 and J.A.B. van BUITENEN, op. cit., p. 41.

59. Cf SatBr XIV.1.1.26 which gives instructions for the *dīkṣā* at the beginning of its exposition of the rite, and ManSS IV. 7. 1ff. (and almost all the other Sūtras) that described the *dīkṣā* at the end.

60. Cf. SatBr XIV. 1. 1. 26 ff. Quoted *in extenso* in note 63.

We really cannot say whether this special initiation was already known at the time of the first Vedas, when *pravargya* was offered at dawn and evening to the Aśvins but probably was not yet linked with *Somayajña*. We get to know about it as soon as *pravargya* is linked to the equally potent Soma sacrifice, and when the doctrine regarding the conjunction of the two rites, considered to be a 'mystery' (*āraṇyaka*), needs to be explained and handed down. This *dikṣā* appears to be a *unique* phenomenon in the world of the Vedic ritual in which an initiation is generally given, at the beginning of every sacrifice, to the *yajamāna* who arranges for the sacrifice and not to the priests whom he invites to officiate at it. In this particular case, on the contrary, the Sūtras and, to a lesser extent, the Śatapatha Brāhmaṇa, insist that it is the officiating priest who is to undergo this initiation. We can deduce that this priest is the one who acts as *adhvaryu* from the fact that it is only in his texts that we find the rules for the initiation, while the Brāhmaṇic texts of the other Vedic groups practically ignore them.[61] This initiation could be interpreted to be a special consecration to render the officiating priest fit to deal with greater ritual energy and to enable him to counteract the excess of the sacredness which he will have to contact during the celebration of *pravargya*[62]. A closer look at the texts, however, gives one the impression that it is disconnected from the actual performance of the rite. It seems to be concerned more with teaching the enquirer its 'mysterious' meaning than with giving information about the subtleties of its material performance. It remains true, however, that many of these initiatory rites also aim at concentrating on the person being initiated a quantity of ritual energy, much greater than the normal one, to enable him to officiate with greater efficiency and bear the burden of his deepened mystical knowledge.

We have already said that the master who gives instruction during the *avāntaradikṣā* is directly responsible for the moral

61. Cf. SatBr XIV. 1. 1. 27 ff. The two Brāhmaṇas of the RV ignore it. The Sūtra, however, mentioned the rules for the initiation, those of the RV included.

62. This interpretation can be allowed if one takes into consideration SatBr XIV. 1. 1. 27 ff. It appears also in J. A. B. van BUITENEN, op. cit. app. I.

and spiritual welfare of his disciple—who, in any case, must already be a person highly skilled in the technique of handling sacred things and endowed with great moral virtues. Hence the master must be particularly careful whom to choose as his disciple. It is for this reason that the Śatapatha Brāhamaṇa warns: "One must not teach this (i.e., *pravargya*) to any and every one, lest Indra should cut off his head; but one may only teach it to one who is a member of his family, or a well-known friend or who is well versed in liturgical matters"[63]. The initiation is as difficult for the master as it is for the disciple. It is the master who is to observe under vow certain rules of abstinence for three nights, for it is he who is to be interiorly fortified to be able to utter a secret so charged with sacrality. The number three is significant for it stands for the three principal seasons of the year which, in their turn, stand for the sun. Thus, by his abstinence, a further idenification is brought between the *gharma* and the sun[64]. Moreover, the master must reinforce his vow by 'taking a sip of hot water'[65] to witness to his resolution 'to teach as a *tapasvī*'. It is he, more than the disciple, who must refrain from eating meat, precisely for the same reason.[66] On the contrary, it is the disciple who is to observe certain tabus—but even here it is not said that these rules are not to be observed by both master and disciple. In any case, these tabus, and other prescriptions, are to preserve the purity of the disciple (and also of the master) by keeping him away from impure objects and persons and to accumulate in him the sacred energy of the sun. Since *pravargya* is centred on the *gharma* and the *gharma* is identified with the sun, all the ceremonies are carried out in strict relation to the sun. Hence the *dīkṣā* of *pravargya*, where the disciple seeks to enter into a direct and personal contact with the sun, is parallel to the *dīkṣā* of *agnicayana* where the *yajamāna* seeks to be

63. SatBr XIV.1.1.26 *tan na sarvas mā'anubrūyāt / enasyaṃ hi tad atho nenma'indraḥ śiraś chinadad iti yo nveva jñātas tasmai brūyād atha yo 'nūcāno atha yo 'sya priyaḥ syānna tveva sarvasmā 'iva //* (mentioned in notes 7 and 33 and 59 and 60).

64. Cf. SatBr XIV.1.1. 28 *tisro rātrīr vrataṃ carati / trayo vā 'ṛtavaḥ saṃvatsarasya ṣaṃvatsara eṣa ya eṣa tapati eṣa u pravargyas tad etam evai tat prīṇāti tasmāt..*

65. Cf. SatBr XIV. 1. 1. 29 *taptam ācāmati tapasvy anubrava iti*....The water used in the *pravargya* is always hot. Cf. also BharSS XI. 5. 4.

66. Cf. SatBr XIV. 1. 1. 29 ..*amāñsāśy anubrūte tapasvy*....

identified with his fire. Here also, one of the 'mysteries' of *pravargya* and its *dīkṣā* is this identification of the initiate with the sun. However, because the sun is a centre of sacrality which is much more powerful and dangerous than the fire, the intiation to *pravargya* must necessarily be different from that to *agnicayana*. The initiate cannot surely acquire the same confidence with the *mahāvīra* as the *yajamāna* can with the *ukhy-agni*[67]. In the two cases, in fact, the relation is quite different: in the former case, the initiate is to be related to nothing less than the sun, while in the latter case, the *yajamāna* is to be related to a fire 'made according to the measure of a man' (which explains why the measurements of its vessel are taken from those of the palm of his hand). It is with the sun that the initiated must cover himself now, in a kind of disguised assimilation with it, to ensure an effective exchange of sacred energy with it, and it is the sun which he will later have to manipulate to make, venerate and offer as the *mahāvīra*. However, the sun, as a source of sacred energy, is more difficult to handle than the fire. To accumulate in himself this energy, the initiate must not even look at anything which is associated with darkness like, for example, the uninitiated or those who, in any case, cannot be initiated such as women and *śūdras*[68]. For the same reason, he cannot look at impure animals (such as dogs and crows), blood, corpses and food which is unsuitable to be offered in sacrifice. Women, *śūdras*, impure animals and the like represent evil and darkness. To avoid them is to avoid "mingling good and bad, light and darkness, truth and falsehood"[69]. Moreover, he must not weaken the effect of the heat of the sun on him by wearing sandals, using umbrellas, riding on wheel-carts[70] or wearing clothes[71]. It is clear that by this injunction nothing is allowed to come between the initiate and the sun or between him and the earth which is the

67. Cf. previously ch. VII, p. 209 ff.

68. Cf. ApSS XV. 20.

69. SatBr XIV. 1. 1.31 ..*necchriyaṃ ca pāpmānaṃ ca nej jyotiś ca tamaś ca net satyānṛte saṃsṛjānīti* //

70. Cf. ApSS XV. 11-12 (cf. a summary in J.A.B.van BUITENEN, op. cit, app. I.)

71. Cf. SatBr XIV.1. 1. 33.

recipient of the sun's rays. It is for this reason that a Sūtra prohibits him from climbing trees (for these offer shade) and another from going down into a well[72]. Significantly enough, the novice is not allowed to take a bath or study with wet clothes on[73]—actions which, on the contary, are meritorious in normal *dīkṣā* of a *brahmacārī*. If he accidentally gets wet in the rain or finds himself in places still wet because of rainfall, he has to immediately expiate his fault by reciting a suitable *mantra*.[74] The Śatapatha adds that, during the day, he should neither spit nor urinate lest he should defile the sun, or weaken it[75]. Finally, many texts forbid him from drinking from earthen vessels[76]. The Śatapatha explains the reason for this last prohibition by saying that on earth many lies are told and by drink- from a vessel made of earth, one comes in contact with untruth[77]. We have just seen how the initiate must always keep in touch with the earth and avoid even wearing sandals ! This apparent contradiction could be explained by the fact that while the earth is the recipient of light and solar heat, an earthen vessel is made of earth which is mixed with water which diminishes the earth's power and heat. For sacred use, such an earthen vessel must first pass through the fire but, as we have seen, it is probable that for natural use it was only dried in the sun[78]. Hence the prohibition clearly concerns earthen vessels made of 'raw' earth which has not been baked. It is from such vessels that the initiate and his master are forbidden to drink. Another prohibition imposed on the initiate is that he should not sleep during the first night of his *dīkṣā* and during the more important lunar phases of the year of his instruction. This prohibition is somehow intended to instil in the disciple

72. Cf. respectively Baudh SS IX. 19 and BharSS XI.21.

73. Cf. BaudhSS IX. 19 and also J.A.B. van BUITENEN op. cit., app. I, par 6, note 4, p. 139.

74. Cf. J.A.B. van BUITENEN, op. cit, app. 1, par 7, p. 139.

75. Cf. SatBr XIV. 1. 1.33.

76. Cf. SatBr XIV. 1. 1. 30 ..*amṛṇmayapāyī*...

77. Cf. SatBr XIV.1. 1. 30..*asti vā'asyāṃ saṃsṛṣṭam iva yad asyām anṛtaṃ vadati tasmād amṛṇmayapāyī* ..

78. Cf. above ch. IV, especially p. 94 ff., fn. 34.

a kind of rejection of the night and its power to weaken solar energy[79].

Also to reject the night and intensify the power of the sun and of the initiate, rites are performed the first evening of the *dīkṣā* and the following morning. After the afternoon prayers in his place of seclusion in the jungle, the disciple is led blindfold to his master's house where he is not allowed either to sleep or lie down during the whole night. On his being led back to the jungle the following morning, his eyes are uncovered and he is made to rest them on six or seven objects designed to augment his spiritual power, such as, the sun, the fire, water (probably hot), gold, etc.[80] At night, he must not touch food or, if he does, the food must be illumined by a fire.[81] The Śatapatha Brāhmaṇa on the contrary enjoins him to eat only at night, the food being illumined by a fire[82].

When all these conditions have been fulfilled, the instruction is imparted by the master to his disciple and repeated, verse by verse, by the latter, both of them sitting around the fire ritually lit in the morning, and holding in their hands *darbha* or *dūrvā* grass. Since this *dīkṣā* ends with the teaching of the texts which concern *pravargya*, one could very well ask whether the previous strengthening of the disciple was meant to counter-balance the burden to be imposed on him by this sacred knowledge, or whether it was meant to prepare him as future priest for the performance of *pravargya.* In any case, during the course of instruction and at the end, the disciple must offer his master certain gifts as recompense (*dakṣiṇā*) which the master is not to pass on to anybody else immediately but only after a day or two have elapsed so that they have time enough to leave on him the imprint of their luminous energy[83].

This intermediate initiation, as we have said, may last a whole year. Actually it generally lasts a whole year, that is, the mea-

79. Cf. the comment of J.A.B. van BUITENEN op. cit., p. 40: "..a denial as it were of the night when the sun's power vanishes".

80. Cf. ApSS XV. 30.9; BharSS XI.21 (J.A.B. van BUITENEN, op. cit. p. 138 f.).

81. Cf. Ap SS XV.20. 11.

82. Cf. SatBr XIV.1. 1.33 towards the end.

83. Cf. SatBr XIV. 1.1. 32.

sure of time the sun takes to make a complete revolution. A year is therefore taken to be the standard duration of this initiation, and this has a further means of strengthening the identification of the year with the sun, the sun with *pravargya*, and *pravargya* with the future officiating priest[64]. However, some Sūtras allow that it be prolonged till the instruction be completed, and this can take upto seven years[85].

A rite, among the preliminaries of *pravargya* and very significant from our point of view, is that which concerns the making and baking of *mahāvīra*. It is this rite which we shall now proceed to examine.

### 3. *Mahāvīra and How to Make and Bake it*:

*Mahāvīra* is the vessel around which revolves the entire ceremony of *pravargya*.[86] It is through it that the identification of the priest with the sun, about which we have spoken so far, takes place. Thus, all the efforts of the priests to put in concrete practice the mystical teachings are concentrated on the way it is made.

*Mahāvīra* reminds us very much of *ukhā* of *agnicayana*, so much so that it is difficult not to see a reciprocal influence of the one on the other. Even though this may be true of their preparation and the process of baking, their distinct shape and use clearly testify to their distinct and independent origins. Each one undoubtedly gets its distinctive characteristics from within the context of the rite in which it is used—characteristics, therefore, which are peculiar to one and not to the other. This is particularly true of *mahāvīra* which, as *gharma*, goes certainly much further back in the history of the Vedic cult. It is the original tripartite form of *mahāvīra*, unquestioned by any Brāhmaṇa, which is to be held responsible for the attempt, not always accepted, of making three *ukhās*[87]. Again most likely it is

84. Cf. SatBr XIV.1. 1.27 *saṃvatsaravāsine 'nubrūyāt / eṣa vai saṃvatsaro ya eṣa tapaty eṣa u pravargyas tad etam evaitat prīṇāti //*

85. Cf. ManSS IV. 7. 8 where the option is of one year, three, five, and even seven. Cf. also ApSS XV. 21.2.

86. Cf. for a complete description of the making of *mahāvīra* J.A.B. van BUITENEN, op. cit., ch. 3, p. 9 ff. and p. 55 ff.

87. Cf. previously in ch. VII, p. 195 and note 83.

the material out of which *ukhā* is made that provides the alternative for making *mahāvīra* out of clay, when the metal, of which it was originally made, is found no longer suitable for the modified form of the ritual.

When the *Pravargya* rite was included in *Somayajña* in the general movement of systematization of the cult, through which Vedic culture passed in a certain period of its history[88], it was already undergoing an internal metamorphosis. Its profound symbolism demanded greater heat than before, to translate it into practice, greater than the melting point of gold or of other metal used up to then. We have seen how priestly reflection on the liturgy led to the realization that sacred heat is one of the most tangible bases for the efficacy of the rite which led the experts to consciously augment this heat to extreme degrees. One of the rites in which this heat was concentrated more and more was precisely *pravargya*, a rite which already from ancient times demanded extra heat[89]. Now its incorporation into the Soma sacrifice, where its significance as 'head' of the sacrifice is further emphasized by a new identification with the sun—not only as the *gharma* of the Aśvins[90] but also as the head of Viṣṇu shot out in the sky and turned into the sun[91]—brings forwards its newly found mystical significance by an increase in heat during the heating of the offering. The only material which can resist this amount of heat is this mixture of clay used to make *ukhā* and the bricks for *agnicayana*. The same mixture, more or less modified to meet the liturgical requirements, is therefore substituted as material for the three *mahāvīras* and the other implements of the rite. That this material is a substitution for the original metal can be inferred from the fact that its substitution must be duly justified by the Brāhmaṇic authorities. Since "some ask, 'Seeing that the offering to the gods is made in wooden vessels (*vānaspatya*), how is it that this (*gharma*) is offered in one of clay?' "[92] the Brāhmaṇic theore-

88. Cf. previously in ch. II, p. 27, fn. 12. where the offering to the Aśvins is mentioned as being hot as its specific characteristic. Cf. also p. 224ff. above.
89. Cf. e.g. AV XI.5.11.
90. Cf. RV V.30.15 quoted in note 12 of ch. II, p. 27.
91. Cf. SatBr XIV.1.1.11 quoted above.
92. SatBr XIV. 2. 2.53 : *tad āhuḥ / yad vānaspatyair devebhyo juhvaty atha kasmād etaṃ mṛṇmayenaiva juhotīti..*

tician replies on the basis of the Foundation-myth which we have just described and by recalling the life-sap which flowed from the severed head of Viṣṇu and fell to the ground, so that only by gathering it from the earth—hence the clay—can it be reintegrated into the divine body[93]. But he suggests also a more subtle and at the same time more practical reason, namely, the inadequacy of the original metallic material to bear the high degree of heat which is now required in the rite: "If in fact it were made of wood, it would burn; if of gold, it would dissolve; if of copper (*loha*), it would melt; if of stone, it would burn the handling-sticks"[94].

Once the change of material is approved and sanctioned, the making of the implements is added to the group of preliminary rites, adequately modified partly on the pattern of *ukhā*[95]. The material is ritually collected (*sambhāra*) more or less in the same way as for *ukhā*, only that the animals which accompany the procession to the place where the clay and the various types of soil are to be dug out are more suited to the internal requirements of the rite. These animals are a goat suckling a male kid, which will be particularly used for milking later, and the unfailing horse[96]. The *mantras* which are recited during the collection are slightly different from those recited for *ukhā* and invoke Savitṛ, the Aśvins, Pūṣan, all of whom are more or less linked to *pravargya* either as recipients of the offering or as personifications of the Sun with which the *gharma* which is to be constructed will be later identified[97].

This material consists, more or less as in the case of *ukhā*, of clay, earth dug out by a wild boar (which is associated with

93. Cf. SatBr XIV.2.53 (end) : ....*yajñasya śīrṣacchinnasya raso vyakṣaratesa ime dyāvāpṛthivī 'agacchad yan mṛd iyantad yad āpo'sau tan mṛdaścāpāṃ ca mahāvīrāḥ kṛtā bhavanti*..

94. SatBr XIV.2.2.54 : *sa yad vānaspatyaḥ syāt / pradahyeta yad hiraṇmayaḥ syāt pralīyeta yal lohamayaḥ syāt prasicyeta yadayasmayaḥ syāt pradahetparīśāsāvathaiṣa evaitasmā/atiṣṭhata* ("he himself submitted") *tasmād etaṃ mṛṇmayenaiva juhoti //* (that is why they offer by means of an earthen vessel).

95. Cf. SatBr XIV.1.2.1 ff. till the end of XIV.2.4.17. Cf. also J.A.B. van BUITENEN, op. cit., p. 55 ff. Cf. also Ch. VII, p. 192 f.

96. Cf. ApSS YV. 1.6.

97. Cf. SatBr XIV.1.2.7 f. J.A.B. van BUITENEN, op. cit., p. 56, par. 2 quotes prayers addressed also to Indra and to the Maruts.

Viṣṇu of whom it will be an *avatāra*)[98], earth taken from a termitary (in honour of the mythical ants which helped to cut off the head of Viṣṇu)[99], certain plants sacred to Indra (these vary according to the schools), hairs of the goat which provides the milk, and hairs from a black antelope's skin which, spread out on the place of the collection of the material, receives the ingredients[100]. Everything is collected with the recital of formulas which link the ingredients to Prajāpati and his creative seed[101]. To these should be added the goat milk which will be used, after the vessel is made and baked, to cool *mahāvira* and which is linked to the heat (*śucā*) which poured out from the severed head of Viṣṇu[102]. Thus, the clay, the earth of two kinds, the plants, the animals' hairs and the goat milk amount to the same number of elements (that is, five) which, at least according to the Śukla School, is the characteristic number of the *sambhāra* of the first Fire-altar[103]. And here too—and we are following here the same school as represented by the Śatapatha Brāhmaṇa—the reason is the same: the identification of the collection with the year (which is composed of five seasons), and the year is the Sun[104] and Bṛhaspati[105].

98. Cf. SatBr XIV.1.2.11: *atha varāha vihatam* / The legend which follows, connected also with the *mantra* pronounced during the collection of this type of earth (VajSam XXXVII. 5), recalls the story of the mythical boar Emusha who raised the earth from the water (Cf. ch. VI, note 20).

99. Cf. SatBr XIV.1.2.10 giving as meaning the legend previously reported (cf SatBr XIV.1.1.8 quoted in this chapter in note 19).

100. Cf. SatBr XIV.1.2.12. The black antelope's skin is assimilated to the sacrifice itself in SatBr XIV.1.2.2 (*yajño vai kṛṣṇājinaṃ*); Manu II.23 connects it geographically with the 'country of sacrifice' contrasted with the 'country of the foreigners' (*mleccha*) : *kṛṣṇasāras tu carati mṛgo yatra svabhāvataḥ / sa jñeyo yajñiyo deśo mleccha deśastataḥ paraḥ //*

101. Cf. BharSS XI.2.7.

102. Cf. SatBr XIV.1.2.13 : *athājākṣīraṃ / yajñasya śīrṣacchinnasya śugud akrāmat tato 'jā samabhavat tayaivainam etac chucā samardhayati kṛtsnaṃ karoti....*

103. Cf. SatBr II.1.1.12 previously quoted in ch. VI note 30. The ingredients collected for the *ukhā* have, however, somehow different characteristics; cf. ch. VII, p. 192 ff., notes 69 and 70, 71.

104. Cf. SatBr XIV.1.2.14 : *tānvā'etān pañca sambhārāntsambharati / pāṅkto yajñaḥ paṅktaḥ paśuḥ pañcartavaḥ saṃvatsarasya saṃvatsara eṣa ya eṣa tapaty eṣa u pravargyas tad etam evaitat prīṇatī..*

105. Cf. SatBr XIV.1.2.15 : *..eṣa vai brahmaṇaspatir ya eṣa tapaty eṣa u pravargyas tad etam evaitat prīṇāti tasmād..*

Finally, the material is wrapped in the antelope skin and taken to the sacrificial hut, within a special enclosure, to be handled and cooked safe from the prying eyes of the uninitiated, especially of those who can in no way be initiated, such as *śūdras* and women[106]. At least according to some schools, the earthen pots can be then prepared and made only by the *adhvaryu* to the exclusion even of the *yajamāna*. In fact, one Sūtra begins its description of *pravargya* by the formulas which are to be recited by the *yajamāna* after the rite of the preparation and baking of these pots is already completed—which is a sign that the *yajamāna* appears on the scene only at this precise moment of the ceremony[107]. This is well in accordance with the secrecy and the mysteriousness of the rite, particularly where *mahāvīra* is concerned.

When the material is deposited in its assigned place, the horse which by now has already taken a great part in the rite, is led to it and made to breathe on it while the priest recites a verse. This verse gives us to understand that it is this very breath of the horse which gives the material all it needs to become the head of the sacrifice: "give life, *prāṇa*, *apāna*, *vyāna*, sight, hearing, mind, voice, body, strength..."[108] After the clay has thus been further strengthened with vital energy, the *adhvaryu* begins to knead the clay, softening it with boiling water perfumed with resin (whenever water is used in *pravargya* it must be boiling) and with the goat milk which, originally, was perhaps directly milked on to it.

The kneading of the clay is performed with a series of precautions which are not required anywhere else. This is already indicative of the profoundly sacred character of the vessel which is being made. Not only is it made in a secluded place – even if

106. Cf. ApSS XV.1.1-6 summarized in J.A.B. van BUITENEN, op. cit., pp. 55-57.

107. Cf. J.A.B. van BUITENEN, op. cit., p. 55, par. I, note 3. "BaudhSS has the 'formal opening' after II.1 [i.e. after the preparation of the *Mahāvīra* ]. This means that the [Yajamāna ] had no need to appear until after all of I. [namely the making of *mahāvīra* ], which in turn means that the rites of the I were strictly the Adhvaryu's office, or, more likely, simply not held, as the paraphernalia was already there".

108. BharSS XI. 2.9.

not in a place covered with a roof because the sun must always shine on *mahāvīra*—and far from the inquisitive eyes of the uninitiated, but also the *adhvaryu* himself, who, in making it, must observe special regulations. He must not breathe over it lest he should pollute it, and therefore he must keep his face turned away from it. He must not handle it with his bare hands but must use a pointed stick made for the purpose[109]. He must see to it that it is always in the sun and that he does not let his shadow fall upon it while he is working on it[110]. If he does not succeed in finishing his work before sunset, he must interrupt everything and take up his work again the following day when the sun is shining[111]. No darkness, not even the suspicion of the approaching night, can overshadow the making of the vessel.

There are three *mahāvīras* to be made, and, although in the rite only the first is really used, this number is never brought into question, in contrast to what we have seen is the case with *ukhā*. Moreover, each one of them is equated with one of the three worlds, the terrestrial, the atmospheric and the heavenly[112] and linked, from the very beginning, with one of the three famous metres which accompany the offerings of Soma in the morning, noon and afternoon, that is, with the *gāyatrī*, the *triṣṭubh* and the *jagatī* respectively[113]. Their shape is characteristically theirs and differs both from that of *ukhā* and from that of any other container of libations. *Mahāvīra*, faithful to the name "head of Makha" given to it by the *Śukla* School, resembles a head, whose top part, wide enough to receive the offerings, is slightly round.[114].

109. Cf. J.A.B. van BUITENEN, op. cit., p. 59, I, par 7, (end) where these restrictions are summarized from various Śrauta Sūtras (as BaudhSS, BharSS, ApSS, etc.) but omitted by ManSS and KatyaSS.

110. Ibidem.

111. Cf. BharSS XI. 2.18 ff. and ApSS XV.2.4-13.

112. Cf. SatBr XIV.1.2.22 ff...*ṛjave tvety asau vai loka ṛjuḥ satyaṃ hy ṛjuḥ satyam eṣa ya eṣa tapaty eṣa u prathamaḥ pravargyas*....(same for vv 23 and 24 for the '*antarikṣa*' represented by Vāyu and for this world represented by Agni).

113. Cf. BharSS XI. 2.24.

114. Thus is the form of a *mahāvīra* I saw in the Museum of the Vaidika Saṃśodhana Maṇḍala (Pune, Tilak Vidyapeetha Nagar) and this is also stated

Only when the shape is ready, does one proceed to hollow out its interior, with the same bamboo stick which served to knead and give shape to the clay, so as to make a place for the offering. Thus hollowed out, the three parts of the vessel are joined from the inside forming one container[115].

When the first *mahāvīra* is finished, it is set apart in the sun so that this solidifies, strengthens and infuses its energy into its own symbol,[116] while the *adhvaryu* proceeds to make the other two as well as the spoons for the offering and the other implements which have to be made of baked clay including some bricks for *agnicayana*, if this is going to take place[117]. But not all of these implements are made to the accompaniment of the recital of formulas. Silence and the recital of formulas alternate, and this has for its purpose—as we said already when we were dealing with *ukhā* and its accessories—to incorporate into the implements of the sacrifice both the visible and manifest part of prajāpati and his transcendent, undefined and ungraspable part[118] after which the implements are cleaned by means of intertwined stalks of grass recalling, here again, the Foundation-myth when the sap which flowed from the severed head of Viṣṇu propped and was gathered in the grass[119]. Finally, the implements are ready for their great trial by fire when they are put into the furnace. As usual, however, they are first fumigated—the significance of which, as we have already explained, is to avoid the sacred fire entering into direct contact with something which is still raw, that is, with what still totally belongs to the profane world[120].

in SatBr XIV. 1.2.17 which maintains that the *mahāvīra* is the head of Makha. J.A.B. van BUITENEN, op. cit., p. 11, suggests that it is "the rough form of a man sitting crosslegged....".

115. Cf.BharSS XI.3.1.

116. Cf. BharSS XI.3.2. Cf J.A.B. van BUITENEN, op. cit. p. 59 for a complex description including many Śrauta Sūtras.

117. Cf. BharSS XI.3. 3-8 and also Ap SS XV.3.8. ff.

118. Cf. SatBr XIV.1.2.18.Cf. the same alternation of silence and formulas in ch. VII, note 95 for the *ukhā's* and the *agnicayana's* bricks.

119. Cf. ApSS XV.3.15

120. Cf. ApSS XV. 3.15. As parallel of this fumigation see ch. VII, p. 198. And for the avoidance of the contact of the 'raw' with the sacred fire, see my already quoted article "The Role of Heat...."

The fumigation is carried out, as for *ukhā*, with horse dung.[121] However, here the required number of dung balls to be burned is not laid down, nor is anything said about the need to have a kind of combustible material which, while associated with the Sun, is at the same time devoid of power. Rather the stress here is on the energy which the horse dung has in itself. It must be of a horse in its full physical vigour and particularly strong[122]. The *mantras* recited on this occasion call on Mitra and Varuṇa, the protectors of the Law, to strengthen the sacrificial implements by their power[123]. The fire used to burn the dung is taken from the *gārhapatya*[124]. To be fumigated, the three *mahāvīras* are held by special tongs on the smoke. From now on, they can no longer be touched by hand and when they have to be moved for any reason whatsoever they have to be carried by means of a special kind of gripping tool. In fact, its process of divinization has now begun and no matter how consecrated the priest might be, he can no longer touch it. And this is one point wherein *mahāvīra*, about to be ready, begins to be clearly distinguished from *ukhā* while, so far, the manner of making both has been similar. *Mahāvīra* has its own history and its own function and, if, for the reasons mentioned earlier, it had to borrow from *ukhā* the material of which it is made and the manner in which it is made, nothing hinders it now from re-asserting, at the right moment, its own nature and inserting itself, in its own way, into *pravargya* of which it forms part. Thus, while *ukhā* remains a mere container and not only can it be touched by the *yajamāna* but must, as it were, be 'put on' by him and made his to effect the latter's identification with the fire it contains, *mahāvīra* becomes so sacred and potent that nobody dares to touch it directly, not even the *adhvaryu* who is specifically initiated for the purpose and already fortified by his being assimilated to the sun.

121. Cf. Ch. VII, p. 198.

122. SatBr XIV.1.2.20 : *athainān dhūpayati | aśvasya tvā vṛṣṇaḥ śaknā dhūpayāmīti vṛṣā vā'aśvo vīryaṃ vai vṛṣā vīryeṇaivainam etat samardhayati kṛtsnaṃ karoti. . . .*

123. Cf. BharSS XI.3.10; ApSS XV.3.17 f. etc. Cf. J.A.B. van BUITENEN op. cit., p. 60, pt. I, par. 10.

124. Cf. ibidem, the summary of the texts.

The cause of the change from a profane (or semiprofane) object, that is an object still belonging to the transitory, *saṃsāric*, world, to a sacred object, that is an object transformed into the Divine, is, once again, its being baked in a furnace especially prepared for the purpose and dug in the earth to the North of the *gārhapatya*, still safe from the inquisitive eyes of the uninitiated[125]. The hole, dug out in the shape of an oven, is filled with material, and the sacrificial implements are ritually placed in it with appropriate formulas. First is placed the first *mahāvīra* with the words: "You are a flame" (*arcir asi*), then the second with: "You are splendour" (*śocir asi*), the third with: "You are light, you are heat" (*jyotir asi, tapo'si*).[126] Then are placed the other implements but without any formulas[127]. However, the Śatapatha, faithful to its Foundation-myth, has only one formula "You are for Makha, you are for Makha's head !" (*makhāya tvā makhasya tvā śirṣṇa*)[128]. Moreover, it justifies the baking of the implements by saying: "for what is baked, belongs to the Gods"[129].

Once the implements are placed in the furnace, other combustible material is added and the fire is lit by means of a sheaf of *muñja* grass which, in its turn, has been lit, according to the *Kṛṣṇa* School, from the *gārhapatya*[130] but according to the *Śukla* School, from the *dakṣiṇāgni*[131]. In spite of the fact that one *Sūtra* allows the baking to go on also at night[132], the Śatapatha strongly insists that it should be done only during the day and that during the day too the implements have to be taken out of the furnace "because the day belongs to the Gods"[133]. In fact, it is their world that *mahāvīra* is about to join.

125. ibidem.

126. Cf. BharSS XI. 3.14 f.

127. Cf. BharSS XI.3.16.

128. Cf. SatBr XIV.1.2.20. The text also refers to an attempt by the more fastidious theoreticians to regulate the order in which to put the implements in the backing, but then common sense prevails and the implements are put wherever it is most convenient for a good result.

129. SatBr XIV. 1.2.21 (*athaināñ chrapayati*)/*śṛtaṃ hi devānām*..

130. Cf. BharSS XI.3.16.

131. Cf. KatyaSS XXVI. 1.23 which have it lit. on tne Dakṣiṇāgni for similarity with the *ukhā*.

132. Cf. J.A.B. van BUITENEN, op. cit., pt I, par 11, note 7, who mentioned the BaudhSS telling "they baked by day or by night".

133. SatBr XIV.1.2.21 (fine) ..*divodvapeda harhi devānām* //

When they are taken out of the furnace, their transformation is complete. The new implements, and among these especially the three *mahāvīras*, have ceased to belong merely to this world and to him who made them. They have become red, strong—and divinized. The *mantras* to the recital of which they are taken one by one out of the furnace, always by means of the intermediary tool, declare their accomplished assimilation to the three worlds and to their presiding deities, Savitṛ, Vāyu and Agni, who in the Śatapatha are represented by truth (*satya*), courage or efficiency (*sādhu*) and goodness (*sukṣitiḥ*)[134]. The *adhvaryu*, then, deposits them in the place reserved for them, to the North or North-East of the *gārhapatya* and cools and further strengthens them by pouring on them fresh goat milk[135]. The formulas which are pronounced at this moment and the gravel which is strewn around them are intended to impart to them strength and stability through the identification especially of *mahāvīra* with the Sun and its heat, and the confirmation of the ritual link between the one and the other[136]. Moreover, the *mantras* serve to fill the *mahāvīra* with all kinds of wealth so that the new Deity thus arisen, or if one prefers, this new sacrificial mediator thus divinized, may be in a position to preserve and multiply them in favour of the *yajamāna*[137].

When all these preliminaries are over, all the implements are again wrapped in the black antelope skin to shelter them from the gaze of those who are not supposed to look at them. Thus wrapped, they are left hanging somewhere in the sacrificial hut

134. The *mantras* are from VajSam XXXVII.10 : *ṛjave tvā sādhave tvā sukṣityai tvā* commented upon by SatBr XIV.1.8. 22-24: *sa udvapati / ṛjave tvety asau vai loka ṛjuḥ satyam hy ṛjuḥ satyam eṣa ya eṣa tapaty eṣa u prathamaḥ pravargyas tad etam evaitat prīṇāti tasmād āhar'jave tveti / / 22// sādhave tveti / ayaṃ vai sādhur yo'yam pavata'eṣa hīmāṃ lokānt siddho 'nupavata' eṣa u dvitīyaḥ pravargyas tad etam evaitat prīṇāti tasmād āha sādhave ti //23//sukṣityai tveti / ayaṃ vai lokaḥ sukṣitir asmini hi loke sarvāṇi bhūtāni kṣiyanty atho'agnir vai sukṣitir agnir hy evāsmin loke sarvāṇi bhūtāni kṣiyaty eṣa u tṛtīyaḥ pravargyas tad etamevaitat prīṇāti tasmād āha sukṣityai tveti....*

135. Cf. SatBr XIV.1.2.25 for the *Śukla* School, and BharSS XI.4.1-11 for the *Kṛṣṇa*, for the complete process of the taking out of the furnace.

136. Cf. SatBr XIV.1.3.6 (from VajSam XXXVII. 11) : *sūryasya tvā tapasa iti / eṣa vai sūryo ya eṣa tapaty eṣa u pravargyas..*

137. Cf. a summary in J.A.B. van BUITENEN, op. cit., pt I, par 13, p. 62.

itself, or in the hall of the firealtars, to wait their turn to be used in the rite[138]. The Śatapatha Brāhmaṇa brings to a close this description of the preparation of the implements by the mystical remark regarding the identification with, or at least the participation in, life and light of *pravargya* on the part of him who teaches or performs it : "Truly, this life and this light enters into him who teaches or partakes of this (*pravargya*)"[139].

4. *Heating of Mahāvira and Its Place in the Rite :*

Now begins the ceremony of *pravargya* in the strict sense. Up to now, the preparation of *mahāvira* which has taken place in a corner within the enclosure of the altars erected for the occasion has been the work solely, or principally, of the *Adhvaryu* and clearly belongs to the preparatory phase. Moreover, as we have already suggested, it could very well be that one did not have to make new implements, *mahāviras* included, every time one wanted to perform *pravargya.* Since at the end of the ceremony the implements did not have to be destroyed but only set apart, the custom could have easily been introduced of making use of them—they were indestructible even if breakable—again and again in the performance of other *pravargyas.* If such were the case, the rite of the preparation of the earthen vessels would be performed at most once or twice during the life-time of an *Adhvaryu* and of a *yajamāna*, and, at all the other times, the ceremony of *pravargya* would begin directly, during the second day of the Soma sacrifice, before and in connection with the *upasad*[140].

We must not forget that, ever since the time when the Vedic ritual was systematized and fixed with its various modalities once and for all in the Brāhmaṇas and the Sūtras, *pravargya* is no longer an independent rite but forms part of the whole complex of one or other of the Soma sacrifices where it takes its place within the sequence of orher rites. This is one more reason which explains the fact that both, the priestly initiation for *pravargya* and the making of *mahāviras* themselves and of the other imple-

138. Cf. BharSS XI.4.13.

139. SatBr XIV.1.2.26 : *athaitad vai / āyur etaj jyotiḥ praviśati ya etamanu vā brūte bhakṣayati vā....*

140. Cf. W. CALAND & V. HENRY, op. cit., vol. I, par. 51.

ments, should not interrupt the sequence of the other rites of the Soma sacrifice. Therefore, whenever they take place (both seem, in fact, to be optional), they are performed principally if not exclusively, by one of the priests—the *Adhvaryu*—without his interfering in the continuation of the principal rite, namely, the offering of Soma. This means that while *avāntaradīkṣā* is undergone, by the priest who desires to penetrate into the 'mysterious' (*āraṇyaka*) meaning of *pravargya*, completely independently of the Soma sacrifice, the implements for *pravargya* are made, if and when they have to be made, in a discreet manner during the course of the day when the initial preparations for the Soma sacrifice are carried out.

In any case, whatever place is to be assigned to its preparatory rites, *pravargya* begins, strictly, at this point. On this, all or nearly all the texts are in agreement[141]. In fact all of them begin here a new chapter in the liturgical description of *pravargya*, taking up again its connection with the Soma sacrifice, and express themselves in such a way to give one to understand that it is now that *pravargya* proper begins. *Pravargya* has two parts : the first consists in the transformation of *mahāvīra* into a concrete manifestation of the Divine (a hierophany), and the second in the actual offering of this selfsame Divine.

(a) *Preliminaries of the Rite* :

The first act of the ceremony, almost unanimously prescribed by the texts, is to shut the gates of the place where the offering is to be made. Now, since during the preparation of the implements, if it has taken place, the gates were already carefully closed, one can presume that within the enclosure there have since taken place other rites to receive Soma and the rites connected with this, for which the gates were opened to allow all kinds of people to assist. But now that *pravargya* is about to begin, almost everybody, except those who are truly authorized to be present, is invited to leave the place and the gates are once again carefully closed behind them[142]. The wife of the

141. Cf. SatBr XIV.1.3.1; TaittAr IV.1.1; BharSS XI.5.1 ff.; ApSS XV.5.1 ff; ManSS VI.2.1 ff; BaudhSS IX.5.1 ff; KatyaSS XXVI.2.1 ff; etc.

142. Cf. BharSS XI.5.1: *pravargyeṇa pracariṣyantaḥ saṃvṛṇvanti dvārāṇi*/ Cf. a summary of the texts in J.A.B. van BUITENEN, op. cit., p. II, par. 1.

sacrificer is also confined to her own hut and the curtains lowered[143]. The 'mystical' secrecy of *pravargya* continues to be observed even when this forms part of a much vaster ceremony like the Soma sacrifice which is open to all and where the wife of the sacrificer is present and active to a large extent. However, according to the Śatapatha Brāhmaṇa, the wife of the sacrificer is allowed to attend and is only asked to cover her head at the culminating moment of the rite[144].

When the gates are closed and secrecy assured, all those attending the rite are ritually given their place and proceed, with the recital of special *mantras*, to the performance of a reconciliatory act by touching hot water[145]. After this the three *mahāvīras*, always held by the special tongs and handled with special care, are deposited on sacred grass strewn in front of the *gārhapatya* and duly sprinkled with hot water[146]. Then are deposited, in an orderly manner from West to East in front of the *gārhapatya*, the other earthen utensils, and also all the objects of the *sambhāra* which will be used in the rite, such as the stakes and ropes to tie the cow and the goat which will have to provide the milk for the oblation, the three fans made of antelope skin which will serve to stir up the fire, the golden plate to be used as cover and the silver plate on which will be placed *mahāvīra*, the various types of combustible material and of sacred grass, sand with which to make certain mounds to the north of the firealtars, etc.[147] While the *adhvaryu* is occupied

143. Cf. BharSS XI. 5.2: *pariśrayanti patnyāḥ*; and also BaudhSS IX. 5.1; ApSS XI, XV.5.1; etc.

144. Cf. SatBr XIV.1.3.16 : *tasmin pravṛjyamāne patnī śiraḥ prorṇute tapto vā'eṣa śuśucāno bhavati nenme 'yaṃ taptaḥ śuśucānaś cakṣuḥ pramuṣṇād iti* // (mentioned again in note 160 of this chapter). Here the woman is sympahetic with the earth and is afraid to be injured by the suffering of the heated *mahāvīra*. See the last part of my quoted article "The Role of Ritual Heat.."

145. Cf. BharSS XI. 5.4; ApSS XV.5.4; etc.

146. The water is not said explicitly to be hot, but the accompanying *mantras* quoted by the SatBr XIV.1.3.4 ff. connect the act of sprinkling (*prokṣati*) with heat : *yamāya tveti / eṣa vai yamo yā eṣa tapaty eṣa..u pravargyas tad etam evaitat prīṇāti tasmād āha yamāya tveti* // The same is repeated in v. 5 for the heading *makhāya tveti* and in v. 6 for the heading *sūryasya tvā tapasa'iti*. Each verse is addressed to one of the three *mahāvīras*.

147. Cf. BharSS XI.5.10 ff. Cf. an exhaustive list of the *saṃbhāras* collected for this rite in J.A.B. van BUITENEN, op. cit., pt. II, pr. 7 d.

in gathering and spreading out these objects, the exponents of the other Vedas recite in their proper tone of voice their respective *mantras* indicating that heat is now about to enter the rite.[148]

(b) *Kindling of the Sacred Fire* :

After two mounds are made with the sand just mentioned[149] and other rites performed which are of no great interest to us, the silver plate is placed on the mound made to the North of the *gārhapatya*. This plate serves a double purpose, namely, to protect *mahāvīra* when it is placed on it[150] and to protect the sand from its contact with it.[151] On this plate the *adhvaryu* puts, after some other rites, a certain number of *muñja* grass sprouts—which are said to have grown from the sap which flowed from the severed head of the sacrifice[152] (that is, the head of Viṣṇu)—lit at both ends from the *gārhapatya*[153] while the formulas, already used before, are recited: "You are a flame (*arcir asi*), you are splendour (*śocir asi*), you are heat (*tapo'si*)"[154]. Then, after having already begun

148. Cf. SatBr XIV.1.3.2; AitBr IV. 1 (end) (IV.1.18) which specifies the chant of the Hotṛ at this point.

149. North of the two main fire-places. Cf. J.A.B. van BUITENEN, op. cit., pt II, par 10, p. 71.

150. Cf. SatBr XIV.1.3.14 : *tad rajataṃ hiraṇyam adhastād upāsyati pṛthivyāḥ saṃspṛśaspāhīty*..; cf. also BharSS XI.7.7; etc.

151. The protection that the Earth asks against the contact with the *mahāvīra* is motivated according to the SatBr XIV.1.3.14 by 'fear' for the suffering the *mahāvīra* has to endure during the process of heating: *atho pṛthivy u ha vā 'etasmād bibhayāñcakāra yad vai māyaṃ taptaḥ śuśucāno na hiṃsyād iti tad evāsyā' etad antar dadhāti*... The same fear is attributed, with the same words to the sky in v. 29. The sky is protected by a golden plate which covers the boiling *mahāvīra*. The implications of this will be studied in another book.

152. Cf. SatBr XIV.1.3.15, on the same line of the etiological myth : "..*yajñasya śīrṣacchinnasya raso vyakṣarattata etā oṣadhayo jajñire tenaivainam etad rasena samardhayati kṛtsnaṃ karoti* //

153. Cf. SatBr XIV.1.3.15 (before the text of note 152) : ..*tad ubhayata ādīptā mauñjāḥ pralavā bhavanti tān upāsya teṣu pravṛṇakti*.... (these pieces of grass kindled on both sides, throwing them (on the mound), he puts (the *mahāvīra pot*) on it.)

154. SatBr XIV.1.3.17 : *sa pravṛṇakti / arcir asi śocir asi tapo'sītyeṣa vai gharmo ya eṣa tapati sarvaṃ vā 'etad eṣa tad etam evaitat prīṇāti tasmād āhārcir asi śocir asi taposīti* // The portion not translated in the text enphasizes how the formulas strengthen the identification between the *gharma* and the sun, "he who heats".

to smear with ghee the principal *mahāvīra* while it is being held on the *āhavanīya*[155], the priest solemnly places it on the glowing silver plate while in unison with the *Hotṛ* he recites : "Sit down, you are great, be pleasing to the Gods. O Agni, worthy of praise and oblation, emit your beautiful red smoke"[156]. However, according to the *Śukla* Yajurveda School, the mantras "*arcir asi, śocir asi, tapo' si*" are recited on the *mahāvīra* when, full of ghee and not only smeared with it, it is placed at the centre of the silver plate[157]. Also after having been put into the fire, the *mahāvīra* is again abundantly smeared, on both the inside and the outside, with the usual ghee so that it is completely covered with it, so much so that the *mantra* which is recited while this is being done, taken from the Ṛgveda, likens the ghee to the *omentum* which envelops the oblation when this is put on the fire : "The priests smear it (i.e. the cauldron) when they have strewn the grass as when they heat on the fire the oblation enveloped in the *omentum*..."[158] The same *mantra* then concludes : "O *gharma*, which serve *ṛta*, sit on this fire as a son sits on the lap of his father"[159]. So, at the beginning of its metamorphosis into the Divine, a kinship is established between the *mahāvīra* and the Fire which precisely is its divinizing element. Father Agni, by taking his son, the *mahāvīra*, on his lap, ratifies his direct relationship to him at the precise moment when the son is about to pass into a divine state. In many traditions of the world, it is only after this fatherly gesture that the child is considered to be truly born, and it is by that gesture

155. Cf. SatBr XIV.1.3.13 : *tad etaṃ pracaraṇīyaṃ mahāvīram ājyena samanakti*.... ("he anoints that mahāvīra, which is to be used, all over with ghee..") (tr. EGGELING).

156. TaittAr IV.5.2 : *saṃsīdasva mahāmasi śocasva devavītamaḥ / vidhūmamagne aruṣaṃ miyedhya sṛja praśasta darśatam //* Cf. also BharSS XI.7.13.

157. Cf. KatyaSS XXVI.3.4 where it is said "to fill' (*abhipur*) besides "to anoint" (*añjati*)

158. RV V.43.7 ab : *añjanti yaṃ prathayanto na viprā vapāvantaṃ nāgninā tapantaḥ /*

159. RV V.43.7 cd : *pitur na putra upasi preṣṭha ā gharmo agnim ṛtayannasādi //* quoted by SatBr XIV.1.3.13; ApSS XV.7.4; etc. ("the vessel which the priests celebrating (it) supply with butter, as if roasting a marrow-yielding animal with fire, has been placed desiderous of sacrifice upon the fire, like a son upon the lap of his father") (in the translation of H. H. WILSON)

that the father confirms his paternity with regard to the son. To recall the paternity of Agni with regard to the *mahāvīra* at this precise moment means to emphasize more strongly the divinized condition to which the latter is about to pass as both, it itself and the offering, are being exposed to such great heat. It is at this moment that the *Śukla* Yajurveda School asks the wife of the sacrificer, allowed to be present sitting in her place, to cover her head and especially her eyes[160]. This culminating moment of the whole rite, when the *mahāvīra* is put into the fire till it becomes enflamed, signals the beginning of the metamorphosis of the offering as well as of its container, leading to a truly authentic theophany. It is therefore particularly delicate and full of difficulties. Any interference by outside elements can jeopardize the result. At the same time, the accumulation of such an intense heat during an operation so particularly sacred as this one, and especially at its beginning, can prove fatal to one who, like the women, is unable to bear it. So, to spare her eyesight, at least, some kind of precaution is prescribed for her even by those schools which are not so exigent in demanding that the wife of the sacrificer, mistress of the house, should withdraw[161]. Moreover, by covering her head and deliberately turning her eyes away from the *mahāvīra* as it is being born to a transcendent life, she avoids, as much as she can, involving herself in its trial, and clings to Mother Earth while she too, by means of the interposition of the silver plate between her and the *mahāvīra*, openly declares her intention of detaching herself from the unavoidable suffering to which is subjected the "divine child to be born"[162].

160. Cf. SatBr XIV.1.3.16 quoted previously in note 144 of this chapter.

161. In the *Kṛṣṇa* School she is secluded, while in the *Śukla* she only covers her head, but remains at her place. (Cf. previous note 151 of this ch. referring to the position of the SatBr XIV.1.3.14, and note 146 referring to the position of the *Kṛṣṇa* School in BharSS XI.5.2 etc.). The *Śukla* School seems somehow less interested in the secrecy of the ritual than in the possibility that the woman be injured by the excess of heat which is bound to be developed in the ritual. In a certain sense she is also initiated with her husband, and in the whole ceremony of Soma her presence is necessary if she now has to be covered or secluded this needs to be explained, as it is in the Śatapatha.

162. Cf. SatBr XIV. 1.3.14 quoted in note 151. This text, one of the most important which explains the damage provoked by excess of heat is discussed in my quoted aricle and awaits to be commented in another research.

While, as we said, the *mahāvīra* begins to be heated "on the lap of the Father", placed as it is on the silver plate, the *yajamāna* advances towards it and asks its blessing before it becomes so sacred that it loses all contact with the terrestrial world. He does this by placing on its aperture the palm of his hand which he points towards six directions (the four cardinal points plus the Zenith and the Nadir) and reciting *mantras* which guarantee him (in accordance with the respective power of each of the directions) life, offspring, *prāṇa*, hearing, splendour, power, fame, energy, intelligence, and protection against enemies of all kinds and against any eventual damage caused by the sacrifice itself[163]. In the meantime, the *hotṛ* is busy reciting other Ṛgvedic formulas to divert the violence of the first fire away from the sacrificer and turn it towards eventual enemies and sly, false, friends[164]—which shows how the fire, when it is lit, is so dangerous that one cannot take any chances with it, seeing that it has to have somebody against whom to discharge its power. At the same time, moreover, before they proceed to increase beyond measure this sacred heat, precursor of the theophany, the priests take all possible safeguards, by means of *mantras*, ritual actions and invocations to Agni himself, to ensure that, when it is so increased after having discharged its violence elsewhere, it be beneficial, fertile and full of creative power without causing to the sacrificer that harm which a great concentration of sacredness can normally do. The priests, in fact, are aware that they are handling an energy which can be as harmful as it can be beneficial and therefore they seek to ensure its greatest services while stemming its possible dangers[165].

At this point, there seems to be no longer any reason for hesitation and the rite can proceed to create the greatest possible

163. Cf. VajSam XXXVII.12ff. (here we quote only vv 14-16 concerning heat): ..*saṃ devo devena savitrā gata saṃ sūryeṇa rocate / sam agnir agninā gata saṃ daivena savitrā saṃ sūryeṇāsrociṣṭa / svāhā sam agnis tapasā gata saṃ daivyena savitrā saṃ sūryeṇārūrucata*..... Cf. also SatBr XIV.1.3.19-25 commenting on these verses, and KatyaSS XXVI.3.5-8 giving their practical application. Cf. also SankhSS V.9.11 and ApSS XV.7. 6; etc.

164. Cf. RV IV.4.1-5 referred to by ApSS XV.7.6.

165. The entire ceremony at this point is continuously under the spell of fear of the possibility of damage caused by an excess of heat, which we cannot tackle at present.

amount of sacred heat. In fact, after the *yajamāna* has ensured the blessing of the *mahāvīra* and the priests have taken proper safeguards, the *adhvaryu* and his assistant, the *pratiprasthātṛ*, take charcoal from the *gārhapatya* with the poker and lay it all around the *gharma* still at the centre of the silver plate[166]. Every piece of charcoal is laid with its proper *mantra* with which its calorific power is strengthened and at the same time the violent and destructive force of the fire is turned towards the enemies of the *yajamāna*[167]. Then are added thirteen pieces of *vikaṅkata* wood, pointing to the cardinal points, while formulas are recited to give prower to the heat to reach the required temperature[168]. The Maruts are invoked to assist and protect this whole process[169], but the *hotṛ* recites Vedic verses only when the first and thirteenth pieces are laid[170]. The pieces are obviously thirteen in number because, according to the always recurring refrain, "thirteen are the months of the year, and the year is the sun and pravargya is the sun"[171]. This theme regarding the identification of *pravargya* with the sun is continuously brought up and stressed at every occasion as if it were an explanation to repeat which is to intensify the union and assimilation of one with the other.

The *mahāvīra*, surrounded as it is now by burning charcoal, pieces of wood and grass which ensure a great heat all round it, and continually smeared with ghee, gradually begins to gather heat. At this point it is covered with the golden plate which, as we recall, was included in the *sambhāra*. The reason for this, as given by the *Śukla* Yajurveda School, is parallel to that for the

166. Cf. SatBr XIV.1.3.26; ApSS XV.8.1-4; BharSS XI.8.1-5; etc.

167. Cf. BharSS XI.8.1 referring to TaittAr. IV.5.5. Cf. also ApSS XV.8.1.

168. Cf. ApSS XV.8.2-4 prescribing *mantras* for the pose of all thirteen pieces of wood (cf. J.A.B. van BUITENEN, op. cit., pt. II, par 17, p. 76 f). Cf. *contra* SatBr XIV. 1.3.27 preferring to have the *mantras* pronounced over the first and the last and having the middle ones placed in silence two by two towards the main cardinal directions.

169. Cf. SatBr XIV.1.3.27 with KatyaSS XXVI.3.9; and also TaittAr IV.5.5 with BharSS XI.8.2-5.

170. The *mantras* are taken from RV I.10.12 and RV I.83.3 used respectively for the first and the last branch.

171. SatBr XIV.1.3.28 : ..*trayodaśa vai māsāḥ saṃvatsarasya saṃvatsara eṣa ya eṣa tapaty eṣa u pravargyas*..

silver plate : the sky too wants to protect itself from the contact with the *mahāvira* which is now becoming incandescent, because it is afraid of its suffering.[172]

(c) *Stirring the Sacred Fire* :

When this final precaution is taken, all the efforts of the attending priests can, rightly and without fear of any further possible harm, be concentrated on the fire and the *mahāvīra* so that heat might reach its highest possible temperature and power. The *hotṛ* who represents the Ṛgveda, now begins a long recitation of various hymns sewn together[173]. At the same time, it seems, the *prastotṛ*, who represents the Sāmaveda, intones two *sāmans*, also taken from the Ṛks[174], in which *soma* and *gharma* are conjointly praised and the gradual increase in the latter of liquified ghee, being melted by the heat, is glorified. During these recitations, the priests who are taking an active part, namely the *adhvaryu* and his assistants, after having ceremoniously taken hold of three fans and walked all around the *gharma*, sit down on three sides of it—the *adhvaryu* on the East side, the *pratiprasthātṛ* on the South side and the *agnīdhra* on the North side[175]—and begin to fan the fire vigorously. As he was walking around the *gharma*, the *adhvaryu* already fanned the fire three times and it was only after having gone around it that did he ritually give the fans to his priest-assistants who now, together with him, continue to fan the fire. At this point, the uninterrupted recital of the *hotṛ* takes up the praises of the Aśvins, recalling their feats. It is to the Aśvins that the offering of the *gharma* was made ever since the time when this rite was perhaps still independent, and now they are invoked at a time when the rite resumes, more than

172. Cf. SatBr XIV.1.3.29 using the same words as SatBr XIV.1.3.14 quoted in note 151, with the difference that the word *pṛthivī* (earth) is constantly substituted with that of *dyaus*, Heaven (or sky).

173. Cf. e.g. TV X.177.1-3; RV IX.73.1-9; RV IX.83.1-2; RV X.123.1-5 and 7.9 just to mention the more significant for our study. See an exposition of the whole text in J.A.B. van BUITENEN, op. cit., pt II, par 20,pp. 18-88 with all the Ṛgvedic references.

174. The two *sāmans* called *gharmasya tanvau* are reconstructed from the Ṛgvedic original RV IX, 107.12.

175. Cf. e.g. BharSS XI.8.8-13; ApSS XV.8.8-10; etc.

at any other time, its specific nature. And it is precisely during the recital in honour of the Aśvins that the fire, stirred physically by the fans and spiritually by the *mantras*, bursts forth with all its force, engulfing the *mahāvīra* and attaching itself to the ghee with which it is anointed every time the *hotṛ* pronounces '*aum*'.[176]

(d) *Hierophany* :

We have now reached the culminating point of the rite. When the fire bursts forth, the *adhvaryu* rises, takes away the golden lid and announces : "the *gharma* is aglow" (*rucito gharma*)[177]. This is one of the key-moments of the whole rite, if not its culminating point. The heat has now reached its Zenith, as also the light which is emitted from the fire. It is in fact the heat which guarantees the hierophany which at this moment takes place in the *mahāvīra*--in the 'Great Hero'—which becomes divine. And it is in this highest degree of incandescence that the Sacred appears with all its force and power, assuring its actual divine presence which the sacrifice—*sacrum facere*—intends to effect and make manifest. The sacrifice, in fact, as a bridge between the 'human' and the 'divine' spheres of the global Reality, has the power, as we have previously seen[178], to transfer every offering from the mortal, impermanent and immanent sphere, to the immortal, eternal and transcendent sphere without having it lose its quality as 'Unique', 'One without a second', as 'Independent' and therefore 'Ab-solute'. But the sacrifice is capable too of acting in the opposite way so that it is by its means that the Incommensurable can at times be reduced "to the measure of man" even without losing its 'sacred' dimension, that is, its 'separate', 'eternal' and 'immutable' character. In a rite which brings about a 'theophany', the '*theos*' is revealed ('*phainein*') in all its splendour and power. But at the same time, the Sacred

176. Cf. the ceremony in J.A.B. van BUITENEN, op. cit. pt. II, par 19, p. 78 f.

177. Cf. SatBr XIV.1.3.33 : *sa yatraitāṃ hotān vāha / apnasvatīm aśvinā vācam asme'iti tad adhvaryur upottiṣṭhann āha rucito gharma iti*.. ("and when the Hotṛ recites this (verse RV I.112.24) 'successful O Aśvins make ye our voice' the Adhvaryu steps up and says, 'the gharma is aglow'..") (tr. EGGELING).

178. Cf ch. I, p. 11 f. and ch. II, p. 51ff.

must be able to leave on him who has invoked It and entered in contact with It as a proof of its power as well as of its presence on earth, a perceptible sign of its action in his life, status and property. It is thus that the incandescence of the fire must be able to bring about for the *yajamāna* the desired wealth as a tangible sign of its divine presence in the *mahāvira*. That it is really the heat in which and by means of which the metamorphosis of the vessel, and through this that of the whole ritual action is accomplished and its power to give is asserted, is clearly stressed by the comment of the Śatapatha Brāhmaṇa, previously quoted, which, at this culminating point of the rite, says that "If it (i.e. the *gharma*) is aglow, let him (i.e. the *adhvaryu*) know that the *yajamāna* will become better (i.e. more prosperous); if it remains *arucita* (i.e. at a lower degree than the required calorific power), (the *yajamāna*) will become worse (i.e. poorer, in a worse condition than before, contrary to his expectations of improving it); and if (one has not succeeded in obtaining either the one or the other condition) and the *gharma* is neither aglow nor not aglow (*naiva rucito nārucitaḥ*), (the *yajamāna*'s position will remain stationary and he will be) neither better nor worse"[179]. In case the rite fails to obtain its result, the fire is to be fanned till the vessel is aglow[180].

(e) *Adoration* :

In any case, it is at this instant that the ghee inside the *mahāvira* catches fire and the vessel is one whole flame—*gharma rucita*—acknowledged, by the *mantras* of all the priests who are present, as a Deity. These priests with the Sacrificer—who together are up to six "for six are the seasons of the year"[181]—rise and go to gaze upon and pay homage to the divine epiphany which at this moment takes concrete form in front of them. The verses of praise, taken from the Yajurveda, which all of them recite in unison, presumably in a high tone of voice, greet

179. SatBr XIV.1.3.33 (continuation of the preceding text) quoted in note 26, ch. IV, and mentioned previously in ch. II, note 17.

180. Cf. SatBr XIV.1.3.33 (end) :.. *yathā tveva rucitaḥ syāttathā dhavitavyaṃ* //

181. SatBr XIV.1.4.1.

the *mahāvīra*, now become *gharma* (hot, incandescent), with epithets which clearly recognize his Lordship over the world, over the elements, over the spirit and over the word, and exalt his presence among the Gods who are entrusted to his protection[182]. "Fire united with fire, with God Savitṛ, with Sūrya, he shines"[183]. "Svāhā' ! Agni, united with Tapas, with God Savitṛ, with the Sun, he shone"[184]. "You who are resplendent, who brilliantly shine, sustainer of the sky, sustainer of the earth, sustainer of the vast atmosphere, God, sustainer of the Gods, immortal, born of Tapas"[185]. The *gharma* has been, so to say, transubstantiated into Divine Power by means both of the concentration of incandescent heat on its 'being' and of the words which were pronounced on it, words which have the double function of honouring him as God and of establishing him as such.

We are here in the presence of a religious inversion, a phenomenon common to some religions of the world where, at a given moment of their history, the sacrificial offering, or any other offering which represents it, after having sought to establish a bridge to the Absolute, finds that it has become itself that bridge, that point of contact with the Absolute. This means that the sacrificial offering which nearly everywhere begins by being something 'pertaining to the human world' which, after a special preparation or consecration, is 'sent', 'offered', 'transposed' to the 'divine world'—or, in other words, which begins by being an 'ascent' from the human to the divine world to which it offers power and glory in exchange for help and graces—ends

182. For the hymn of praise to the *mahāvīra-gharma* we prefer to follow the *Kṛṣṇa* School of the TaittAr IV.7.1ff. to give a vision of both the traditions. Till now we have mostly followed the *Śukla*.

183. TaittAr IV.7.1. : *sam agnir agninā gataḥ saṃ devena savitrā / saṃ sūryeṇa rocate //* SatBr XIV.1.4.2 ff. reverses the order : *saṃ devo devena savitrā gateti* is at v. 4 and *sam agnir agninā gateti* v. 5.

184. TaittAr IV.7.2. : *svāhā sam agnis tapasā gata / saṃ devena savitrā saṃ sūryeṇārociṣṭa //* Same SatBr XIV.1.4.6.

185. TattAr IV.7.2. : *dhartā divo vibhāsi rajasaḥ pṛthivyā dhartā / uror antarikṣasya dhartā / dhartā devo devānām / amartyas tapojāḥ iti //* Cf. SatBr XIV. 1.4 .8 (based on VajSam XXXVII. 16) with the variant *vibhāti tapasas* for *vibhāsi rajasaḥ*.

up by being transformed into something 'pertaining to the divine world', the Deity itself to which it was offered, a 'descent' of the Transcendent in the form of a passing epiphany in a contingent world. The sacrifice becomes then a 'sacrament', an efficacious religious sign, the central pier of the bridge across the two opposite banks of the Total Reality, the concrete and visible 'locus' where the Divine reveals itself in all its power. Fire united with the eternal Fire, Agni with Agni, Savitṛ, Sūrya, the Sun in all its divine splendour. But as the central pier of the bridge, it is also the main support of the Deities as it is of men. The passage from the 'human' to the 'divine' world, the new birth, is due to the heat which once again reveals its creative and divinizing power to transform whatever comes into contact with it and, in a certain sense, also to destroy its mortal body. The *gharma*, born of *tapas*, is now immortal and the base which supports not only the world which at its contact is recreated and renewed, but also the Sky, the Earth and the Atmosphere, the primordial elements.

And yet the *gharma* continues to be, at the same time, a sacrificial offering which carries the human prayer to its heavenly destination : "You (are offered) for the heart, you for the mind, you for the sky, you for the sun. Carry on high this Soma sacrifice (*adhvara*) ; carry these hymns to the Deities in heaven"[186]. All this means, therefore, that the *gharma* is at one and the same time both an Offering and the Receiver of the offering, both Messenger and Lord. He is the Mediator who by means of the Fire transforms his own mortal substance and reveals himself as the Lord of all that exists, Father and Protector of the inhabitants of the two 'worlds' which find in him their common support.

In fact, the hymn which the priests continue to sing in reverent homage to it, goes on like this : "O Lord of all the worlds, Lord of all the earth, Lord of all the mind, Lord of all speech, Lord of all *Tapas*, Lord of all *Brahman*, renowned among the Gods, O God *Gharma*, protect the Gods. Bring us the Word, born of *Tapas*, which goes to the Gods. (You are) Embryo (or, womb,

186. TaittAr IV.7.2f. : *hṛde tvā manase tvā dive tvā sūryāya tvā //2// ūrdhvam imam adhvaraṃ kṛdhi / divi deveṣu hotrāṃ yaccha //*

*garbha*) of the Gods, Father of speech, Lord of creatures, inspiration of poets"[187]. Then follows the almost never-failing ending of all the hymns and invocations to the Divine : Let us too partake of what you are ! "God beat against the God Savitṛ, he flared up with the Sun ! O *Gharma* give us life (*āyur*), you are the giver of glory. To us you are father, like a father awaken us (to understanding). Giver of life, giver of the body, giver of space, giver of wealth. (You are) higher than the heavenly spaces. May we join you. Do not cause us harm"[188]. "You are Agni, you are master of the house of all the tribes of men...protect us"[189]. And the wife of the *yajamāna*, uncovering now her eyes, reverently recites the last verse of the series[190] in which she asks fertility for herself and her husband, thus establishing herself, a female, with the *mahāvīra* of *pravargya*, a male, as a productive couple—as the Brāhmaṇa explains[191].

The ritual which we have just described, where the sacrificial offering is transformed and made divine to be then consumed by the faithful, is not, as we have already pointed out, exclusive to Brāhmaṇism. The two principal motifs, namely, sacrality as effected by means of heat, and the transformation of the sacrificial offering into a divine being who becomes present in it to be consumed by the faithful so that these may, in their turn, be internally transformed, can be found in many religions. In fact, sacrality is often measured in terms of light and intensity of heat[192]. The most intense heat belongs to the Divine and from

187. TaittAr IV.7.3f. : *viśvāsāṃ bhuvāṃ pate / viśvasya bhuvanas pate / viśvasya manasas pate / viśvasya vacasas pate / viśvasya tapasas pate / viśvasya brahmaṇas pate // devaśrūstvaṃ deva gharma devān pāhi // tapojāṃ vācam asme niyaccha devāyuvam //3// garbho devānām / pitā matīnām / patiḥ prajānām / matiḥ kavīnām //*

188. TaittAr IV.7.4 f. *saṃ devo devena savitrā 'yatiṣṭa / saṃ sūryeṇārukta / āyuṛdāstvam asmabhyaṃ gharma varcodā asi / pitā no'si pitā no bodha / āyurdhāstanūdhāḥ payodhāḥ/ varcod avāriyodā / draviṇodāḥ //4// antarikṣa pra urorvarīyān/ aśīmahi tvā mā mā hiṃsīḥ /..*

189. TaittAr IV.7.5 : *tvam agne gṛhapatir viśām asi / viśvāsāṃ māṇuṣīṇām.. ·bāhmaṃ hasaḥ /....*

190. Cf. TaittAr IV.7.5; VajSam XXXVII.20

191. Cf. SatBr XIV.1.4.16 ..*atha patnyai śiro'pavṛtya / mahāvīram īkṣamāṇāṃ vācayati*....and the *mantra*. Cf. also BharSS XI.8.21 : *anuvākaś eṣaṃ tu pratiprasthātā pariśrite patnīṃ vācayati*.... (cf. also SK vol. II, pt. I, p. 169 and 176).

192. Cf. a brief summary of the sacrality of heat in many religions in D.K. KNIPE, op. cit., pp. 79-89.

the time of the Ṛgveda, as we have seen, the essence of the Deities consists in their *tejas* and in their *tapas*. It is precisely *Tapas*, their most intimate and most profound heat, the sustainer and signifier of their specific divine power, which once was raised to Absolute Power when the *ṛṣis*, moved by their unquenchable desire to know the Unity which is subjacent to all that there is, ventured to go beyond the name and form of the divine to feel, by a direct experience, their most intimate essence. Now this *Tapas*, this Heat, 'goes back', as it were, to concentrate itself, by means of a special rite, on a vessel which the rite identifies with the Sun, the Year, the Universe, the All.

(f) *The Sacrificial Offering as a Sacramental Meal* :

We have seen how this process of divinization of the sacrificial offering and of its container—a process which is dramatic, long, difficult and also painful—led to *pravargya's* interpretation as a fusion of a rite which consisted in the adoration of a divine image (*mūrti*; Gk. *eidolon*) with the other classical rite of Vedic origin which consisted of an offering of hot milk to the Aśvins[193]. This interpretation has well brought into focus an important point of the whole ceremony, namely, the divinization of *mahāvira*, but perhaps it has not brought out all its philosophico-religious implications. *Mahāvira* is not the prototype of a *mūrti*. If it were, there would be no need, as we saw when we were discussing *agnicayana*, of so much secrecy and of so many precautions. The *mūrti* is a concrete but exterior epiphany of the divine, at a determined point of space and time, and can be seen by all. Here, however, we are dealing with something which is much else.

We are, in fact, dealing with an epiphany which certainly is concrete but without a stable form, and which, moreover, takes place in the course of a sacred act by which the sacrificial offering is internally transformed into the Absolute Itself who absorbs the human in order to be, in Its turn, absorbed by it. In other words, here the Divine Fullness assumes and annihilates the mortal element of the sacrificial offering in Itself and

193. Cf. above note 9 of this ch.

transforms the offering into its Absolute self. Man, on his part, by pronouncing the consecratory words at the end of a liturgical and sacrificial action performed by himself, feels that he is the material instrument in the transformation of the 'human' into a 'divine' object through the unapproachable and unbearable intensity of the ritual heat. The priest, therefore, as the material instrument or human agent of the sacrificial action, adores and prays, offers and expects to receive, prepares and brings about a *theophany* destined to shift the sacrificial implement to a sphere of Reality different from his own—that is, the divine. But immediately afterwards he sets about offering it again to the formless and nameless Godhead, partaking of it himself by consuming a part of it. Such a ritual act which renders present the Divine "here and now" in all its intensity, purity, transcendence and sacrality, in an offering destined to be consumed by the faithful, is so bold that it needs to be protected by the initiatory secrecy, and, to be understood and faced, it requires a high degree of spiritual maturity which only few can possess. As for that matter, it is not without reason that the rite, whereby the offering is divinized, generally remains secret and esoteric, and that it usually enters relatively late in the history of a religion and its conception of the relation between man and God.

To remain within the ambit of the two religions which have served us so far as terms of comparison, the religion of ancient Greece and the semitic religion of Israel, we find that the 'transubstantiation' of the sacrificial offering into the Divine is a relatively late rite in both, and in both too it remained exclusive to a particular group within the larger religious tradition. In Greece, the sacrificial offering and libation are, generally speaking, human gifts intended to please the Gods and then to disappear. It was only for a small group of the faithful, which remains a 'separated', and therefore 'esoteric' group, that the Deity not only accepted the offering but incarnated himself into it and revealed himself to the faithful in a way which invites them to an intimate communion with him, offering himself to them in a sacramental meal. The goat of the orphic-dionysian mystery-religion represents—indeed, becomes or is—Dionysius in person and it is he who, as God, is chased, dismembered and consumed in a direct communion of the faithful with him, whereby the faithful is trasmuted into him.

In the Israelite religion, strictly so called, such a transformation does not take place; however, it does take place in the spiritual and religious movement which originally appeared to be one of its sects but which soon afterwards detached itself from the mother religion to become an independent religion by itself, namely, Christianity. Here, the victim of the cosmic Sacrifice of reconciliation, the Lamb of the Second Passover, is the bread and wine transubstantiated into the divinized Body and Blood of Christ to be consumed in a sacramental meal by the circle of the faithful who obtain a right of access to it by means of their acceptance in the community by baptism[194]. The bread and wine "fruit of the earth and work of human hands"[195] are transformed, in virtue of the words of consecration in the course of a liturgical action, into the divine body of the Mediator who both as victim and as Son of God, joins in his epiphany the two levels of the global Reality, on one hand reducing to the measure of Man, visible on the altar, the incommensurable and ungraspable Divine Transcendence, and on the other hand, placing man in a position to be able to consume God, eating and drinking Him in a communal meal, so that he himself be divinized.[196]

*Pravargya* is to be interpreted much more in this light than in that of an earthen 'idol', an exterior image, anointed and consecrated, to be adored in the presence of a living flame. The God, born of *tapas* and emerging as an epiphany from the intensity of the ritual heat, is not a congealed exterior apparition, worthy of adoration and full of largesse, but a Power, an interior Energy which sustains the very depths of the Gods and men who consume It. It is the very Might of the Universe which inhabits the heart, the mind and the poetic inspiration of

194. The fact that today a lot of people can approach the Eucharistic meal does not mean that its 'exclusiveness' is overshadowed but only that the circle of the faithful has become too vast. This shows once more that if the 'sacred' is not 'protected' in its 'mystery' it risks becoming diluted into 'profanity'.

195. The words of the 'Offertory' in the Catholic Mass of Roman rite.

196. Cf. e.g. my comments on this point in R. PANIKKAR, *Il Silenzio del Buddha*, in collaboration with U. M. Vesci, op. cit., pp. 251 and 428.

those who partake of It; He is the spirit of the Sun, revealing itself as the Sun itself which rises in all its splendour on the morning horizon; He is the strength of Savitṛ, identified with Savitṛ himself who moves and sustains the world with his fervent power. At the same time, this God *Gharma* is also the offering of hot milk[197] poured into the divine vessel immediately after an interval during which this is adored, and libated successively to the Aśvins, Indra and the other Deities all of whom are more or less mythically related to *pravargya*. Thus the Aśvins, the original recipients of the offering, are further associated with it inasmuch as they restored its head[198]; Indra who conquered it from Viṣṇu before the rest of the Deities[199] and Sarasvatī who, as Word, must be integrated into it[200], etc. Twelve are the Deities who are thus honoured[201] and who with *Gharma* make thirteen—since thirteen are the months of the year...[202]. In fact, after *Gharma*, the new God, is adored, the rite resumes and the whole liturgical action is shifted to a level which is no longer the merely terrestrial. It is God himself who is libated and offered to the other Gods. And, moreover, this divinized offering, before it is definitely libated in Agni to the honour and glory of these Gods, is ritually raised towards heaven and permanently placed there with the help of the *mantras* recited for the purpose[203]. This symbolic gesture of

197. Also for this offering there is the need to know through a formula that the milk is cooked (or boiled): cf. SatBr XIV.3.1.30 : ..*hy atra hotāthopottiṣṭhann āha śrātaṃ havir iti*..

198. Cf. SatBr XIV.2.1.11: *atha pinvane pinvayati | aśvibhyāṃ pinvasvety aśvināvevaitad āhāśvinau vā'etad yajñasya śiraḥ pratyadhattān tavevaitat prīṇāti tasmād āhāśvibhyāṃ pinvasveti ||*

199. Cf. SatBr XIV.2.1.13: *indrāya pinvasveti | indro vai yajñasya devatā sā yaive yajñasya devatā tayaivaitad aśvinau yajñasya śiraḥ pratyadhattāntāvevaitat prīṇāti tasmād....*

200. Cf. SatBr XIV.2.1.12: *sarasvatyai pinvasveti | vāgvai sarasvatī vācā vā'etad aśvinau yajñāsya śiraḥ pratyadhattāntāvevaitat prīṇāti tasmād....*

201. Cf. SatBr XIV.2.2.12 with SatBr XIV.2.2.1 ff. where the names of the Deities to whom libation is offered are given.

202. Cf. SatBr XIV.2.2.13 where it is specified that the thirteenth Deity making up for the thirteenth lunar month of the year is the *Gharma* itself.

203. Cf. SatBr XIV.2.2.17 *atha hutvordhvam utkampayati | divi dhā imaṃ yajñam imaṃ yajñaṃ divi dhā ity asau vā'ādityo gharmo yajño divi vā'eṣa hito divi pratiṣṭhitas tam evaitat prīṇāti tasmād āha divi dhā imaṃ yajñām imaṃ yajñaṃ divi dhā ity anuvaṣaṭ kṛte juhoti ||*

raising heavenwards the *gharma* which either as the severed head of Viṣṇu or as the ritual vessel of the Aśvins is the sun, is the dramatic representation of the direct relation existing between the two spheres of the Total Reality, a relation which is precisely established in the sacrificial action and in the liturgical gesture of placing the offering in Heaven.

(g) *Sacrificial Creation Through the Three Phases of the Boiling Process* :

That this relation which is established between the two spheres of the Total Reality, including the complete identification between the terrestrial and the heavenly elements, is principally (even if not exclusively, of course) due to the ritual heating process, and that the fusion which is effected of the three worlds (the terrestrial, the atmospheric and the heavenly) is directly due to the high degree of heat sought in *pravargya*, is further made clear by the exegete himself. In fact, in his final explanatory summary of his exposition of the rite, the Śatapatha Brāhmaṇa relates the three essential cosmic moments with the three more significant liturgical moments, namely, when *mahāvīra* full of milk, is put into the fire; when it becomes incandescent just before the milk starts boiling; when the milk, boiling and superabundant, overflows. Thus the overheated *pravargya* is said to be All (*sarva*), and it is so under the form of a 'year' (*saṃvatsara*) which is preeminently the standard measure of time. This is because *pravargya* represents the year's major seasons in the following manner: it represents Spring when *mahāvīra* is put into the fire; it represents the summer (the hot season) when *mahāvīra* is all aflame and the milk begins to rise; it represents the rainy season (a season of overabundance) when *mahāvīra* lets the milk in full boil overflow[204]. These three moments identify *pravargya* also with 'these worlds' (*ime vai lokāḥ*) since *mahāvīra*, with the milk it contains, is the terrestrial world when it is put into the fire, it is the atmospheric world when it becomes incandescent and it is the celestial world when it super-

204. Cf. SatBr XIV.3.2.22: *saṃvatsaro vai pravargyaḥ / sarvaṃ vai saṃvatsaraḥ sarvaṃ pravargyaḥ sa yat pravṛktas tad vasanto yad rucitas tad grīṣmo yat pinvitas tad varṣā yadā*. . . . Cf. Ch. III, fn. 16.

abounds[205]. Naturally, in these three moments, *pravargya* is as well the three major Deities who preside over these three worlds, namely, Agni, Vāyu and Āditya respectively[206]. But if the process of identification stopped here, how would the *yajamāna* derive benefit from the good that *pravargya* does to the world? So the three ritual moments are again identified respectively with the *yajamāna's* own self, his offspring and his property, especially his cattle. It is the cattle which are the more valuable form of wealth, and which, it is said, will become as abundant as the over-flowing milk[207]. Finally, *pravargya* is said to include and incorporate in the three phases of its boiling process, as if to recapitulate in itself all the liturgical activity of the sacrificer, the whole Soma sacrifice of which it forms part and then, by extension, every other type of sacrifice in such a way that no sacrifice is offered which is not included, at least 'mystically', in *pravargya* in its spiritualized form[208].

This means that because of the intensity of the sacred heat which *pravargya* produces and absorbs in the course of its ritual performance, it is 'mystically' present in every Brāhmaṇic cultic activity in all its forms, representing the 'head' of the Sacrifice, that is its most sacred and 'spiritualized' part.

205. Cf. SatBr XIV.3.2 23 : *ime vai lokāḥ pravargyaḥ| sarvaṃ vā' ime lokāḥ sarvaṃ pravargyaḥ sa yat pravṛktas tad ayaṃ loko yad rucitas tad antarikṣaloko yat pinvitas tad asau loko yadā....*

206. Cf. SatBr XIV.3.2.24: *etā vai devatāḥ pravargyaḥ | agnir vāyur ādityaḥ sarvaṃ vā 'etā devatāḥ sarvaṃ pravargyaḥ sa yat pravṛktas tad agnir yad rucitas tad vāyur yat pinvitas tad asāvādityo yadā..*

207. Cf. SatBr XIV.3.2.25: *yajamāno vai pravargyaḥ| tasyātmā prajā paśavaḥ sarvaṃ vai yajamānaḥ sarvaṃ pravargyaḥ sa yat pravṛktas tad ātmā yad rucitas tat prajā yat pinvitas tat paśavo yadā vai paśavaḥ pinvante'thainānt sarve devāḥ sarvāṇi bhūtāny upajīvanti pinvante ha vā'asmai paśavo ya evam etad veda ||* The end is the same for all the preceding verses quoted from note 204 ff., with some variants according to the cases.

208. Cf. SatBr XIV.3.2.30: *somo vai pravargyaḥ | sarvaṃ vai somaḥ sarvaṃ pravargyaḥ sa yad abhiṣutas tat pravṛkto yad unnītas tad rucito yaddhutas tat pinvito yadā vai somaḥ pinvate'thainaṃ sarve devāḥ sarvāṇi bhūtāny upajīvanti pinvate ha vā'asmai somo ya evam etad veda na ha vā 'asyā pravargyeṇa kenacana yajñeneṣṭaṃ bhavati ya evaṃ etad veda ||*

Cf. also G. U. THITE, op. cit. ch. IX where the mystical and spiritual character of the Pravargya is stressed.

5. *Pravargya as Mystery about to Surpass the Ritual* :

*Pravargya*, therefore, confirms its intrinsic unity. But at the time when the Brāhmaṇic cult was being re-organized at Kurukṣetra simultaneously with the re-systematization of the Sacred texts, it was not considered self-sufficient. This is clear from the fact that for some reason or other—no matter which—the need was felt to annex it as an ancillary rite to more conspicuous and complicated sacrificial complexes, such as *agniṣṭoma*. But in spite of this it will always remain a 'mystery', which by means of the divinization of the offering, Mediatrix between the Human and the Divine, introduces into the traditional religion essentially founded on the ritual, an element of high spirituality leading man directly to the very heart of the Absolute without having him—at least for the time being—renounce his specific human nature. And it is also because of this, in fact, that *pravargya* is performed behind closed doors: nobody can come close to it if he cannot understand it and bear its concentrated Power.

Because of the intense accumulation of 'sacredness' which it produces by means of the excessive heat bordering on the 'limit' of bearability, *pravargya* needs to be contained and handled by one who is equipped with supra-normal understanding. Hence the necessity of the initiation wherein the priest does not merely learn the material techniques of how it is performed but is also introduced to the obscure labyrinth of its profoundest meaning. But the more one begins to have an inner understanding, the more the exterior action begins to be surpassed. It begins to be seen as an exteriorization of a process which would even be more efficacious if it remained confined to a spiritual interiority. What is more, this is confirmed by the position which the Brāhmaṇic texts assign to *pravargya*, a position which, as we have seen, brings out clearly its role as a *link* between the ritual and the Upaniṣadic spirit in which the ritual will soon be surpassed[209].

The purpose of the sacrifice is to divinize man, and when this divinization, wrought by means of the exterior action itself, is sufficiently intense, man, having come into contact with the Divine, is transfigured. But this kind of transfiguration is at first limited to the time during which the ritual action is per-

209. Cf. previously in this same chapter, p. 216 f. with the notes 4, 5, 6.

formed; nevertheless with the passage of time and the continuous accumulation of sacred energy both on one's person and on the rite itself, it tends to last longer and to become a permanent state, in such a way that there will no longer be any need of its periodical renewal by the performance of the rite. Hence, *pravargya* already contains within itself the potential by which the ritual will be eventually surpassed.

6. *Other Rites in Pravargya* :

Just for completeness' sake, we might as well mention here that though the libation of hot milk contained in *mahāvīra* is the central and more important offering, it is not offered alone but is in fact accompanied by two wheat-cakes, the *rauhiṇas*, which are considered to be its complement. They are placed around the *gharma* like heaven and earth, day and night, thus providing it with the existential spatio-temporal dimensions[210]. They are also the two eyes which are ritually given to the 'head' of the sacrifice which *pravargya* is[211]. The inclusion of the vegetable kingdom as a corrective and complement of the animal kingdom, in the sacrifice, is a ritual phenomenon which, as we have earlier seen, is common not only to the other Vedic sacrifices but also to the sacrifices of many other religions of the world, perhaps inherited from pre-historic times.

We recall too that when *pravargya* comes to an end, at noon of the third day of the *upasad*, the rites which are rendered necessary to dispose of the sacred implements are of special interest for us. The concentration of the 'sacredness' and of the heat—especially on *mahāvīra*, has been such that they cannot be disposed of in the usual way like other implements used in other rites. They cannot be burnt, nor can they be buried except in specially fixed places and with all due precautions[212]. But

210. Cf. SatBr XIV.2.1.2 : *tad yad rauhiṇau juhoti / agniś ca ha vā 'ādityaś ca rauhiṇāvetābhyāṃ hi devatābhyāṃ yajamānāḥ svargaṃ lokaṃ rohanti //* ("And as to why he offers two Rauhiṇas (cakes)—the two Rauhiṇas doubtless are Agni and Āditya (the sun), for by means of these two deities sacrificers ascend (ruh) to heaven".) (tr. EGGELING).

211. Cf. SatBr XIV.2.5. Cf. p. 223 of this ch.

212. Cf. for a complete exposition of the rite J.A.B. van BUITENEN, op. cit., pt. V, pp. 124 ff.

since such precautions are due to the dangerous nature of the 'sacred' when it exceeds the limit, we hope to treat of the closing ceremonies of *pravargya* in another, more appropriate, study[213].

213. The closing rites of the *Pravargya* revealing the fear of an excess of heat will not be dealt with in this volume. Cf. the last part of the quoted article of mine "The Role of Sacred Heat.."

# CONCLUSION : BRĀHMAṆIC COSMOLOGY

## 1. *Transformation of the Divine*

With the *pravargya* we arrived at the end of our concrete examples chosen to describe the effects of the calorific energy on the sacrificial action in the Brāhmaṇic period. We saw how in each case, that is, in the *paśuyajña*, *agnyādhāna*, *agnicayana* and *pravargya* (all of which, except for the second, are ancillary rites of the Soma Sacrifice), by means of a strictly traditional liturgy one reached the point where the fullness of the rite led to its own transcendence, when the intricacies and difficulties of the cultic actions called for reflective consciousness. The rite, by now independent of a divine figure to whom it would be addressed and superior to it, is to be known in its minutest details if one is to be able to face all its internal exigencies, since these are no longer imposed by a divine will. This need of knowing the rite itself, at first of an essentially practical order, immediately leads the priest to search deeply into the profound significance of every gesture and every word in the rite. With this search there also arises the need of an explicit and conscious identification of man with the sacrality which is at work in the sacrificial action if one is to receive its salvific benefits. Thus the point is reached where the rite, and all that goes with it, is transformed on a spiritual level. It is not without reason that the Āraṇyakas and the Upaniṣads are incorporated into the Brāhmaṇas and are their logical continuation.

This spiritual transformation of the sacrifice, which we have been tracing so far, has had profound repercussions not only on man and on his newly born reflective consciousness, but also on the philosophy and cosmology of the Divine. As we have seen, the sacrifice performed on earth is raised, by means of the divinization of the offering and of the ritual implements, to a divine Cosmic Action containing within its ritual centre the entire universe and being the centre of attraction where the two poles of global Reality find their complementarity in a mutual assimilation.

But at this point the cosmological transformation extends its effects also on the sphere of the Deities who are also gradually attracted towards the irresistible and magnetic, unique and absolute Sacred Action. In fact, when the sacrifice becomes important in itself and no longer as an offering to somebody greater than it, it becomes the only determining Act of the world, the only guarantor of its creation and maintenance. At the same time it becomes also the means to obtain immortality. The Deities, therefore, finding themselves mortal[1] by this very fact, are now obliged to acquire immortality by such a rite no more and no less than the Demons, men and even the Supreme God Prajāpati.

This transformation, already anticipated in the speculative hymns both of the Ṛgveda and of the Atharva, is now an accomplished fact. In the diagram drawn earlier[2], the centripetal force of S is now very great and S, as the Cosmic Sacrifice, has absorbed all the power, the strength, the "essence" (*medha*) of the Divine, so to say, thus radically changing the direction of the arrow. Sacrifice is, therefore, no longer an action which is directed *towards* the Deities, but an action which *draws* the Deities *towards its* Centre. Henceforth it is simply the very source of the existence of the Deities as also of men and of all the created in general. The clearest sign of this change in the status of the Deities and of the corresponding change in

1. Cf e.g. SatBr XI.2.3.6: *martyā ha vā'agre devā āsuḥ / sa yadaiva te brahmaṇāpur athāmṛtā āsuḥ....//* Cf TaittSam II. 3. 2.1: *devā vai mṛtyor abibhayus .. niravapat tayaivaiṣvamṛtam adadhāt..* PancBr XXIV. 19.2: *devā ha vai mṛtyor abibhayus te prajāpatim upādhāvaṃsa tebhya etena..amṛtatvaṃ prāyacchat..*; etc.

2. Cf. ch. II, pp. 52 and 55.

the Brāhmaṇic conception of them can be found in the attitude towards the Deities which is shown, as we have seen, in the *paśuyajña*. Here the Deities lose even their dignified aloofness to rush in the house of the sacrificer before they are invited by the usual various formulas of invocation[3]. Indeed, the formulas which are here recited are no longer of an "invitatory" but rather of a "regulative" nature meant to avoid rivalries and fights among the illustrious divine guests[4]. This is a sign, then, that Sacrifice has now gained so greater dimensions than before, and that the Deities themselves are now so dependent on It that they have lost their natural reserve and have therefore become more subject to human blackmail. The *do ut des* of the historico-religious definition of sacrifice is here rendered easier since it is the Deities themselves who placed themselves in the condition of having to be grateful for what they receive. The only thing is that their power of giving is somewhat limited and that they too are bound by the cosmic law of Sacrifice. There takes place a process similar to the one which happened in Ancient Greece where the power of Zeus, and the Greek deities in general have become subjected to the unremovable, omnipotent and impersonal law of the *anañche* (Necessity)[5]. In India, however, the supreme Power is not attributed to an anonymous Necessity, but is assumed by a Sacred Action which is also abstract and impersonal but which preserves a vital internal Dynamism of its own expressing itself in its laws. These laws too are subject to certain difficulties and contain within themselves the seed of success or failure. This, therefore, supposes an attitude on the part of man, and of the Deities, which is quite different from that prevalent in Hellenism. The Sacred Action, even

3. Cf. SatBr I.1.1.7: ..*mano ha vai devā manuṣyasyājānanti ta' enam etad vratam upayantaṃ viduḥ prātarnno yakṣyata' iti te'sya viśve devā gṛhānāgacchanti te'sya gṛheṣ ūpavasanti*..// and almost *verbatim* SatBr II.1.4.1 and GopBr II.1.6.

4. Cf. SatBr I.1.2.18 f.: *atha devatāyā' ādiśati / sarvā ha vai devatā adhvaryuṃ havir grahīṣyantam upatiṣṭhante mama nāma grahīṣyati mama nāma grahīṣyatīti tābhya evaitat saha satībhyo' samadaṃ karoti* //18// *yadyeva devatāyā' ādiśati / yāvatībhyo ha vai devatābhyo havīṃṣi gṛhyanta' ṛṇam u haiva tās tena manyante yad asmai taṃ kāmaṃ samarddhā veyur yat kāmyā gṛhṇāti tasmād*....*evam eva yathāpūrvaṃ havīṃṣi gṛhitvā.*

5. Cf. this evolution into an Impersonal Necessity in Greek Pantheon in poetic and dramatic literature of the ancient Greece, with Sophokles and especially Euripides.

though rigid and universalized, somehow or other contains a voluntary aspect in such a way that he who performs it does not feel as if he were a mere passive object in the Great Theatre of the World. This means that instead of finding in the Universal Principle which stands above him an unmoving Order at variance with his own will—as in Greece where Zeus himself has to adapt himself, againt his will, to the decrees of Fate, and finds himself impotent against them to succour one of his faithful or even his own son—the sacrificer, in India, whether human or divine, feels that he is himself the master of his own destiny and of that of the world. It is through his efforts that he can determine the regularity of the seasons, of the year, of the days and nights, of the length of his life, etc. He who offers Sacrifice, controls it—or at least believes that he does[6]—and, therefore, even though he may fail to obtain what he wants, does not feel that sense of frustration as the one who is subject to a blind Destiny which has to have its way in spite of the despair of men and Gods. In case of failure, the fault lies with the sacrificer (or his priests), who can always remedy the fault by means of a counter-ritual.[7] Sacrifice is a Power in itself, but it is also an arm since it is the means—and a means in the hands of the celebrants—by which this Power acts for good or bad. By its performance the very Cosmic Order is created in such a way that the brāhmaṇa can say, with justified pride, that when "the celebrant offers the *agnihotra* early in the morning, he generates this (sun) which having become luminous energy (*tejas*), rises radiant and continuously. However, it would not rise at all if he (the priest) did not offer it. And it is for this reason that he offers it."[8] The Action with which the Deities have entrusted man as their agent is so decisive in the smooth running of the cosmic events that the very equi-

6. Since we could not include here the effects of excess of sacred heat, we do not have for the moment elements to show how not even the greatest skillfulness of priests could avoid some catastrophes.

7. The difficulties incurred by the priests in handling the sacrifice have to be taken into consideration in a conclusion, although they have not been shown here.

8. SatBr II.3.1.5: *atha yat prātar anudite juhoti / prajanayati evainam etat so 'yaṃ tejo bhūtvā vibhrājamāna udeti śaśvaddha vai nodiyād yad asminn etām āhutiṃ na juhuyāt tasmād vā etām āhutiṃ juhoti //*

librium of the succession of days and nights depends on the correct performance of the sacrificial Action.

The responsibility of the sacrificer, therefore, is immense both for good and bad. He who knows the secrets of the rites and can make use of them can control the course of nature, and of his own life, either to prolong it or to destroy it. Men and Deities are now nearly on the same level since both can, at least in theory, make use of the same means to dominate and control their own destiny. It is not without reason that the *devas* are less and less referred to as the passive recipients of the offering and more and more as those who offer it. As they too have to offer Sacrifice, they begin to be seen by man more as models to imitate than as bestowers of favours in return for gratifications received. To share actively in the Sacred Action, the best way for them is now to take it in hand by performing it rather than to wait for someone to offer it to them. This leads to a new interpretation of the mythological conflicts between the *devas* and the *asuras*. The reason for these conflicts is no longer the conquest of heaven as in other mythologies,[9] as also in the Ṛgveda itself,[10] but it is the acquisition of the sacrificial benefits and the appropriation of the formulae for the correct performance of Sacrifice. Both owe their respective status to the fact that the former are successful and the latter not. In fact, he, who is in possession of Sacrifice, knows its secrets and is able to perform it perfectly, is master of existence and of the entire world,[11] and the *devas*, unlike the *asuras*, have secured for themselves, in that way, all their divine privileges : immortality, creative power, wisdom and even their position in heaven.

On the other hand, since to a certain extent they remain still recipients of man's offerings, the Devas remain to this effect so dependent on such offerings that they gradually lose both their status as major Deities and their very power—except, at

9. Cf. e.g. the Greek mythology with the Titans and the Jewish one with Satan.

10. Where the rivals of Indra and Agni are on a different plane with respect to the following anonymous masses of Asuras.

11. Cf. the texts in S. LEVI, op. cit., p. 27 f. The Asuras do not gain immortality due to faults in their rites.

least for a time, an Agni or an Indra. Their place is, then, taken by another Entity endowed with universal and creative powers and directly emerging from Sacrifice itself. Such an Entity, already perceived by the ancients as *Tapas* which energized the sacrificial offering, is now personified in *Prajāpati*, the *Puruṣa* immolated at the beginning of existence.[12] In fact, in spite of the Brāhmaṇic intuition that there is a Cosmic Action which transcends any divine figure, the necessity of the existence of a Divine Power which is able to enter into personal relationship with the world is felt once again. However this Divine Power could only grow from the interiority of Sacrifice itself. More precisely It has to emerge from the sacrificial victim, because it was that consecrated being which more than any other has undergone that transformation through cooking which we have followed in the course of our study[13], a transformation which was gradually extended to the sacrificial action as a whole and to its various implements. It was then but natural that it was precisely the sacrificial victim which should become the focus of the sacrificial theophany. Hence, if on the speculative level, the *devas* have lost their specific status as Deities, their divine nature has emerged in all its power in the Victim which, having now become the axis on which the whole Cosmic Sacrificial Action revolves, acquires in the dismemberment of its mortal and immolated body, such a creative power as to assume the dimensions of a First Principle. Thus it becomes the non-temporal cosmic Goat,[14] the *Odana* without beginning or end,[15] and especially the *Puruṣa* called also *Prajāpati* because Lord of all **creatures** produced by him in his self-immolation.[16] Theoretically, any sacrificial victim can become *Prajāpati* since it is dismembered in creation. Still, practically, it is only the victim which from a certain point of view is the most important, that is the human victim,[17] which is

12. Cf. RV X.90.1 ff. and also RV I.164. 1ff.; etc.

13. One has to take into consideration the difference occurring in the destiny of the victim in RV I.162.21 or that in AitBr VI. 6 (II.1.6) where the victim was going to the Gods, and the complete divinization of the offering in *pravargya*.

14. Cf. AV IX.5, variously quoted in ch. III.

15. Cf. AV IV.34, and AV XI.3.

16. Cf. SatBr X.2.2.1.

17. That is, more important from a 'sentimental' point of view, not ritually.

normally called *Prajāpati* : "Now the one person (*Puruṣa*) which they made out of those seven persons became this *Prajāpati*. He produced living beings..."[18] And this title soon assumes the meaning of a primordial Supreme Being : "in the beginning *Prajāpati*, this one, was alone."[19]

But when *Prajāpati* becomes the personification of Sacrifice as the universal and sacred Act, he stops being a mere divinized victim but personifies Sacrifice as a whole. He himself is the Sacrifice *par excellence*[20], embodying within himself the three functions, of victim, of immolator and of receiver of the Sacrifice, at the same time. *Prajāpati* is somehow a creation of the Brāhmaṇic speculation, still on the borderline between myth and philosophy,[21], whose role is to 'save' the Cosmic Action from its inherent tendency to become impersonal. In fact, having arrived at a point where it now represents the totality of Reality—human, terrestrial and divine—Sacrifice has practically become the only thing which is responsible for its creative dynamism. But such an abstract Action needs, in its turn, a new sustainer. Hence it reprojects its personalized self in the figure of the Lord of Creatures and, in the speculative realm, it appears as the new recipient of its self-immólation. This God, supreme and superior to all, is the specific Brāhmaṇic Deity, to whom the other Gods pay homage and to whom they owe their very origin. He is that Being whom the more ancient speculation had sought beyond the singular figures of the divine Pantheon, present at the origin of the world and of creation which gradually extended beyond the limited sphere of activity of the single

18. SatBr VI.1.1.5 : *sa puruṣaḥ prajāpatirabhavat.*

19. SatBr II.2.4.1 : *prajāpatir ha vā idam agra eka evāsa.* Cf. also SatBr VII.5.2.6; AitBr X.1.5; PancBr XVI.1; etc.

20. Cf. *prajāpatir yajñaḥ* in AitBr VII.7 (II.2.7) and similar in GopBr II.2.18; SatBr I.7.4.4, ; etc. The same identification will occur for Viṣṇu (cf. ch. VIII, note 17).

21. Prajāpati is a Philosophical Entity entering in the Vedic religion as an anonymous figure (his name is an attribute pointing to a function) which personifies sacrifice. But he has also myths and rituals (these last characterized through silence instead of *mantras*). Cf. S. LEVI, op. cit. ch. II; R. PANIKKAR, *Myth, Faith, Hermeneutics*, op. cit., ch. on Prajāpati; id. *Il Silenzio del Buddha*, pt. III, ch. III.

Deities.[22] However, true to his nature, *Prajāpati* does not become Supreme God independently of that Cosmic Act which he personifies and represents.[23] His activity, splendour, authority and power continue to be derived from the fact that he *is* the Sacrifice and that he can act correctly only by its means.[24] That is, he is never characterized except as a Creator, and, in the ultimate analysis, he is and remains essentially an Act more than truly and properly a Person even though he can become the object of various myths which describe his activity. The rite itself witnesses to this undefined character of his with its alternation of silence and the recitation of formulas during the presentation of offerings which bear his name.[25] *Prajāpati,* as Lord and Supreme Act, cannot be defined and delimited in a figure which is too concrete and which has clear-cut boundaries. He must be able to include in himself both what can be expressed and what has to remain unexpressed, both the limited and the unlimited.[26] Indeed, He is seen as the eminently unlimited : *aparimito vai prajāpatiḥ.*[27] And in fact, soon enough, nearly as soon as his figure emerges, this indefinite character of his—which is more consonant to philosophical speculation than to religious imagination —is betrayed and emphasized by one of its more common and more repeated epithets : *kaḥ.* This is a simple interrogative pronoun which, in the myth describing the origin of the name, is the crystallization, as it were, of the question asked by

22. Since Ṛgvedic times, cf. e.g. RV. X.129.6 : ..*arvāg devā asya visarjanenā 'thā ko veda yata ābabhūva*..whose answer is Prajāpati. Cf. also the 'birth' of Prajāpati in AV in ch. III, p. 75 with notes 47 ff. of this book.

23. In order not to create misunderstanding we do not intend to minimize Prajāpati by saying that he is not independent from the cultic action, but on the contrary we want to sublimate the Sacred Act as such. It, being 'universal' cannot have anyone 'above' or 'beyond', the same as in a theistic mentality there is no sense in saying that there is 'something' 'above' or 'beyond' God.

24. Cf. a characterization of Prajāpati through the texts quoted in S. LEVI, op. cit., ch. I, p. 13 ff.

25. Cf. the texts on the cult of Prajāpati with silence in R. PANIKKAR, *Il Silenzio del Buddha,* op. cit., ch. III, pt. III, par. a, p. 430 ff. and also in ch. VII of this work, note 96.

26. Cf. e.g. SatBr VII.2.4.30 *ubhayametat prajāpatir niruktaś cāniruktaśca parimitaś cāparimitaś ca....*

27. AitBr VII.7 (II.2.7).

Prajāpati regarding his own identity,[28] but which, in the liturgy, ends up by being his most frequently used epithet : *Prajāpati vai kaḥ.*[29] This Brāhmaṇic myth links the origin of this epithet with the loss of creative power, thus perhaps implying that the personification of Sacrifice is due to its effects (multiplicity and its maintenance). But when *Prajāpati* loses his creative power (Indra asks him for his splendour and grandeur, i.e. his creative attributes), his name too is voided of its meaning and is replaced by a pronoun which insinuates that now thathe is no longer connected with the Act of creating, his very identity is put into doubt. In other words, the speculative origin of this divine figure is mirrored also in the vicissitudes of his name : from a *function* ("Lord of his creatures") it is turned into a *question* ("Who?").

We can therefore ask : what is the philosophical and religious attitude of that people which finds not in a name but in a pronoun—and an interrogative pronoun at that—its way of "defining" and calling its God ? If the name reveals the divine personality, what personality lies hidden behind a pronoun expressive of a doubt ? Has speculation, still expressed in mythical terms, no other way than to crystallize and personify once again its own doubt when it seeks to go beyond the function and the proper name of the Divine and to attain the unfathomable depths of the Source? *Prajāpati*, as the Lord ofSactifice at the time when Sacrifice, the Creative Action, becomes ritually and philosophically the Absolute, transforms his very name into its substitute, an interrogative pronoun, even before the philosophical doubt becomes conscious of itself in the mind of the philosophers. His new name, *Kaḥ*, represents the first step, still on a mythological level, towards the philosophical doubt at which reflection invariably arrives when it turns to religious

28. Cf. AitBr XII.10 (III.2.21). At the request of Indra to hand him over Prajāpati's own greatness Prajāpati asks:" 'then who shall I be?' and Indra answered 'he whom you said'. Thus Prajāpati received the name of Who?" (*sa prajāpatir abravīd atha ko 'ham iti / yad evaitad avoca ity abravīt tato vai ko nāma prajāpatir abhavat //*). Cf. a variant in TaittBr II.2.1.1 f. Cf. a comment on my art. "*Kah,* le nomme de Dieu.." quoted.

29. Cf. e.g. TaittSam I.7.6.6; SatBr IV.5.6.4; etc. The epithet is very common in the Brāhmaṇas. It continues, but more rarely in the Purāṇas as epithet of Brahmā.

matters. It is a first step, as yet still timid and expressed in a question, towards search and desire of an Absolute which is not bound to a world which is transient, always unstable and continuously in need of being sustained in existence by means of the Sacrificial power. But when the Supreme God becomes an interrogation mark to Himself and to His faithful, his domain in the field of religious practice cannot last long. The question will sooner or later demand an answer, and this answer will be Brahman, the One without a second, unmovable and perfect, but without any contact whatsoever either with the transient world, now seen as mere heavy and opaque matter, or with the living world of the Deities.[30] This therefore means that earthly creation, once exalted as the highest good, will find no place in the new philosophical conception of Reality. In an immobile and perfect Absolute, a creation in becoming and imperfect does not have any meaning. It would not even be looked upon as something desirable. Apart from the fact that such a creation would be an obstacle for the realization that only the Absolute is and that It alone is pure, its very conception is not unproblematic. When philosophy, in fact, begins to question, consciously, and explicitly the reason of existence and considers Sacrifice as a necessary means for its continuance, it soon becomes aware of the immensely difficult task required from Sacrifice to achieve its purpose, namely to empower existence to survive its transiency and to reach an ever-coveted and an ever-eluding immortality. A new philosophical attitude, therefore, arises, at first imperceptibly, which begins to assume that if a final dissolution is inevitable, if Sacrifice continues to suffer resistance in the pursuit of its task, existence (the world) might as well be allowed to have its own mortal destiny in the full consciousness of its 'inexistence' in front of the Only Existent which really matters, that Absolute which only was before the world detached itself as independent multiplicity with a self-consistency difficult to maintain.

Thus the way is laid open for a re-consideration of Sacrifice

30. Cf. the entire Upaniṣadic philosophy which continues this point, in e.g. S. RADHAKRISHNAN, *Philosophy of the Upaniṣads*, London, (Allen & Unwin), 1958.

in the economy of religious salvation. This may seem, at first sight, somewhat surprising. The Brāhmaṇic Sacrifice is now at its apotheosis. It has reached its highest peak. For a people which loves life, it is the means of creation, it is what renders the One fertile and productive of multiplicity and it is what allows this multiplicity to maintain itself in existence. Still, in the midst of this exaltation of Life, of Reality and of Action, there appears, imperceptibly, and covertly a crack : reflection ! The human mind begins to want to account for everything...not only for human life and existence but also for the intimate Essence of the Absolute. This latter, however, continues to elude it and becomes for it a questioning mark (*Prajāpati vai kaḥ*) while that Reality which has to be continually re-created by means of Sacrifice, with its negative and terrifying aspects, begins to be looked down upon.

The exigencies of speculative thought, however, are not always in agreement with the exigencies of a living religion which has to keep its values intact if it has to survive. The Brāhmaṇic theorists themselves became promptly aware of what threat *Prajāpati*, this abstract figure, imposed upon them as the personification of Sacrifice, could be to their cult. This time the reaction comes from the traditional Deities of the Vedic Pantheon who unlike the evasive figure of *Prajāpati*, a figure too 'philosophical' to resist the attraction of the Absolute, provide, in their mythological concreteness, a much more solid basis for the religious and cultic life. But, significantly enough, the new figure which now makes its appearance to assume the cultic heritage of *Prajāpati* is relatively new in the Vedic world where it previously occupied only a minor and less important place. It is that of *Viṣṇu* whom we saw engaged in the divine strife for the acquisition of the sacrificial knowledge.[31] The Deities who were previously at the zenith of their fortune, Agni included, were too mythologically well-defined—where Prajāpati was too little—to be in a position to assume the new role imposed on the Divine by the changed understanding of Sacrifice. After all, a theological gain, as powerful as this Brāhmaṇic one which has seen the Sacred Act assuming universal proportions, cannot easily remain unheeded even by the most popular mentality. Hence any new

31. Cf. the myth in SatBr VI.1.1.1 ff.

Deity who aspires to become the Supreme must be able to follow the new direction given by speculative thought. This explains why *Viṣṇu*, as we have seen, to obtain superiority over the other Deities had to identify himself with the Cosmic Sacrifice in his ritual struggle to obtain a deepened and direct knowledge of Sacrifice[32] as such. Henceforth only a victory of this kind can place him above the other Deities and endow him with the character of the Supreme God in the cultic and popular religion —a character he continues to enjoy even today.[33]

## 2. *Transformation of Man : His Immortalization and Divinization*

If the stature of the personal Deities decreases with the emergence and universalization of Sacrifice, this is not the case with man and his destiny. Here we must recall that one of the principal aims of Sacrifice—apart, that is, from the increase and maintenance of man's present life—is the attainment of immortality. For the Deities, this means a come-down since now they have to pass through the offering of Sacrifice if they want to obtain immortality—something which so far was considered a natural attribute of theirs. For man, on the contrary, this means a gain because now they are in possession of a concrete means to obtain it—since immortality is normally and naturally denied to him. The sacrificer, therefore, in the manner of the sacrificial victim which ascends to the world of the Deities,[34] and indeed in the manner of the Deities

32. The difference with Prajāpati is that, this one is the result of an inner development of sacrifice as such and therefore is bound to follow its dynamism while Viṣṇu is a divine figure originally external to sacrifice which has conquered his identification with the sacred act through an act of knowledege and of will (cf. SatBr VI.1.1.1 ff) and Indra never reached such identification (and therefore could not remain in later Hindu cult) because his victory was through the meditation of Viṣṇu (Cf. SatBr VI.1.1.12).

33. In the Viṣṇuitic religion, where Viṣṇu is the main figure in the Trimūrti. But also Śiva is connected with Vedic sacrifice since early times, cf. e.g. VajSam XVI.1 ff. and the SvetUp. III.1 ff. etc.

34. Cf AV IV.14.6 quote in ch. III, note 2. Cf. also the other texts quoted in that note.

themselves,[35] is gradually placed in a position where he is able to transform his body and enter into a new life beyond any grasp of death.

But the Brāhmaṇic Sacrifice, if well understood, can offer much more than mere immortality. And the celebrating priests, obliged by liturgical necessity to reflect on the deeper meaning of Sacrifice to make sure of its complete efficacy, have certainly seen this. They have seen that after all immortality is not such a big gain. In fact, the Deities themselves who obtained it through Sacrifice had to pay dearly for it. They had to give up a great part of their power—something which was perhaps greater than the acquired gain. Besides, such an immortality has proved to be, in the long run, a good which is not acquired once and for all. As the transient world, so too the divine world has to be continuously sustained in existence by means of Sacrifice, and this Sacrifice becomes more and more difficult and complicated as new obstacles to the conquest of a definitive and perpetual life after death are encountered.[36] And so the sacrificer, as well as the philosopher, look beyond the deities and their desire for immortality and fix their gaze directly on that Absolute with which the Cosmic Action (i.e. Sacrifice) has been gradually identified and which is All-Powerful by definition.

As *Viṣṇu* has done before him, during the sacrificial session at *Kurukṣetra*, man now understands that the highest good is his identification with Sacrifice and that he, mortal though he is, has the same possibilities of doing so as the Deities. In his meditations, the priest has understood, first of all, that by the very fact that he can offer the Sacrifice on which the Deities themselves depend, man as such has risen to a very high position at the very centre of the Cosmic Dynamism. If Sacrifice is the recapitulation of all creative activity, the priest who offers it finds himself, at least during the time that he does so, to be the co-creator of the universe, the controller of all phenomena, the

35. Cf. TaittSam VI.2.2.6 f. where the officiant priest sips the *tapta vrata* (the hot milk of the oblation) following the example of the Gods who did it at the beginnng of time (text quoted in ch. IV, note 28); or SatBr I.7.3.26 where priests and sacrificer cook the offering on fire because the Gods made the same and from there went to heaven (text quoted in ch. IV, note 28); etc.

36. In the performance of sacrifice there is a whole problematic with respect to the possible final victory of death over life, both in the lacking of heat in the sacred act, and in its excess. Cf. II and III parts of my article "The Role of Sacred Heat....".

mediator between heaven and earth. The knowledge of the sacrificial ritual is, therefore, the key to acquire mastery over Life, to conquer Death, thus assuring for oneself a continuity within the devastating alienation brought about by Time, and above all to identify oneself with the sacrificial Power. It is the means for the sacrificer and the priest to realize that during that time man becomes the equal of the Deities and even superior to them : he becomes at one with the Cosmic Action which he performs, and thus he places himself at the centre of the primordial Creative Act. For as long as the Sacrifice lasts, man as sacrificer is identified with *Prajāpati* and plays his role in 'the Great Theatre of the World' almost on the same level as the Cosmic Powers. The priest knows, in fact, that he is dependent on the 'Divine' for his own existence, but he knows at the same time that the Deities depend on him for the offerings they receive and indeed that they have to offer the same type of sacrifice for their own existence since every existence and its maintenance including their own, depends on Sacrifice. The sacrificer and the priest are aware of their 'sinfulness', of their weakness, of the possibility of losing their sacred power at any time and for the least mistake they commit in the ritual. But they are aware too that during the time in which they are consecrated and called upon to offer Sacrifice, they perform an Act with cosmic dimensions and are therefore in possession of a power which is superior to that of the single Deities. Still, in most cases, this is true, as we are saying, only for the time while the Sacrifice lasts, after which, the sacrificer and his priests purify themselves, shed off their sacrality and return to the world of men.

But even then, the fact that they have 'tasted' their participation of the Absolute instils in the Brāhmaṇa the desire to secure for himself this state of his in a permanent manner. In most cases, the sacrificer contents himself with having obtained immortality—either by begetting offspring which prolongs his life on earth[37] or by becoming an ancestor (*pitṛ*) having transformed his mortal body into an immortal one on the pyre of his last sacri-

37. The often repeated request in the sacrifices to obtain children has the goal to continue life on the earth and amounts in a certain sense to be the same as 'immortality'.

fice.[38] But he who has handled the Sacred, who has performed the Sacrifice in all its details with full knowledge of its powers, its hidden meanings and far-reaching effects, is likely to beget the desire of acquiring a state which is far superior to that conferred by immortality. The *ṛṣis* and the priests who have transformed the world and the 'divine' with their sacrifice would want to be enabled to transform themselves too by identifying themselves, on a permanent basis, with the supreme Creative Power. The first step in this process has been in fact to divinize the first Vedic *ṛṣis* and to identify them with the Absolute Power so as, then, to extend the process and apply it to themselves. Throught the centuries, in fact, the more recent *ṛṣis* celebrated, in their hymns and philosophical speculations, their more ancient predecessors as primordial cosmic Powers beyond the power of the Deities themselves. The *Sapta Ṛṣis,* for example, became in the eyes of their successors those who alone existed at the beginning (*agre*), indeed who were beyond existence, identified with the "Non-Existent".[39] In the eyes of their successors—that is, of those who follow in their footsteps and continue their task of unfolding the Sacred on earth—they could not but have been fully divinized as a result of their having partaken of the Cosmic Sacrifice. Otherwise, all the theological speculation regarding the effects of Sacrifice would have remained unproved and therefore vain. That means that Sacrifice which lies at the basis of all the created worlds and which has transformed Itself into a Cosmic Action, transforming, at the same time, all the single Deities into an all-comprehensive Absolute, must have—according to the philosophers—effected the same transformation, in a concrete manner on the first offerers of that very Sacrifice, i.e. the first *Ṛṣis,* making them the co-creators of the Universe and placing them, therefore, beyond its very existence.[40]

38. Cf. ch. II, p. 41 ff. about the funeral rites and its aims.

39. Cf. SatBr VI.1.1.1: *aum asad vā'idam agra'āsīt / tad āhuḥ kiṃ tad asad-āsīd ity ṛṣayo vāva te'gre 'sad āsīt tad āhuḥ ke ta 'ṛṣaya iti prāṇā vā ṛṣayas te*.. ("Aum, verily, in the beginning there was here the non-existent. As to this they say, 'What was that non-existent ?' The Rishis assuredly,—it is they that were the non-existent, (in the beginning). As to this they say 'who were those Rishis ?' The Rishis doubtless were the vital air..") (tr. EGGELING).

40. For this it was not necessary that they should have been 'moral' in the sense we ask today; what it was needed was for them to be 'perfect' both ritually and religiously.

After this first step—the divinization of the *Ṛṣis* of the past, of the famous seven ancestors of the Vedic *gotra* (*gentes*, families)—the second step is to extend this divinization to the priests and philosophers of the 'present time'.[41] But now the divinization which is sought does not stop at an identification with the Creator or with the First Powers which were responsible for creation. Now it is no longer enough to attain the position of conscious co-creator of the world. In fact the philosophy of the world and of its existence is now in a process of change. The created world now no longer enjoys those positive characteristics with which it was endowed at the time of the Hymns and of the initial period of their *Brāhmaṇas*. To the inquisitive human mind the world reveals itself for what it really is, namely something terribly unstable which continuously needs to be sustained by repeated dismemberment of sacrificial victims. Besides—as one can easily realize if one studies the difficulties entailed in the performance of Sacrifice—every new effort to sustain such a created world invariably ends up in the complete exhaustion of the sacrificial Victim even in its universal and cosmic form.[42] Why, therefore, should the aim of man be to create and sustain such a world whose origin and continuance in existence costs so much? Besides, it is not as creator that man, more specifically the priest, can experience that bliss of identification with the Absolute; he can experience that bliss and sense of fulness only when he is busily engaged in building up again the body of *Prajāpati* after it has been dismembered and before his new creative act. In fact, the various fragments of multiplicity, dispersed throughout the visible world, can be gradually

41. That is to say 'contemporary' to those composing the Brāhmaṇas. Even for them perfection in rituals was more important than perfection in 'morality'. Yet SatBr XI.8.4.1ff. relates a story according to which a Brāhmaṇa priest performs his moral duty (*dharma*) although to his personal detriment in this world. He expected a kind of reward, perhaps, in an after-life, because to his advisors he answers: "I will tell (him) surely because 'there' there are more nights" (v. 5 : *sa hovāca vakṣyāmy evām ūrvai rātrayo bhūyasya iti*).

42. Cf. e.g. SatBr X.4.2.2ff. where Prajāpati, having created the beings (that is to say, having performed the creative sacrifice) is afraid of dying because he feels empty: ; or SatBr VI.1.2.12 ff. PancBr IX.6.6 f.; or the many cases we have met with where the *rasa* or *medha* runs away. Cf. the implications of this fact in my same quoted article.

re-gathered through the effort and mediation of man to re-construct the body of the Creator "who dies for having created." One could say, in accordance with the myth, that after the dismemberment of *Prajāpati*, multiplicity which estranges itself from its Creator returns to Him by means of the same Sacrifice which had produced it. But to the philosopher who partakes of this Sacrifice, this process of having always to start afresh, of having to re-construct again and again the unity long-wished for only to destroy it again and thus to sustain the world at the cost of the very life of Prajāpati—seems absurd. And what is more, he feels himself to be necessarily caught up in this cycle—with the consequent periodical loss of his own unity which he so laboriously acquires. In fact, he loses his unity and identification with the Absolute at the end of every Sacrifice in the same way as *Prajāpati* loses his wholeness when he is dismembered. *Prajāpati* is bodily dismembered and his interior energy exhausted at the end of the creative Sacrifice, while his priest loses his identification with the Divine as soon as he stops officiating. The latter's state is as precarious as that of the Sacrificial Act itself since it has to be renewed again and again. However, the *dīkṣā*, even though it is linked to the practical performance of Sacrifice, preparing and consecrating those who are about to offer it, has a more personal influence on the sacrificer and on the priest since it infuses directly in them that energy which enables them to encounter the Sacred and consequently to assimilate themselves with the Divine with which they have to come in contact by means of Sacrifice. The *dīkṣā* is the beginning of man's self-transformation into the Divine—not through any exterior action but through an interior change entailing a certain amount of *tapas*. Hence, to achieve this end, the more obvious measure which now imposes itself on the philosopher-priest would be to strengthen himself ever more in his *dikṣā* till his interior transformation leads to his identification with the Absolute independently of any further sacred activity, an excess of which could only result once again in the production of multiplicity.

This new attitude taken by the philosophical speculation prepares the ground for the spiritual transformation as found in the *Upaniṣads*. The Upaniṣadic great mystical personalities are the same great ritual masters of the Brāhmaṇas, as, for example, Yājñavalkya, Uddālaka, Śāṇḍilya, etc. Having experienced the possibility of his becoming God, of identifying himself with the Absolute, man is not content with such a state for only as long as his participation in the Sacrifice permits but seeks to prolong it for the duration of all his life and beyond his life to reach that eternity which is now open to him. By having divinized the first ancient *Ṛṣis*, the Brāhmaṇic philosopher rendered them equal to the First Creative Principle—which, however, exhausts Itself in that same activity by which It is then to re-create Itself. But by his own divinization, the philosopher identifies himself with that Absolute which revealed Itself to him beyond the cosmic activity, in the Silence and Non-Activity of the by now Immobile Perfection as described in the Upaniṣads. Thus the philosopher gradually arrives at a stage where he stops offering sacrifice, at first simply to avoid any external activity and to interiorize its effects by meditation, but then to deliver himself totally to the pure awareness of the Perfect Unity. In this perception he can then contemplate, in an unmoved and detached manner, the flow of the world and of the universe which unfolds itself in front of him without touching him, and in his experience of the Absolute remains forever identified with It.

In this way, therefore, man finds himself once again in the position, even without his wanting it, of a creator in much the same way as the ancient *Ṛṣis* divinized by him but, still, on another level. In fact, his creative activity is not actualized in Sacrifice, but by his partaking of the ultimate Immobility of the global Reality and by his ability to *see* the point of origin of the world's independent flow. His activity, therefore, is not a creative activity in the strict sense but an act of *seeing*, an act of conscious awareness regarding the moment in which creation or multiplicity, detaches itself from the Absolute Reality. And in this act of conscious awareness, man accepts, contemplates and perhaps sustains too the transient world, but does not bring it into being. He makes use of Sacrifice as a point of departure for his meditation—and even then only to reconstruct the unity of *Prajāpati* now become *Brahman*, and stopping at the zenith of this reconstruction before its next disintergration.

But this means that he has to abstain, in a sense, from the celebration of Sacrifice in a concrete and practical way, and to prefer to interiorize it in his intuitive (mystical) perception, since sacrifice, if peformed has to reach its due creative dismemberment. However, to abstain from the liturgical celebration of Sacrifice could mean that the philosopher would have to renounce the share of the energetic effects of heat which is the heart of every Sacrifice and the source of all its divine benefits. But the philosopher simply cannot renounce that: to do so would mean to renounce partaking, in any manner whatsoever, in that Absolute which the power of Sacrifice has revealed to him. The Upaniṣadic philosopher, therefore, even if he renounces the celebration of Sacrifice, does not renounce its calorific energy, the divine *tapas* which he finds above all in the sacrificial preliminaries and which he can now kindle most of all in his *dīkṣā*. He thus makes use of the fury of his, by now, interiorized fire to burn the dross of contingent matter which binds him to the world's becoming, and, letting himself be driven upwards by the ascensional force of *tapas*, he lets himself be transformed in such a way as to finally disappear in the immensity, the vacuity and immobility of the cosmic Absolute.

Thus, at a time when Sacrifice reaches its zenith and the positivity of material creation is unquestioned, we arrive too at the full blossoming of Upaniṣadic mysticism which considers multiplicity no longer as a good, as indicative of the fertility of the One but rather as an aberration from the One's solemn and immobile Perfection. In the new philosophical circles, formed among the religious sages themselves, the idea is now to transcend this kind of sacrificial cult retaining from it only the fortifying energy of *tapas*—not as a creavtive means but as a means to purify oneself from whatever keeps multiple reality from its First and Unique Source—and its ascensional force which is now used for one's absorption into the Absolute.[43]

43. The process we have sketched here is the one followed by the philosopher and the mystic, not by the whole Brāhmaṇic religiosity. The mystical exigency which is developing out of popular religion will since early times take the form of *bhakti*, that is to say of the adoration to a Supreme God. But this part does not fall into the boundary of the present research.

And so we come to the close of this part of our study of the Brāhmaṇic Sacrifice, which we have pursued by tracing the role and function which heat has in it. We have seen how the Sacrifice, as the dynamic Cosmic Action, on the one hand, has swept away the single Deities and absorbed them in the form-less and attribute-less Absolute, while, on the other hand, it has offered man an immortality and a divinization in such a way as to place him in a condition of becoming himself that Absolute.

## GLOSSARY

ADHYĀYA A section in *Brāhmaṇas* (q.v.), *Upaniṣads* (q.v.), etc.

ADHVARA Another name for Soma (q.v.) Sacrifice.

ADHVARYU An officiating priest in the sacrifice, from among the Yajurveda group. He is in charge of the material performance of most of the ritual actions.

ADITI Lit., infinity. Name of the Great Goddess, Mother of Gods.

ĀDITYA Lit., son of Aditi. Name of a group of Gods the most prominent of whom is the Sun.

AGNI Lit., fire. Name of one of the principal Gods of the Vedic world. He is especially linked to sacrifice. The name is also used to indicate Fire-Altar.

AGNICAYANA Lit., construction of Fire-Altar. *Cayana*, n., from the root *ci*, means to build, edify, heap up.

AGNICITI Lit., a constructed Fire-Altar. *Citi*, f., from the root *ci*. The term has the same meaning as the preceding and in our study we use the two terms synonymously.

AGNĪDHRA The priest in charge of the fire. He is one of the assistants of Adhvaryu (q.v.).

AGNIHOTRA An important Vedic sacrifice though very rarely performed today, consisting of an offering of hot milk to the Aśvins (q.v.) in the morning and to Agni (q.v.) in the evening.

AGNIṢṬOMA One of the names of Soma (q.v.) sacrifice, perhaps the most common.

AGNYĀDHĀNA or AGNYĀDHEYA The ceremony of the building and lighting of the first fire of the sacrificer.

ĀHAVANĪYA One of the Vedic Fire-Altars. It is square in shape and situated on the east side of *vedi* (q.v.). It is on it that the gifts of the offering are placed.

ĀHUTI Oblation.

AJA Lit., non-born. Name given to goat, the victim par excellence, of animal sacrifices which are often included in more sacrifical complexes. It is the principal victim in *ajamedha* (q.v.).

AJAMEDHA Lit., sacrifice of the non-born. It is a sacrifice in which the principal victim is a goat.

ĀMA Cold.

AMṚTA Lit., immortality, deathlessness. Also a name given to the "nectar of immortality" of Gods, ambrosia. In this second meaning it is given especially to Soma (q.v.) but also to ghee (*ghṛta*, q.v.)

ANAÑKE A Greek word which means "necessity". It is a name used in the Hellenic world to designate the Absolute Necessity of Cosmic Fate to which even Zeus, the head of the Pantheon (q.v.), is subject.

AṆVA An interstice in the filter which serves to purify Soma (q.v.).

APĀNA one of the five vital airs, or breaths, which circulate in the body.

ARAṆI Name of two pieces of wood having a particular shape, which when rubbed together produce fire (*Agni*, q.v.). Hence they are also called "the parents of Agni".

ĀRAṆYAKA Lit, belonging to the forest, that is, the place where normally the Indian wise men and hermits retire. By extension, the word came to mean also "myster ious", "mystical". As neuter noun, it is the name of a part of the Brāhmaṇas (q.v.) which must be read and meditated upon in the solitude of the forest. They stand midway between the Brāhmaṇas properly so called and the Upaniṣads (q.v.), and are of a philosophico-spiritual character.

ARCIS Flame.

AṢĀḌHĀ Lit., unconquerable. A name given to a special brick used in *Agnicayana* (q.v.).

ĀSANDĪ Name of the ritual seat on which *ukhā* (q.v.) with its fire (*ukhyagni*, q.v.) is placed during moments of rest while Fire-Altar is being constructed (*Agnicayana*, q.v.).

ASURA Lit., Lord. In the initial Vedic period, the word was

used to designate a group of Deities whose head was Varuṇa (q.v.). Later, in the Brāhmaṇas (q.v.) the meaning is entirely changed and the word comes to designate a category of Demons and malign spirits who are the chief enemies of Devas (q.v.).

AŚVA Horse.

AŚVAMEDHA Horse Sacrifice. A great sacrificial complex consisting of many rites including the offering of many animals. It was the privilege of a king to perform it for which he gained a high esteem.

AŚVATTHA *Ficus religiosa*, the banyan tree.

AŚVIN Name of the twin Deities; heralds of the rising sun. Wonder-workers and heavenly healers, they are the Twin Gods; the equivalent of the Greek and Latin Dioscuri.

ĀTMAN A word which is difficult to translate. It means the soul, the self, the 'I' and also the Universal Spirit. All these meanings are only approximative.

AVĀNTARADĪKṢĀ Lit., intermediary initiation. It is a special initiation (*dīkṣā*, q.v.) given on the occasion of *Soma* (q.v.) Sacrifice in connection with *Upasada* (q.v.). and therefore also with *Pravargya* (q.v.). But the word is also used to refer to a more complicated initiation of a priest during the course of which the secrets of Pravargya are learnt.

ĀVASATHYA One of the Vedic Fire-Altars. It is of a minor importance and is constructed only rarely. It is small and round in shape, situated to the north of Āhavanīya (q.v.) with which it is directly linked.

AVATĀRA Generally translated as "incarnation", it stands for the descent of *Viṣṇu* (q.v.) in various animal and human forms. Tradition ended up by fixing the number of times of this descent to ten, the last one still to come.

AYAS "Metal" in general (it is difficult to be more specific).

ĀYUR Life. More exactly, the life-span of a man. It corresponds, even though not exactly, to the Greek word, *aiôn*.

AUM Sometimes written also as OM. A Vedic sacred syllable expressing the Absolute in Its essence.

BAAL A Cananean Deity whose prophets were challenged by Elijah, a prophet of Israel.

BHAKTI Lit., division, but also devotion, love, adoration, from the root *bhaj*. A form of cult consisting in loving devotion and dedication to a personal God. It developed roundabout the 15th century of our era perhaps under the influence of Islam. But it has its roots in much more ancient times. In fact, it makes its appearance already with *Kṛṣṇa* (q.v.) in the Epics, and it is *Kṛṣṇa* to whom this cult is mostly addressed. The same cult however is also addressed to other Hindu Deities.

BHŪR, BHUVAḤ, SVAḤ The three potent sacred formulae, or utterances, collectively known as *vyāhṛti* (q.v.). They represent the three worlds, the earthly, the atmospheric and the celestial, respectively. They contain, as in a nutshell, the whole essence of Vedic wisdom.

BRAHMĀ (m.) The first Deity in the Hindu *Trimūrti* (q.v.). He is eminently the Creator. In India his cult is today limited to one temple alone and somehow linked to the cult of *Viṣṇu* (q.v.) of whom Brahmā is born at the beginning of every new era (*kalpa*).

BRAHMAUDANA Lit., rice-pudding (*odana* q.v.) of Brahmā (q.v.). It is the name given to the rice-pudding which is to be offered to the priests (cf. *Brāhmaṇa*). It is cooked on a provisional fire at the end of the initiation of the sacrificer on the occasion of the establishment of his first fires.

BRAHMACĀRIN A student of *Brahman* (q.v.), one who practices *Brahmacarya* (q.v.).

BRAHMACARYA The period of religious studies. It is the first of the four stages of life (*āśramas*) in which the life of a *Brāhmaṇa* (q.v.) is, according to tradition, divided. The other three are: *gṛhastha*, the stage of the householder, of the married man; *vānaprastha*, the stage of the forest dweller, the hermit—after having performed his worldly duties, the householder retires into solitude to give himself to meditation and spiritual things; *saṃnyāsa*, the stage of the wandering monk, a stage of complete renunciation. In this fourth and last stage, the householder renounces his sacrificial fire also, which is now interiorized in *tapas* (q.v.), and hence its profane benefits too. He does not eat cooked food and after his death his corpse is not cremated.

BRAHMAN (n.) Initially, a sacred formula recited during sacrifice. Later, raised to stand for the Absolute, the Ultimate Ground of all things.

BRĀHMAṆÁ A member belonging to the priestly caste, the highest of the four Vedic and Hindu castes; a brahmin. Also a specific type of priest whose duty it is to supervise sacrifice and whose Veda is the Atharva.

BRĀHMAṆA A collection of texts, of an explicative and philosophical character, forming part of *śruti* (q.v.). They are divided according to the types of hymns in which the Vedas are themselves divided. So there are Ṛgveda Brāhmaṇas (two), Sāmaveda Brāhmaṇas (many), Yajurveda Brāhmaṇas (one according to the *Kṛṣṇa* school, and one according to the *Śukla* school) and Atharvaveda Brāhmaṇas (one).

BRAHMAṆASPATI (also BṚHASPATI) Name of a Deity, the "Lord of the Sacred Formula."

BRAHMAVĀDIN A *Brāhmaṇa* (q.v.) who studies, speculates and explains the sacred texts and spiritual matters. In our study we have generally translated the term by "theologian".

BRAHMAVARCAS Lit., splendour of *Brahman* (q.v.). A quality which man can acquire by means of sacrifice and which seems to have been very ardently desired.

BṚHAT A sacred formula.

CARU A type of cooked offering, generally vegetal, of rice or grain.

CARUṆA Rice-pudding. A cooked offering which is poured in oblation on the sacred fire at times together with the offering of animal victims.

CĀTURMĀSYA Lit., four months. A type of sacrifice which lasts four months, performed in accordance with the phases of the moon, especially the new moon and the full moon of all the four chosen months.

DAKṢIṆĀ (m.) (dakṣiṇa) the South; (f.) recompense, honorarium, of the priest.

DAKṢIṆĀGNI Lit., the southern fire. Name of one of the Fire-altars, having the form of a half circle, situated to the south of *Gārhapatya* (q.v.). In place of or together with Gārhapatya, it serves to cook the offerings, but its building is optional. Specially used to cook the *Brahma-udana* (q.v.).

DARŚAPŪRṆAMĀSA As the word itself indicates, a name of a sacrificial rite to be performed on a new and full moon.

DEVA God, deity, cosmic power. In the early Vedic period, when the term is applied to the major figures like Indra, Agni, Soma, it retains all its meaning as a personal God. In the Brāhmaṇic period, however, the term is used to designate a category of generally anonymous Divine Beings, opposd to Asuras (q.v.).

DHARMA Lit., Order. Complex term, meaning also 'religious duties'.

DĪKṢĀ Initiation, consecration. Within the sacrificial context, the undergoing of certain preliminary rites, especially of purification, for a specific end which often is the participation in a sacrifice, particularly *Somayajña* (q.v.) or any other rite of some importance (e.g. *agnihotra*, q.v.).

DIŚ The cardinal points. These are very important in the Vedic religion and are even worthy of sacrificial offerings.

EIDOLON A Greek word which literally means "image of a God". It is the equivalent of the sanskrit *mūrti* (q.v.). We avoid using its usual English translation as "idol" because of its pejorative connotation.

ELIJAH One of the great prophets of Israel.

EPIPHANY A Greek word which literally means "manifestation". It is used especially to indicate a divine manifestation or appearance.

GARBHA Lit., embryo. It is a term whose metaphorical meaning is very important in the Vedic-Brāhmaṇic spirituality and philosophy. At times, it also means "womb".

GĀRHAPATYA One of the two principal Fire-Altars used for the Vedic sacrifice. Circular in shape and situated on the west side of the sacrificial ground, it is used to cook and prepare the offerings which will be poured on the *Āhavanīya* (q.v.). From it also is lit the fire which serves the daily needs of the family of the *yajamāna* (q.v.), during sacrificial performances.

GĀYATRĪ The most sacred Vedic *mantra* (q.v.) formed of eight 'feet' of twenty-four syllables each. Divinized as a Goddess.

GHARMA Lit., heat, from the root *ghṛ*. It is also the name of the cauldron which is a special receptacle used mainly in *Pravargya* (q.v.) and in *Agnihotra* (q.v.).

GHṚTA Clarified butter. One of the most sacred offerings in India from Vedic times end throughout its history. It is the "immortal" food of the Gods.

GOSAVA The Ox or Cow Sacrifice.

GOTRA Family or clan, equivalent to the Latin "gens". A collectivity of families, especially belonging to the Brāhmaṇic caste, but also to the two other higher castes, tracing its ancestry to one of the great Vedic *ṛṣis* (q.v.).

GURU Master, especially spiritual guide.

HAVANA The act of pouring the offering in the fire as an oblation, generally performed with the palm of the hand turned upwards.

HAVIS Sacrificial offering. The best and main part of the animal or vegetal victim to be poured in oblation on the sacred fire. At times the term is uesd for the victim as a whole, whether animal or vegetal.

HEPHAISTOS The God of Fire in the Greek *Pantheon* (q.v.), called by the Romans *Vulcanus* (God *Vulcan*).

HERMES A Greek God, called *Psychopompos* because of his specific task among many others of accompanying the souls of the dead to their destination beyond the grave. He is called *Mercurius* (*Mercury*) by the Romans.

HESTIA A Goddess, called *Vesta* by the Romans, who in the Greek and Roman *Pantheon* (q.v.) supervises the Fire.

HINDUISM A term which is inexactly but by now commonly used to refer to the Brāhmaṇic religion. Like the term "India" itself, it originated in the Greek literature where this country, with its language, culture and religion, is referred to as the land "beyond the river Indus (Sindhu)". In our study we have employed the term a few times only to refer to the religious tradition which developed after the time of the *Upaniṣads* (q.v.) basing itself above all on the Epics and the *Purāṇas* (q.v.). We do so to distinguish this religious tradition, perhaps in a too simplified but certainly clear way, from the more ancient religious tradition which is known to us above all from the texts of *Śruti* (q.v.).

HOMA A type of oblation.

HOTṚ Priest in general, but more precisely the principal priest of the Ṛgvedic group whose main task it is to recite his, i.e. the Ṛgvedic, *mantras* (q.v.) especially during sacrifice. *Hotrā* is the function of the Hotṛ.

INDRA The greatest God in the Vedic *Pantheon* (q.v.). He is the King of Kings, the mighty warrior fighting against enemies and demons. Even after the decline of the personal deities, he retains a certain prominent position.

ĪŚĀNA Lit., Lord. The God who rules the North-East, sometimes identified with Śiva who is often considered to be the Lord (*Īśa*) *par excellence.*

IṢṬA A technical Sanskrit term for "offering".

IṢṬAKA Brick.

ITARAJANĀḤ Foreign peoples.

JAGATĪ A Vedic meter of four feet with twelve syllables each. The *mantra* (q.v.) which has this meter is proper to the members of the Vaiśya caste.

JĀTAVEDAS Lit., the knower of the people. A title of *Agni* (q.v.).

JIGHARTI "It Warms." From the root *ghṛ*, from which *gharma* (q.v.) too is derived and which is linked to the Indoeuropean root *guer* from which comes the germanic *warm.*

JYOTIS Light.

KAḤ Interrogative pronoun, "who?". A name given to *Prajāpati* (q.v.) in the Brāhmaṇic literature. It is also given, a couple of times in the Purāṇic literature, to *Brahmā* (q.v.) who as Creator sometimes assumes the title of *Prajāpati* not as a name but as an attribute.

KĀṆḌA A division in chapters, in the Brāhmaṇas, Upaniṣads, etc.

KRAVYĀDA Lit., "eater of corpses". Title of *Agni* (q.v.) as the funeral fire. Such a title, however, is not proper to Agni alone but to any eater of corpses, e.g. the vulture.

KṚṢṆA Lit., black. One of the two great divisions of the Yajurveda (the other division being the *Śukla*, lit., white). It comprises four Schools of which the Taittirīya is the most important and which we have followed in our study. Descendants and followers of the Taittirīya are to be found today mostly in the South of India.

KṚṢṆA Name of one of the most adored and loved Indian Gods. Probably of a local origin (in Mathurā), he soon became the principal object of bhakti cult all over the country. Official Hinduism absorbed Him and made of Him an *avatāra* of *Viṣṇu* (q.v.).

KṢATRIYA A member of the second Vedic caste, which is that of the warriors, that is, of the nobility, out of which the kings are normally chosen. It is for this reason that this caste is sometimes called "of the *rājās*" or kings.

KUMBHA A round jar or vessel, like an amphora without neck.

KŪRMA Tortoise. An animal with a great cosmogonic symbolism. Since it is also a symbol of life, it is walled up in the first layer of the bricks of *Agnicayana* (q.v.). Because of its cosmogonic symbolism, one of the first incarnations of *Viṣṇu* (q.v.) is said to have taken the form of a tortoise.

KURUKṢETRA Lit., field of Kuru. The name of a place, to the north of Delhi, where, according to tradition, the battle between the sons of Dhṛtarāṣṭra and the sons of Pāṇḍu was waged. This battle is described in one of the greatest Indian Epics, the *Mahābhārata* (q.v.). It is also the place where, according to tradition too, a sacrifice was performed during which the Vedas were systematized, and the just mentioned Epic was written by Vyāsa. It is there too that, always according to tradition, the Purāṇas were rearranged by the same Vyāsa.

LOṢṬACAYANA The rite of building a tumulus on the ashes of the cremated body of the dead sacrificer who had in his life constructed the *Agnicayana* (q.v.).

MAGHAVAN Lit., munificent. One of the titles of *Indra* (q.v.).

MAHĀBHĀRATA The title of the greater of the two Indian epics. (See under *Kurukṣetra*.)

MAHĀTMĀ Lit., great soul. Title of a sage or a saint.

MAHĀVEDI Name of very big (*mahā*) altar (*vedi*) used for the ceremony of the Pressing of Soma (q.v.) and situated between the usual altar and the *uttaravedi* (q.v.).

MAHĀVĪRA Lit., great man. Name of a special vessel used to boil milk in *Pravargya* (q.v.). When it is intensely heated, it stands for an epiphany of the Divine. At times, it is also called *Gharma* (q.v.).

MAHĀVRATA Lit., great vow. Name of a ceremony which is a ritual itself.

MAKHA Name of a Deity linked to Indra. The term is explained as an esoteric form of *Maghavan* (q.v.). It is to his head that *Pravargya* (q.v.) is addressed.

MANAS Mind in the broadest sense, intellect, spirit, etc.

MANOTĀ The beginning of a Ṛgvedic hymn dedicated to *Agni* (q.v.). It becomes the technical term for the offering of an animal victim at the moment of its being oblated on the sacred fire.

MANTRA A sacred verse usually taken from the Saṃhitās. The repetition of such a verse confers a certain power on him who recites it.

MARUT A type of deity—always spoken of in the plural—associated with Indra and manifesting itself in impetuous wind (but not, as is often understood, in a naturalistic sense).

MATHITA Past participle passive of the root *math* which means "to run around", "to batter very fast". Hence when the term is applied to fire, it means "produced by friction" in the context of the sacred rite. Another word, therefore, for the sacrificial fire itself.

MEDHA Lit., sap, and therefore essence. In particular, the essence of the sacrificial victim, often used as a synonym of the sacrificial victim itself.

MYTH From the Greek *mythos*. As the term is used in different meanings in the History of Religions, we point out that in our study we understand it in its original sense as a "narrative of sacred themes" with the view of explaining the origin of certain rites, the reason for certain events and for the existence of certain phenomena.

MITRA Lit., friend. The name of a God in the Vedic *Pantheon* (q.v.), often invoked in association with *Varuṇa* (q.v.). When they are so associated, Mitra represents the light of day and *Varuṇa* the darkness of night.

MUÑJA A type of sacrificial herb. This long-stalked herb has an important and multiple function in the Vedic rite.

MŪRTI Lit., image. Mostly used for an image of a God, as a kind of *theophany* (q.v.). The cult which is offered to the God represented in the image is quite different from that offered with the sacrificial victim, and follows different rules.

NĀBHI Lit., navel. Used synonymously for "centre".

NĀKAM Firmament. In the Vedic cosmology, there exist many firmaments.

ODANA A vegetal offering, generally a rice-pudding. It may be either a secondary offering in a blood sacrifice or the principal offering of self-standing liturgical complex. Some hymns are sung in its praise in a deified form.

OMENTUM A Latin word used to indicate the fatty net which covers the kidneys, and surrounds the intestines.

ORPHISM An ancient Greek religion for its purificatory and sometimes orgiastic rites.

PAKTI (f.) cooking. From the root *pac*. All the preliminaries of sacrifice are indicated by this comprehensive term.

PAKVA Adj. and p.p. passive (f. *pakvi*), cooked. From the root *pac*.

PALĀŚA An Indian sacred tree with broad leaves and red flowers (*butea frondosa*).

PAÑCAUDANA A quintuple rice-pudding (*pañca+odana*, q.v.). Often used as a side-offering in big sacrificial complexes.

PAÑCAVIṂŚA BRĀHMAṆA Lit. "of twenty five chapters". The name of one of the Brāhmaṇas of the Sāmaveda, called also Tāṇḍya Mahābrāhmaṇa.

PANTHEON A Greek word derived from *pan+theion* indicating the collectivity of the deities. For convenience's sake, we use it in our study, even if inexactly, to indicate the collectivity of the Vedic deities forming, as it were, an organic and organized body.

PĀPMAN Evil, and by extension, also sin.

PARYAGNI Lit., circumambulation of the fire. It is a rite performed prior to the immolation of the victim, consisting in going around the victim with a burning torch in hand before it is immolated or, by extension, around any other type of offering. Today it is still performed around the body of a deceased person and funeral pyre.

PAŚUBANDHA Lit., the binding of the animal victim. It is used synonymously for "animal sacrifice", an ancillary rite of great sacrificial complexes.

PAŚUPURODĀŚA (Ṛgvedic: *paśupurolāśa*) A pudding of baked grains, in the form of an animal, offered immediately after that of the *omentum* (q.v.). It replaced the bloody offering, with which it is identified, when the blood sacrifice was abandoned.

PAŚUŚRAPAṆA The name of the so-called 'profane' fire, lit near the place of the immolation of the victim. It is also called "the fire of the immolator". It serves to cook the omentum (q.v.) and other parts of the victim while they are still raw so that by this first cooking it does not let the consecrated fire to come in contact with still raw—and therefore impure—things.

PAŚUYAJÑA Animal sacrifice.

PAVITRA Lit., filter. Therefore, the purifier and, by extension, the saint, the sanctified, the pure *par excellence*.

PELOPE Son of Tantalus, in the Greek mythology.

PIṆḌA Small round balls. It is in this form that every part of the sacrificial offering is offered even today, so that it can easily be consigned to the sacred fire.

PRAJĀPATI Lit., Lord of creatures. Initially only an attribute of the creating deities, it later becomes the name of the Supreme God, Father of Gods and Demons, particularly active and adored in the Brāhmaṇic era. In the Purāṇic literature, the name still appears every now and then but once again as an attributive and applied to *Brahmā* (q.v.).

PRĀṆA One of the five kinds of breath of which it is the most important and represents also the vital spirit, the interior pneumatic force. The term is used also comprehensively for all the five, and to represent life as such.

PRASĀDA Gift. It is that portion of an offering made to a God (present in the *mūrti*, q.v.), a Master, *Guru* (q.v.), a *Mahātmā* (q.v.), which is then returned to the offerer charged with the spiritual power of him to whom it was offered.

PRATIPRASTHĀTṚ One of the priests who help the *Adhvaryu* (q.v.).

PRAVARGYA A Vedic rite, linked to the *Soma* sacrifice(q.v.), which consists in three offerings of very hot milk to the *Aśvins* (q.v.) in the morning, to *Indra* (q.v.) at noon and to *Viśvedevāḥ* (q.v.) in the evening. It is an optional rite but when it is performed, it is performed immediately before the *Upasada* (q.v.). It is through it that a kind of spiritualization enters in the performance of sacrifices, through the interpretation of the Atharvan priests.

PRAVṚJE A word which appears only once in the *Ṛgveda* (see under *Ṛk*) and presumably is the ancient form of *Pravargya* (q.v.).

PROMETHEUS A giant (Titan) who, in the Greek mythology, was the founder of civilization and stole fire to give it to man for which he was punished by *Zeus* (q.v.).

PŪJĀ A form of cult addressed to a God present in his *mūrti* (q.v.), consisting in the offering of flowers, fruit or other things held on the palm of both hands moved in a circular movement. The washing of the *mūrti* often forms part of the *pūjā*.

PURĀṆA Lit., old things. The literature comprising the Indian mythology, perhaps of a popular origin but difficult to date. The extant manuscripts are mostly recent, the older ones going back to the 15th or 16th century of our era, and even earlier in Nepal (xi-xii cent.). Internal evidence traces their origin to *Vyāsa* (q.v.). Traditionally they are eighteen in number as eighteen too are the minor purāṇas.

PUROḌĀŚA (Ṛgvedic *purolāśa*) A cereal cake (q.v. *paśu-puroḍāśa*).

PUROHITA A court priest. A term commonly used for priest in general.

PURUṢA Lit., man. The primordial Man with cosmic dimensions, divinized as the Creative victim, the first to be immolated by the Gods for the purposes of creation. Later, especially in the *Upaniṣads* (q.v.), it is the Absolute Itself of which only the fourth inferior part corresponds to the visible world.

PURUṢAMEDHA Human sacrifice.

PŪṢAN A Vedic Deity, associated with the Sun at its noon zenith.

PUṢṬA Lit., wealth. A Vedic term. The sacrificial victim is called "the wealth of the Gods."

RĀJĀ King.

RĀJASŪYA Sacrifice performed at the coronation of a king.

RAKṢAS-S Bad, malevolent spirits.

RASA Lit., sap. Hence the intimate essence of something. Also, savor. When applied to the sacrificial victim, the term indicates its essence.

RETAS Seed, semen. Its symbolism is very great in the Brāhmaṇic ritual and cosmology.

ṚK A specific kind of song or hymn. The first collection of such *ṛk* hymns is called the *Ṛgveda.*

ṚṢI Seer, wise man. The poet-sage of the Vedic hymns.

ṚTA The cosmic order. In the Vedas, it has the characteristics of a First Principle. Often associated with sacrifice. Its opposite is *anṛta* which is the evil *par excellence.* In the first Vedas, it figures very often, but with the passage of time it gives way to an "Order" which is more of a moral type: the *Dharma* whose opposite is *adharma.*

ṚTVIJ An officiating priest.

RUDRA A Vedic God, head of a class of Gods called by the same name. Bordering on the demonic, he is the Śiva of the Purāṇic mythology (see under *Trimūrti*).

SABHYA One of the five fireplaces of the Brāhmaṇic altar. It is of minor importance and built only rarely and only for specific sacrifices. It is linked to the *Āvasathya* (q.v.): both are asociated with the *Āhavanīya* (q.v.), built of the same material as the latter, and situated to the north of it.

SACRIFICE Sacred action (from Latin, *sacrum facere*). We translate by this word the Sanskrit term *yajña* (q.v.).

SADASYA One of the officiating priests in the Brāhmaṇic rites. He is the seventeenth of the regular group of priests and his presence is optional.

SĀMAN Sung hymns. A term applied especially to the hymns of the *Sāmaveda*.

SAMBHĀRA Lit., collection. Used especially to refer to the collection of the material needed for a sacred rite.

SAMITṚ The immolator. Forms part of the team of priests officiating at the sacrifice, himself enjoying the dignity of a minor priest. Sometimes he may not belong to the Brāhmaṇic caste.

SAṂVATSARA Year. Standard measure of ritual time. Equivalent to *Prajāpati* (q.v.), to *Agni* (q.v.), to the Sacrifice, etc.

SARASVATĪ The Goddess of Wisdom in Hindu mythology. In the Vedas hers is the name of a sacred river later on believed to flow underground.

SARVAM The "All", understood also in a cosmic sense.

ŚATARUDRĪYA A litany of one hundred verses dedicated to *Rudra* (q.v.) found in the Yajurveda. It is still recited today (with additions) on various occasions.

SATTRA One of the technical terms for the *Soma* (q. v.) sacrifice.

SATYAM (n.) The true, truth. A name of the Absolute. One of the cosmic and moral entities associated with sacrifice.

SAVITṚ The Sun, a Vedic God.

SMṚTI Lit., memory, what is retained in memory. Hence, Tradition, that is, those texts which though not canonical like the *Śruti* (q.v.) were "remembered" by those who wrote them down. The Epics, the Law Treatises, the *Purāṇas* (q.v.), etc. form part of *Smṛti*.

ŚOCIS Lit., flame, intense heat. That was the meaning of the term especially during the period of the first Vedas. With the passage of time, from the *Upaniṣads* (q.v.) onwards, it came to mean almost exclusively "pain", "suffering".

SOMA (m.) A plant from whose root an intoxicating drink is extracted, a drink used in the Soma sacrifice. The name can stand either for the plant itself, or for the drink, or for the God who is manifested in the plant and who is often identified with the Moon.

SOMAYAJÑA The Soma sacrifice. Another name for this is *Sutyayajña,* sacrifice of the Pressing (or Extraction).

ŚṚTA Cooked, prepared, from the Vedic root *śra.*

ŚRADDHĀ (f.) Faith, confidence.

ŚRAMA Lit., to toil hard. Mostly used in an ascetical sense, to toil, strive, in performing ascetical practices. When used in a sacrificial context it denotes the laborious pains undergone by the sacrificer in performing the rites.

ŚRUTI From the root *śru* which means "to hear", "to listen". The Sacred Texts which were "heard" by the *ṛṣis* (q. v.) at the beginning of time. The whole body of the Vedas. The Sacred Texts, traditionally and even today, are transmitted orally, learned by heart and are not considered as "written".

SUBANDHU Good friend.

ŚŪDRA A member of the fourth caste in the Brāhmaṇic social division, comprising artisans, peasants, servants, etc.

ŚUKLA Lit., white. One of the two great divisions of the Yajurveda which includes two principal versions : the *Mādhyandina* and the *Kāṇva.*

SŪRYA The sun, also a Vedic God.

SŪTRA Treatises on ritual, mostly in the form of short aphorisms. Each of the four Vedas has its *sūtras.*

SUTYAYAJÑA See under *Somayajña.*

SVĀHĀ An exclamatory word pronounced at the end of the recitation accompanying the oblation. It is addressed to the Gods.

SVARGA Heaven, the highest of the three worlds. The dwelling place of the blessed and of the Gods.

SVARGA LOKA Heavenly abode, the place of recompense for the blessed and the Gods, the goal of him who offers the sacrifice. With the change of spiritual horizons wrought by the *Upaniṣads* (q.v.), *svarga* will be seen to be included in the cycle of rebirths and stops being the ultimate spiritual goal.

TAD Lit., that. A pronoun often used to indicate "the world

beyond" in opposition to *idam*, that is, "this terrestrial and visible world".

TANTALUS Titan; a figure in ancient Greek Mythology.

TANŪ A solid body.

TAPAS Etym., heat. In the first Vedas, the term has generally this meaning—a meaning which we have retained in our study. Today, however, it has come to mean austerity, asceticism, works of penance and the like.

TAPASVIN He who possesses *tapas* (q.v.), who is powerful through *tapas*. The one who subjects himself to arduous ascetical practices is called by this name. In Vedic times, the *tapasvin* par excellence was *Agni* (q.v.), the "possessor of heat".

TAPTA Adj. from the root *tap*, hot. It often qualifies *Gharma* (q.v.).

TAPUS Adj., intensively hot. A Ṛgvedic term which gradually disappears in the other Vedas and their literature.

TEDOFORUS A Greek-derived Latin term for torch-bearer.

TEJAS Calorific energy. A force of heat and light which emanates from a human or divine personality, externally visible as an aura.

THEOPHANY Divine manifestation (from the Greek *theos*, God and *phanein*, to appear).

TRIMŪRTI The Indian Divine Triad, consisting of *Brahmā* (q.v.), the Creator, *Viṣṇu* (q.v.), the Sustainer of the created, and *Śiva*, the Destroyer.

TṚṢṬUBH Vedic meter consisting of four feet (*pāda*) of eleven syllables each.

TŪṢṆĪM Adv., in silence. Silence is a ritual element of great importance. In the offering, its alternation with the spoken formulae is indeed very significative.

UCCHIṢṬA Left-over, that is, what remains of the sacrificial victim after the Gods have taken the part due to them, to be shared by the sacrificer and his priests. It corresponds, to a certain extent, to what is meant today by *prasāda* (q.v.) but it retains, in common usage, the idea of 'left-over' in the pejorative sense of the term.

UDGĀTṚ One of the main officiating priests at the sacrifice, whose function is to sing the *sâman* (q.v.) during the offering.

UKHĀ A sacrificial vessel in the form of a square pot. In the animal sacrifice, it serves to boil the greater part of the flesh of the victim. During the construction of the Fire-Altar, it serves to contain the fire during all the time when the sacrificer is being initiated.

UKHYAGNI The fire which is kept in *ukhā* (q.v.) and which is very important for the initiation of the sacrificer. In classical Sanskrit, it is a term of comparison for feminine beauty and masculine nobility.

UPADIKĀ A species of ants which dig the earth in search of water.

UPANIṢAD A collection of texts of a spiritual and philosophical nature, included in the *Brāhmaṇas* (q.v.) but isolated because of their peculiar character. Each of the Ṛk, Atharva, Sāma and Yajus (with its two schools), has its *Upaniṣads*.

UPASAD/UPASADA Lit., vow of honour. A preliminary rite connected with the Soma (q.v.) sacrifice, consisting of a triple offering of ghee to *Agni* (q.v.), *Soma* (q.v.) and *Viṣṇu* (q.v.). It immediately precedes the *Pravargya* (q.v.) whenever the latter is performed.

ŪRDHVANABHAS The name of the son of the *Maruts* (q.v.).

UTTARANĀBHI The centre of *Uttaravedi* (q.v.), on which *Agnicayana* (q.v.) is, on occasion, constructed.

UTTARAVEDI An altar, smaller than the normal one, built during the Soma (q.v.) sacrifice, to the East of the *Mahāvedi* (q.v.). See also under *Uttaranābhi*.

VĀC Word. A very important ritual element. It is because of the Word of the offertory formulae that the oblation is carried to the Gods. In both the Brāhmaṇic myth and speculation, it assumes the dignity of being "Second" to *Prajāpati* (q.v.) and sometimes is the means through which or with the help of which *Prajāpati* creates.

VĀJAPEYA One of the seven great sacrifices of the Soma (q.v.) From it is derived the modern brāhmaṇa family name *Bājpeyi* indicating that one of the family's forebears must have offered the sacrifice at least once in his life.

VĀMANA Lit., dwarf. One of the incarnations of *Viṣṇu* (q.v.) who, as a dwarf, takes the three cosmic steps. (See under *Viṣṇuvikrama.*)

VAPĀ See under *Omentum.*

VARĀHA Wild boar. An animal whose symbolism is very significant in Vedic mythology, perhaps because of its habit of digging furrows in the earth with its snout. Its significance is retained in the Purāṇic mythology.

VARUṆA A Vedic God, belonging to the *Asura* (q.v.) group when no negative character was yet attached to it. Upholder of the Law (see under *Ṛta*), he has as weapon the slip-knot with which he binds its transgressors. (See also under *Mitra.*)

VAIŚYA Lit., prosperity. The third caste which, according to the Brāhmaṇic social division, includes the merchants and the peasants.

VĀTSAPRA A rite linked to *Viṣṇuvikrama* (q.v.) and consisting of the repetition of certain sacred formulae of praise, believed to have creative power.

VĀYU The God of the Wind. He presides over the middle kingdom, the atmospheric; as *Agni* (q.v.) he presides over the terrestrial, and as *Āditya* (q.v.) over the heavenly.

VEDA Lit., knowledge. The ancient Indian sacred Scriptures. Also, "what is known" (in the same way as *Śruti* [q.v.] means also "what is heard"). The Vedic Corpus comprises the Hymns (*Saṃhitās*), and their Commentaries (*Brāhmaṇas*), which include also texts for reflection for the ascetics (*Āraṇyakas*), and texts of a philosophical and mystical nature (*Upaniṣads*). Attached to them are also the Sūtras (both Gṛhya and Śrauta) cotnaining ritual rules (domestic and sacrificial ones). The Vedas are four: *ṚK*, *Sāma*, *Yajus* and *Atharva*; each one having the just mentioned four-fold division, with the Sūtras as well.

VEDI (f.) Altar. Sacrificial platform which generally lies between the *Gārhapatya* (q.v.) and the *Āhavanīya* (q.v.).

VIKAṄKATA A kind of thorny tree which furnishes wood for the fire used in certain rites.

VĪṆĀ A musical string instrument, like a lute. Still used today in Indian classical music of a more ancient type.

VIRĀJ Lit., splendour. (m.) A deity sometimes identified with *Puruṣa* (q.v.) or *Prajāpati* (q.v.). (f.) The daughter of either of these Gods.

VIṢṆU The central God of the *Trimūrti* (q.v.), the Sustainer of the created. Of Vedic origin, he has initially little or no significance, but gradually gains in importance in the time of the *Brāhmaṇas* (q.v.) till he becomes one of the major Gods in Purāṇic literature. Apt to incarnate himself in different forms for the benefit of mankind (see under *Avatāra*), he is the Brāhmaṇic figure most apt to incorporate the various local and even tribal deities in the official Hindu religion and give them an orthodox stamp. Tradition has fixed the number of his incarnations to ten among which is *Kṛṣṇa* (q.v.) and even Buddha.

VIṢṆUVIKRAMA Lit., steps of *Viṣṇu*. The famous three steps which, according to Purāṇic mythology, Viṣṇu takes to conquer the worlds. In the Brāhmaṇic mythology, however, it is the Gods who perform this action for a creative purpose.

VIŚVAJYOTIS Lit., all light, or the light of All. Name of three special bricks used in *Agnicayana* (q.v.).

VIŚVADEVA Lit., all the Gods. Can be understood either as a collective term for all the Gods of the Vedic *pantheon* (q.v.) or, as has sometimes been suggested, as a proper name of a particular God.

VRATA A complex term from the root *vṛ*. It has been translated from time to time as vow, to want, religious and ascetical observance, intention (with which a sacrifice is offered), order, command, obedience, moral and religious behaviour, way of religious and ascetical life.

VYĀNA One of the five forms of vital air or breath, collectively called *prāṇa* (q.v.).

VYĀHṚTI Mystical exclamation of certain words, especially of the syllables *bhūr*, *bhuvaḥ*, *svaḥ*.

VYĀSA Lit., systematizer, compiler, or commentator. Name of the mythical author or systematizer of the *Mahābhārata* (q.v.), *Purāṇas* (q.v.) and also re-arranger of the *Vedas* (q.v.).

YAHVEH Principal name of the God of the people of Israel.

YAJAMĀNA Sacrificer. More precisely, the one who has a sacrifice performed, who pays its expenses, and in which he acts personally, together with his wife.

YAJÑA (m.) Sacrifice, from the root *yaj*, to offer a sacrifice, or, to perform a cult.

YAJUS Sacrificial formula or utterance. See also under *Veda.*

YONI Lit., Matrix, vulva, feminine organ, and, by extension, origin, place where something is produced. In the *Vedas* (q.v.) the term is nearly always masculine; in the *Ṛk* (q.v.) always. In classical Sanskrit, however, it is mostly feminine.

YŪPA Sacrificial pole to which were tied the victims to be immolated and also the animals to be milked during the rite. Because of the great influence sacrifice had on the Indian culture, *yūpa* came to stand for the "cosmic column" and corresponds to what in other religious cultures is conceived as the "cosmic tree" or the "axis of the world". In greek sacrifice this "tree" is present but with a different function; it is the tree of meat where the meat to be offered is hanged before sacrificial cooking and consumption.

WELTANSCHAUUNG A German term which means "vision of the world" proper to a certain philosophy or culture.

ZEUS Principal God of the Greek *pantheon* (q.v.); the King of the Gods.

## BIBLIOGRAPHY

### A. VEDIC TEXTS

*Ṛgvedasaṃhitā* (ṚV), edited by Shripad Damodar Satavalekar, Bombay (Swādhyāya Maṇḍala, Pāraḍī), 1957.

*Atharvavedasaṃhitā* (AV), edited by Shripad Damodar Satavalekar, Bombay (Swādhyāya Maṇḍala, Pāraḍī), 1957.

*Yajurvedasaṃhitā* (*Vājasaneyi*) (VajSam), edited by Shripad Damoder Satavalekar, Bombay (Swādhyāya Maṇḍala. Pāraḍī).

*Taittirīyasaṃhitā* (TaittSam), edited by Shripad Damodar Satavaleker, Bombay (Swādhyāya Maṇḍala, Pāraḍī), 1957.

*Aitareyabrāhmaṇa* (AitBr) with the *Vṛtti Sukhaprada* di ṢAḌGURUŚIṢYA, edited by R. Ananta Krishna Shastri, Vol. I (Adhyāya 1-15), Trivandrum (University of Travancore Sanskrit Series No. 139), 1942.

id. vol. II (Adhyāya 16-25), edited by P.K. Narayana Pillai (Trivandrum Sanskrit Series No 167), 1952.

id vol. III (Adhyāya 26-32), edited by S.K. Pillai (Trivandrum Sanskrit Series No. 176), 1955.

*Śāṅkhāyanabrāhmaṇa* (KausBr), or *Kauṣitakibrāhmaṇa* (KausBr), edited by H.N. Bhattacarya, Calcutta (Sanskrit College) (Calcutta Sanskrit Research Series No. LXXIII), 1970 (Sanskrit text with Bengali trans.).

*Aitareya Āraṇyaka* (AitAr), edited by A.B. Keith (Sanskrit text with English trans.), Oxford (Clarendon Press) in *Anecdota Oxoniensia,* 1909 (reprinted by Oxford University Press, 1969).

*Gopathabrāhmaṇa* (GopBr) (of the *Atharvaveda*), edited by R.L. Mitra, Delhi-Varanasi (Indological Book House) (Bibliotheca Indica—A Collection of Oriental Works), 1972.

*Śatapathabrāhmaṇa* (SatBr) (of the *Śuklayajurveda*), according to the *Mādhyandina School* edited by A. Weber, Varanasi (Chowkhamba) (Chowkhamba Sanskrit Granthamala No. 96) 1964.

*Taittirīyabrāhmaṇa* (TaittBr) (of the *Kṛṣṇayajurveda*), edited by Narayana Shastri, vols. 1&2 (Anandasrama Mudranalaya, Anandasramam Sanskrita Granthavali) (Series 36 & 37), 1938.

*Kṛṣṇayajurvedataittirīyāraṇyaka*, Ganapata, edited by Yadava Natu in 2 vols. Anandasrama Mudranalaya, (Anandasrama Sanskrita Granthavali) 1937-1939.

*Pañcaviṃśabrāhmaṇa* (PancBr), or *Tāṇḍyamahābrāhmaṇa* (of the *Sāmaveda*), trans. into English by W. CALAND, Calcutta (Asiatic Society of Bengal) (Bibliotheca Indica—A Collection of Oriental Works No. 255), 1931.

## CONSULTED TRANSLATIONS

*The Hymns of the Ṛgveda*, trans. into English by R.T.H. GRIFFITH, Varanasi (Chowkhamba Sanskrit Series Office), vols. XXXIV & XXXV, 5 ed. 1971.

*The Hymns of the Atharvaveda*, (trans. into English with a popular commentary by R.T.H. GRIFFTH), edited by M.L. Abhimanyu, Varanasi (Master Khelari Lal & Sons) 3ed. 2 vols., 1962.

*The Text of the White Yajurveda*, trans. into English by R.T.H. GRIFFITH, edited by M.L. Abhimanyu (B.N. Yadav & E.J. Lazarus& Co., Medical Hall Press), Varanasi 1957.

*The Veda of the Black Yajus School : Taittirīya Saṃhitā*, trans. into English by A.B. KEITH (Harvard Oriental Series Vols. XVIII XIX,1914), reprinted(Motilal Banarsidass, Delhi), 2 vols. 1967.

*Rigveda Brāhmaṇas: The Aitareya and Kauṣītaki Brāhmaṇas of the Rigveda* trans. into English by A.B. KEITH (Harvard Oriental Series Vol. 25, 1920),reprinted (Motilal Banarsidass, Delhi), 1971.

*Śatapatha Brāhmaṇa according the Text of the Mādhyandina School*, trans. into English by J. EGGELINC, Motilal Banarsidass, Delhi (Sacred Book of the East Series, Nos. XII XXVI, XLI, XLIII, XLIV), 5 vols.

ŚRAUTA SŪTRA

*Śrauta Paitṛmedhika* & *Pariśeṣa Sūtra* of BHARADVĀJA, (of the Taittirīya school) vols. 2, critical edition and English trans. by C. G. KASHIKAR, Poona (Vaidika Saṃśodhana Maṇḍala), 1964.

*Mānava Śrauta Sūtra* (of *Maitrāyaṇī Saṃhitā*), trans. into English by J.M. van GELDER, New Delhi (international Academy of Indian Culture), 1963.

*Śrautakośa* (*Encyclopaedia of Vedic Sacrificial Ritual*) so far in six vols., Poona (Vaidika Saṃśodhana Maṇḍala).

*Sanskrit Section*, Vol. I, edited by D.G. Bapat, C.G.KASHIKAR and others, 1958.

*English Section*, Vol. I, pt. 1, trans. into English by R.N. DANDEKAR, 1962.

*English Section*, Vol. I, pt. 2, edited translated into English by R.N. DANDEKAR, 1960.

*Sanskrit Section*, Vol. II, pt. 1, edited by C. G. KASHIKAR and others, 1970.

*English Section*, Vol. II, pt. 1, edited and translated into English by R.N. DANDEKAR, 1973.

*English Section*, Vol. II, pt. 2, edited and translated into English by DANDEKAR, 1980.

*Āśvalāyana-Śrauta-Sūtram*, Vol. I, translated by H.G. RANADE, Poona (Ranade Ed.), 1981.

*Kātyāyana Śrauta Sūtra*, edited and translated into English by H.G. RANADE, Poona (Ed. Ranade), 1978.

*Vārāha-Śrauta Sūtra*, criticatly edited by Dr. W. CALAND and Dr. RAGHUVIRA, Delhi (Meharchand Lachhmandas), 1971.

*Śāṅkhāyana Śrautasūtra*, ed. W. CALAND and LOKESH CHANDRA, Delhi (Motilal Banarsidass), 1980.

B. SECONDARY WORKS

H. AGUILAR *Sacrifice in the Ṛg Veda*, Delhi (Bharatiya Vidya Prakashan), 1976.

S. BHATTACHARJEE *Hindu Theogonies*, New York (McMillan), 1970.

Ch. BLAIR *Heat in Ṛgveda and Atharvaveda*, New Haven, Conn. (AOS), 1961.

A. BRELICH *Dispense sul Politeismo*, Roma (Ed. dell'Ateneo), 1958.

id *Introduzione alla Storia delle Religioni*, Roma (Ed. dell 'Ateneo), 1966.

id "Comment se forme un Dieu", in *Proceedings of the XII International Congress of the International Association for the History of Religions*, edited by C. J. BLEEKER, G. WIDENGREN, E. J. SHARP, Leiden, (Brill) (Suppl. to "Numen", no. 31), 1975, p. 136.

J.A.B. van BUITENEN *The Pravargya (An Ancient Indian Iconic Ritual Described and Annotated)*, Poona (Deccan College), 1968.

W. BURKERT Homo Necans : *Interpretation en altgriechischer Opfer riten und Mythen.* Berlin-N York (Walter de Gruyter), 1972.

W. CALAND & V. HENRY *The Agniṣṭoma*, 2 vols., Paris, 1906-7&1907

P. CARACCHI "La presenza divina della *mūrti* secondo i Purāṇa" in *Indologia Taurinensia*, Torino, 1978, p. 1.

G.V. DEVASTHALI *Religion and Mythology of the Brāhmaṇas*, Univers. of Poona (The Bhau Vishnu Ashtekar Vedic Research Series Vol. No. 1), 1965.

P.E. DUMONT *L'Agnihotra*, Baltimore, 1939.

id. *L'Aśvamedha (Description solennel du cheval dans le culte vedique)*, Paris-Louvain, 1927.

M. ELIADE *Patterns in comparative Religion*, London (Kegan Paul), 1958.

M. ELIADE *De Zalmoxis à Gengis Khan*, Paris (Payot), 1970, Chap. III

J. GONDA *Brahman*, L'Aia (Moulton), 1961.

id. *Change and Continuity in Indian Religion*, The Hagen (Moulton), 1965, Chap. X, *Dikṣā*, pp. 315ff.

id. *Aspects of Early Viṣṇuism*, Delhi (Motilal Banarsidass), 2nd ed. 1969 (1st, 1954).

J.C. HEESTERMAN *The Ancient Indian Royal Consecration (The Rājasūya described according to the Yajus Texts and annoted)*, The Hagen (Mouton), 1957

J. C. KAELBER "Tapas, Birth and Spiritual Rebirth in the

Veda", in *History of Religions*, Chicago, XV, 4 (May 1976), pp. 343-386.

A. B. KEITH *The Religion and Philosophy of the Veda and Upaniṣads*, (Harvard Oriental Series, 1925) reprinted (Motilal Banarsidass, Delhi), 1976.

C. KERENYI *La mitologia dei Greci*, trans. into Italian and edited by A. Brelich, Roma (Astrolabio), 1952.

D. K. KNIPE *In the Image of Fire* (*The Vedic Experience of Heat*), Motilal Banarsidass, Delhi, 1975.

H. KRICK Das Ritual der Feurgründung (Agnyâdheya) (Ost, Akadamie der Wissenschaffen), Wien 1983.

C. KUNHAN RAJA *Poet-philosophers of the Ṛgveda* (*Vedic and pre-Vedic*), Ganesh&Co., Madras, 1963.

S. LEVI *La doctrine du sacrifice dans les Brāhmaṇas*, Paris 1898, reprinted, Paris (P.U.F.), 1966.

CI LEVI STRAUSS *Le cru et le cuit*, Paris (Plon), 1964.

Ch. MALAMOUD "Cuir le monde", in *Puruṣārtha*, *Researches de Sciences sociales sur le Asie du Sud*. Paris (Centre d' Etudes de l' Iude etde l' Asie du Sud), 1975, pp. 91-135.

R. PANIKKAR *Le Mystère du Culte dans l 'Hindouisme et le Christianisme*, Paris (Ed. du Cerf), 1970.

id. *The Vedic Experience, Mantramañjari* (*An Anthology of the Vedas for Modern Man and Contemporary Celebration*), London, (Longmann, Darton&Todd), 1977.

id *Myth, Faith&Hermeneutics*, New York (Paulist Press), 1978.

id. *Il Silenzio del Buddha. Studio su alcuni aspetti dell 'Ateismo modern e buddista*, with the collaboration of U.M. Vesci.

J. POKORNY *Indogermanisches Etymologisches Wörterbuch*, Bern (Francke), 1959.

K.R. POTDAR *Sacrifice in the Ṛgveda* (*its nature, influence, origin and growth*), Bombay (Bharatiya Vidya Bhavan) 1953 (Bharatiya Yidya Series Vol 16).

S. RADHAKRISHNAN *Philosophy of the Upaniṣads*, London (Allen&Unwin), 1958.

L. RENOU *La Vocabulair du ṚgVeda*, Pondicherry.

V.G. RAHARKAR *The Seers of the Ṛgveda*, Poona (Univ. of Poona), 1964.

W. RAU *Töpferei und Tongeschir in Vedism*, Marburg, 1971.

U. RUSTAGI *Darśapūrṇamāsa* (*A Comparative Ritualistic Study*), Delhi-Varanasi (Bharatiya Vidya Prakashan), 1981.

R. SABBATUCCI *Saggi sul Misticismo Greco*, Roma (Ed. dell 'Ateneo), 1968.

V.R. GAUḌA SHARMA *Yajña Mīmāmsā*, Varanasi, 1970 (3rd ed.), (In Hindi).

N.J. SHENDE *The Religion and Philosophy of the Atharvaveda*, Poona (Bhandarkar Oriental Research Institute), 1952 (Bhandarkar Oriental Series No. 8).

L. SILBURN *Instante et Cause*, Paris (Vrin), 1955

G. SCHWAB *Das Alt Indische Tieropfer*, Erlangen, 1888.

F. STALL *Agni*, vols. 2, Berkeley (Asian Humanities Press), 1983.

G.U. THITE *Sacrifice in the Brāhmaṇa-texts*, Poona (Poona Unv. Press), 1975).

J.P. VERNANT, *A' la table des hommes*, in M. DETIENNE & J. P. VERNANT, *La cuisine du sacrifice en pays greque*, Paris, 1975, ch. II.

U.M. VESCI "Der Begriff der Tapas", *Kairos*, Salzburg 3/ 1968, pp. 186-192.

id. "Kah, le Nome de Dieu comme Pronome Interrogatif," in *Archivio di Filosofia*, edited by E. Castelli, Roma 1968.

id. "Ritual as Mirror Reflecting Ṛgvedic Life" in *Bharati*, (Prof. V.S. Agravala vol.), Varanasi (BHU) 1968-1971, No. 12-14, pp. 281-289.

id. "The Role of Ritual Heat in Vedic Sacrifice" (The place of pain in the act of Creation)", in *Bijdragen* (Negen en Dertigste Deel), 4/1978, pp. 399-423.

id. "Sacrifice seen as an ambivalent action" Summary in *History of Religions : Proceedings of the XIII Congress of the International Association for the History of Religions*, Lancaster 1975, edited by M. Pye&P. MacKenzie, Leichester (Dept. of Relig. Univers. of Leichester), 1980 (Series : Leichester Studies and Religions No. 2), pp. 115 ff.

# INDEXES

# I. INDEX OF NAMES

## II. INDEX OF REFERENCES

# III. INDEX OF SANSKRIT WORDS

# IV. GENERAL INDEX